GENERATIONS OF EXCLUSION

GENERATIONS OF EXCLUSION

MEXICAN AMERICANS, ASSIMILATION, AND RACE

EDWARD E. TELLES AND VILMA ORTIZ

Russell Sage Foundation • New York

Russell Sage Foundation

The Russell Sage Foundation, one of the oldest of America's general purpose foundations, was established in 1907 by Mrs. Margaret Olivia Sage for "the improvement of social and living conditions in the United States." The Foundation seeks to fulfill this mandate by fostering the development and dissemination of knowledge about the country's political, social, and economic problems. While the Foundation endeavors to assure the accuracy and objectivity of each book it publishes, the conclusions and interpretations in Russell Sage Foundation publications are those of the authors and not of the Foundation, its Trustees, or its staff. Publication by Russell Sage, therefore, does not imply Foundation endorsement.

Library of Congress Cataloging-in-Publication Data

Telles, Edward Eric, 1956-
  Generations of exclusion : Mexican Americans, assimilation, and race / Edward E. Telles, Vilma Ortiz.
     p. cm.
  Includes bibliographical references.
  ISBN 0-87154-848-8
  1. Mexican Americans—Ethnic identity. 2. Mexican Americans—Cultural assimilation. 3. Mexican Americans—Interviews. 4. Mexican Americans—Longitudinal studies. 5. Social surveys—United States. 6. Intergenerational relations—United States. 7. United States—Race relations. 8. United States—Ethnic relations. I. Ortiz, Vilma, 1954- II. Title.
  E184.M5T45 2007
  305.8968'72073—dc22

                                                                    2007027804

Text design by Suzanne Nichols.

RUSSELL SAGE FOUNDATION
112 East 64th Street, New York, New York 10021
10 9 8 7 6 5 4 3 2 1

To the memories of: Raymond L. Telles
and Beatriz Ochoa Telles
E.T.

Antonio Serrata
V.O.

$=$ Contents $=$

== About the Authors ==

Edward E. Telles is professor of sociology and Chicano studies at the University of California, Los Angeles, and recipient of the 2006 Distinguished Scholarly Publication Award from the American Sociological Association.

Vilma Ortiz is associate professor of sociology at the University of California, Los Angeles.

Joan W. Moore codirected the original Mexican American Study Project (MASP), and is Distinguished Professor Emeritus of Sociology at the University of Wisconsin, Milwaukee.

= Acknowledgments =

The second wave of the Mexican American Study Project has had a fifteen-year history leading up to the publication of this book. Along the way, we have had many people to thank. Our apologies if we missed anyone—likely given the long and collective nature of our research project. First, we acknowledge the construction workers who in 1992 found the 1965 questionnaires and research materials of the original Mexican American Study Project and Charlotte Brown of the University Research Library for bringing them to our attention. These questionnaires became the baseline data for our longitudinal study, in which we re-interviewed almost 700 of the original respondents in 2000 as well as around 750 of their children. Most importantly, we thank our 1,442 respondents in Los Angeles, San Antonio, and wherever else we found them, for giving generously of their time, opinions, and hospitality.

From the time we first went into the field in late 1993, this has been a team effort. Estela Ballon started with the project back then and served as project director until 2002. She supervised numerous assistants during the laborious and lengthy searching for the original respondents, was our go-between with the two different survey efforts (Los Angeles and San Antonio), coordinated the data management, conducted data analysis, and did much more. Without her dedication and creativity, this project would never have been completed. When Estela left in 2001, Katy Pinto took over as project director and did an awesome job of coordinating data management and analysis.

The core research group that searched for respondents from 1994 to 2001 consisted of Bertha Cueva, Ana Delatorre, Norma García, Gilda González, and Katy Pinto and for shorter periods: María Arias (in San Antonio), Cynthia Feliciano, Daniel Malpica, Gilda Ochoa, Ricardo Ramírez, Carlos Ramos, and Margie Zamudio. Olivia Carvajal, Edna Molina, and Kris Zentgraf provided administrative support at different points in the project. Daniel Malpica ably translated and pretested our instruments in Spanish. Most of the graduate students working with us have since received their Ph.D.s and we are proud to see many of them become professors at various universities.

We also had the short-term assistance of several undergraduate students, some of whose surnames we were unfortunately not able to recall. These included Obed Agredano-Lozano, Alicia Alvarado, Belia, Dean Cheley, Elizabeth Cornejo, Gudiel Crosthwaite, Michelle Lilienfeld, Marci, María (a high school student), Maricela, Alvaro Mejía, Evangelina Meza, Felicia Ortiz, and Mercedes Zavala.

The survey interviews were carried out in Southern California by UCLA's Survey Research Center under the expert direction of Eve Fielder and Tonya Hayes and with the administrative assistance of Daria Galindo. In Texas, interviews were conducted by NuStats under the leadership of Carlos Arce (former director of the 1979 National Chicano Survey) and his helpful and hardworking staff, including Lilian Hogenmiller, George Uribe, and Kelly Govea.

As part of our follow-up study, we also interviewed some of our respondents in greater depth. We plan to report on those in a separate volume in the future. Bert Cueva, Daniel Malpica, and Katy Pinto conducted the interviews in Los Angeles. The San Antonio interviews were done by University of Texas at San Antonio students Alicia Guerrero and Antonio García under the direction of Pablo Vila. Those respondents generously gave of their time and we are especially grateful to them. The interviews were transcribed by Rocío Carrillo, Mónica Cervantes, Elizabeth Delgado, Kenia Rivera, Marco Durazo, José González, and Steven Rubalcava.

During the data analysis and writing stage from 2004 to 2007, we were assisted by UCLA students Jennifer Flashman, Amy Hsin, Kelly Nielson, Chinyere Osuji, Heidy Sarabia, Cristina Solis, and Christie Sue. Wesley Hiers gave a thorough read to a near-final version of the manuscript.

We owe much to Joan Moore, the only surviving author of the original study, for her support throughout the life of the project. Joan was always available to provide missing background information and she reviewed our questionnaires and later read manuscript drafts. We also thank her for the heartfelt foreword she wrote for this book. She provided helpful words of encouragement throughout, even though she initially thought a follow-up study was "overly ambitious and not doable." Well, Joan, here it is!

Along with Joan, Ralph Mittelbach, Georges Sabagh, Alfonso Cárdenas, and Nicandro Juárez, who were involved in the original project, also provided useful background information and told wonderful stories about the project effort in the 1960s. We especially thank Ralph for a number of methodological insights that he recalled and for several copies of *The Mexican American People*. Walter Allen, Leo Estrada, Robert Hauser, David López, Don Treiman, and Diego Vigil gave valuable advice as we wrote our proposals and developed our questionnaires. Arturo

Madrid, Ed Murguía, and especially Lalo Valdez helped us Angelenos to better understand San Antonio. Robert Mare was very generous with his time and statistical expertise, especially on the thorny issues of weighting and the presentation of regression results.

We are grateful to a great set of friends and colleagues who read earlier drafts of chapters, provided much advice and certainly improved the quality of this book. Bryan Roberts and Rogelio Saenz, as the outside reviewers for Russell Sage, provided useful comments and recommended its publication. We are indebted to Laura Gómez, who read the first draft and gave us extensive and honest comments on the entire manuscript. Roger Waldinger, Andreas Wimmer, and Howard Winant read several chapters and helped extensively with drawing out the book's contribution. As sociologists, we were particularly challenged with both history and politics and thus particularly appreciate the sage advice of historians Albert Camarillo, David Montejano, and especially Vicki Ruiz and political scientists Rodolfo de la Garza and Louis De Sipio. We also received advice and insight from Mark Alvarez, Frank Bean, Sylvia Hurtado, Kelly Lytle-Hernández, Reynaldo Macías, Lionel Maldonado, Julie Mendoza, Luis Ortiz-Frano, Jaime Pacheco, Devah Pager, Raymond Rocco, Renato Rosaldo, Otto Santa Anna, Mark Sawyer, Denise Segura, Danny Solórzano, Diego Vigil, and René Zenteno. Robert Smith provided important "eleventh-hour" comments.

From 1994 to 2001, we housed the project at UCLA's Institute for Social Science Research, under the leadership of David Sears and, from 2001 to 2007, at the Chicano Studies Research Center with Chon Noriega at the helm. We thank the talented administrative staff at both centers: Jacqueline Archuleta, Rick Ackerman, Madelyn De Maria, Alain De Vera, Carlos Haro, Charles Kim, Luz Orozco, Antonio Serrata, and especially Tana Wong.

We appreciate the comments on our presentations at the following universities: Albany, Brown, Cal State Fullerton, Cal State LA, Princeton, Pomona, Stanford, Texas A&M, UCLA, UC Santa Barbara, USC, and Vanderbilt, as well as the Russell Sage Foundation, the UC MEXUS Latino Policy Conference, and annual meetings of the American Sociological Association, the National Association of Chicana and Chicano Studies, and the Population Association of America.

We are indebted to numerous programs and foundations that provided funding for this long and expensive survey project as well as to individual program officers who convinced them of our worthiness. The Ford Foundation, which bankrolled the original study in the 1960's, was our first major funder. We appreciate the support of Ford program officers Cristina Cuevas and Anthony Romero for a planning grant and later, Taryn Higashi and Melvin Oliver for data collection. Tomas Ybarra-Frausto and Aída Rodríguez at the Rockefeller Foundation, and Diane

Cornwell of the Haynes Foundation, also bet on our project in its early stages and provided funding for data collection. Finally, we received a major grant from the National Institute of Child and Human Development [1 R01 HD33436-01A2] and we are thankful for the work of our program officer, Rose Li. That grant allowed us to continue searching for respondents and to conduct all the survey interviews, so we did not have to worry about funding for a long time.

The Russell Sage Foundation provided support in various ways over the years. First we acknowledge its president, Eric Wanner, for his unwavering support throughout the life of the project. RSF provided grants during the data collection stage and during the data analysis and writing stage. Our program officers over the years, Aixa Cintron-Vélez, Nancy Cunniff Casey, and Stephanie Platz, were always helpful. Telles was a visiting scholar at RSF in New York from 2004 to 2005, which proved invaluable as we began writing the book. There he was aided by talented colleagues too numerous to mention and excellent research assistance by Sarah Lowe, Galo Vale, Nicole Radmore and Katie Winograd. As we finished the book, we benefited greatly from their thoughtful and experienced editor, Suzanne Nichols, and her able assistant, Matthew Callan.

The many small university grants we received were indispensable, especially as we were getting started or waiting for major funding. From the University of California system, we secured funds from the University of California Mexico-U.S. program (UC-MEXUS), the California Policy Seminar, and the UC Committee on Latino Research. At UCLA, funders included the Institute of American Cultures, the Chicano Studies Research Center, the California Center for Population Research, the Center for American Politics and Public Policy, and the Committee on Research of the Academic Senate. Also, Chancellor Charles Young, Vice Chancellor for Research Kumar Patel, Social Sciences Dean Scott Waugh and Associate Vice Chancellor Raymund Paredes provided discretionary funds at critical times.

We thank Judy Baca, director of The Social and Public Art Resource Center (SPARC), for generously providing the cover artwork from the "History of Highland Park" mural she painted in 1976. We also appreciate the assistance of SPARC staff, particularly Pilar Castillo and Debra Padilla.

Finally, our families helped make this possible. As we struggled with meeting both professional and personal commitments, their love and support for us made us better professionals and persons. Julia G. Telles and Ana María Goldani showed considerable patience and provided cover so that Eddie, their father and spouse, could finish the manuscript. Ana María also provided wise personal and professional advice. Miguel Serrata must be commended for never compromising his high expectations of his mother, Vilma, as she struggled to find the right balance between single parenting and productive academic work. Vilma also appreciates the unwavering love and support from her family, parents José and Haydee Ortiz and sister Rebeca Romain, and the emotional and logistical support from friends Rebecca Emigh, Laura Gómez, Victor Narro, and Nanci Strum. Lastly, she thanks the Vista staff, in particular KC Hurst, for providing a safe place for Miguel on a daily basis.

We dedicate this book to deceased loved ones. V. Ortiz dedicates this to her late husband, Antonio Serrata, a third-generation Mexican American from Brownsville, Texas, and transplant to the San Francisco area. He is remembered for his unwavering support, warm and open manner, and calm dignity. E. Telles dedicates this to his father, Raymond L. Telles, descendant of early Santa Fe and Paso del Norte settlers, and mother, Beatriz Ochoa Telles from Chihuahua, Mexico. Both struggled so that their children could achieve their dreams. In life, Antonio, Raymond, and Beatriz all looked forward to this book's long-awaited appearance but unfortunately passed on before it was completed. We can see their smiling (and relieved) faces as if they were still with us.

═ Foreword ═

Joan W. Moore

UCLA's Mexican American Study Project is the ancestor of the study you hold in your hands. Born in the politically charged environment of the mid-1960s, the UCLA study was a massive effort to help put Mexican Americans on America's social and political map. I served as its associate director.[1]

Household surveys of the Spanish-surnamed population,[2] then overwhelmingly of Mexican origin, were a major aspect of the research. The interviews were conducted in Los Angeles and San Antonio, the two cities with the greatest numbers of Mexican Americans. We also contracted for a dozen or so specialized studies and enlisted the aid of academics and community leaders throughout the Southwest.[3] Leo Grebler, the housing and urban land economist who directed the project, expected the study to be a benchmark.[4] He hoped that later studies of Mexican Americans would show that the population had prospered, and he expected that their progress would be measured against our findings. With the usual caution of academic researchers, we were careful to hedge our optimism, but I think we all felt it.

This book is evidence that the benchmark part of Grebler's wish came true. A generation after our study was published, our original interview forms were peacefully gathering dust at UCLA when they were rediscovered by Vilma Ortiz and Edward Telles, who decided to trace our respondents and interview them again. That was exciting for people from the original staff, like me, who believed that the study had been permanently mothballed. Our old interviews would actually become the first round in that rare phenomenon, a longitudinal study. But when the early findings came in, I was deeply disturbed that the progress we had hoped for was clouded. Telles and Ortiz tell us the details of both progress and struggle in this book, but in this introductory note, I would like to lay out what I think were some of the grounds for our initial optimism. This essay is a purely personal perspective. I do not speak for other participants in the study, and when I use the term *we* I do not mean to imply consensus.

Life in the mid-1960s was different from what it was to become some thirty-five years later when this book was being prepared. In the nation as a whole, what it meant to be a minority was defined by the great divide between blacks and whites. The concepts used by social scientists to deal with other ethnic groups were quite different from what they are today, as were the social scientists, conditioned by the social realities of the time. There were very few Mexican American social scientists. Our colleague Ralph Guzmán was to become the very first Chicano political scientist, and there weren't many more Mexican American sociologists or economists. By the 1960s, even though most Mexican Americans were living in cities, the existing literature about the population was heavily weighted in favor of studies of rural and traditional life. Our project was specifically aimed at correcting that imbalance by focusing on cities—a focus that was all the more critical because it might help shape the new activism on the part of the federal government. The war on poverty was getting under way, with all the optimism of a long-delayed crusade. We assumed that federal concern with ameliorating the condition of poor urban minorities would continue, and that we were contributing to it by showing that Mexican Americans were indeed deserving of help.

But we made some other assumptions—never clearly articulated—that were to prove wrong. For one, even though we knew about and analyzed the fluctuating flow of immigrants from Mexico, we never really expected that there would be an enormous increase in immigration in later decades, and we certainly would have dismissed the notion that a wider Latin-American diaspora would become significant. Further, we had no inkling that our sturdy American industrial economy would soon be fractured, with devastating effects on the prospects of all urban minorities.

We were also not well attuned to what was happening in San Antonio. We were based in Los Angeles and spent a great deal of effort trying to understand the complexities of Chicano life in that very complex city. We probably didn't know enough to recognize the extent to which Los Angeles was anomalous in the Southwest. The depth of poverty we saw among Chicanos in San Antonio bothered us, but there were some paradoxical strengths of Chicano cultural life in that Texas city that eluded us.[5]

The Changing Meanings of Ethnicity

For most Americans, the 1960s was an era of black protest, of white southern resistance—often accompanied by shocking violence, and of unprecedented accomplishments in civil rights. Race became a pressing political issue. Researchers were beginning to craft a wide array of alternatives to the prevailing models of acculturation and assimilation, and conflict models were being revived. Both nationally and locally in Los Angeles and San Antonio it seemed that the country was at long last ready to alleviate the struggles and injustices experienced by all people of color, not just blacks.

We subtitled our book "the nation's second largest minority" in an open effort to redefine Mexican Americans in terms of race. The struggles of this southwestern population had gone almost totally unrecognized by the rest of the country—including its social scientists. Too much of the existing literature concentrated on quaint beliefs and archaic practices, while too little documented the obstacles facing Mexican Americans. They were generally portrayed as one of many American ethnic groups, one that was peculiarly attached to the Spanish language and to unusual cultural behaviors. Our book would provide evidence that they should no longer be dismissed as tourist-worthy attractions to be discovered in back-country Texas or New Mexico or the California of John Steinbeck. Mexican Americans were a heavily urbanized minority, and though their struggles were distinctively their own, they paralleled those of blacks in some ways. In fact, blacks were literally living up the street from Chicanos in many of the big cities of the Southwest. In 1965, our interviewers were knocking on doors in Watts the day the riots broke out there.[6] I, for one, felt that in addition to our scholarly goals it was incumbent on us to promote the kind of dialog that would—finally—include Mexican Americans in the national civil rights fervor.

We had good antecedents to follow. Black Americans had long recognized that good social science can be put to political use. Black colleges may have been resource-poor, but they nurtured a steady stream of social scientists and historians. These researchers developed authentic portraits of the burdens of African American life in the urban North as well as in the deep South. In default of actual political representation, black advocacy organizations such as the Urban League and NAACP employed Ph.D.-level researchers to get the facts straight and get them out, and many of the black civil rights leaders had backgrounds in the social sciences. The drama on the streets of Birmingham was backed up by substantial data on the living conditions of blacks.

No such reserve of academic strength existed among Mexican Americans, despite a few outstanding individuals who had gained positions in mainstream universities. UCLA, our home base, had no Chicano faculty in any of the social science departments, and this meant that our senior Chicano colleague, Ralph Guzmán, faced demands on his time and energy that none of us anticipated. Ralph had a long background in journalism and in political activism, and was working on his dissertation when he joined the staff. His task was to develop material on politics and leadership, to supervise the Los Angeles survey interviewers, and, less formally, to enlighten the Anglo members of the staff, like me. He had other demands to meet as well, however. Most of the interviewers for the survey were Chicano graduate students in the social sciences, and Ralph became, *de facto*, a mentor for a group of future Chicano social scientists. He enjoyed that role, and I think that he enjoyed serving as a kind of in-house ethnographer for the Anglo staff. More painfully, he found himself whipsawed between the project and an advocacy organization that had very little understanding of or interest in our goals and techniques. His later career flourished, but his travails reflect the enormous strains involved in being a Mexican American social scientist in that era of intense demands and challenges.

At the time, many Mexican Americans rejected the term *minority* and its implied association with black America. Remember, the only large-scale data source for Mexican Americans was the U.S. census tally of "White persons of Spanish Surname" in five southwestern states. Local euphemisms prevailed. Mexican Americans in San Antonio were proudly Latin Americans, and Mexican restaurants advertised Spanish food.[7] These practices equated middle-class respectability with whiteness, and advocacy organizations emerged after World War II to challenge them. Later, in the civil rights era of the 1960s, the younger militants actively rejected the drive for whiteness. They insisted on being called Chicanos, a term that embarrassed many in the older generation, even though it was often an in-home label. Being a minority had important implications, given the potential role of the federal government. It was all tied up with the politics of ethnicity.

The Political Context for MASP

Our project was funded primarily by the Ford Foundation. Although I did not know how they planned to use our study, I hoped that they would spearhead a movement to bring Mexican Americans more effectively within the purview of federal policy makers. Meanwhile, our findings would speak for themselves. As the political climate changed, politicians were becoming more and more interested in Mexican Americans. In 1960, the Viva Kennedy campaign had made the first serious national effort to harness the voting strength of the sleeping giant, as the Mexican American population had been called for decades. When he became president, Lyndon Johnson followed through—somewhat. He was intimately familiar with the political potential of Mexican Americans in Texas, and when he assumed the presidency it looked as if the population might at long last get some attention.

Federal help was critical because Mexican Americans were isolated and excluded from mainstream politics and had made only small gains in local politics. Outside of New Mexico, only a tiny handful served in state and local legislative bodies. In 1967, there was not one Chicano representative in California's state legislature. Edward Roybal had been the lone Chicano on the Los Angeles City Council (and the first since 1881) when he was elected to Congress in 1962, but no other Chicano would serve on the council for more than twenty years after that. Even as I write these facts, I find them hard to believe: there were so many Chicanos in the city. San Antonio was different. A business-controlled coalition had granted a kind of token representation to Mexican Americans, but they served under an agenda that ruled out attention to community issues (such as paving streets and taking care of periodic flooding in the barrios). A few independent Chicano politicians increasingly made waves in San Antonio and, along with a few representatives from South Texas, in the part-time state legislature. Actually, Mexican Americans had a pretty lively political life in the border areas of that state. There were not, though, many substantive victories statewide.

To fill the void, Mexican Americans formed advocacy organizations after World War II that were designed to confront discrimination and political exclusion. They were particularly active in California and Texas, and had some influence in the Democratic party at both the state and the national level. By the late 1960s, when our project was in mid-stride, openly militant groups had become even more conspicuous. Chicano militancy paralleled the activism of the black civil rights workers, but with a distinctive twist. Except for César Chávez's farm workers and their nationwide move to boycott grapes, the substance of most Chicano claims was probably unintelligible to the rest of the country. Aggressive protests were mounted against the historical injustice of land-grant grabs in New Mexico. An advocacy organization (PASSO) won an unprecedented electoral victory in Crystal City, a small Texas agricultural fiefdom, and out of that victory a militant new political organization was formed—the Raza Unida Party. The RUP, as it was known, went on to mount a full slate of Chicano candidates in Texas and a few more elsewhere in the Southwest. Chicano priests organized PADRES to press for change in the Catholic Church.[8] The Chicano Moratorium rallied some 30,000 Angelenos to protest disproportionate death rates of Chicanos in Vietnam. The Brown Berets and UMAS (United Mexican American Students) organized young people on the streets and on college campuses.[9] UMAS later became MEChA (Movimiento Estudiantil Chicanos de Aztlán), dropping the assimilationist-sounding Mexican American, and choosing a name that was redolent of militancy, cultural nationalism, and historical legacies (compare Vigil 1988). So we were doing our research in an era of unprecedented political activism for Chicanos.

The results of our study were published in 1970.[10] Our hopes for the future progress of Mexican Americans rested on several assumptions: about the federal government, about the economy, and about immigration.

The Federal Government   Our optimistic assumptions about the role of the federal government proved justified, if only in the short run. Federal actions on behalf of urban minorities would continue for almost a decade, and urban Mexican Americans would benefit. Programs like Model Cities and the Comprehensive Employment and Training Act (CETA, passed in 1973 and replaced in 1982 by the Job Training Partnership Act [JTPA]) flourished, emphasizing the empowerment of neighborhoods and creating community-based organizations that met needs systematically overlooked by existing agencies. These ranged from health care for the Spanish-speaking to services for undocumented immigrants and newly released prisoners. Core institutions, such as county hospitals, would become more responsive to their Latino clientele. Even in education, that most localized of all institutions, the federal influence could be felt both in bilingual education and in efforts to increase the number of Chicano teachers.[11]

But it didn't last long. Looking back, our faith in federal influence now seems naive. In the decades that followed, funding for grassroots community-based organizations was deliberately dismantled to clear the way for what were called market-based solutions. Though the electoral potential of the Chicano population grew, accessible local agencies—especially those designed to help "problem" populations—faded. Some survived, vastly transformed. Sometimes those that disappeared left traces in mainstream institutions, but usually they did not.[12]

Economic Restructuring   These local resources vanished at an unfortunate moment, just as economic conditions were undergoing dramatic transformation. But during the 1960s, we had no real sense of these impending shifts. There were a few portents. We knew that the economy of the Southwest, which was then home to almost all of the country's Mexican Americans, had been expanding, but social scientists had to wait until the late 1970s, well after our study was published, before the shift from the Rustbelt to the Sunbelt became obvious enough to provoke national attention and a catchy label.[13] We knew that the proportion of Mexican Americans employed in agriculture had been declining and that by 1960 almost 80 percent of all Chicanos in the Southwest were living in urban areas: after all, that's why we were doing the study. We knew that government and service industries were growing, but our interest in government employment was limited.

Our attention was firmly fixed on the promise offered by our industrial economy. For example, our discussion of industrial concentration opens with an analysis of the benefits of unionization. Unions were considerably more important in the 1960s than they were by the time Telles and Ortiz did their interviewing. Among our respondents, a whopping 54 percent of employed household heads in Los Angeles worked in manufacturing or construction, and there is no doubt in my mind that they would have been better off with easier access to stronger unions. Strong and effective antiunion traditions prevailed in both Los Angeles and San Antonio, though San Antonio again was different. The industrial sector in that town was thin; Mexican American employment in San Antonio was concentrated in tourism and at local military bases. Despite a history of violent strikes involving Chicanos, unions were even weaker there than in Los Angeles.

The nationwide shift from an industrial to a globalized information and service economy was not widely recognized until the early 1980s. Deindustrialization began to be widely discussed then, and so did globalization, the shift of production away from the United States, and the outsourcing of jobs.[14] By the early 2000s, the new trends had generated reams of popular and scholarly writing. If we had recognized in 1969 that we were in the early stages of major economic restructuring—one that would put poorly educated workers at an even greater disadvantage—we probably would have been far less optimistic. In 1987, William J. Wilson used the term *underclass* to describe a new kind of persistent, concentrated poverty that resulted from Chicago's deindustrialization. He painted a truly bleak picture. A storm of controversy ensued,[15] and whether poor urban Latinos could appropriately be termed an "underclass" was particularly contentious.[16] There were many objections: for example, it's difficult to talk about de-industrialization because so many of the cities in the Southwest, like San Antonio, were never really industrialized to begin with. And one of the strongest objections to the term arose because of the importance of immigration to Latino poverty.

The Surprise: Immigration   When we wrote in the mid-1960s, most Mexican Americans—some 85 percent—were U.S. born. We wrote as follows: "Although immigration from Mexico still continues at a substantial rate, the foreign-born component is declining."[17] This trend was one of the grounds for our interest in what we called "assimilative potential." We should have known better. We had analyzed fluctuations in immigration, and noted that "when immigration was curtailed in 1963 and the Bracero Program terminated [in 1964], one of the immediate results was an increasing number of illegal migrants."[18] As we all know now, immigration from Mexico picked up in the late 1960s, and accelerated in the decades to follow.

Furthermore, Mexico wasn't the only source of Latin American immigrants—especially those heading for Los Angeles. In the 1970s, well after our research was completed, Mexicans began to be joined by Salvadorans, Guatemalans, and other Latin Americans—populations that were virtually unknown in the city when we did our research. Twenty years after our study there were almost a million Latinos in Los Angeles who did not trace their ancestry to Mexico, and *Latino* had become a newly relevant term. Many of the immigrants from El Salvador and Guatemala were refugees, and high proportions—an estimated 40 to 50 percent—came without papers.[19] Though many of these new migrants poured into occupational niches avoided by Mexican Americans,[20] there is little question that Central Americans—young, Spanish-speaking, and poorly educated—competed with the continuously poor and poorly educated U.S.-born Mexicans for many low-wage manufacturing and service jobs. Again, San Antonio was a little bit different: Los Angeles was a magnet for immigrants from all over, but San Antonio exerted very little drawing power.

By the 1990s, undocumented immigration had again become an issue not only in the traditional southwestern home of Mexican Americans, but nationwide. It was painfully reminiscent of the 1950s and Operation Wetback. In 1994, two years after Latinos conspicuously participated in the Rodney King riots in Los Angeles, Californians passed Proposition 187 to deny schooling and public health benefits to undocumented immigrants. Some 60 percent of the state's voters were firmly in support of the proposition. It was declared unconstitutional in 1998, the same year that Californians passed another anti-immigrant proposition, this time to undermine bilingual education. In Arizona, traditional xenophobes gained new standing as organized groups of vigilantes patrolled the border, and in New Mexico, a state of emergency was declared for border problems. By 2006, the anti-immigrant movement was well organized, mounting demonstrations, legal challenges, and political campaigns in inland cities hundreds of miles from the border and far away from the Southwest. The presence of an estimated 12 million undocumented immigrants was fueling controversy, and national politicians were struggling to develop a policy that would be acceptable to all.[21]

Still a Minority?

It's an axiom of social science that social research reflects the preoccupations of the times. We were thinking and writing at a time when race was a major issue and when there was strong political pressure to make things better with the power of the federal government. Americans on the streets of almost every big city were being forced to confront the problems of our urban ghettoes, and Washington was responding. In the national consciousness, Mexican Americans were peripheral at best, but they were clamoring for recognition and using every political strategy creative minds could think of, against any and every available target.

It was—and still is—hard for Mexican Americans to penetrate the cultural screen. Most Americans found them confusing. In much of the Southwest, they were treated like a racial minority. They were the targets of prejudice, racial stereotyping, and vicious discrimination. But they were also original settlers, dating back to the sixteenth century, and descendants of a few of those early Spanish-Mexican colonists occupied positions of real power and prestige.[22] They were work-hungry immigrants, now arriving in cities and towns that had never seen them before.[23] They were desperately poor city dwellers. In the countryside of the Southwest, they were traditionalists, almost like American peasants. In the old movies, they had been sexy senoritas, leering bandidos, and noble fighters for freedom—stereotypes that were hard to erase.

Social scientists were accustomed to dealing with populations that were easier to classify. Immigrants of Caucasian ancestry just needed to acculturate and assimilate, and if they held on to some of their family customs that was nice and showed that America could accommodate diversity. Of course, blacks challenged the conscience of America, and there were too few Asian Americans or American Indians for most social scientists to worry much about them. But in the 1960s, we were riding a wave of change, and long-standing paradigms of ethnicity were being challenged. A wide array of alternatives to the acculturation-assimilation models were being explored. Some had special relevance to Mexican Americans, including a short-lived effort to draw out an analogy with newly decolonized nations. The underclass construct bloomed briefly in response to the devastation of economic restructuring, but morphed into a variant of assimilation theory that seemed to depict a semi-acculturated pan-Latino immigrant proletariat, a population that had neither the personal nor the community or social resources to make it in America.[24] We have shifted from a concern with the position of this population in society to a concern for what it takes for individuals to get ahead. This shift has important policy implications.

It may have been something of a miracle, then, that Mexican Americans in fact came to be defined as a minority. Our effort to redefine the population was a small part of a broad trend, dominated by the efforts of Chicanos themselves—advocacy organizations, movement groups, elected representatives, and outspoken scholars. There were consequences that would make most of us feel good: Mexican Americans became beneficiaries of affirmative action, and their barrios became targets in the war on poverty. In the narrow world of academia, most social scientists began to look at the population differently.

The helpfulness of that definition may have been transitory, however. Thus, in the twenty-first century, it was announced that Latinos had become the largest minority in the United States, outnumbering blacks. If only it were that simple. The term *Latino* covers so much diversity that it is virtually useless for understanding why there are so many poor people of Spanish surname (to revert to an outdated term) whose parents and grandparents were also poor. Mexican Americans are still the largest component of the Latino population, but most sources of data do not permit us to extricate their historically distinctive experience from that of more recent immigrants. The findings in this study permit Telles and Ortiz to do so. For that reason alone, this book is of major scholarly importance.

More important, the authors have used the rare opportunity of developing longitudinal data to create a new way of conceptualizing the population—as a racialized ethnic group. The concept rings true. It captures the undeniable strength of ethnic identification and ethnic traditions, and it emphasizes the importance of external forces that created and perpetuate a minority status.

Our study did, in fact, become a benchmark. More significant for me on a personal level, however, is the sense that the political culture that supported social justice for minorities has itself been swamped. There is little doubt that the economic shifts of the late twentieth century shook some long-standing ladders to mobility, and that a huge influx of immigrants has shifted the opportunity structure for Chicanos. There is even less doubt that the political and social climate of the early twenty-first century is deeply antipathetic to government help for inner-city minorities, and that the vast influx of Latin American immigrants has revived and exacerbated long dormant prejudices. Even if the findings in this book unequivocally linked the continuing problems of Chicanos to their painful history of discrimination, I have no sense—though I did in the 1960s—that the national conscience would find a way to make things better for us all.

= Chapter 1 =

Introduction

In 1993, when UCLA's historic Powell Library was being retrofitted to meet stricter earthquake codes, workers found numerous dusty boxes hidden behind a bookshelf in an unused basement room. The boxes contained the original survey questionnaires taken in 1965 and 1966 that were used to inform Leo Grebler, Joan Moore, and Ralph Guzmán's *The Mexican American People: The Nation's Second Largest Minority*, published in 1970. This path-breaking study had accompanied the national discovery of Mexican Americans, which, they claim, began in 1960 with the presidential campaign of John F. Kennedy. Based on random samples of Mexican Americans in Los Angeles County and San Antonio City, their study concluded that though some sectors of the Mexican American population had entered the middle class and begun to participate in American society, there was still little overall assimilation, even for those who had lived in the United States for several generations.[1]

Library staff soon brought these questionnaires and other project materials to our attention. Sensing a unique opportunity, we seized on the idea of revisiting the original respondents. We sensed that Grebler, Moore, and Guzmán's survey could once again be important if we could examine the lives of the original respondents some three decades later and thus create a longitudinal study. In addition, we thought to make this genuinely intergenerational by interviewing the children of the original respondents, who would now be well into adulthood. This kind of follow-up study would require substantial detective work to find the survivors and a sample of their children, both of whom we knew would be scattered not only throughout California and Texas but also beyond. Several years later, with generous funding from the National Institute of Health (NIH) and several foundations as well as the assistance of many energetic graduate students, we were able to locate and interview 684 of the nearly 1,200 respondents who were younger than fifty in the original survey (nearly 60 percent) and 758 of their children.

We believe that this truly longitudinal and intergenerational design would be especially well-suited to address current debates about the integration of immigrants and their descendants in American society. We were able to design a research study that addresses conceptual and methodological issues that arise in intergenerational and longitudinal research and ethnic integration generally. These include the problems of interviewing respondents who might be so highly assimilated that they no longer identify with the group, tracking intergenerational change with cross-sectional data, and selectivity due to respondent loss over time. Our survey examines a randomly selected sample of persons who identified themselves as Mexican Americans in 1965 and follows them and their children some thirty-five years later, regardless of how they identified in 2000. In other words, our research design allows sampling without an ethnic bias. It also permits investigating actual intergenerational change from adult parents to their adult children a generation later, overcoming the problem of comparing generations with cross-sectional data. Finally, to overcome the loss of respondents over time, we are able to adjust our follow-up data to reflect the entire original random sample, using information from the 1965 survey questionnaires.

In this book, we carefully examine the historical and intergenerational trends along several dimensions used to measure the integration of ethnic groups, as well as several factors that may shape these trends. We investigate the trajectory of integration along the dimensions of education, socioeconomic status, exposure to other groups, language, ethnic identity, and political participation. We look for factors that shape the integration trajectory, including generation, education, household characteristics, and urban and neighborhood contexts. As far as we know, this is the only study of its kind.

Background on the Original Study

Grebler, Moore, and Guzmán's study sought to systematically address the huge gaps in knowledge about "the nation's second largest minority" of the time.[2] It evaluated the condition of the Mexican American population using a 1965 to 1966 household survey of Los Angeles and San Antonio as well as the 1960 U.S. Census information on "white persons of Spanish surname" in the five southwestern states of Arizona, California, Colorado, New Mexico, and Texas. Before "The Mexican American People," the major scholarly work on Mexican Americans was ethnographic and based in rural settings. It generally described the population as almost entirely poor, trapped in their backward cultural traditions, and unassimilable.[3] The 1970 study instead focused on cities, where by then most Mexican Americans resided, and concluded that some had entered the middle class and become part of urban American society. On the other hand, the authors found "astonishingly little collective assimilation" among those tracing their origins to the American Southwest in the former Mexican territories of the nineteenth century.

The 5 million Mexican Americans were hardly known outside the five southwestern states in the 1960s, but with massive immigration since then, the Mexican origin population has roughly tripled in size and dispersed beyond the Southwest. Mexicans have become the leading immigrant group in the United States by far. Most research on Mexican Americans fails to make the important distinctions between immigrants, their children, and later generations-since-immigration. Statistics frequently presented for the Mexican American population are swamped by large numbers of immigrants among the population. For example, the low educational levels frequently include immigrants who were schooled in Mexico, where average education is fewer than nine years. Thus, research on Mexican immigrants arriving before 1970 and their descendants has largely escaped the scrutiny of careful empirical analysis.

Indeed, it seems that many Americans still do not know much of this population and often assume that Mexican Americans or Latinos in general are nearly all immigrants and their children. This has permitted pundits to characterize Mexican Americans as immigrants and make facile analogies to other groups. Most notable is the experience of European and especially Italian Americans, whose forebears were the largest immigrant group a century ago and entered the lower ranks of Americans society, and who eventually succeeded in assimilating to the white American mainstream.[4] Analogies to Italians assume that the structural conditions Italians and Mexicans, who also immigrated in the early twentieth century, faced were similar. However, the historical evidence suggests otherwise. Immigrant Italians may have faced discrimination, but their descendants experienced notably less. The children and grandchildren of Italian immigrants were integrated into the thriving economies of the Northeast and Midwest. Second- and third-generation Mexican Americans, on the other hand, were often classified as nonwhite, faced egregious discrimination and segregation, and worked in segmented and less-developed labor markets in the Southwest.

On beginning our follow-up survey, we became more convinced of its potential usefulness as we read the arguments of Washington-based policy analysts that Mexican American immigrants had become much like their turn-of-the-century European counterparts.[5] These analysts took issue with the civil rights protections that Mexican Americans gained in the 1960s (along with African Americans), claiming that Mexican American leaders sought victim status simply to be included in affirmative action policies. Affirmative action, the analysts continued, proved detrimental to Mexican Americans generally, who would have become upwardly mobile anyway and could have become so without having to bear the stigma that their mobility was attributable to affirmative action. These positions contrasted with a formerly racialist position espoused mostly by insiders and a few outsider social scientists. These scholars argued that racism has been the greatest impediment to the progress of Mexican Americans.[6] Unfortunately, the evidence for both schools of thought has been woefully incomplete.

However, forty years after the Civil Rights Act and the end of the most egregious types of segregation and discrimination, and as the children of the recent wave of Mexican immigrants are coming of age, the question of Mexican American assimilation has returned. Do racial discrimination and an overall system of racism continue to be a major force in determining how Mexican Americans are integrated in American society or is it wearing away in this new era? William Julius Wilson has argued that race is declining in significance for African Americans.[7] According to him, the fortunes of children today are determined less by the color of their skin than by their structural or class position in society. Based on the historical and sociological evidence, we also believe that the fairly rigid racial system of the Southwest, with all its economic, political, and social implications that had been the major impediment to Mexican American progress before 1970, has decreased. Does this mean that Mexican Americans have a chance to assimilate like the descendants of European immigrants did?

Our Study in the Context of an Emerging Debate

Since we began this survey more than ten years ago, an academic debate has emerged about the future the children of today's many immigrants face. The case of Mexicans has taken a prominent place in the debate because today's immigrants, unlike their predecessors a century ago, hail predominantly from Latin American and Asia. The intergenerational integration of these immigrants has come to again occupy a central place in American sociology. Theoretical debates about the importance or nature of assimilation have re-emerged, but with a decidedly more empirical bent. In particular, two book-length studies have become prominent.[8] As the largest group in the new immigration, Mexicans have become a litmus test for the assimilation prospects of the new immigration. With the experience of new mass immigration already twenty some years behind us, immigration scholars have mostly speculated about the sociological outcomes expected for the new second generation. However, because the oldest of these children are only now entering adulthood and gaining a foothold in the labor market, it is still a bit early to analyze outcomes such as occupation, intermarriage, and adult identity, though at least one study has begun to provide some early evidence on the possibilities. Examining the adolescent children of immigrants in San Diego County,[9] Alejandro Portes and Rubén Rumbaut's *Legacies: The Story of the Second Immigration Generation*[10] comes to especially pessimistic conclusions about the children of Mexican immigrants, who they expect will experience downward assimilation. The authors maintain that Mexican Americans have little hope of entering the middle class and a large number resolutely identify as Mexican. Instead of becoming like the assimilating Italian Americans, Portes and Rumbaut predict that they will become more like the stigmatized African Americans.

By contrast, Richard Alba and Victor Nee, in their *Remaking the American Mainstream: Assimilation and Contemporary Immigration*,[11] have tried to resurrect the assimilation model, albeit a more nuanced version. They are guarded in their interpretations of the Mexican American experience, primarily because of evidence of poor progress by the third generation, but think that Mexican Americans and the descendants of today's Latin American and Asian immigrants will eventually assimilate, much like earlier European immigrants, and that the social boundaries between groups will for the most part disappear. Although they recognize race as a formidable impediment to successful integration in American society, they believe it is surmountable.

We believe the experiences of the Mexican American population are likely to be mixed rather than unambiguously assimilated or racialized. Some may do well and more or less blend into mainstream society. Others will not. We know little about the variation in outcomes and even less about what factors best determine outcomes. We see a complex sociological puzzle that needs to be sorted out through careful empirical analysis. That puzzle became apparent to us in at least one incident in our early fieldwork. In the exploratory stages of the search process in 1996, we visited the 1965 and 1966 addresses of the original survey respondents. Although we later discovered that this was an inefficient way to locate respondents, we gathered some insights about variations in integration outcomes and the extent of change over thirty years.

During an exploratory trip into the field, we searched for a Gerardo Loya (not his real name) in a poor and traditionally Mexican neighborhood. We began to ask neighbors if they had any inkling about his whereabouts. One such neighbor was Susie Estrada (not her real name), who was born in the United States, had lived next door since the original survey, and remembered Mr. Loya fondly. She claimed that he had moved away about twenty years ago and said she had no idea where he had moved. Ms. Estrada remained in the neighborhood near her brothers and was both unemployed and a single mother. Judging from her appearance and language, she was apparently associated with a cholo (gang) lifestyle—all symptoms of what W. J. Wilson called the underclass. A couple of months later, we located Gerardo Loya through voter registration files. He informed us that he had since moved to a largely white suburban neighborhood and that his eighteen-year-old daughter was about to begin college at Harvard University. The contrast in outcomes was striking. What factors might account for it: differences in education, parental involvement, immigrant status, the move to the second neighborhood, some combination of these, or something else altogether?

Moreover, what role did their ethnic identities play? Did Mr. Loya, who was an immigrant, come to see himself as Hispanic or American after his move? How did Ms. Loya see herself? Did she speak Spanish, English, or both? If either was bilingual, how fluent were they and in what circumstances did they prefer to speak which language? How did their respective experiences shape their identities? Did they experience discrimination? How did they feel about whites or blacks? How did they feel about the current state of immigration? What were their orientations in American politics? How widespread and generalizable are their respective experiences?

We are interested in describing, first, the patterns of integration for Mexican immigrants and their descendants. To what extent are these different from the dominant explanations of immigrant or ethnic integration in the United States? What are the contours of Mexican American integration and what explains deviations from European or African patterns? How do these patterns vary across social dimensions such as education, economic status, language, residential isolation, and ethnic identity? Do these dimensions proceed at the same pace and in the same direction? How are these dimensions related to one another? To what extent is racial discrimination a factor? We are also interested in variation within the Mexican American population. Are such differences patterned consistently by variables such as urban context or skin color? Who are the most successful Mexican Americans? How is success transmitted across generations? What has changed between 1965 and 2000? Is ethnic retention a more likely outcome on some dimensions for Mexican Americans with particular characteristics? How does the low education of the immigrant generation affect the assimilation of their descendants? Finally, what does this say about our theories of race and ethnicity? In a nutshell, our evidence does point to some optimism in the sense that economic assimilation has improved over the course of the twentieth century, though later generation Mexican Americans—whose grandparents, great-grandparents or earlier were Mexican nationals—continue to lag economically behind Americans of European descent.

Before proceeding, a comment on our terminology for various groups is appropriate. We use the terms Anglo, European American, and non-Hispanic white synonymously. In popular parlance, Anglo has been the term most commonly used by Mexican Americans although the simple term white is sometimes also commonly used. However, some Mexican Americans also consider themselves white, which adds to the popularity of the term Anglo, despite its obvious imprecision. Moreover, scholars writing on Mexican American history have used Anglo extensively. The U.S. Census has used a more precise but clumsy and rarely used term, non-Hispanic white, which we sometimes use especially in reference to demographic statistics. We refer to the population we study as Mexican American because it is the preferred term by that population, it captures the expected integration path from Mexican to American, which is the main focus of this book, and it is consistent with terms used for other ethnic groups, including African Americans and various groups of European Americans. The term Chicano refers to the same population which we use mostly to refer to Chicano history, the Chicano movement, and institutions with that name. The terms Hispanic and Latino are also used synonymously to refer to the larger population of Spanish or Latin American descent, which includes but is not limited to persons of Mexican origin. We recognize that Hispanic and Latino do not always refer to exactly the same populations but for the intents and purposes of this study, they are roughly the same.

No Americano Dream

In 2004, as we were getting ready to write this book, along came Samuel P. Huntington, a prominent Harvard professor and former coordinator of security planning for the National Security Council during the Reagan administration, with *Who Are We?: The Challenges to America's National Identity.* Using an argument stressing ethnic identification that was reminiscent of his (also) polemic book *The Clash of Civilizations and the Remaking of the World Order* (1996), in which he predicts that mostly religious identities will determine the new phase of global politics and conflicts, Huntington argues that Hispanics and especially Mexicans pose a threat to American national unity and their large presence in the Southwest "blurs the border between Mexico and America." With his highly selective use of often anecdotal evidence, Huntington concludes that "Mexicans and their progeny have not assimilated into American society as other immigrants did in the past and as many other immigrants are doing now." He goes on to claim that the "unassimilable" Mexicans along with the large numbers of mostly illegal immigrants are leading to a demographic reconquista of the American Southwest. Huntington further concludes by saying that Mexicans lag on every indicator of assimilation and thus calls for a massive reduction in Mexican immigration: "There is no Americano Dream. There is only the American Dream created by an Anglo Protestant society. Mexican Americans will share in that dream and in that society only if they dream in English."[12]

Failing to use basic social science principles, Huntington, at best, only further muddies any understanding of Mexican immigrant integration. For example, he is quite misinformed about the tremendous body of research on the economic and fiscal impacts of immigration, the history of Mexican Americans or Mexican immigration to the United States, and how diverse immigrant groups have affected American culture and politics.[13] The cited passage also suggests that he does not know that virtually all Mexican Americans are fluent in English by the second generation. However, given his prominence as a social scientist and his high profile in Republican administration policy circles, Huntington has strongly fanned the flames of anti-Mexican nativism. The American public and policy makers are likely to take his opinions very seriously, especially given that these often fit with their own commonsense notions.[14]

Huntington's remarks have closely paralleled and reinforced a renewed immigration debate in the Unites States Congress and American society generally. In 2006, Congress sought to pass a major immigration reform bill in response to public pressures, including those by border vigilantes, to reduce illegal immigration and build up border enforcement. However, Congress deadlocked between a Senate bill to grant amnesty to millions of undocumented workers and a House resolution to deny amnesty, enforce employer sanctions, and wall-off large sections of the United States-Mexico border. In response to the drastic measures proposed in the House of Representatives, millions protested in several cities between March and May 2006. At a single march in downtown Los Angeles, for example, half a million marchers, largely immigrants, rallied in protest. The debate continued in 2007 with little resolution except to further extend the border wall.

Our Study Design

We hope to provide a sober analysis based on systematic and well-grounded evidence. We take an empirically based and multidimensional approach to examining the multigenerational status of Mexican Americans, using our unique intergenerational and longitudinal data, which we have compiled over the past decade. Specifically, we follow the original respondents from the 1965 interview and re-interview a random sample of them and their children, regardless of where they moved. We believe that our data allow us to overcome many of the biases in data used to study Mexican Americans or, for that matter, other ethnic groups. Furthermore, we have new data to more fully address competing hypotheses. Our intergenerational design overcomes many of the deficiencies of previous data that are unable to examine true change between parents and children. The data set is large enough for systematic statistical analysis, is based on random samples of two quite distinct metropolitan areas, and has questions appropriate to studying ethnic retention and change.

With our unique study design, we explore sociological indicators, such as economic status and language use, to describe the extent to which the grandchildren and great-grandchildren of immigrants (or descendants of the pre-1848 Mexican settlers in formerly Mexican territory) have been integrated into American society. To what extent have they taken on the cultural or social traits of the American mainstream? Have they assimilated or do they continue to hold low status positions, speak their native language, or see themselves more as foreigners or ethnics than Americans? The answer may lie somewhere between the experience of blacks and whites or it may point to a trajectory quite unlike either group. We believe, as Alba and Nee do, that not all immigrants and their descendants will be integrated into American society to the same extent and at the same rate.[15] We also believe that integration will not always be linear and toward assimilation and that it will be affected by various characteristics or contingencies. Race, place, and human capital are only some of the contingencies that shape the integration of different groups and for individuals within groups.

Our study extends Grebler, Moore, and Guzmán's by thirty-five years, just more than the average generation,[16] which allows us to track the progress of this population. With a sizable adult population in the United States for at least four generations, it seems that a compelling test of successful integration is now possible. As important, these thirty-five years represent the end of legal segregation and egregiously discriminatory laws and policies that had directly impeded progress. We have also benefited from great strides in social science methodologies since the 1970 volume. In particular, we integrate social statistics and longitudinal methods into our analysis. We review these methods in chapter 3. Moreover, the social history of the American West and Southwest, the context of our study, has blossomed in recent decades and provides important information used to set up appropriate hypotheses. We review that history in chapter 4. Finally, several new theoretical developments, related to understanding status attainment and how the large new wave of immigrants is becoming American, have been proposed since the 1960s. We cover these in chapter 2.

Disentangling generation-since-immigration from historical or family generations is an important part of our analysis. For Mexicans, constant immigration throughout the twentieth century has led to repeated first generations throughout the twentieth century, each of which has spawned later generations. Consequently, by the late twentieth century, Mexican Americans of four (or more) different generations-since-immigration intermarry, live together, interact, and, often share a common ethnic identity. This makes the Mexican case quite unlike the European experience on which assimilation theory is modeled. Generational change occurs over time or family generations but, at the same time, each period has families with various numbers of generations removed from the immigration generation. These two conceptions of generation have been treated as equivalents in the past because of the European experience in which mass immigration was followed by a hiatus.

For many European ethnics in the United States, the immigration experience often occurred in a very short time frame, and the descendants of these immigrants at a particular point in time thus tended to be similarly distant from the experience. Family or historical generation and generation-since-immigration were tightly linked. Because previous analyses have generally focused on European immigrants, the Mexican pattern of ongoing immigration—which is likely to become a more common pattern—has eluded previous scholars of assimilation. Most Italians, for example, came to the United States from 1900 to 1915, so that cohorts of Italian Americans in any particular period were generally of the same generation-since-immigration. That is, a cross-section of young adults of Italian origin in 1910 were typically immigrants, in 1940 were second generation, and by 1970 were third generation or more. Thus, each generation-since-immigration tended to experience similar historical events. The New Deal and the early labor movement, which were critical for successful integration,[17] for example, were limited largely to second-generation descendants. By contrast, in studying Mexican Americans, it is important to disentangle family generational status from generation-since-immigration to understand their integration experiences. Both types of generations must be understood to present a full picture of the Mexican American integration process.

In sum, our goal is to investigate the intergenerational integration of the Mexican origin population into American society during the second half of the twentieth century. We ask whether the cultural, economic, and political characteristics of Mexican Americans change in any patterned way the longer families have been in the United States. We take the generational approach that has become the sociological standard for understanding immigrant integration. Our primary stratifying variables are therefore generations over time (family generations) and since immigration. As explained earlier, we divide generation into historical or family generations and generations-since-immigration, which have been largely confounded in the academic literature. We also examine variations in integration among members of this population, differentiated not only by generation but also by other variables, including urban context, parental background, and skin color. This book thus takes a very long view of immigrant integration, investigating the effects of four generations or more of residence in the United States. Ultimately, then, this is a story that is more than a century long, in which fourth-generation persons are unlikely to have ever known their immigrant great-grandparents, who were often Mexican nationals.

Why Study Mexicans?

As a wide variety of scholars—from the most nationalist of Chicano historians to nativists like Huntington—have noted, no other ethnic group in the United States has had the same relation with its origin country. Through ideas of race and manifest destiny, the United States appropriated nearly half of Mexican territory in 1848 following the Mexican-American War and that history has shaped subsequent relations between the two countries and arguably the social and economic position of Mexicans in the United States. This conquest and "annexation" subsequently set the stage for a tension-filled relationship between the two countries. Since then, Mexicans have become the largest immigrant group in American history and the largest contemporary immigrant group.[18] United States immigration policies have long treated Mexican immigration in a distinct manner, largely in response to economic interests that have long relied on this large, low-skilled labor pool. These policies have led to the creation of an undocumented status category of workers, the so-called illegal, which has produced an especially exploitable labor pool since the 1930s.[19] This has major implications for Mexican American integration into American society.

A shared 2,000-mile land border and starkly contrasting levels of development have long made immigration to the United States attractive to the Mexican poor. Along with a history of conquest and the geographic proximity of Mexico, this low-skilled and continuous immigration has shaped American images of Mexicans as well as the experiences, collective memory, and self-image of Mexican Americans. The century-long immigration, preceded by conquest and an additional sixty years of low intensity circular immigration,[20] is unlike that of any other ethnic group in the United States. Among other things, it has resulted in a large and multigenerational presence in the United States. Those identifying as Mexican origin in the 2000 census constituted 28 percent of the population in the five southwestern states.[21] The ethnic dominance of a single group in the Southwest is quite unlike the East and Midwest of a century ago, which was characterized by multiple national groups of European immigrants, whose mass movement had mostly halted by the 1920s.

Another justification for studying Mexican Americans is their wide internal variation. This heterogeneity helps us explain why some may assimilate more than others. Theories that explain why some national groups are slower to move up the occupational ladder or shed their ethnic identities and behaviors generally ignore such internal variation and thus may be of limited value. The Mexican American experience covers a broad range—from growing up and living in segregated barrios to mostly white suburbs, from unskilled manual worker to professional, from Spanish monolingual to English monolingual, from identification as Mexicano to American, from recent immigrant to descendant of Spanish land-grant families, and from light skin with blue eyes to dark brown skin with Indian features. By examining the relationships of these variables to such outcomes as ethnic identity, language use, and education, we can begin to understand which factors might best explain different rates and paths of assimilation.

Finally, given the media attention to Hispanics or Latinos in recent years as they have become the largest minority, we should explain our focus on Mexicans. We hesitate to conflate them and generalize about their presumed pan-ethnic experience, as is fashionable today, even though there are some similarities between Mexicans and other Hispanics. For one, the public's recognition and treatment of them seems to often be the same. The unique histories, culture, and immigration contexts of each group need to be understood, however. We believe that this is especially true for Mexicans.

First, as we have noted, the historical depth and demographic size of the Mexican population is unlike any other national group from Latin America. Second, the circumstances of Mexican immigration are unique. We note that Puerto Ricans are American citizens before their migration, which began only in the 1930s. Cubans have been largely middle class and were given refugee status since they began arriving in large numbers in the 1960s. Based on the evidence thus far, the descendants of Puerto Ricans seem to have been racialized, whereas Cuban-Americans have been more successfully assimilated.[22] Other groups—such as Salvadorans and Guatemalans—may be more like Mexicans in that they are labor migrants but their immigration is only recent and considerably smaller. Still others, like Dominicans, are also relatively recent and mostly labor migrants but often experience racialization as blacks.

Finally, whether Hispanics can be considered a single ethnic group is itself questionable given that few prefer to identify that way[23] and that there are also large differences culturally, racially, and otherwise.[24] On the other hand, Latinos or Hispanics have been collectively categorized and often racialized as such in the American mind. The fate and image of Mexican Americans, who comprise 62 percent of all Latinos, is often generalized to other Latinos, and vice versa. Certainly, in the American Southwest, at least, other Latinos are often perceived, labeled, and perhaps treated as Mexicans. The historical stigma of being Mexican is thus often pinned on persons from Latin America generally. In this study, we do not make arguments about the racialization or assimilation of non-Mexican Latinos but do not deny the implications of the Mexican American experience and similarities for other groups.

Race and Ethnicity in American Sociology

Although we seek to track the particular situation of Mexican Americans in the latter third of the twentieth century, our study has implications for understanding race and ethnicity in general. The area of race and ethnicity has long occupied center stage in American sociology as researchers throughout the twentieth century have sought to understand how immigrant, racial, or ethnic groups are integrated into the host society. Since the field's inception, American sociologists, based mostly in the Northeast and Midwest, have been largely concerned with the social dynamics of immigration and race and ethnic relations in the rapidly changing cities around them. They have sought to understand how European immigrant groups and their descendants, through an often competitive and intergenerational process, were able to eventually become fully or nearly fully American. In contrast, many also became concerned that a phenotypically distinct group—African Americans—seemed unable to assimilate. Some analysts thus began to study how racism and racial discrimination limited the life chances of some Americans and prevented them from receiving the full benefits of American citizenship. This dual American experience of assimilating European Americans versus excluded African Americans in Midwest and Eastern cities therefore became the dominant models for understanding race and ethnicity in America. These models still dominate today.

Certainly, those of European and African origin comprised the vast majority of Americans until the 1970s, though there have long been significant numbers of Mexicans and Asians, not to mention the once-predominant Native Americans. However, these groups were generally concentrated in the West, far from the Midwest and Eastern social laboratories that most American sociologists found in the cities around them. It was only with large-scale immigration of Asians and Latinos since the 1970s that mainstream American sociology became concerned with the integration experience of other groups of Americans. Immigration from Latin America and Asia would also become more geographically dispersed. By then, major universities had also emerged throughout the United States and research had become increasingly national in scope.

In recent years, a lively debate has ensued about the future of these new immigrants and their descendants, but unfortunately it has formed around the classic divisions of assimilation versus the persistence of race cast by the sociologists of the earlier era. Although some expect that Latinos and Asians will assimilate like the Europeans before them,[25] others expect that the traditional racial categories of white and nonwhite, the latter would include Asians and Latinos along with blacks, will continue to predict their experiences in American society.[26] On the other hand, the multigenerational outcomes of the descendants of immigrants from Asia and Latin America may fall somewhere on a relational continuum between African Americans on one end and the assimilated European Americans on the other.[27] Still another possibility is that the experience of immigrants and their descendants will vary across the white-black spectrum according to national group or perhaps according to still other characteristics.

A global perspective on race and ethnicity will reveal that European American assimilation and African American racialization are not the only two possible outcomes in plural societies. The nature of race and ethnicity in diverse contexts extends well beyond the framework provided by mainstream American sociology. Blacks and mixed race people in Brazil, for example, are largely assimilated in terms of marriage, residential integration, and feeling part of the Brazilian nation, but are mostly excluded in education and the labor market.[28] This is distinct from the experience of the descendants of African slaves in the United States. The Roma in Central Europe, though often physically indistinguishable from other Europeans or gadje, are often stigmatized as poor and petty criminals. In most historical periods, they have been excluded from formal employment, though during the socialist period, they were fully employed.[29] Koreans in Japan are yet another example.[30] To take an extreme case, Jews became explicitly and fully racialized in Nazi Germany and were nearly exterminated on the basis of their ethnicity or race.[31]

These and many other examples show that race and ethnicity have many more manifestations than the two dominant American perspectives can account for. For one, racial exclusion and assimilation often coexist. Additionally, race is often based on perceived cultural differences, rather than merely on phenotype. Moreover, the intensity of exclusionary experiences based on race or ethnicity may vary over time or across geographies, as the cited examples have shown. Indeed, the national context, social institutions, and attitudes about immigration affect ethnic integration, as the case of Moroccan and Turkish persons in European countries reveals.[32] These variations show that historical, political, economic, and ideological contexts or circumstances have shaped the nature of race and ethnicity in numerous ways.[33]

Even though it is an American experience, the case of Mexican Americans also does not seem to fit well into either of the two dominant race and ethnic paradigms in American sociology. The reason often implicit in the literature is that they, like many other non-European immigrants, are recent arrivals and thus we can only speculate on their intergenerational experience. The empirical verdict for the integration of the new (post-1965) immigration is not yet in because the oldest U.S.-born children of immigrants in this wave are barely still young adults. These speculations are—somewhat surprisingly—made despite the fact that some of these groups predated the new immigration, sometimes by as much as a century or more. Mexicans in the United States, like Africans and Europeans, have had multiple generation experiences. Mexican Americans have had a significant presence in the United States throughout the twentieth century, and well before. As we will show, that pathway is one that features a multigenerational persistence of ethnicity that combines elements of the assimilation and the persistence-of-race paradigms, but contains other unique elements as well.

Assimilation and Racialization

Assimilation and racialization have both been used to describe how American society has integrated those of Mexican origin. In popular conversations, both race and assimilation commonly describe Mexican

Americans, but those terms are often both ambiguously and unevenly used, and not based on evidence to support the various arguments. Instead, we focus on sociological definitions of the terms and examine the extent to which these concepts might apply based on systematic examination of hard evidence. By assimilation, we do not refer to the often desired but contentious goals set by some, better referred to as assimilationism. Instead, assimilation refers to the actual social process by which immigrants and their descendants may become integrated with and more like members of the host society through prolonged exposure and socialization to them and their institutions. There are several versions of assimilation theory, which we review in chapter 2. Assimilation often occurs whether or not those affected or anyone else wants them to. Assimilation would seem to be a reasonable expectation especially in a society like the United States, with its characteristically strong institutions (such as a formal democracy), public education, and its mass consumerism and culture, which all arguably promote homogeneity. However, the strong force of assimilation in American society may be slowed or even halted by the counterforce of racialization. Racialization may act to maintain or strengthen ethnic boundaries despite the forces of assimilation.

Like assimilation, racialization—designating people by race, thus implying their position in a social hierarchy—is also a sociological process. The idea of race was once based in biology and assumed that the human species could be subdivided into races, and that intelligence and other characteristics could be ranked on the basis of race. Today, race no longer has scientific validity, but society continues to commonly sort people into racial categories, according to assumed physical, ancestral, or cultural characteristics. Racialization creates images or stereotypes about people that are used to evaluate them and thus to guide social interactions with them.[34] The idea of racialization as a process is also useful because it recognizes that these categories and placement in them change over time and across societies.

Today, racial distinctions continue to be popularly accepted as natural divisions of humanity with an implicit racial hierarchy that largely defines one's place in society. The accumulation of racially discriminatory treatment disproportionately sorts those stigmatized into the bottom strata of society even as it privileges others.[35] Moreover, this hierarchy is generally accepted as a natural aspect of society and thus may lead individuals to find their place in it regardless of direct discrimination. All this occurs despite a common ideology today that the United States is color-blind.[36] American society often stigmatizes those of Mexican origin, regardless of whether Mexicans are considered or consider themselves white, whether they are physically distinct, or whether they speak Spanish or have a Spanish surname or accent. This racialization also creates shared personal and political identities, which often become the basis for collective political action.

Whereas European ethnics assimilated into mainstream (white) American society, African Americans have long been racialized into a subordinate status and have thus been largely unable to assimilate. Although European immigrants were often racialized as nonwhite, they were largely accepted as white by the second or third generation, which allowed them to fully or nearly fully assimilate. For Mexican Americans, though, we find racialization especially in education well into the fourth generation, even though cultural and other forms of assimilation may occur.

Our data directly show that economic integration, the most desirable aspect of assimilation, stalls after the second generation while cultural, social and political assimilation occurs slowly but constantly over generations-since-immigration. As we will show, a sorting into the lower ranks of American society is mostly through public education. Moreover, persistently poor education over several generations-since-immigration largely accounts for the slow or interrupted assimilation of Mexican Americans in socioeconomic, cultural, residential, and other dimensions of life. Thus, poor educational opportunities, more than any other factor, exclude many Mexican Americans from successful integration into American society.

The Mexican American case shows that low education is not the only factor that slows assimilation. The size of the Mexican American population in the American Southwest and continuing immigration further promote residential isolation and ethnic persistence. These two factors make the Mexican American experience unlike that of African Americans and thus complicate our understanding of race in the United States. The large demographic presence and continuing immigration are products of a historical American dependence on Mexican labor. In addition, a continuing immigration of Mexican workers creates a largely Mexican context in many southwestern cities, such as Los Angeles and San Antonio, which regenerates ethnicity among Mexican Americans. These factors are likely to strengthen ethnic identity and ethnic behavior. One might argue that they also increase racialization by making the group more visible, ethnically distinct, and ethnically cohesive, as they respond politically to shared issues.

Assimilation and racialization may both be useful for understanding the Mexican American case, though neither term can be applied to Mexican Americans as they are to the European and African American experiences, respectively. Mexican Americans do show signs of assimilation on some dimensions but the process is inconsistent and slower than for European groups. Whereas European Americans assimilated on most dimensions by the third generation, Mexican Americans do not. Indeed, there are no signs of complete assimilation on any dimension even by the fourth generation, though loss of Spanish comes closest. Indeed, one can easily point to dis-assimilation, such as the increasing residential isolation from 1965 to 2000, or to the fact that education worsens from the second to the third generation-since-immigration. If assimilation happens slowly and direction is often uncertain, can we even call it assimilation?

On the other hand, should we refer to the Mexican American pattern of integration as racialized? If we limit ourselves to the African American model of racialization, then we probably should not. Mexican Americans out-marry and are residentially integrated much more than African Americans, and Mexican American ethnic and racial identities and political affiliations are also much more fluid than those of African Americans. Boundaries with other groups are far more permeable, a fluidity often determined by generation-since-immigration. To the extent it occurs, racialization may have quite different sources and current manifestations.

Racialization is thus more complex than it is for blacks in the United States. The idea of race also may arise from the changing nature of immigration. Also, racialization and the creation of racial stereotypes emerges in nineteenth-century conquest and continues afterward. The stigma is reinforced by the defining characteristics of Mexican immigration to the United States—low-wage labor and illegal status—and from the asymmetric relations between the two countries. Discrimination against Mexican Americans focuses particularly on the immigrants, but frequently extends to anyone of that origin. Substantial racial or ethnic boundaries may thus arise even for culturally assimilated U.S.-born Mexican Americans because of societal racism or nativism directed at Mexican immigrants but felt by all persons of Mexican origin.

In many ways we show the glass as both half full and half empty. Some Mexican Americans have done well and most do better now than their parents did when they were young in the 1960s. Those are signs of partial assimilation. However, they continue to lag well behind their Anglo counterparts, which also reflects a process of racialization. Our title *Generations of Exclusion* conveys the problematic fact that a large part of the Mexican American population has not been allowed the same opportunities that have been given to mainstream America and these disadvantages tend to get reproduced across generations. In a country as wealthy as the United States and one that holds fairness and equality as fundamental, how is it that many Mexican Americans fall behind? Even if we consider the assimilation stages that many believe are necessary for immigrant groups to become fully integrated, how then do we explain that the U.S.-born children of U.S.-born parents (and often U.S.-born grandparents) that are of Mexican origin have among the worst educational levels in the country? Moreover, their low educational status has kept them from becoming fully integrated in American society in many other ways. That, in our judgment, reveals a fundamental dilemma in a society that considers itself inclusive.

Organization of Chapters

We lay out our theoretical, methodological and historical background in chapters 2 to 4, our findings in chapters 5 to 10, and our conclusions in chapter 11. Specifically, chapter 2 begins by reviewing theories and important findings that have guided scholarly understanding of ethnicity, assimilation, and race. It summarizes previous and current debates about the process of immigrant integration, including several versions of assimilation and racialization theories but also other perspectives about the role of national borders and state policies. It pays special attention to how Mexican origin persons might fit into these conceptual frameworks. Thus chapter 2 guides our analysis and sets the foundation for the rest of the book.

Chapter 3 describes our study design, including the sample, research methodology, and the longitudinal and intergenerational approach. In the interest of providing a transparent and scientifically based analysis, we specify our methodological steps. These, we believe, have yielded highly reliable data for our analysis. First, our study is based on a 1965 random sample of Mexican Americans in the two largest counties where they were represented. Second, we searched over a period of five years and eventually interviewed nearly 60 percent of the original sample (who were age fifty or younger in 1965) as well as a sample of their children. These data were then carefully weighted to compensate for respondents we were unable to locate and for self-selection bias in interviewing original respondents and their children. Chapter 3 is thus critical to demonstrating the strength and, particularly, the representativeness of our findings.

Chapter 4 provides context by exploring key trends in the history of Mexican Americans and by specifying how historians have come to view their position in American society. We begin with the 1830s, when Anglo Americans first began to dominate in northern Mexican lands and then launched a war to occupy them in the 1840s. Since that time, Mexicans were explicitly depicted as an inferior race—an idea that continued to sort the descendants of various waves of Mexican immigrants into subordinate positions throughout the twentieth century. At the same time, Americanization campaigns sought to assimilate Mexicans and Mexican Americans struggled for acceptance and equal opportunities. Legally, they first sought classification as white and then simply equal protection under the law, both to improve their lot in American society. Interestingly, their political and legal struggles often focused on education, which we find continues to be the central factor that keeps Mexican Americans disadvantaged. We emphasize how tensions between assimilation and racialization have contributed to the economic and political outcomes of Mexican Americans today.

Chapters 5 to 10 present the results of our survey and focus on intergenerational change from parents to children and over generations-since-immigration. We examine several dimensions involved in the integration experience of Mexican Americans, focusing on structural factors in chapters 5 through 7, and on culture, identity, and political issues in chapters 8 through 10.

Chapters 5 and 6 are concerned with the hierarchical or vertical issues of socioeconomic assimilation, which captures the core concerns of fairness and the American dream. Chapter 5, which explores education, turns out to be particularly important. It shows relatively low levels of education for Mexican Americans, which persist for generations beyond the immigration generation. Educational disadvantage or exclusion impedes social mobility and produces economic disadvantage for Mexican Americans throughout their adult lives, which we explore in chapter 6. In a stratified society such as the United States, socioeconomic status or hierarchical boundaries between ethnic and racial groups are arguably the most salient indicators of successful integration. In the case of Mexican Americans, their persistently low socioeconomic status reveals poor integration or assimilation.

Chapter 7 examines the social relations of Mexican Americans with other groups. We focus on intermarriage and residential segregation but also examine friendships and interracial attitudes. Mexican Americans are much more likely than African Americans to intermarry and live near whites and other groups, though rates of intermarriage and residential integration are far from random. Even into the fourth generation, many Mexican Americans continue to live in barrios and marry other Hispanics. Like status generally, exposure and relations outside the group are determined by education. The low levels of education that persist across generations impede this kind of assimilation.

Chapter 8 investigates cultural integration, particularly in language. Although nearly all Mexican Americans are proficient in English by the second generation, we discover substantial Spanish language persistence into the fourth generation. By the fifth generation, however, few children learn Spanish at home. The progressive loss of Spanish language proficiency over generations reveals a clear linear trend of linguistic assimilation, though a slow one relative to other groups. We find similar patterns regarding the naming of children in Spanish, a practice which does not require fluency in Spanish but does indicate ethnic attachment. We also find that Mexican Americans remain mostly Catholic by the fourth generation, though significant numbers have switched to being Protestant. Many also participate in ethnic culture, including celebrating holidays and listening to ethnic radio or music.

In chapter 9, we explore Mexican American identities or, more specifically, the subjective making of ethnic differentiation from the perspective of Mexican Americans. We examine how Mexican Americans self-identify and understand their position in American society. We examine whether a shared collective identity sets the population apart as a group. We find that, even into the fourth generation, identification with Mexicans or Mexican Americans remains strong, though for a minority, American identities have become stronger. Finally, racial identification as nonwhite is strong and increases from parents to children. However, even among those who identify as white, perceptions of discrimination are common.

In chapter 10, we then examine politics and political identities, investigating whether Mexican Americans are assimilating politically and whether they can be seen as a voting bloc. We also explore what common interests might underlie political boundary formation, especially in regards to presumably ethnic issues like immigration, affirmative action and bilingualism. We find that Mexican Americans, especially immigrants, were almost entirely Democratic in the 1960s but that Democratic partisanship diminished notably by the 1990s, especially among later generations-since-immigration. We also find surprisingly strong support for immigration, affirmative action, and bilingualism even into the fourth generation, suggesting that generational differences have failed to create ethnic group cleavages in attitudes regarding ethnic issues. Mexican Americans are clearly pro-immigration compared to blacks and whites, regardless of whether they or their parents or even grandparents were immigrants.

We summarize the results in chapter 11 and propose a new understanding of Mexican integration in the United States. To what extent are existing theories of integration able to explain the case of Mexican Americans and what are the shortcomings of these theories? To what extent are Mexicans exceptional in the American experience? How does the Mexican American experience inform sociological theories of race and ethnicity? First we summarize the conclusions from the earlier chapters into an account of how those of Mexican origin become Americans, providing a mixed picture of assimilation (e.g., language) or persistent disadvantage (e.g., education). However, we also find large differences in outcomes among our respondents, some of which are explained by their varying experiences such as growing up in either San Antonio or Los Angeles. We differentiate interpretations based on historical or family generations from those based on generations-since-immigration. We also articulate an explanation premised on how significantly a century or more of American dependence on Mexican labor has contributed to the unique position of Mexican Americans. We then speculate about the future of Mexican Americans. Ultimately, we hope to have contributed not only to a sociological understanding of immigrant integration in general but also to the experience of the descendants of the longest and largest immigrant group in the United States.

═ Chapter 2 ═

Theoretical Background

How ethnic groups are integrated in national societies and why they take particular paths are subjects of considerable debate. In the United States, the literature on their integration often revolves around a tension between assimilation and racialization perspectives. Even though Mexicans are the largest immigrant group with the longest duration in the history of the United States, little is known about their integration trajectories. Do the descendants of Mexican immigrants assimilate into mainstream society, like the descendants of European immigrants have, does race come into play, or is there another path? There is no consensus but much debate about which path they did or will follow, if indeed only these two paths exist. Where some analysts cast Mexican Americans as ethnics who follow the assimilation experience of European immigrant groups, albeit more like the slowly but surely assimilating Italians, others see them as a group that has been marginalized on the basis of race, much like African Americans.

We believe that a simple assimilation or racialization hypothesis may oversimplify reality. For one, it requires fitting the Mexican American experience into either the African American or European American box. Mexican Americans, like Native Americans or Asian Americans or ethnic minorities in dozens of countries across the globe, are unlikely to fit entirely into either. Furthermore, factors besides racialization or assimilation may define their experience and there may be important variations within the group. Ideas of race and assimilation, at least as they have been formulated so far, may be artifacts of a social science built largely on one empirical model (the United States), and, moreover, mostly on either the experiences of those of African or European origin. Drawing from realities throughout the globe, Stephen Cornell and Douglas Hartmann stress the remarkable "diversity of forms of race and ethnicity, the variety of functions they apparently serve and the quite different kinds of attachments that claim the ethnic label."[1]

In recent years, the debate on ethnic integration has focused mostly on the economic dimension, drawing heavily from the debate on the significance of race for African Americans and other groups. On the racialization side, scholars have often assumed that Mexican Americans have been discriminated against and that their mobility has thus been blocked. Evidence based on national statistics show that Mexican Americans, like Puerto Ricans and African Americans, have persistently low socioeconomic status even by the third generation.[2] Since at least the 1970s, many scholars, working largely from an ethnic studies perspective, have argued that racism has been the greatest impediment to Mexican American progress.[3] They claim that Mexican Americans have experienced such ills as discrimination in labor and housing markets, inferior and segregated education, tracking into manual jobs, and exclusion from voting rights. In contrast, the historiography of earlier European immigrant groups suggest that the children of immigrants made impressive gains over their parents, with continuing economic and social gains by the third generation.[4] Scholars of assimilation have generalized these findings to Mexican Americans, while conceding the process is slower for them.[5]

Immigrant or ethnic integration may also vary by social dimension, so that the nature of integration may differ along them. We examine ethnic integration broadly and beyond the issue of economic status, as many contemporary accounts tend to do.[6] The noneconomic dimensions of the integration process, including the cultural, linguistic, and political, are less well theorized and analyzed but are often assumed to go in the same direction as economic assimilation. A high degree of language retention, for example, may reflect the residential and educational segregation of Mexicans and the availability of Spanish language media, which is often made possible through the large presence of immigrants. We may find evidence of assimilation on some dimensions, such as language, but not others, such as identity.[7] For example, we might expect a strong sense of ethnic consciousness and progressive political behavior if Mexican Americans perceive racial discrimination as limiting their chances of success.

Based on the experience of European ethnics, for which there is ample evidence, we could expect almost complete erosion of ethnic traits by the fourth generation. The third and fourth generation descendants of European immigrants to the United States are often depicted as having only symbolic ethnicity,[8] in which the ethnicity is not accompanied by cultural and social distinctions that matter in the real world, such as language, but is instead often limited to symbolic acts, such as celebration of national holidays or cuisine. That is, ethnicity is no longer particularly important for these individuals or for society. In contrast, however, it might have greater significance in arenas where it results in inequality or social divisions. Indeed, ethnicity varies in intensity from strong, such as regional minorities like the Basques in Spain or Kurds in Turkey, to symbolic, such as most

European Americans. The former have developed strong nationalist projects and some members have maintained their native languages despite assimilatory pressures, while the latter's attachment to their backgrounds is generally nothing more than occasionally celebrating ethnic holidays or preparing ethnic foods. As John Comaroff puts it, "Why is ethnicity sometimes the basis of bitter conflict, even genocide, while at other times, it is no more than the stuff of gastronomic totemism?"[9]

Unfortunately, the tension between assimilation and racialization has over-simplified the many possible manifestations of ethnicity. The debate thus far has been largely grounded on studies of the eastern half of the United States involving the contrasting experience of Europeans, on which models of assimilation are drawn, and African Americans, from which we base our theories of race. In the Mexican case, we discover assimilation, although slow, on cultural dimensions like Spanish language maintenance, but we simultaneously find strong evidence of racialization influencing educational attainment, which in turn stunts economic integration. Certainly, we borrow heavily from theories of assimilation and racialization as our guide-posts to understanding the Mexican American experience, but as this study will show, we also need to go beyond these traditional explanations.

Ethnic and Racial Boundaries

Fundamentally, we examine ethnic and racial boundaries. Ethnicity and race, whether or not created through racialization, assimilation, or any other process, necessarily involves social boundaries. Fredrik Barth argued that ethnicity is largely created when establishing boundaries between groups during social interaction, contrary to earlier assumptions that ethnicity merely reflects cultural differences.[10] Race, a concept that overlaps with ethnicity, also involves boundaries established in social interaction. Racial boundaries, however, tend to be more rigid because they involve strong doses of discrimination and idea of social hierarchy. Race refers to a group that is defined as culturally or physically distinct and, furthermore, ranked on a social hierarchy of worth and desirability.[11] This is similar to the distinction between caste and ethnicity Max Weber proposed in 1922.

Our book follows in this tradition. It is largely an empirical analysis of how social boundaries between Mexican Americans and other groups, especially the dominant group, are enhanced, persist, blur, or disappear over time and between generations. Alba and Nee's use of assimilation relies on the concept of social boundary, which they define as "a categorical distinction that members of a society recognize in their quotidian activities and that affects their mental orientations and actions toward one another."[12] Jimy Sanders similarly defines ethnic boundaries as patterns of social interaction that give rise to and reinforce in-group members' self-identification and outsiders' confirmation of ethnic distinctions.[13] We find the boundary concept particularly useful, especially because it allows a holistic analysis of the multiple dimensions that comprise ethnic retention or complete assimilation. Some of these dimensions, which we examine in this book, include ethnic identity, which are distinctions made by the in-group that set them apart from others; language, which marks a largely impenetrable boundary that separates insiders from outsiders; residential concentration, which also limits social interaction with other groups; and politics, which is often contested by ethnic groups in ways that reinforce some boundaries but erode others. Clearly, ethnic boundaries on all these dimensions exist between Mexican immigrants and mainstream American society, as they do between most immigrant groups and the mainstream. Mexican immigrants, in particular, see themselves as different: they speak a different language, often live in segregated barrios, and have generally quite distinct political views. But what do we make of ethnic boundaries for their descendants? Do they persist or eventually erode over the generations that follow?

The societal treatment of Mexican Americans has, at least historically, rested on a scientific and popularly accepted idea of race that has legitimized the subordination of nonwhites throughout the Western world, at least since the early nineteenth century.[14] Although Mexican Americans are often referred to as an ethnic group and not as a race, they were referred to as the latter in earlier times and arguably continue to be referred to and treated as such in societal interactions today. The ethnic boundary between Mexican Americans and the mainstream may thus persist largely because of race. Certainly, the history of conquest and colonization of former Mexican land and people was legitimized on racial grounds and since then, Mexicans have sometimes sought to negotiate out of their nonwhite status, as we show in chapter 4. This includes the individual strategies of passing as white through high societal position or light skin[15] and the collective strategies of Mexican American leaders in the past who sought to reposition the entire group as white to escape segregation and restrictive immigration laws.[16] At other times, though, Mexican American leaders have also argued that as Americans, and despite their race or ethnicity, Mexican Americans deserve fairness and full citizenship rights. For Mexican Americans, race has thus been somewhat malleable, which reflects the dynamic process of racialization.

Social boundaries may exist at several levels and together capture the extent of ethnic group distinctions. In the classic anthropological literature, ethnic group distinctions were mostly based on differences in cultural traits such as languages and traditions. However, Fredrik Barth recognized that the boundaries societies established, including how societal members identified and were classified in particular categories, were at least as important as the cultural content thought to define ethnicity.[17] Cornell and Hartmann explain that social boundaries and culture are not independent, and in fact reinforce cultural and racial distinctions.[18] Richard Jenkins and others have discussed in depth how identities are constructed on the basis of social interactions,[19] which are in turn affected by the identities and by the way in which others create categories and then treat people accordingly. Intermarriage and friendships, for example, are not random but rather often patterned by the way in which individuals ethnically or racially classify and evaluate each other, as well as by social patterns that result from these distinctions, such as residential, educational, and occupational segregation.

Employers and educators often treat employees and students differently by ethnicity or race so that labor and educational markets sort groups into different levels on the basis of prestige or status. Such discriminatory treatment racializes the ethnic group and hardens the ethnic boundary. In addition, the group's actual or perceived modal socioeconomic status is also often associated with its alleged intelligence, aspirations and abilities, which further racializes ethnic group boundaries. The Mexican American example seems to follow this pattern, in that their status is largely defined by racial discrimination against them and the low status of the large numbers of unskilled immigrants among them.

Insiders, outsiders, and institutions each shape the nature and rigidity of ethnic boundaries.[20] In turn, group classification and treatment generate differences in whether those being classified think of themselves as different or equal, and shape how the discriminated respond, including "performing" their differences through language, celebration of ethnic traditions, and politics.[21] Economic domination, reinforced by an ideology about race or the proper role of particular groups in society, for example, may create and reinforce such boundaries. The rigidity of boundaries is reinforced by social structures and institutions such as residence, labor markets, schools and state policies that shape and maintain differences and inequalities, which themselves create boundaries among groups. The media, popular culture, and an accepted moral discourse further delineate particular groups by making ethnic or racial distinctions apparent or natural.[22] These boundaries may be extremely rigid, permeable, or nonexistent, depending on the group in question. Mexican Americans may see themselves as similar or different and may seek to maintain boundaries by developing strong ethnic identities or bridge them through American or white identities. Mexican Americans may also reflect the high profile and rigid national boundaries between the United States and Mexico, which reinforce ethnic boundaries within the United States.

The rigidity of social boundaries between the descendants of immigrants born in the United States is the focus of a long-standing assimilation versus race debate. Following the expectations of classical sociology and economics, many have questioned whether race and ethnicity can endure in modern societies. Theories of race and ethnicity deal largely with why ethnic boundaries remain salient for identity and for allocating opportunities in a modern industrial society. As early as 1926, Robert Park expected that modernizing forces would "dismantle the prejudices and boundaries that separated races and peoples," and eventually lead to "progressive and irreversible assimilation."[23] Modernization expects greater universalism and therefore a decreasing significance of ethnicity and traditional values.[24] Modernization and, more specifically, its ethnic variant assimilation have long been prominent in the social sciences and continue to drive the study of ethnicity in American life.

By contrast, the racial-ethnic competition perspective expects that with modernization, ethnicity will become more salient because ethnic competition and conflict increase as groups are increasingly thrown into greater competition over scarce resources, thus heightening ethnic identification and ethnic boundaries. As a result, some individuals will mobilize and join with others of the same mind to use ethnicity as a resource for personal and group advancement.[25] In the process, some groups are racialized or stigmatized as nonwhites, thus naturalizing their inferiority in relation to whites and automatically disqualifying them from competition for economic resources.[26] Also, where discrimination blocks economic assimilation, racialized ethnics may seek to maintain ethnic distinctions and resist assimilation. These processes seem to be important for understanding how Mexican Americans and other ethnic groups build or break down ethnic boundaries. In the following pages, we examine the development of this literature.

Assimilation Theory: Erosion of Boundaries

Ethnic group boundaries are often thought to be worn away with increasing exposure to another culture. In the United States, this is often expressed as assimilation or Americanization and often involves a process over several generations, but may also occur in the lifetime of an immigrant. Theories of assimilation underlie most concepts of ethnicity in the United States. Park and his colleagues had scientifically sought to confirm the general idea of the United States as a melting pot capable of assimilating the many distinct ethnic groups that immigrated to the United States a century or more ago. Milton Gordon's *Assimilation in American Life* has been the canonical treatise on ethnicity in American life and is consistent with the classical liberal and modernist tendencies of the social sciences, which expected that race and ethnicity would eventually dissolve with the extension of rationality and universality in a modern industrializing society.[27] Gordon and others suggested a progressive, if not linear, movement from foreign to eventually complete acculturation and from lower to the higher status of members of the host society. Based on the available research evidence, which focused on European immigrants, Gordon expected widespread structural assimilation, which he defined as full participation into the social networks of the host society,[28] which in turn naturally led to all other forms of assimilation. For Gordon, group boundaries were set by the lack of interaction and spatial isolation but once these barriers are broken, full assimilation was likely.

Gordon's formulation of assimilation continues to be important for its many dimensions[29]—cultural, structural, marital, identity, prejudice, discrimination, and civic. In laying these out, Gordon recognized and proposed that assimilation could occur more in some social spheres than others, though he expected all groups to adopt the cultural patterns (except religion) of Anglo American society. These dimensions are also important because they would permit the growing field of quantitative sociology to specify and analyze specific outcomes of assimilation. Gordon's model was mostly based on the immigrant experiences of European arrivals to the American Midwest and Northeast.[30] Despite the persistent low status of blacks in the United States, Park's[31] and Gordon's predictions of eventual assimilation held to the predictions of the classical European sociologists, whose ideas dominated early American sociology.[32]

Park and the Chicago School of Sociology in the 1930s and 1940s and Gordon's classic *Assimilation in American Life*[33] in the 1960s had profound influences on the field, institutionalizing assimilation as a rule for immigrants and their descendants, even though the Mexican group received little attention. Indeed, the assimilation model has been so powerful that its followers generally have accepted it as the pattern all immigrant groups and their descendants experience,[34] with the possible exception of African Americans. More to the point, Mexicans (and Asians and Indians) were well off of the radar screen of the largely eastern and midwestern-based social sciences.[35] At best, they were viewed as some inexplicable frontier anomaly.

According to Alba and Nee,[36] Gordon emphasized only the last stage of Park's race relations cycle—assimilation—as developed by the Chicago school, whereas Tamotsu Shibutani and Kian Kwan's *Ethnic Stratification: A Comparative Approach,* published around the same time, integrated Park's fuller process of contact, competition, conflict, and accommodation.[37] Specifically, Shibutani and Kwan's theory elaborated on the processes that may hinder assimilation, including power differences between different groups, barriers based on white supremacy discriminatory institutions and the role of racial classification and ideology in which people are treated according to the racial categories they are fitted into.[38] Moreover, Shibutani and Kwan were sensitive to the apparently distinct ethnic issues of the western United States, not to mention their understanding of the rest of the world. Their own ethnic experiences and location in California certainly helped them understand the wider range of ethnic phenomena in the United States. Shibutani was the son of Japanese immigrants, grew up in Stockton, California, and taught at the University of California, Santa Barbara. Kwan, a Chinese national, grew up in the Philippines and was later studying under Shibutani when they wrote *Ethnic Stratification*.[39]

Nonetheless, Gordon's book would have much greater influence on the subsequent social science literature on immigrant integration, perhaps not surprising given academia's eastern United States bias. Although Grebler and his colleagues[40] provided little discussion of the mechanisms that led to their findings, their emphasis on stratification and their integration of concepts such as social isolation and social mobilization seem to closely reflect Shibutani and Kwan's[41] and thus Park's[42] research interests. Joan Moore, a University of Chicago-trained sociologist like Shibutani and the only sociologist on the original Mexican American study, rejected Gordon's emphasis on acculturation, which she felt was not important in itself, and had little to do with the far more important issue of successful economic integration.[43]

In a sociological sense, Grebler and his colleagues were primarily concerned with the extent of social interaction between Mexican Americans and the dominant group.[44] They sought to "depict factually and analytically the present realities for Mexican Americans," which they believed depended on their "interaction with the dominant system."[45] They found that a large part of the Mexican American population remained on the lowest rungs of American society, resided in ethnic enclaves, and retained their language more than any other group, despite several generations in the United States. They also saw greater assimilative potential for Mexican Americans than for blacks, with whom they shared many characteristics of low socioeconomic status. They discovered substantial socioeconomic diversity within the Mexican American population, which they attributed to growing structural diversification and urbanization. Among the young, better-educated, and residents of mixed neighborhoods, they described— contrary to previous accounts—"considerable social interaction of Mexican Americans with Anglos." Grebler, Moore, and Guzmán thought that assimilation was incipient for Mexican Americans, noting that, for the most part, they may not have had enough time to assimilate like "the longer resident minorities."[46] This was in apparent contradiction to their findings of especially low status for many of the "charter members," that is, those of the fourth generation or more in 1965.

Internal Colonialism: Persistence of Racial Boundaries

Gordon's classic on assimilation was released in 1964, just as the civil rights movement was getting into full swing. The role of race and the experience of subordinated groups other than blacks were becoming the subject of academic inquiry for the first time. Social scientists sought alternative models to the dominant expectation of a common American experience of assimilation for racial minorities and European immigrants. The American experience with race, at least on the black-white cleavage, was simply difficult to explain with the European-inspired social theories of ethnicity, including not only assimilation and modernization but also Marxism.[47] Italians, Poles, Jews, and other immigrant groups and their descendants had assimilated by the 1950s.[48] The Mexican American picture, however, also looked quite different to scholars familiar with the Mexican experience, as it did for blacks and American Indians. Many of these scholars were in fact members of these groups, which were entering American universities for the first time in significant numbers.

The internal colonial model of the 1960s and 1970s was an early attempt at an alternative explanation. Although internal colonial scholars often referred to Mexican Americans and others as "ethnic groups," they would generally describe their situations in a racialized manner. Sociologists writing in the late 1960s looked to Latin America for inspiration in the theories of Andre Gunder Frank, Pablo Casanova, and Rodolfo Stavenhagen. The economic theories of the time expected a burst of industrialization and economic development in the region, such as had occurred in Western Europe. New theories, however, explained underdevelopment as a result of the colonial and exploitative ties that poor nations had with Europe and the United States. With that inspiration, and with the perceived failure of the assimilation model to explain the case of blacks and other groups, several scholars in the United States developed theories of internal colonialism to account for persistent racial oppression, poverty, segregation, and white skin privilege.[49] They theorized that the cheap labor the indigenous populations offered served the economic interests of domestic metropolitan elites and induced capitalists to maintain a rigid system of racial stratification.[50]

In sociology, Robert Blauner gave one of the most systematic accounts, claiming that "people of color" in the United States are embedded in historical-structural circumstances that include conquest and colonization rather than voluntary immigration, subjection to labor regimes that limit mobility and a colonizing policy that destroys or transforms ethnic culture.[51] Political and educational institutions and a racist ideology, reinforced by state police and bureaucracies, act to reinforce the subordination of minorities, thus furthering the economic interests of the colonizer. Blauner considered Mexican Americans a hybrid between a racialized minority and voluntary immigrants to a land historically and still, in many ways, culturally and socially Mexican.

Internal colonial theorists suggested that this ethnic division of labor would also lead to persistence of ethnic differentiation in various dimensions. Blauner, for example, painted a picture of significant cultural autonomy for groups such as Mexican Americans, who were not differentiated by generation but whose culture was devalued and reduced to stereotypes by dominant group members.[52] At the same time, Blauner claimed that cultural imperialism in the internal colony sought to break down ethnic culture and ethnic ties of solidarity to facilitate exploitation. Forced Anglicization served the goals of the colonizing group in the United States. In perhaps the most fully elaborated and nuanced account of internal colonialism, Michael Hechter argued that Celtic minorities in the English periphery maintained their culture because their labor was subordinated on the basis of culture and they collectively responded to their marginalization.[53] According to historian Ramon Gutiérrez,[54] the internal colonial model would serve as the theoretical framework for a new generation of empirically based Chicano history in the 1970s and 1980s, most clearly seen in Rodolfo Acuña's[55] sweeping account of Chicano history in *Occupied America*[56] and Mario Barrera's[57] class-internal colonial account in *Race and Class in the Southwest.*

However, Moore, armed with the recent findings of *The Mexican American People*, cautioned against the internal colonial model.[58] She noted how these theories neglected the regional diversity and considerable stratification of the Mexican American population, but her warnings seemed to go unheeded. It took until the mid-1980s, perhaps with Albert Camarillo's careful empirical study of southern California, for Chicano scholars to begin to realize that they had gone too far in emphasizing racial oppression, resistance, and conflict as they had sought to refute the accommodation and assimilation theories they had so strongly disagreed with.[59] Tomas Almaguer, a leading exponent of internal colonialism in the 1970s, recanted his earlier support for the theory, claiming that it was empirically inaccurate but a necessary break from the overdetermined assimilation theory. Among his arguments, his own work demonstrated that Mexican status fell somewhere between that of whites and both Asians and blacks in the nineteenth century, when they received full legal citizenship and were perceived as assimilable. Moreover, internal colonial theories could not account for differences in the social treatment of Mexican Americans by gender, phenotype, class, generation, and region.[60] Also, substantial intermarriage gave proof of well-established and fairly fluid relations among at least some Mexican Americans and whites. Finally, the idea of Chinese, Filipinos, and particularly Mexicans as involuntary minorities, as opposed to voluntary immigrants, was beginning to be seen as a weakness of internal colonialism, as massive immigration from their homelands was re-emerging.

Assimilation Theory Reformulated: Diversity in Boundary Erosion

The changing composition of the new wave of immigration—primarily from Latin America and Asia, has again raised questions about the extent and nature of economic adaptation for the descendants of immigrants including those that were already well represented before post-1965 immigration. As a result, a new generation of scholarship emerged that was primarily concerned with the fate of the new immigrants and their descendants. Both the assimilation and racialization arguments have been made with new immigrants in mind, but because of growing empirical evidence, these positions are less polarized. Revisited, the debate has focused largely on whether the mostly Asian and Latin American immigrants and descendants of the current wave of immigration will assimilate more like Europeans or African Americans.

Assimilation theory has had a major shift since Milton Gordon's classic, mostly because of the work of Alba and Nee in 2003.[61] Their idea of assimilation follows the more nuanced work of Shibutani and Kwan[62] and the earlier work of the Chicago school. Unlike Gordon,[63] their theory of assimilation emphasizes a process of becoming similar rather than any ultimate state, and makes room for the possibility that assimilation works for some groups more than others. They also stress that assimilation is involuntary, such that a series of economic motives, rather than a decision to become like dominant society, lead to behaviors that are considered assimilative. For example, seeking mobility opportunities is fairly universal and generally implies learning English and trying to access mainstream social networks. Agreeing that Gordon's formulations were inappropriate for the experiences of many groups, Alba and Nee's work has recast assimilation's basic premises for the new era of mass migration. They argue that assimilation "will be a force of major consequence" though it may not be the "master trend" it was for the descendants of earlier immigration.[64]

Whereas Gordon identified the target of assimilation as an Anglo-Saxon core, Alba and Nee argue that the endpoint is a changing mainstream defined as "that part of the society within which ethnic and racial origins have at most minor impacts on life chances or opportunities"[65] and constituted by diverse ethnic elements. Like Shibutani and Kwan, Alba and Nee bring the notion of power and the role of institutions into their analysis, where subordination of minorities is largely maintained through the institutionalized power and outright coercion often directed at racial minorities.[66] They also introduce the idea that assimilation depends on the rigidity of social boundaries that keep particular ethnic groups from entering the mainstream.[67] They describe how a process of social exclusion against African Americans and an enduring and rigid black-white boundary has kept them out of the assimilation process, at least economically. Alba and Nee acknowledge mechanisms that explain the "coexistence of both blending and segregating processes" such as the extent of shared identity versus racial exclusion and the ability of dominant groups to wield power. They cite early evidence that some new immigrant groups and their children are held back because of race. West Indian immigrants, for example, must constantly emphasize their acceptable immigrant identities so as not to become perceived and thus treated as African American. Their children, unfortunately, have less of a choice.[68]

Despite this, Alba and Nee are guardedly optimistic about the long-term integration prospects for Mexicans. They observe that despite a relatively high degree of speaking Spanish into the third generation, there is a clear erosion in retaining it over the longer term. They also argue that residential segregation for Mexican Americans and other Latinos is moderate and that attitudes toward them may be improving. They also speculate that the assimilation prospects of light-skin Latinos may be particularly good. However, they are less optimistic when it comes to schooling, recognizing that low educational attainments, even for the third generation, may be due to racialization.[69] This lack of achievement gives Alba and Nee pause for concern, but they seem to hold off their verdict regarding educational assimilation in the long term.[70] Alba and Tariq Islam, however, later contend that Mexican American education may not be so low, implying that poor data might be yielding artificial results.[71]

With Alba and Nee's new formulation, their more nuanced perspective can accommodate a greater diversity of experiences among immigrant groups.[72] They recognize the apparently complex and contradictory patterns of different groups, which include rapid assimilation and integration as racialized minorities.[73] They note that racism and the ability of immigrants to accumulate human capital are significant contingencies. If rates of assimilation differ widely and may even be avoided, however, how robust a theory can this be? If the conditional "most groups" comes into play, as it does for Alba and Nee, then how do we predict or differentiate those who will assimilate from those who will not?

Segmented Assimilation: Boundary Erosion for Some, Maintenance for Others

With the recent emergence of a young cohort of children of post-1970 Latin American and Asian immigration, some sociologists have begun to document early signs of educational failure among particular ethnic groups. Assimilation theory, at least in its classical form, is unable to account for the poor schooling and early labor market experiences of particular second generation nationalities, including West Indians and Mexicans, although the children of many Asian immigrants and some Latin American groups have revealed encouraging to very positive outcomes. Herbert Gans noted "second generation decline" among nonwhite immigrant children who were relegated to bad schools and jobs and experienced downward assimilation compared to their parents.[74] Alejandro Portes and Min Zhou then incorporated three paths—the possibility of "downward" assimilation, the traditional assimilative path of intergenerational success and a third path of economic success but within an ethnic economy[75]—into a more general theory of segmented assimilation.[76] Portes and his colleagues hypothesize that the outcomes for the second generation of various national origins depend on the human capital of the first generation, how those immigrants were received by the United States government, and whether vibrant ethnic communities awaited them.[77] These factors determine the extent of access to social networks and financial resources for immigrants and their children. For those who do not have such access, vulnerability to downward assimilation is compounded by proximity to the minority experience in the United States.

Portes and Rumbaut pay special attention to the Mexican case and come to especially pessimistic conclusions.[78] For them, the children of Mexican immigrants are embedded in a particularly negative context in which the parents' low human capital combines with hostile government immigration policies and a history of racial stigmatization to impede school performance and reinforce strong Mexican identities, despite the positive orientations of parents to school. At the same time, the loss of the Spanish language among a large proportion of second-generation respondents reveals not only Americanization but also an inability to communicate with immigrant parents whose limited English is further impeded by their low socioeconomic position. A dissonance between parents and children thus accompanies child acculturation. Moreover, Portes and Rumbaut show that those early signs of educational problems for the second generation are replicated in the third generation. Using findings from the U.S. Census, they show apparently even worse outcomes among the third generation, as others have also shown.[79]

While other groups tended to have relatively positive experiences, Portes and Rumbaut do not expect conditions for Mexicans to improve over time; in fact, they expect downward assimilation for future generations.[80] These findings mirror other evidence showing especially high dropout rates and substandard school performance for Mexican American youth, leading them to accept a reactive ethnicity perspective in which stronger ethnic identities form in opposition to perceived constraints on social acceptance. Portes and Rumbaut affirm John Ogbu and Maria Matute-Bianchi's racialization claims that Mexican American youth develop oppositional identities that emphasize loyalty to one's group and "collective dignity," which draw from internal colonialism perspectives.[81] Thus, Portes and Rumbaut's explanation of Mexican American integration emphasizes the role of racism, specifically a hostile context of reception for Mexican immigrants and their children, overwhelming the positive influences of high educational aspirations and immigrant optimism.

Although Alba and Nee and Portes and his colleagues take distinct positions on the possibilities of upward mobility for the children of immigrants, and on the role of race, they both greatly advance the simpler models of assimilation and racialization perspectives by introducing important contingencies in their respective explanations of intergenerational progress.[82] They do not simply predict or assume assimilation or racialization but also seek to understand the conditions under which ethnicity would be most or least salient. These authors, despite their distinct conclusions, recognized how the integration of immigrants and their descendants is affected not only by national origin but also by factors such as human capital, the structure of urban areas, the extent of segregation and skin color, acknowledging that assimilation is a more complex process than previously believed. Although these contingencies lead to different outcomes under segmented assimilation theory, Alba and Nee believe that they merely hasten or hinder eventual assimilation but accept that African Americans are an exception.[83] A subsequent piece by Rumbaut and Portes, possibly reacting to earlier work by Alba and Nee,[84] is critical of "too many contingencies" in assimilation theory "to render the image of a relatively uniform and straightforward path as unconvincing."[85]

On the other hand, Portes and Rumbaut's very negative account of the Mexican experience may reflect an unusual context, which is based on the educational performance of a sample of youth in San Diego in 1996.[86] About half of those youth were born in Mexico, suggesting that integration difficulties may be due to very recent immigration. Additionally, respondents are all adolescent, a particularly difficult and an often rebellious life stage. Whether these young persons are able to bounce back in later years is not clear, but schooling performance at that age is certainly vital to adult life outcomes. The very dissonance they experienced with parents may partly reflect the differences between adolescence and adulthood. Similarly, Alba and Nee argue that Portes and Rumbaut treat urban youth culture as constant and assume that race-ethnic boundaries are static throughout the life course.[87] In addition, San Diego at the time of their study may have represented a particularly hostile context for Mexicans as an English-only movement spread in that area and two statewide anti-immigrant initiatives (Propositions 187 and 227) were endorsed by a conservative California governor and former San Diego mayor. Finally, they do not account for the fact there may be wide variation in the Mexican American experience. A few of Mexican origin may become solidly middle class and show signs of thorough integration in American society.

Status Attainment

An important component of contemporary assimilation theory, whether straight or segmented, is the status attainment model. This is concerned with how parents transmit their social and economic standing to their children and how education determines adult socioeconomic or occupational position.[88] Indicators of the family's socioeconomic status—

especially parent's education, father's occupation, and family income—significantly predict the educational status of offspring and other human capital variables, which in turn predict occupational and income status. Many contemporary analysts of immigrant integration consider that Mexican Americans are disadvantaged and take long to assimilate because of their immigrant ancestors' low human capital.[89]

Straight-line assimilation theorists add to the status attainment model by explaining that status improves over generations as immigrants and descendants learn English, acquire human capital, and become increasingly integrated into mainstream American institutions and culture. Low human capital leads to low earnings and an inability to secure housing in middle class and predominantly white neighborhoods, thus limiting intermarriage and promoting residential segregation. Isolation in predominantly ethnic neighborhoods, by contrast, would likely reinforce continued use of the ethnic language. Nevertheless, these theories would expect Mexican Americans to accumulate enough human capital by the third or fourth generation that the social boundaries between them and the dominant group would greatly erode.

Education also greatly affects one's adult socioeconomic status. This is consistent with human capital theory. Status attainment describes how highly educated students get access to professional networks and mainstream institutions. A related theme found in much of the assimilation literature is how higher socioeconomic status also facilitates assimilation by improving access to mainstream networks and institutions. A spatial version posits that higher incomes allow ethnics to afford more integrated neighborhoods, which in turn provide greater access to members of other ethnic and racial groups as well as to better and more integrated schools, which facilitates the assimilation of their children. The status attainment model considers that nonwhite race may also impede success.[90] However, some analysts in the status attainment tradition argue that race tends to be overplayed in the sociological literature, especially for nonblack immigrants, whereas the role of human capital is often overlooked. They contend that the low status of Mexican Americans has been empirically shown to result from education deficiencies rather than from discrimination in the labor market, which largely accounts for the low status of African Americans.[91] Of course, such analysts often overlook that discrimination may also occur through education. Education—measured by years of education, high school drop-out rates, and other indicators—is especially low for Mexican Americans, even compared with African Americans.[92]

Race and Racialization: Maintaining Boundaries

The path that Portes and Rumbaut specified for Mexicans in their segmented assimilation model largely involves the stigma of race. Whereas Alba and Nee see race as only slightly and perhaps temporarily significant in the assimilation of most Mexicans and other Hispanics, Portes and Rumbaut seem to give it central and lasting importance. The role of race for nonblacks and nonwhites has consequently occupied a central place in the study of new immigrant groups. Although sociological theories about race developed primarily in relation to African Americans and in contrast to the experiences of European Americans, other theories about how and why racial identity form have been applied to a wider range of groups. Most prominent were the internal colonial theories, which were developed in the 1960s and 1970s, largely in response to classic assimilation theories. For example, Herbert Blumer's theory of Race Prejudice as a Sense of Group Position, which Lawrence Bobo and his colleagues have extended, claims that modern racial prejudice results largely from normative ideas about "where one's own group should stand in the social order vis-à-vis other groups."[93]

Another prominent theory is Michael Omi and Howard Winant's racial formation, which argues that meanings and ideologies of race in the United States are widely shared and shape individual identities as well as political and economic relations, both collectively and individually.[94] Similar ideas, collectively called racialization theories, also emerged mostly through British sociology.[95] Racialization naturalizes social distinctions and creates stereotypes that guide individuals in how they interact with or value others. To understand racialization as a process moves us away from the traditional approach to race as a static variable, which often seems to refer to an unquestioned or essential attribute of birth, much like the racial scientists had it a century ago. Although race is a biologically invalid concept but important socially, racialization refers to the sociological process that makes racial differences meaningful. The idea of race and racially discriminatory practices are often deeply embedded in society, but they can change, albeit slowly, as particular groups or individuals may have their position shifted on a racial hierarchy. Also, racialization varies in intensity. It may be particularly intense, for example, among persons who are perceived as distinct physically or culturally from the dominant group.

Racialization and Mexican Americans

Racialization seems particularly appropriate for describing the changing experiences of groups such as Mexican Americans, whose treatment on a racial hierarchy has varied over time and place and who sometimes may be perceived as not racially differentiated from the dominant group. While race often refers to a predetermined set of fixed categories decided by 19th century biological scientists, racialization is a process in which racial categories themselves change as well as the meanings, value or stigma given to them also change. Racial characteristics are often physical but they may also be based on cultural or other criteria commonly associated with ethnicity. For example, Jews were clearly racialized in Germany in the 1930s and 1940s and often racialized in the United States at the time of mass immigration but they are generally accepted as part of the white population today. Officially, Mexican Americans have not been classified as a race in the U.S. Census since 1930, and in 1977, the U.S. Congress passed the Office of Management and Budget's (OMB) Statistical Directive 15, which deemed that racial and ethnic categories should be collected separately and that for data collection purposes, Hispanics were an ethnic but not a racial group.[96] Despite its limited scope, OMB Directive 15 became an important standard for how groups are to be classified in general. Regardless of this edict, much evidence indicates that Mexican Americans have been popularly classified and treated as nonwhite. Moreover, the U.S. Census tends to exclude Hispanics in its official tabulations of the so-called racial groups (e.g., non-Hispanic whites and non-Hispanic blacks) and reports statistics for them separately and in addition to the other groups, thereby treating them as a de facto racial group. By contrast, the descendants of various European immigrant groups, many of which were previously racialized as nonwhite, are now popularly labeled and treated as white, a cause and consequence of rising to the top ranks of the American socioeconomic structure, as well as in their generally lighter appearance.

Social linguists have also shown that societal racism is reinforced through debasing metaphors, often conveyed through the mainstream media. Otto Santa Ana shows how these images establish the public's commonsense view of Mexican immigrants in the United States. These media metaphors treat Mexicans as lawbreakers, burdens, noncitizens, unpatriotic, and unable to ever become fully American or even humans despite the polite denials of other Americans. Although often directed at immigrants, they limit Mexican (and often Latino) social identities, regardless of one's immigrant status. As George Lakoff and Mark Johnson have noted, metaphors define societal understandings of reality and thus guide its behaviors towards an understanding of others.[97] Metaphors about Mexicans may be more subtle than the explicit racial slurs of the past but they nonetheless may stigmatize or racialize those of Mexican origin. Richard Flores shows how the pervasive Alamo myth has defined the Mexicans as enemies of the United States, established a stigmatized identity for Mexican Americans, and led to rigid ethnic boundaries between the conquered Mexicans and the patriotic whites, which it decrees as the legitimate Americans.[98]

Overall, these theories refer to how race is an important organizing principle in American society. However, we prefer the concept of racialization over race because it refers to an often-changing process that hardens or softens such boundaries. Racialization gives particular meaning to racial identities and the idea of race as varying across societies and over time, rather than as being an unchanging fact of birth. Thus we find the concept of racialization particularly useful for discussing Mexican Americans regardless of (baseless) official or biological classifications of race.[99]

Social scientists often employ the concept of ethnocentrism, or the belief in the normality and superiority of one's people and their way of doing things.[100] It is often applied to foreign-born groups but, unlike racism, allows that foreigners and their descendants may change or assimilate, as in the case of European Americans. Ethnocentrism of the first generation often gives way to assimilation of the second. In American sociology, racism often refers to the ideas that whites have of blacks and ethnocentrism to ideas about foreigners, especially European immigrants, even though attitudes about the latter were often clearly racist.[101] That is, racism and ethnocentrism have gone hand in hand. The Mexican American experience, though, defies this dualism. Many Americans are ethnocentric in their attitudes about the large and often undocumented Mexican immigrant population, but their ethnocentrism and related nativism often translate into stereotypes and racialized attitudes about those of Mexican origin generally. On the other hand, others are ethnocentric about immigrants and perhaps some of their descendants, but believe that they can nonetheless change over time and become ordinary Americans. Our point is that the distinction between racism and ethnocentrism is derived from a model that contrasted the experiences of European immigrants with African Americans. But about Mexican Americans, boundaries are established based on both ethnocentrism and racism.

Beyond the Traditional Paradigms

Mexico-United States relations, and particularly United States immigration policy regarding Mexicans, also may have large implications for how Mexicans are integrated into American society. The United States-Mexico border and the asymmetry between the two countries would seem to be an important factor. National and thus ethnic boundaries are particularly strong, given Mexico's geographical proximity and unequal relation with the United States, and the consequent century-long historical dependence on Mexican labor. Mexico's history has been more intertwined with the United States than any other country's. The annexation of nearly half of Mexico in 1848 and the creation of a militarized border make the relation arguably more antagonistic than any other. Mexican nationalism since then has often been framed in these terms, and Mexican immigration to the United States has arguably been the dominant issue in relations between the two countries.

Mexican Americans are often defined by the experience of their immigration and thus immigration policies may be particularly important in their integration.[102] States define who become members of American society by restricting immigration.[103] Societies thus decide who belongs and who doesn't. Exclusionary immigration policies signal to co-ethnics already entrenched in American society that they are not fully American, despite the principles and rights declared in the constitution. This is particularly true of immigration policies that identified and stigmatized Mexicans and some Asians as illegal immigrants.[104] From the perspective of the immigrants, established minorities serve "as instruments of Americanization, while also providing a counter-community, which proves attractive when the majority is unwilling or reluctant to let individual immigrants make their own way upward."[105] Thus, it would seem that for those of Mexican origin in the United States, hostility aimed at immigrants in general and Mexicans in particular hurts natives but the (limited) political and social gains of ethnic natives reduces immigrant exclusion. Based on extensive interviews with U.S.-born Mexican Americans, Tomás Jiménez finds that continuing Mexican immigration sharpens their racial and ethnic identities through the indirect effects of nativism.[106]

An immigration policy that makes hierarchical distinctions about immigrant treatment with designations of refugee, legal immigrant. and undocumented immigrant is also likely to create different kinds of ethnic boundaries. Portes and his colleagues emphasize how distinct contexts of reception further or impede the comparative assimilation experiences of immigrants to the United States. For example, Cubans fleeing Castro received generous housing, loan, and employment assistance, despite the fact that those immigrating tended to already have high levels of human and social capital. By contrast, Mexican immigrants today are mostly undocumented because of a state policy that has radically limited the number of work-based visas to Mexicans.[107] Mexicans applying for United States visas today can expect up to a forty-year wait, although amnesty laws and family reunification visas have shortened the wait considerably for some.[108] Consequently, Mexican immigration is unregulated, the source of a very large, inexpensive, and tractable labor force that serves American employers and consumers very well. This ultimately shapes the nature and salience of ethnic distinctions for Mexican Americans.[109]

In addition to immigration policies, social boundaries involving Mexican Americans are also affected by domestic laws and other state decisions. That is, the state creates racial or ethnic categories for official or census recordkeeping. The Hispanic distinction, though considered an ethnicity rather than a race, has nonetheless been treated as a racial category, as previously discussed.[110] More explicitly, Washington implemented and enforced exclusionary policies such as segregation, poll taxes and segmented labor markets for Mexican Americans that remained in place into the 1960s. It then created race-specific policies such as affirmative action and the Voting Rights Act, which sought to include Mexican Americans and other groups. Other policies, though they may not necessarily name particular groups, may also be racially based. This is particularly apparent in the funding patterns of public education, both among and within schools.

Finally, the state's approach and capability to integrate immigrants also changes over time in the United States and other Western democracies.[111] In the United States, the official policy of Americanization to encourage rapid assimilation has shifted to an emphasis on multiculturalism, even though rapid assimilation may occur nonetheless.[112] Also, democratic openings have allowed racialized groups to ease some of the most egregious affronts. Largely through the efforts of the excluded, racial boundaries may be dissolved, transformed, and reorganized. In the United States, the civil rights movement has arguably attenuated the rigidity of the boundaries. Mexican American ethnic political entrepreneurs and civil rights organizations have also sought to defend the population against discrimination since at least the 1940s. Although blatant racism may have diminished, the political polarization of the groups may have also further reinforced ethnic distinctions.

Forgotten Within-Group Variation

Comparing ethnic group experiences is standard in American sociology. Far less is known, however, about differences in the experiences of individuals within the group. Assimilation and racialization theories emphasize integration processes for particular groups, and thus have largely neglected variation within the groups. Why are some individuals economically successful and assimilate, and others not? As we noted earlier, Mexican Americans have a diversity of characteristics that may affect their integration, including their family background, where they live, and their skin color. Certainly, authors such as Alba and Nee and Portes and Rumbaut have argued that these are important for the direction and pace of integration but may also be important in understanding in-group differences.[113] Such factors may hasten or constrain the assimilation or racialization process for particular individuals.

We have reviewed issues of parental education under the status attainment perspective. We expect that parental education will also affect variation among Mexican Americans. We also examined how changing industrial structure is theorized to affect the future integration prospects of the new immigrants. We contend that our Los Angeles–San Antonio sample from 1965 to 2000 allows us to directly tap the effects that an industrialized labor market in 1965 (Los Angeles) and a service-oriented labor market (San Antonio) had on Mexican Americans. Whereas Grebler, Moore, and Guzmán's 1970 study emphasized the extent to which the two locales represented modernization or cultural development, we focus on how their distinct structures have shaped integration outcomes in 2000. In the following paragraphs, we examine how these urban distinctions, neighborhood segregation, and skin color may influence the varied experiences of Mexican Americans.

Urban Context: Geographical Distinctions on Ethnic Boundaries

Contrasts between Los Angeles and San Antonio include industrial differences, but other urban distinctions may also be significant. Grebler, Moore, and Guzmán stressed the range of Mexican American experiences using Redfield's modernization-inspired continuum, in which Los Angeles is considered more modern and acculturated and San Antonio more traditional and unacculturated.[114] This focus reflected communal rather than individual foundations of social change, particularly Robert Redfield's "folk to urban continuum" and Louis Wirth's classic statement on "urbanism as a way of life."[115] Redfield, who largely shared the ideas of his colleague Robert Park, observed that in the most traditional and remote villages as well as in the neighborhoods of modern societies, such communities of small numbers were easily identifiable by outsiders and fellow community members. These communities tended to be quite homogenous. To examine such communities, Grebler, Moore, and Guzmán would often stratify Mexican Americans in their tabular presentations according to residence in Los Angeles or San Antonio and from more to less segregated areas. They found that San Antonians were more traditional than Angelenos, as were those in more segregated areas.[116] They also characterized San Antonio as being more egregiously and formally racialized, and having a weaker labor market than in Los Angeles.

Several changes have occurred since then. First, formal and explicit racism have mostly if not entirely disappeared in both places. Also, post-1965 immigration to Los Angeles has been significant, in contrast to surprisingly low levels in San Antonio. Today, both urban areas have large Mexican-origin populations, but these are largely immigrant with young second-generation children in Los Angeles and a mostly settled population in San Antonio. Finally, heavy industry with highly paid blue-collar jobs has been replaced by light industry with poorly paid jobs since the 1970s in Los Angeles, whereas San Antonio has had an underdeveloped industrial structure and depended on poorly paid service sector work all along. In both places, Mexican Americans continue to predominate in working class jobs, with immigrants in the lowest strata of the labor force.

Neighborhood Context: Boundaries Through Childhood Ethnic Isolation

Urban experiences are also captured as segregation at the neighborhood level. The study of neighborhoods has been a focus of sociological inquiry, at least since the Chicago school of the 1930s. From community studies, we have learned of the ways in which neighborhoods create or limit economic opportunities and forge or dissipate a sense of identity.[117] Grebler,

Moore, and Guzmán recognized that the degree to which a society was traditional or modern depended largely on the degree of isolation of the population.[118] Those who resided in barrios were more likely to hold traditional behaviors and values. Grebler, Moore, and Guzmán described San Antonio and Los Angeles as "sharply differing social worlds,"[119] with the social isolation and poverty of Mexican Americans far greater in San Antonio than in Los Angeles. Such isolation continues to be an important variable, though the interest in traditional or modern values has waned and that in adult socioeconomic outcomes has increased. Recent sociological research has shown the detrimental influence of concentrated neighborhood poverty, which fosters social isolation, social disorganization, and weak social ties, on the economic status of children in poor neighborhoods, especially for African Americans.[120] However, the characteristics and behaviors associated with concentrated poverty and underclass often do not hold up for Hispanic groups,[121] which analysis of our data confirms.[122] The effects of residential segregation, though, are likely to extend well beyond the economic dimension, and are associated with reduced contact with other groups and fewer assimilative opportunities.

A spatial assimilation theory argues that immigrants and their descendants move away from such neighborhoods gradually and over time and thus evade their deleterious consequences.[123] Immigrants and their descendants move up in the social structure and, in the process, integrate spatially with the dominant group. Consequently, they interact with, increasingly share the values of, and eventually identify with the dominant group.[124] Settlement in integrated neighborhoods before marriage also leads to greater chances of endogamy, or intermarriage. Alba similarly claims that the declining salience of ethnicity among European ethnic groups is related to the decline of white ethnic neighborhoods.[125] By contrast, among Mexican Americans, continuing immigration and high fertility have led to a growth of ethnic neighborhoods. Our study examines how later generation Mexican Americans are affected by this.

Skin Color: Negotiating the Boundary

The process of racialization, to the extent that it occurs, may affect some more than others because particular individuals may be closer to a stigmatized stereotype. Furthermore, skin color has been a prominent feature of racialization in the United States. African Americans are the darkest of the major ethnic groups and darker African Americans often suffer the worst discrimination. However, persons of similar skin color may also be racialized on the basis of different culture or religion (for example, Jews in Nazi Germany). The historical record shows the granting of white or near-white status to particular Mexican Americans at particular times and places. Skin color has been a key marker of racial status and varies widely among Mexican Americans because they are products of a long history of miscegenation between a mostly indigenous population, a relatively small African-origin population,[126] and the Spaniards, the colonizing group in Mexico.

Mexican Americans may use light skin color to negotiate the racial or ethnic boundary (to the extent it exists) and try to reposition themselves as long as they can also hide other ethnic signals, such as an accent or a Spanish surname. In addition to marking whether one is in the Mexican category, skin color may also be used to place those of Mexican origin along a racial continuum within the Mexican category. Specifically, teachers, employers, and even family members might perceive those with darker skins or more Indian features as less capable or worthy than lighter skinned Mexicans, even if both are considered equally Mexican. Previous research shows that such individuals may be at an educational or socioeconomic disadvantage, net of other factors.[127] Similar evidence has been shown for African Americans, who are also products of many generations of race mixture. Recent empirical findings for blacks and Hispanics, however, question this earlier finding. This more recent work shows that skin color sometimes may have no effect on status.[128]

Discussion

Unlike the 1965 study, ours takes advantage of a highly developed set of theoretical tools that enable us to conceptualize race, ethnicity, and immigrant integration and propose numerous outcomes. Mexican Americans—as the largest immigrant group and the consensus litmus test of integration theories—are an important case to understand. More important, though, we argue that they are a unique case and do not easily fit the prevailing theories. We therefore set out to conduct an in-depth empirical analysis of the Mexican American experience based on a unique and especially appropriate data set to examine intergenerational issues in immigrant integration. Based on that evidence, we hope to flesh out new empirical findings that will provide a solid base for theory development. Unfortunately, the lack of adequate empirical data in the past has allowed theorists much leeway in fitting the Mexican case to their own hypothesis. We thus strongly heed Charles Hirschman's 2005 call as president of the Population Association of America to go beyond additional theory development in understanding ethnic integration. Hirschman begs instead for compelling interpretations of how and why ethnicity matters for particular groups and bring data and empirical analysis to test the developing new and competing theories.

We explore the possibility that the nature of ethnic boundaries involving Mexican Americans may be quite complex. Perhaps such boundaries have disappeared on some dimensions but persist in others. Whereas other studies have focused on a more limited set of dimensions, we integrate dimensions of identification, culture, economics, segregation, intermarriage, language, and politics into an overall assessment of intergenerational change. For example, we question rather than assume that fourth-generation Mexican Americans identify with immigrants and their plight. Indeed, we question the very basis of assuming either homogeneity among Mexicans or complete assimilation with the native white population in later generations.

Unlike previous studies, ours is a study of the long term, multigenerational experience of an ethnic group. We also closely examine variation within the group, and are guided by sociological literature suggesting that parental characteristics, metropolitan area, neighborhood, skin color, and other factors may be important. Rather than suggest that all of these factors are responsible in some collective but mysterious way, we empirically and systematically investigate the role of each of these factors, especially as they relate to generational change. We seek to posit explanations of the causal mechanisms for change and demonstrate the extent and direction in which change may occur, if at all. We also distinguish between various social dimensions that all define the nature of multigenerational integration and we do not assume that the degrees of assimilation vary together among them. Rather, we recognize that ethnic integration experiences may vary greatly from one dimension to the other across groups as well as among individuals within groups.

Methodologically, we go beyond previous studies by using actual generational and representative data from 1965 to 2000 and over for four generations since immigration. This allows us to distinguish between historical trajectories of integration from the examination of generation-since-immigration at the same point in time. Our sample of roughly 700, who were randomly selected and interviewed in the 1965 to 1966 study, closely represents the population of Mexican American household heads or their spouses that resided in Los Angeles County and San Antonio City in 1965. In addition, we have also collected data from a similarly sized sample of their children. Thus, we have a data set that includes information on the original respondents in 1965 and 2000 and on their children in 2000. We examine these methods in more detail in the following chapter.

= Chapter 3 =

The Mexican American Study Project

The 1965 Mexican American Study Project was designed as the first comprehensive study to "depict factually and analytically the present realities of life for Mexican Americans in our society."[1] Using the latest scientific methods at their disposal, Grebler, Moore, and Guzmán collected random sample surveys of Mexican Americans in Los Angeles County and San Antonio City, the two largest concentrations of Mexican Americans and together 25 percent of all Mexican Americans in the Southwest and 37 percent of all Mexican Americans in urban areas.[2] The samples represented the wide diversity of Mexican Americans in the two metropolitan areas on various characteristics including class, levels of segregation, and generation-since-immigration.

Fully thirty-five years later, we have completed a second wave of that study, by interviewing the original respondents and their adult children. Our study is thus intergenerational and longitudinal, providing a research design that is especially well suited for examining the theoretical debates regarding ethnic integration. Specifically, our data consist of the 1965 to 1966 random sample of Mexican Americans in Los Angeles County and San Antonio City age eighteen to fifty,[3] a 1998 to 2002 follow-up of the original respondents, who are by then fifty-three to eighty-five years old, and a sample of their children, who are between thirty-five and fifty-four when they are interviewed in the same period. Parent and child data are linked by families. Because we depend on the original random sample in 1965 for representation, we develop a weighting scheme to maintain the same randomness, inasmuch as possible, in the 2000 follow-up. This controls for selectivity bias resulting from the loss of a numerical minority of the cases in the intervening thirty-five years and a similar bias in child interviews.

Advantages of our Research Design

Grebler, Moore, and Guzmán noted that a cross-sectional study such as theirs "does not take the place of a longitudinal study."[4] Nonetheless, such conventional data have been the main source of information about immigrant integration, but cross-sectional comparisons by generations-since-immigration are only a simulation of a dynamic process. Immigrant integration is an intergenerational process and is modeled better through longitudinal and intergenerational information. Our study design captures the dynamics of longitudinal and intergenerational change, thus providing unique data for addressing the important sociological questions we posed in chapter 2. Although census and other official national data are important because they are widely representative and include numerous cases, they are not designed to capture information on many of the pressing questions in the field of race and ethnicity.

Specifically, our survey design offers several benefits. First, it preempts the effect of identifying as other than Mexican origin. It includes information on children and parents to establish actual generations. It includes information on parental attitudes and behavior at time one. Children, on average, are at time two roughly the same age as their parents were at time one. It includes information on the fourth generation. It covers two metropolitan areas. Last, it focuses solely on the Mexican-origin population.

Preempts "Opting Out" of Mexican Origin Identity   A major advantage of the follow-up survey is that respondents who identified as Mexican origin in 1965 and 1966 may no longer identify as such, and thus wouldn't fall into a new cross-sectional sample. They may identify as American or as Hispanic or Latino, with no identifier that permits placing them in a Mexican origin sample. This might occur because of extensive cultural and economic assimilation in which there is no longer an attachment to Mexican roots, including living in a mostly white neighborhood or having no contact with the Spanish language or Mexican culture, or because of parental intermarriage. Because such individuals might not be captured in a cross-sectional study of the Mexican American population, such data could not fully measure the extent of real-world change for the Mexican-origin across generations. We study ethnicity or ethnic change on the basis of a sample that does not have such an ethnic bias.

In our study, we use a random sample of Mexican Americans—that of the original respondent sample—and choose a random sample of their children, regardless of how they identify in 2000. Indeed, we find that more than 10 percent of the children of the 1965 sample identify primarily as white or American rather than Mexican, Mexican American, Hispanic, or Latino. This suggests a potential problem with studies of ethnicity more generally.

If respondents must self-identify as group members to be included, then they represent a select group. By taking a sample of the ethnic group at one point, following them over time, and studying their children, we have an ideal design for determining the full range of symbolic and behavioral expressions of ethnic identity, which may be truncated in a cross-sectional survey. This method also overcomes the problem of changing definitions of ethnic categories across censuses, such as relying on the proxies of Spanish surname, place of birth, or Spanish language use in the 1960 or 1970 censuses, which is often compared to direct questions on Mexican origin in more recent censuses.

Actual Parental-Child Generations   Generations-since-immigration are generally captured through cross-sectional designs that compare immigrants (first generation) to children of immigrants (second generation) to the native stock (third or later generation), often under the assumption that these are proxies for generational change from parents to children. With cross-sectional data, those in the so-called parent generation are not really the parents of the so-called child generation. Rather, the children of immigrants are the progeny of immigrants from an earlier cohort and may have different characteristics from those of the current population of immigrants. For example, higher levels of education among the second generation, compared with immigrants, using a single cross-sectional data point is commonly assumed to mean that children of immigrants have higher education than their parents. Our data will show, however, that the second-generation parents had only ten years of education and that their children had fully thirteen. Because schooling for whites also increased, we then show how the Mexican-white gap also changed. Cross-sectional methods thus cannot truly capture these generational changes within families.[5]

Parental Behaviors and Attitudes of a Generation Ago   Many items of interest cannot be reliably captured in retrospective questions about events that occurred many years earlier. This is particularly true of characteristics that change throughout one's life course or that one may forget. This includes attitudes about politics, race, education, and childbearing as well as individual characteristics such as language use, income, and wealth. Retrospective questions about previous behaviors and attitudes often cannot be accurately recollected. We therefore do not need to limit ourselves to behavioral indicators that can be recalled. We can include variables such as parents' attitudes toward schooling and level of involvement in schooling, when children were growing up. We also have information on the location of residence in the 1960s, which we link to 1970 census tract data to give us information on the neighborhood context, among them the extent of residential segregation.

Age Similarity   The children in our study, when interviewed, are on average roughly the same age as their parents were when they were interviewed. This is important because it generally controls for factors which change throughout the life course. If we consider that a typical generation from parents to children lasts thirty years,[6] then the children in our sample, who are interviewed thirty-two to thirty-seven years after their parents, will only be slightly older, on average, than the parents when they were interviewed in 1965. For example, political attitudes often change over time—as the person moves from young adulthood to parenthood to retired status, for example. Thus a comparison of parents and children at roughly the same age is ideal.[7]

Fourth Generation   Our study is also an improvement over other data sets, particularly official data, because it captures the fourth (or later) generation. This is rarely found in other studies. Much available data on Latinos or Mexican Americans provide only country of birth, which permits distinctions only between immigrants and those born in the United States. Other data specify parents' place of birth, which permits a three-generation breakdown. Data with four generations, which depend on information about grandparents' place of birth, are rare. Respondents sometimes simply do not have that information, as we found in our study. Because we surveyed parents, however, we could secure reliable information. We might, incidentally, have divided the four-plus generation into a fourth and a fifth-plus generation because we had asked the parental generation where their grandparents were born. We decided against this on the basis of relatively weak information on birthplace of grandparents and a relatively small fifth generation.

Two Urban Areas   We have a random sample of Mexican Americans who grew up in Los Angeles and San Antonio in the mid-1960s, despite their place of residence at the time of the follow-up survey. We tracked and interviewed the original respondents and their children. This allows us to examine how conditions in particular places affect outcomes years later. Although national samples are preferable for generalizing about ethnic group experiences, rarely are there enough cases for researchers to examine the effects of growing up in a particular place. An important part of our study is based on how local context is important for immigrant integration.

Mexican Origin Population   Although some may see this as a disadvantage of our study design, we considered it an advantage. An intra-ethnic study on the dynamics of generation change among Mexican Americans permits insight into their unique experiences. In contrast, many comparative studies with Mexican Americans, Puerto Ricans, and Cubans and other major racial-ethnic groups have been undertaken. Such efforts are important when assessing the relative status of groups, but they are less useful when examining the overlap of particular historical and contextual conditions and how individual characteristics might influence certain outcomes. In the case of Mexican Americans, we believe there was substantial heterogeneity within the population on most outcomes. We therefore examined the characteristics that lead to wide ranging levels of mobility and the extent to which ethnic persistence or assimilation carries from parents to children. By contrast, the more common research design that compares groups is less likely to tell us about why certain outcomes have occurred among some Mexican Americans but not others. Finally, our sample would have been impossible to replicate for other groups in the absence of an earlier sample, such as ours.

The Original 1965 Data

UCLA library employees discovered the original questionnaires of the Mexican American Study Project in 1992, when the university cleaned out its holdings from the old Powell Library during a building renovation. The original investigators had donated them to the UCLA library sometime in the 1970s but they had never been archived—few mechanisms for archiving data were available at the time—and by the 1990s no one was even aware of them.

Within a few months of our discovery, we decided that it would be worthwhile to at least analyze some of the data again, especially in light of theoretical and methodological developments since the original study. We were particularly interested in using multivariate statistical techniques (since user-friendly programs and high-speed computers were not available to the original authors) to reveal some of the complex patterns in the data. We thus accounted for and organized the original questionnaires and set out to digitize the information. We were in communication with Joan Moore, who had held onto a computer tape of the data for the Los Angeles sample. Fortunately, we were able to access the Los Angeles data from the tape and to re-enter the San Antonio sample in a matching electronic format, creating the full original data set. This has been made available to other researchers through UCLA's data archives at the Institute for Social Science Research. Finally, we archived the questionnaires, establishing procedures for ensuring the confidentiality of respondents.

The original survey included a random sample of 973 households in Los Angeles County and 603 households in the City of San Antonio.[8] The larger sample of Mexican Americans in Los Angeles reflected the larger overall population in that county compared to San Antonio. The City of San Antonio rather than Bexar County was chosen because the large majority of Mexican Americans in that county lived in the city and the remaining population was either rural or lived on military bases surrounding the city. The original survey sample was randomly selected within census tracts stratified by the proportion of "white persons of Spanish surname" as recorded in the 1960 census, which was the best proxy for Mexican American at the time. Fifty-one census tracts were selected in Los Angeles and twenty-nine were in San Antonio.

To draw the sample, 1960 census information was used to select tracts, the primary sampling units, and blocks, the secondary sampling units. Spanish-surname households, the tertiary sampling units, were selected from reverse directories in Los Angeles and San Antonio city directories. At that time, the sampling procedures were state of the art. A comparison to 1960 census distribution indicates that the Los Angeles and San Antonio samples were representative of the population in the respective places.[9] For instance, the educational, occupational, and income distribution between the samples and respective populations were similar. Thus this sample is an excellent one for a long term follow up.

Density (percent Spanish surname) and imputed home value were the major strata in the sampling design. Primary sampling units (PSUs), at the level of census tracts, were chosen with probabilities proportional to size, with the measure of size being the number of Spanish-surnamed households within the PSUs. In Los Angeles, census tracts were classified as high density (43.9 percent or more Mexican American), medium density (between 15.2 and 43.8 percent), or low density (less than 15.2 percent). In San Antonio, tracts classified as high density (65.1 percent or more Mexican American), medium density (between 38.2 and 65.0 percent), and low density (less than 38.2 percent). The greater proportion of Mexican Americans in San Antonio (about 40 percent versus about 10 percent in Los Angeles according to the 1960 census) and their greater segregation in San Antonio led to density thresholds that were inevitably quite different in the two places.

Once the census tracts were chosen, particular blocks or street segments were then selected as secondary sampling units to further obtain proportionality, according to a fairly elaborate procedure. Tertiary sampling units, or households, were then chosen by either screening for self-identified Mexican American households from among all households in high density tracts or selecting from among Spanish-surname households using reverse directories in Los Angeles and city directories in San Antonio in low- and medium-density tracts. The interview was given alternatively to males and females who were heads of households or spouses of the head of household. In households not consisting of husband and wife, the head of household was interviewed. In each secondary sampling unit, a random selection was made of the first person to be interviewed. The final sample overrepresented females because single-parent households tend to be headed by women.

Mexican American households were those in which either the head or spouse of identified as Mexican American or Spanish. Mixed-ethnic households fell into the sample if the targeted respondent was Mexican American even if the spouse was not. Those identifying as Spanish were included in the sample because some preferred that term over the highly stigmatized *Mexican,* especially in Texas. This is probably more true when respondents made initial contact with the screener or interviewer, whom they did not previously know. In the Southwest, Spanish or Latin American has often been used as a euphemism for Mexican and, because direct descendants of Spanish immigration in this century are rare, the screen for Spanish was unlikely to include anyone not of Mexican origin.

Households were selected on the basis of Spanish surname in low- and medium-density tracts, which meant that the few who did not have Spanish surnames were undersampled. This bias will be more likely for women, given that they often acquire a non-Spanish surname from intermarriage. We realize that those with non-Spanish surnames in largely white neighborhoods may be among the most assimilated elements of the population (because they have intermarried or are descendants of an intermarriage and live in largely white neighborhoods). Despite this limitation, Spanish surname was the best proxy for Mexican American at the time this sample was drawn.[10] Moreover, although we may have lost this portion of the population in 1965 and 1966, we will be able to pick up children of original respondents who may have been similarly affected by intermarriage and residential integration between the time of the original study and the follow-up. We are confident that the data represent the Mexican American population in the two urban areas at the time, based on our review of the sampling techniques. The sampling method is also discussed in two articles published in the *Journal of the American Statistical Association* by Raymond Jessen, the statistician who designed the sample for the original survey.[11]

Figures 3.1 and 3.2 show that the selected census tracts were geographically dispersed throughout Los Angeles and San Antonio in proportion to the spatial distribution of the Mexican-origin population and stratified by the percentage Mexican-origin of census tracts. They show that among our child sample, respondents grew up in places as varied as those in which the large majority of their neighbors were Mexican American and those in which only a small minority were. As the figures show, the largest concentration of Mexicans is in East Los Angeles and South San Antonio. In Los Angeles County, areas of low and medium concentration are all represented and dispersed in all directions in and around the city, but particularly on the Greater Eastside, including Montebello, Santa Fe Springs, La Puente, and Pomona, all of which are now predominantly Mexican American. There are also selected census tracts in places as varied as South Central, the San Fernando Valley, the Westside, and the Harbor area.

In San Antonio, about half of the selected census tracts and the majority of the respondents were in high density areas. Only neighborhoods in the southern half of San Antonio were chosen reflecting the area's segregation

Figure 3.1   Selected Tracts in Los Angeles County for 1965 Survey[a]

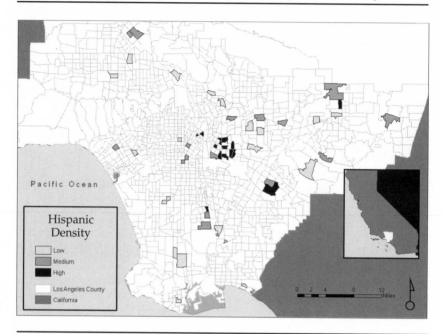

Source: Mexican American Study Project.
[a] Map from national Historical Geographic Information System, Minnesota Population Center, University of Minnesota.

pattern, with the two inner southern rings being high density Mexican American and largely poor, except for the two extreme eastern tracts, which are poor but mostly African American. The next two rings out from the inner city were traditionally white ethnic working class (especially Germans and Czechs) in the 1960s with upwardly mobile Mexican Americans beginning to move in. San Antonio's deep pattern of segregation precluded the selection of Northside census tracts. By now, the entire Southside is predominately Mexican American and the Northwest is also largely populated by Mexican Americans as well as the white working and middle class.[12] For readers familiar with either area, these maps confirm that respondents came from a wide diversity of neighborhoods.

The 2000 Mexican American Study Project

In addition to reanalyzing the 1965 data, we also decided to pursue a far more ambitious goal. We would try to find and interview the surviving original respondents, as well as their children. Based on a pilot test of finding a sample of Los Angeles residents, we came to discover that the

Figure 3.2   Selected Tracts in San Antonio (Bexar County) for 1965 Survey[a]

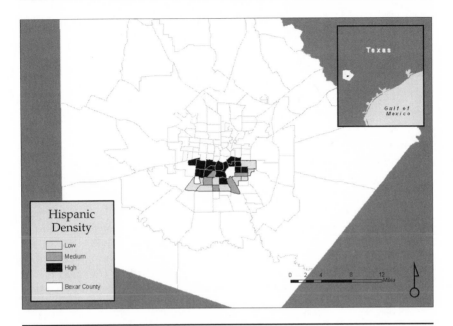

Source: Mexican American Study Project.
[a] Map from national Historical Geographic Information System, Minnesota Population Center, University of Minnesota.

task would require much detective-like work, making it even harder than anticipated. This would be a multiyear project and would require substantial funding. By mid-1994, we had secured enough to hire several graduate students and begin searching for the original respondents. In 1997, a large grant enabled us to conduct the actual interviews. Indeed, the process of finding and interviewing respondents would take several years and involved several arduous tasks, which we will describe.

We set out to reinterview the original respondents who were age eighteen to fifty in 1965 and 1966 and in their early fifties to early eighties during the 1998 to 2000 follow-up. We omitted the 24 percent who were over fifty in 1965 and 1966 because of the high probability that they would have died by 1998. When the original respondents age fifty and younger had died, we searched for family members and conducted an interview about the respondent, which we refer to as informant interviews. In addition, we sought to interview the children of respondents who were younger than eighteen in 1965 and therefore in their early thirties to early fifties in 1998. The selection method for the original respondents was therefore straightforward. The sample had been drawn in the 1960s. Our plan was to simply search for and interview the 76 percent of the sample age fifty or younger at the time. Initially, we were optimistic that we would be able to replicate the original random sample fairly accurately. Our search was thus intensive and lengthy and used more methods than we had anticipated.

Searching for the 1965 Respondents

Searching for the original respondents took considerable effort and nearly five years (from 1994 to 1998). Unfortunately, the original study directors had not instituted procedures for relocating respondents, apparently never having anticipated that anyone would survey the sample a second time. No social security numbers and no information on relatives or friends that might help to track the respondents in the event of an eventual resurvey were collected. We therefore had to rely on respondents' names, which are rarely unique, and a variety of data sources that would help track them. In some cases, we did not even have full names and in many cases, particularly among women, names had changed since the original study. Few of the respondents lived at the original address or had the same phone number, so we set off on a hunt much as a police detective would. In this section, we review only some of our search procedures.[13]

The search process for respondents evolved over time as we added new sources of information. In retrospect, we can group our search strategy into three major stages and types of sources. In the first stage, in Los Angeles, we relied heavily on public sources of information which, for the most part, required travel to government offices. The most important sources during this period were voter registration, property, death, and marriage records, all available at county offices. These, particularly voter registration and property records, provided more recent addresses and information on family members. Also, voter registration, death, and marriage records all provided dates of birth, death, and marriage. To access these records, our research assistants manually searched through the original record books,[14] scanned microfiche, and used agency computers and electronic data bases. We also accessed computerized data sources of death and marriage records at the Family History Center at the Church of Jesus Christ of Latter-Day Saints, which were useful in ascertaining that a death or marriage had occurred. They did not, however, always include complete information, so we followed up by searching for the actual certificates at county offices.[15] To a lesser extent, we used divorce records, available through the court system, but were difficult to find. When available, however, they provided a wealth of information.

Phone directories and directory assistance were also important sources of information, though we did encounter certain difficulties with them. Los Angeles, for example, has numerous volumes and it was nearly impossible to acquire a complete set for our project offices. We had difficulties with local directory assistance when we did not know the respondent's current address because there are more than eighty cities in Los Angeles County alone and many others in surrounding counties. At the Los Angeles Public Library, we accessed historical sources from the 1960s and 1970s—phone directories, city directories from the 1960s for parts of Los Angeles, and reverse directories starting in 1972. These provided far more information than was collected in the 1965 survey, such as names of spouses and children. In San Antonio, on the other hand, a single phone book covered the entire city, which greatly facilitated our searching there.

Searching through county records and address and telephone directories frequently yielded a list of possibilities. In this situation, we would call or mail letters to each individual. If we got no response, we mailed at least two follow-up letters and then visited the address if it was nearby. If we received replies, we spoke with the possible respondent at length to see if they matched on other characteristics of the original respondent.

Occasionally, we searched for a group of respondents simultaneously. For instance, early on, we looked for sixteen respondents who had lived in a single housing project, but no longer did. We contacted the management office of the housing project and found the resident manager quite cooperative. He had been, it turned out, a UCLA undergraduate student at one time and thus was familiar with the original Grebler project and book. He allowed us access to the forms that residents completed when they moved away from the projects. Although many of the forms did not list a forwarding address, many did include information, such as a relative's name or social security number, that helped us locate the respondent. Because most of these respondents were unmarried women, an especially difficult group to search for given remarriage and name changes, this was especially useful.

Throughout the search process, we continued visiting houses when necessary. For respondents for whom we could find no leads, we visited the 1965 address to find long-term neighbors who might provide additional information about the respondent, such as names of spouse or children, or know where the respondent had moved. When we suspected that we had located the respondent but were unsuccessful at establishing contact (no phone number, no response to multiple letters, no response to phone messages), we would visit the home.

We continued looking for alternative sources of information in our quest to find as many as possible of the original respondents. Our work coincided with the development of compact disks, which made large amounts of data available. We were eventually able to purchase CDs of property records in California, voter registration records in California, a national death index, and national phone directories. We also gained access to Trans Union credit headers, which included the name, address, telephone information taken from applications for credit and other finan-

Table 3.1   Sources for Locating Original Respondents in Los Angeles

	Used Source	First Source[a]
Source		
Personal contacts[b]	28%	8%
Directories	14	5
Historical directories	9	8
Voter registration	34	21
Property	33	22
Marriage	14	12
Death	10	6
Drivers license	11	5
Other public[c]	5	3
Credit header[d]	23	4
Internet sources	7	5
Total		100

Source: Mexican American Study Project.
[a] 39 percent of sample located with one source, 36 percent with two sources, 15 percent with three sources, and 10 percent with four or more sources.
[b] Personal contacts include visiting original addresses, contacting neighbors, landlords, family coworkers, church, school.
[c] Other public include birth, divorce, naturalization, and housing records.
[d] Credit headers from TransUnion by modem.

cial sources but do not include any of the financial data. With special permission granted to us as researchers, we also accessed California Department of Motor Vehicles records. Having access to these sources of information shifted most of the searching activities from field work to our project offices.

The final stage of our search process coincided with the availability of information through the Internet, including much information we had previously secured in CD format. The availability had many benefits. First, it was easier to identify and purchase sources of information on compact disks, such as California Property, Texas People Finder, and Texas Property. Second, national phone directories became available. Third, the Internet permitted more powerful and flexible searching strategies. Last, Internet data sets merged large quantities of data from multiple sources.

In sum, technological developments improved our ability to find respondents over the course of our search. Additionally, we had devised many creative ways of searching when we had exhausted the normal search procedures. Table 3.1 presents the sources we used to locate respondents, grouped into broad categories. The first column presents the percentage of cases that we used, by type of source, in the search process. Because multiple sources could be used to locate a respondent, the percentages in the first column add up to more than 100 percent. Voter registration and property records were the most useful in locating respondents, followed by personal contacts and credit headers. What made these sources useful is that they provided additional information on which we could match our respondents and use for further searching. For example, property records frequently provided the name of the spouse or a forwarding address. Voter registration records provided place of birth. The second column presents the first source of information that led us to locate the respondent, which shows that voter registration and property records were also as useful as a first source.

We turned to the San Antonio sample after completing our search of the Los Angeles sample. This allowed us to draw on our experiences in Los Angeles to develop procedures for searching in San Antonio. Many of the same sources of information were available; and fortunately many were more easily accessible. For instance, California Department of Motor Vehicles records were available, but only after a time-consuming application process, whereas similar Texas records were public and readily available. City directories from the 1960s, which are available for only some communities in Los Angeles, were available for all of San Antonio in one volume. Moreover, throughout the search process in San Antonio, we benefited from the Internet and large databases we secured only in the last stage of our Los Angeles search.

Finally, it is important to note that names made a big difference in whether we were able to find the original respondents. In some cases, information on names and addresses in the 1965 questionnaires was incomplete. For example, though fully eighty-three respondents were missing first names and twenty-three were missing both first and last names, we searched for them regardless.[16] We used the historical reverse directories to find names because these are sorted by address rather than by name. We could then gather more information in city directories. Taking this approach, we were able to locate 67 percent of respondents for whom we had only last names. Interestingly, we were able to locate 44 percent of those respondents for whom we had neither first nor last names. By way of comparison, we located 81 percent of respondents for whom we had full names. Those with especially common names, such as Jose García, were especially difficult to find, as one might expect.

The Survey

During the time we were seeking our original respondents and securing additional funding, we had plenty of time to design our survey instrument. The final questionnaire reflected our theoretical interests around various dimensions of ethnic integration, as we outlined in chapter 2. It begins with questions on ethnic identity and is followed by questions on contact with other groups, language, place of birth, education, employment, politics,

Table 3.2   **Stayed or Moved from 1965 Urban Area and Completed
Telephone Interview**

	Distribution			Completed Telephone Interview		
	Stayed	Moved	Total	Stayers	Movers	Overall
Original respondents[a]						
Overall	93%	7%	100%	4%	60%	8%
Los Angeles	85	15	100	7	58	12
San Antonio	98	2	100	0	100	1
Children						
Overall	83	17	100	17	70	26
Los Angeles	78	22	100	27	72	37
San Antonio	89	11	100	2	66	26

Source: Mexican American Study Project.
[a] Informant interviews not included in calculations.

homeownership, marriage, children, household composition, and income. The survey ended up being forty-five to seventy-five minutes long, largely depending on how many questions applied to the respondent. We designed separate questionnaires each for original respondents, children of respondents, and informants for the original respondents. The original respondent and informant questionnaires were made available in English and Spanish.[17]

For original respondents who had died, we interviewed an informant, which was usually the surviving spouse but sometimes an adult child or other close family member. The informant questionnaire was much like that for the respondent, but without attitudinal questions and those for which we believed informants could not provide reliable answers. It included questions on place of birth, language use, contact with other groups, educational level, employment status, marital status, household composition, income, and children.

The Los Angeles interviews were conducted by the Survey Research Center (SRC) of UCLA's Institute for Social Science Research (ISSR), and the San Antonio sample by a Texas-based firm, NuStats Research and Consulting in Austin. Interviews were primarily conducted in respondents' homes. Contact information was forwarded from the UCLA project staff to SRC and NuStats field staff to facilitate appointment setting for interviewing. Contact was first made with the original respondent and after that with randomly selected children of the respondent. Respondents were paid an incentive of $20 for their participation.

In some cases, we were unable to interview respondents face to face, usually for those who moved out of metropolitan Los Angeles or San Antonio. The first three columns of table 3.2 show the proportion of respon-

Table 3.3   Searched, Located, and Interviewed Original Respondents
             by Urban Area

	Total	Los Angeles	San Antonio
a. Searched	1,193	792	401
b. Located	941	614	327
c. Interviewed	684	434	250
Located of total (b/a)	79%	78%	82%
Interviewed of located (c/b)	73	71	76
Response rate (c/a)	57	55	62

Source: Mexican American Study Project.

dents who had moved and the final three show the percentage of movers, stayers, and the overall sample who were interviewed by phone. Anywhere from 2 to 22 percent of respondents moved out of the two metropolitan areas by 2000. Most of those who moved, but only a few of those who stayed, were interviewed by telephone. For three of the four cases, no more than 7 percent of the stayers were interviewed by phone. The exception was the 27 percent of children in Los Angeles, most of whom lived outside of Los Angeles County but within the five-county metropolitan area. Although we consider them stayers, many were often at a considerable distance, making personal interviews difficult.[18]

Success in Locating and Interviewing Original Respondents

We located nearly four of every five (79 percent) of the original respondents, as shown in table 3.3. We did have a higher number of refusals than expected, however, and were able to interview only 73 percent of those we found. In the end, we interviewed nearly three of every five (57 percent) of the original respondents who were age fifty or less in 1965.

Most of our nonresponses were refusals. For the most part, we found that respondents were receptive and often surprised when we located them. Most did not remember being interviewed more than thirty years earlier. Many, however, were curious that we had located them after so many years, especially when they did not recall participating in the original study. Some were suspicious or concerned that we were able to do so and thus sometimes refused to be interviewed. Additionally, by 2000, many of our original respondents had become elderly. We were up against a public service campaign at the time aimed at Latino elderly, which warned them to be careful of solicitors, telemarketers, or any stranger coming to the door or calling.

The field staff at SRC and NuStats used all the standard approaches to convert the refusals into interviews. Project staff who searched for respondents made sure to note any resistance to our calling in our initial contact with them. This information was passed to the interviewing staff at SRC and NuStats. Refusing or reluctant respondent cases were assigned to skilled supervisors or interviewers trained specifically for refusal conversion. Special letters were sent to respondents to assure them of our legitimacy and to attempt to gain their confidence and trust, addressing their individual concerns when voiced. If we had not secured an interview after numerous attempts, we left prospective respondents alone for some time before following up again. In some instances, recalcitrant individuals consented to the re-study but only through a telephone interview. For those interviews, we used a telephone version of the questionnaire originally developed for interviewing with respondents living too far from Los Angeles or San Antonio to be visited in person.

Differences between Los Angeles and San Antonio in success at locating and interviewing further illustrate issues in the field. Table 3.3 shows that we located 82 percent of respondents in San Antonio and 78 percent in Los Angeles. One reason is that more respondents in San Antonio remained at their original address or in the same community. Also, the sources we utilized for searching in San Antonio were more readily available and easier to access. But even more important, more were homeowners in San Antonio than in Los Angeles and homeowners are easier to locate than renters.

Further sample attrition would come with refusals to interview. This was also greater in Los Angeles than San Antonio. In the end, we interviewed 76 percent in San Antonio but only 71 percent in Los Angeles. This may have had something to do with the size of Los Angeles, a city where respondents spend less time at home, more time commuting, and distrust strangers more than in San Antonio. We suspect, however, that some of the difference was mostly attributable to the longer lag-time between searching and interviewing in Los Angeles. We began searching for respondents as many as five years before the interviews but interviewed quickly on locating respondents in San Antonio. Although we searched for respondents who had moved, some were never located. Yet most of the interviews not completed were due to refusals, which we estimate at more than 90 percent.

Selectivity Issues in the 2000 Original Respondent Sample

The greater attrition in the original Los Angeles sample could be indicative of selectivity. To further understand the nature of our selectivity, table 3.4 shows our success at locating and interviewing respondents with particular characteristics as measured in the original survey.[19] We show the results for the two stages: the percent of original respondents that we found

Table 3.4   Located and Interviewed Original Respondents by 1965 Characteristics[a]

	Located	Interviewed of Located	Interviewed of Total
Age			
Eighteen to thirty-five	78%	76%	59%
Thirty-six to fifty	80	69	55
Sex			
Men	81	72	58
Women	77	73	57
Marital Status			
Married	82	73	60
Unmarried	65	71	46
Nativity			
Born in United States	81	72	59
Born in Mexico	69	75	52
Language of interview			
English	84	72	61
Spanish	71	74	52
Years of schooling			
Less than nine	73	75	54
Nine or more	84	71	60
Household income			
Less than $6,000	75	73	55
$6,000 or more	84	72	61
Homeownership status			
Home owner	89	71	64
Renter	68	75	51

Source: Mexican American Study Project.
[a] Among original respondents searched for.

out of the total sample searched for is listed in column 1; the percent of persons interviewed among those whom we found are listed in column 2; the final percent interviewed out of the total sample is shown in column 3. For example, the first row shows that persons age eighteen to thirty-five in 1965 were slightly less likely to be located than those older than thirty-five, but, when they were located, were more likely to be interviewed. Eventually, we ended up interviewing 59 percent of the younger respondents to the original survey and 55 percent of the older respondents. Men were slightly more likely to be interviewed than women. The differences, though, were greater for all of the other variables. Married persons, those born in

Table 3.5   Determinants for Locating and Interviewing Original Respondents[a]

Characteristics	Located	Interviewed
San Antonio	1.05	1.25
Age	0.99	0.99
Male	1.04	0.98
Married	1.51*	1.42*
Born in United States	1.34	1.07
English interview	1.39	1.14
Education	1.04	1.03
Income (thousands of dollars)	1.05	1.00
Home owner	3.22***	1.58**

Source: Mexican American Study Project.
[a] Logistic regression run. Adjusted odds ratios presented. Searched sample of original respondents analyzed. Predictors based on 1965 characteristics. See appendix B, table B.1 for full model.
*p<.05, **p<.01; ***p<.001

the United States, those interviewed in English, the more educated, the wealthier, and homeowners were all more likely to be interviewed than their counterparts.[20]

Because many of these variables are interrelated, effects are not necessarily independent. For example, persons born in the United States are more likely to have answered the interview in English, received more schooling, and owned their homes. It may therefore be that birthplace drives the differences on language, education, and homeownership. It may also be, however, that one or more of these variables have an additional independent effect. To determine which variables are responsible or in statistical parlance, which have an independent and significant effect, we ran a statistical analysis to predict locating and interviewing respondents. Specifically, we used logistic regression analysis to regress a binary variable indicating whether we found a respondent and secured an interview in the follow-up on a set of potential explanatory variables drawn from the 1965 data. The results are shown on table 3.5 (where we present odd ratios). Column 1 shows that only two variables were statistically significant in locating the original respondents: married persons were 1.5 times more likely to be found than unmarried, and homeowners were fully 3.2 times more likely than renters, net of all other effects. The other variables, including city of residence, were not independently influential factors and are apparently correlated with homeownership and perhaps also with married status. In other words, the fact that we found more San Antonio respondents seems largely because they are more likely to be homeowners than respondents in Los Angeles.

The second column of table 3.5 demonstrates which variables predict whether we secured an interview for the sample used in our follow-up study. The results show that we are 1.6 times more likely to have interviewed persons who owned homes in 1965 and 1.4 times more likely to have interviewed married persons. Note that though the effects for homeownership and marital status are statistically significant, they are not large. A large number of renters and unmarried persons were also interviewed, though not at the same rate. Variables such as education, nativity, and language, though apparently important in the bivariate analysis, did not have significant independent effects.

In hindsight, the especially strong effect of homeownership is not surprising. First, it represents stability—homeowners move less than renters. Also, homeowners generally continue to be homeowners even when they sell. Third, transfers in property leave a paper trail, making it easier to locate owners in public records. Our findings are consistent with previous studies on differences between located and nonlocated respondents—showing that homeownership has a strong effect on being located.[21] Similarly, persons who were not married in 1965 were likely to move after marriage, often far from the neighborhoods where they lived, or if they remained single, they were less likely to leave a trail to trace their whereabouts. In the case of women, marriage often implies a name change, which further limited our ability to locate them. Not surprisingly, we found it easier to locate respondents with deeper roots, more family connections, and more stable lives.

Weighting for Selectivity of the Original Respondent Sample

Attrition in the sample is a worrisome problem for social analysis because it implies selective attrition. Selectivity, in turn, means that our sample is no longer random. We have the advantage of the 1965 survey for the original random sample, which provides information to gauge which types of persons fell out of the sample. If we were to use the follow-up sample as is, we would end up with too many original respondents who were homeowners and married in 1965, and too few who were renters and unmarried. To correct for this problem, we created weights to inflate the numbers of those who were underrepresented and deflate the number of those who were overrepresented. With the help of Dr. Robert Mare, a statistical specialist, we assigned weights based on our previous regression analysis. Specifically, the weights are the inverse of the odds that the persons in the original sample will end up in the follow-up sample. We used the two variables that predicted selective attrition (homeownership and marital status) and two additional variables, city of residence (San Antonio or Los Angeles), and family income (less than $3,000 in 1965 dollars, or $16,400 in 2000 dollars), as extra corrective measures.

Table 3.6   **Weights for Bivariate Analyses with Original Respondents**[a]

	Poor		Not Poor	
	Married	Unmarried	Married	Unmarried
Los Angeles				
Homeowner	0.584	0.779	0.949	1.168
Not homeowner	1.103	1.256	1.126	1.244
San Antonio				
Homeowner	0.861	1.635	0.809	0.949
Not homeowner	1.038	2.103	0.883	1.071

Source: Mexican American Study Project.
[a] Based on 1965 characteristics.

Those weights are shown in the matrix on table 3.6. Based on the original respondent's homeownership, marital status, city of residence, and income during the original survey, the values in table 3.6 show the extent to which their representation was weighted in the follow-up sample. At one end, married and low-income homeowners who lived in Los Angeles were especially likely to have been reinterviewed and thus were given the lowest weight (.584). At the other extreme, unmarried and low income renters in San Antonio were least likely to be found in the follow-up survey and thus were given the greatest weight. The representation of such persons was inflated more than two times (2.103). With the exception of these two categories, the other fourteen categories of original respondents fell within a fairly narrow range (.779 to 1.244), which suggests that selectivity was not especially problematic.

The 2000 Children Sample

For the child sample, who were adults in 2000, we selected a random sample of the original respondents' children born between 1947 and 1966. We selected a maximum of two children for each original respondent.[22] When original respondents had one or two children who met the selection criteria, all were selected. When more than two children met the criteria, we chose the most recent birthdate.[23] As can be seen in table 3.7, ninety-two families had no children who met the criteria, 100 had one, 146 had two, and 358 had three or more. In summary, 2,004 children met the age criteria, 1,108 were selected, and 758 (68 percent of those selected) were interviewed.

We selected and located children based on information from the parents we interviewed. First, we completed a roster of all the original respondents' children, with information on sex, name, birth month and year, biological relationship, country of birth, status (employed, in the military, laid off or unemployed, keeping house, in school, in prison or institution, deceased),

Table 3.7   Eligible, Selected, and Interviewed Child Respondents[a]

	Total	No Eligible Children	One Eligible Child	Two Eligible Children	Three to Twelve Eligible Children
a. Families	696	92	100	146	358
b. Eligible children	2,004	0	100	292	1,612
c. Selected children	1,108	0	100	292	716
d. Interviewed children	758	0	65	207	486
Response rate (d/c)	68%	—	65%	71%	69%

Source: Mexican American Study Project.
[a] Among children listed on roster in original respondent questionnaire.

years of education, and whether living with the original respondent parent in 1965 and 1966. We used this information to select children and to determine whether the characteristics of children we interviewed biased the sample in any way. We then determined bias by regressing a binary variable for whether we selected a respondent or secured an interview on a set of potential explanatory variables drawn from the child roster.

The results are shown on table 3.8, where we present odd ratios. Column 1 shows the results for selecting the child respondents and column 2 shows the results for interviewing children out of all eligible children. The number of children in the family had a strong relationship to both selecting and interviewing children, which was a direct result of our selection strategy. In families with one or two eligible children, each child had a 100 percent chance of being selected, whereas in families with three

Table 3.8   Determinants of Selecting and Interviewing Child Respondents[a]

	Selected	Interviewed
Number of eligible children	0.60***	0.69***
Education	1.02	1.08***
Female	0.96	1.28*
San Antonio	0.78*	0.87
Born in United States	1.17	1.25
Birth year	1.00	1.00
Working	0.86	1.11

Source: Mexican American Study Project.
[a] Logistic regression run. Adjusted odds ratios presented. Predictors based on characteristics of children listed on child roster in original respondent questionnaire. See appendix B, table B.2 for full model.
*$p<.05$, ***$p<.001$

eligible children, each child had a 66 percent chance of being selected. As the number of eligible children increased, the chance that a particular child would be selected decreased (with four children, the chances were one in two, with five children, two out of five, and so on). Children growing up in San Antonio were somewhat less likely to be selected, because San Antonio respondents had more children and children in larger families had less chance of being selected. Fortunately, children in San Antonio were neither more nor less likely to be interviewed. No other factors affected selection, which shows that our process was appropriate. On the other hand, column 2 of table 3.8 shows that once selected, the chances of securing an interview were significantly greater for more educated children and for females. Children from smaller families, with more education, and who are female were therefore overrepresented in our child sample. This probably reflects the greater likelihood that women could be found at home and were thus easier to arrange interviews with. Finding more educated children may have been due to their greater stability and willingness of parents to give us their contact information.

Weighting for Selectivity in the Child Sample

In the child sample, as with the original respondents, we also weighted for bias. If we had used the child sample as is, children from smaller families, the more educated, and women would have been overrepresented. To correct for this, we again used weights to increase and decrease the numbers of those who were over- and underrepresented, as we did for the original respondent sample.[24] Specifically, the weights were the inverse of the odds that the child would end up in the child sample.

Table 3.9 shows weight based on family size, education, and gender. At one end, the least-educated males from the largest families were least likely to be found in the follow-up survey and thus are given the greatest weight—inflated in the data more than two and a half times (2.627). At the other, the most-educated women from the smallest families are especially likely to have been interviewed and thus are given the lowest weights. Finally, for the combined selectivity of parents and children, the weight for children was multiplied by that for the original respondent.

Analysis Strategy

We present our results in chapters 5 through 10. We sought to do our analysis in a way that would take advantage of our longitudinal and intergenerational design and a way consistent with our theoretical interests. Theories of immigrant integration or assimilation focus principally on the extent of change across generations since the immigration experience.

Table 3.9   Weights for Bivariate Analyses with Child Respondents[a]

	One Eligible Child	Two Eligible Children	Three Eligible Children	Four or More Eligible Children
Male				
Less than high school	1.663	0.897	0.893	2.627
High school graduate	0.600	0.595	0.820	1.576
Some college	0.475	0.503	1.010	1.540
College graduate	0.493	0.450	0.842	1.478
Female				
Less than high school	0.369	0.480	1.478	1.218
High school graduate	0.517	0.507	0.769	1.671
Some college	0.677	0.465	0.665	1.396
College graduate	0.443	0.458	0.650	0.985

Source: Mexican American Study Project.
[a] Based on characteristics of children listed on roster in original respondent questionnaire.

These theories, however, often treat generation-since-immigration as coterminous with family generation, for example, from grandparents, who are often but not always immigrant, to child to grandchild. A significant overlap between family generation and generation-since-immigration may have been the experience of many European ethnics but it implies some theoretical and methodological confusion. Empirically, it is very troublesome in understanding the Mexican American case.

Parsing family generation from generation-since-immigration is particularly important, and complex, for Mexicans, whose history of immigration has been, for the most part, throughout the twentieth century. For example, the relatively small population born in the United States before 1910 intermarried extensively with the larger population of 1910 to 1930 immigrants, and their U.S.-born children have intermarried with the immigrants from subsequent waves. This generational complexity has been a significant issue in studies even though assimilation theories rarely deal with it. That they do not is not surprising, given the immigration experience of most groups.

The classic road to assimilation involved immigration in a relatively compressed time and thus generational change was generally uniform for entire ethnic groups. Massive immigration from Central and Southern Europe occurred during a short period in the late nineteenth and early twentieth centuries, so that the subsequent history of the group coincided largely with the experience of single generations-since-immigration. Italian immigration, the bulk of which occurred from 1900 to 1914, is a good example.[25] We seek to resolve this problem, which we illustrate in figure 3.3.

Figure 3.3   Two Dimensions of Generational Change

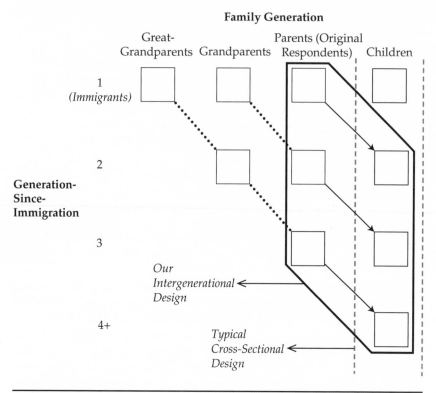

Source: Authors' compilation.

Family generation appears on the horizontal axis in figure 3.1 and indicates historical change. We also break the sample into generations-since-immigration, which is denoted on the vertical axis of figure 3.1. Generation-since-immigration refers to the number of generations since the immigrants arrived in the United States. Figure 3.3 summarizes the relation between the family generation and generation-since-immigration in our study. It shows, for example, that third-generation children had immigrant grandparents and that the fourth-generation children had great-grandparents who immigrated at a still earlier period.

The bold octagon defines the two family generations and four generations-since-immigration used in our study. That is, we capture a more dynamic process of real generational change, as required for testing hypotheses of assimilation or ethnic change. This compares to the standard intergenerational comparisons based on cross-sectional data, which is denoted by the dashed lines on figure 3.3. Such designs are based on synthetic cohorts and thus do not capture real generational change from parents to children. In the absence of better data, they must often assume, for example, that the second generation is the progeny of immigrants captured in the same data set, many of whom arrived well after their parents. Instead, we are interested in intergenerational changes on both dimensions of family generation and generation-since-immigration, as figure 3.3 shows. Specifically, we focus on change from parents of the first generation to their children in the second generation, from parents of the second generation to their children in the third generation, and from parents of the third or more generation to their children in the fourth or more generation.

Bivariate Strategy

To examine generational changes, we present bivariate tables that show generation-since-immigration for both original respondents and their children. For that analysis, we divide the original respondents into first, second, and third generations and their children into second, third, and fourth generations. The first generation among the original respondents consists of those born in Mexico, whose children are second generation. Similarly, the second generation of the original respondents is comprised of those who had at least one Mexico-born parent and whose children are third generation. The third generation among original respondents includes those with two U.S.-born parents and whose children are the fourth generation. Although we have a fourth generation among the original respondents, it is relatively small. We decided to combine these individuals with the third generation to permit a robust enough sample size in our analysis. The place of birth of the nonrespondent parent is ignored for the bivariate analysis.

In addition to weighting to adjust for the selectivity of our samples, we also adjusted for the compositional effects of age, gender, and city, which may affect some of our variables of interest. Specifically, the generational groups differ along these key characteristics that might affect our comparisons. Among both the original respondents and children, the first generation (and their second generation children) is much more likely to be from Los Angeles, and the third generation (and their fourth generation children) is much more likely to be from San Antonio. Also, the first generation was somewhat older and more female while the third generation was somewhat younger and more male. To adjust for these differences, we standardized generational comparisons by city, age, and gender. Specifically, we weighted original respondents by standardizing the first and third generation cases according to the sex-age composition of the second generation. For the children sample, we used the third generation as the standard.

Figure 3.4   Model of Intergenerational Transmission and Change

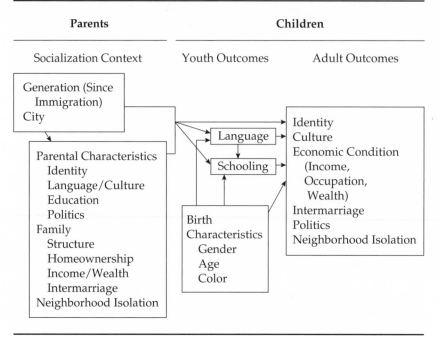

Source: Authors' compilation.

Our Multivariate Model

Aside from examining the extent of change from original respondents to their children, we are also interested in understanding the factors most associated with that change. For example, if children are more likely to attend college than their parents, is it generation that led to the change or some other factor? Could greater college attendance be due to greater resources that later generation parents have accrued and that perhaps permitted them to provide for a better education for their children, either because they moved out of the barrio or because they paid for private education? Similarly, how are changes in ethnic identity or Spanish-language proficiency associated with such factors?

We present our basic model of intergenerational transmission and change in figure 3.4. The model reads from left to right, beginning with the exogenous characteristics of generation and urban area (Los Angeles County or San Antonio City). We are interested, above all, on how generation-since-immigration and, to a lesser extent, urban area are related to the outcomes for both the original respondents and their children. An analysis of these variables seeks to answer the question like, "to what extent does increasing generation-since-immigration erode the ethnic behaviors and attitudes of Mexican Americans?" and, secondarily, "does growing up in Los Angeles or San Antonio make a difference?" The importance of generation-since-immigration and urban area is reflected in most of the descriptive (bivariate) analysis in this book, in which we stratify outcomes mostly on these two variables. However, to understand how generation-since-immigration, urban area, and other factors simultaneously affect integration, we use multivariate statistical analysis, mostly by following the general model shown in figure 3.4.

For the multivariate analysis, we cast our gaze more broadly than in the bivariate analysis to understand the extent to which parental characteristics and the characteristics of children's families and neighborhoods as they were growing up affect the outcomes among the children later in life. Thus we focus on the children's generation to take advantage of the extensive information we have on their parents and their circumstances while growing up, from which we create data for the independent variables. Through multivariate statistical analyses, including multiple regression and logistic regression, we investigate the independent effects of variables representing the socialization context of the children. The research question here is "how does childhood socialization or parental human capital, itself affected by generational change, affect outcomes later in life?" Through a series of such analyses, we can begin to understand the causal mechanisms that lead to the nature of ethnic change among Mexican Americans. We use these regression models to examine several of the outcomes of interest.[26] We use a similar full model in all the regressions to be consistent across chapters, though we recognize that alternative models might produce distinct results. The general trends we describe, though, are unlikely to be significantly different.

On the right side of figure 3.4 are the three types of variables, which we use to examine the child sample. The leftmost box shows birth characteristics for the children generation, namely gender, age, and skin color, that may affect both youth and adult outcomes. Youth outcomes include schooling or educational attainment and language proficiency, which are largely determined during youth. Youth outcomes are the outcomes that other researchers have mostly been able to analyze, as the U.S.-born children of these new immigrants are still quite young.[27] Finally, in the rightmost box are adult outcomes, which are potentially affected by all of the variables that come earlier in the model. Findings on adult outcomes so far have been almost exclusively based on the experience of European ethnics, whose ancestors immigrated before the current wave. We know of no study, even of European Americans, that models intergenerational change as we have done.

In all of the regression analyses, we also present a variable for those we interviewed by telephone. This serves two functions. First, it controls for the quality of the interview, because it is always possible that telephone

Table 3.10   Children's Generation-Since-Immigration by Parents' Generational Status

Original Respondent Parent	Non-Respondent Parent					Simple Definition for Children
	Gen. 1	Gen. 2	Gen. 2.5	Gen. 2 or 3ᵃ	Gen. 3+	
Gen. 1	Gen. 1.5ᵇ (38) Gen. 2ᶜ (60)	Gen. 2.5 (48)	Gen. 2.5 (9)	Gen. 2.5 (18)	Gen. 2.5 (12)	Gen. 2 (185)
Gen. 2	Gen. 2.5 (44)	Gen. 3 (100)	Gen. 3 (27)	Gen. 3 (46)	Gen. 3 (36)	Gen. 3 (253)
Gen. 2.5	Gen. 2.5 (21)	Gen. 3 (40)	Gen. 3 (24)	Gen. 3 (17)	Gen. 4+ (36)	Gen. 3 (138)
Gen. 3+	Gen. 2.5 (14)	Gen. 3 (45)	Gen. 4+ (15)	Gen. 4+ (36)	Gen. 4+ (72)	Gen. 4+ (182)

Source: Mexican American Study Project.
ᵃ Unable to distinguish whether generation 2 or 3.
ᵇ Born in Mexico.
ᶜ U.S. born.

interviews bias the responses. Second, it serves as a proxy measure for persons who moved out of the area. In particular, we expect that those who did may be among the more assimilated sectors of the population, and thus it is important to measure or control for this effect. On an indicator such as residential segregation, for example, we would expect persons who were interviewed by telephone to have moved to neighborhoods with fewer other Mexican Americans, because they are likely to have left the ethnically dense Los Angeles or San Antonio urban areas.

Generation-Since-Immigration of Children as Used in the Multivariate Analyses

For the multivariate analysis, the children are the primary unit of analysis. This permits us to use parental characteristics for determining child outcomes and to examine generation in greater detail. Whereas a child's generation in the bivariate analysis is determined as simply the original respondent's generation plus one, for the multivariate analysis we calculate the child's generation based on birthplace and the generation of both parents. We thus allow for greater generational complexity than in the bivariate analysis by computing half or .5 generations.

Table 3.10 shows the distribution by generation of the 720 U.S.-born children in our sample, according to the generation of both their parents.

It shows how we calculated five generational groups for the children, including a 1.5, a second, a 2.5th, a third, and a fourth generation. Thirty-eight respondents who were born in Mexico but came to the United States with their parents before the 1965 survey are labeled 1.5th generation. These persons were child members of a family residing in the United States at the time of the 1965 survey and thus were probably socialized and completed their education in the United States.

Table 3.10 shows that the U.S.-born children of two immigrant parents are considered in generation 2, and that those with one immigrant parent and a U.S.-born parent of any generation are treated as generation 2.5. Anyone with one second-generation parent and one who was second generation or more is allocated to generation 3. Generation 4 requires that at least three of the four grandparents be U.S.-born. We were unable to determine whether some of the U.S.-born nonrespondent parents were second or third generation. In these cases, we relied mostly on information from the respondent parent to sort children by generation. In sum, among the 758 children of the original respondents, 38 are in the 1.5 generation, 60 in the second, 166 in the 2.5, 335 in the third, and 159 in the fourth.

= Chapter 4 =

The Historical Context

A t the time that Grebler, Moore, and Guzmán were conducting their study, Mexican Americans were beginning to enter universities in significant numbers. These students, along with a tiny cadre of Mexican American professors, were beginning to question the prevailing conceptions of Mexicans in the United States. Reacting to the cultural and ahistorical explanations of the conditions of Mexican Americans, in which they were characterized as fatalistic, apathetic, irrational, sexually irresponsible, and un-American, these scholars would instead emphasize the historical-structural constraints to the progress of Mexican Americans in the American social structure. For example, Octavio Romano concluded that the extant literature suggested that Mexican Americans were trapped in a traditional culture, isolated from the progress of history, and preferring to retreat from American culture and society:

> Contrary to the ahistorical views of anthropology and sociology, Mexican Americans as well as Mexican immigrants have not simply wallowed passively in some teleological treadmill, awaiting the emergence of an acculturated third generation before joining in the historical process.[1]

Romano and others of this new generation of scholars strongly believed that Mexican Americans did not have some kind of cultural resistance to or inability for upward mobility. Instead, they were limited by a structure of racial domination in the American Southwest, one which they actively fought in the pursuit of the full benefits of American citizenship.

Romano was part of the first wave of so-called Chicano university academics.[2] This new presence of Mexican American scholars and students would bring about a revised perspective on their position in American society, one that would challenge the traditional national narrative of assimilation. They would assail both assimilation and cultural deficiency theories and, in the beginning, emphasize racial oppression, often framing their research on the internal colonial model. The early work tended to emphasize a heroic Mexican in the face of brutal Anglo repression and homogeneity in the experiences of Mexican Americans. The bulk of the work since then, however, has been more nuanced and systematic, often stressing the diversity of Mexican American experiences, the formation of distinct Mexican American identities and culture, ethnic politics, and the importance of the immigration experience.

The findings of Chicano history have largely revealed a system of white racial supremacy and domination over colonized Mexicans since the 1830s, which persisted, in changing guises, to affect the descendants of these people and of various waves of immigration until at least the 1930s. Although they have largely discarded the internal colonial model, these scholars also criticize the assimilation assumptions implicit in early work on Mexican Americans, including Grebler, Moore, and Guzmán. David Montejano argues:

> As Grebler and his co-authors put it, contrary to the "stubborn notions" that Mexican Americans were unassimilable, they were merely immigrants who were in need of "assimilative opportunities" . . . Immigrant approaches, such as that of Grebler, Moore and Guzmán, served to shift the emphasis away from war and annexation, denying the memory of these origins for contemporary Mexican-Anglo relations. Rather than a people living under the shadow of the Alamo and San Jacinto, Mexican Americans are now seen as another group marching through the stages of assimilation. For the possibility of full citizenship, such historical revisionism may be a small price to pay.[3]

This history is an essential backdrop for understanding the current status of Mexican Americans. In this chapter, we explore some of it, seeking to provide a sense of the issues central to our research. We emphasize important socioeconomic and demographic trends, racialization and assimilation experiences, political and legal breakthroughs, and the generational differences that reflect and have shaped the incorporation of Mexican-origin persons in the United States, especially in and around Los Angeles and San Antonio. A sociological account today requires an understanding of that history, which featured both moments of intense conflict and attempts to accommodate to mainstream American society.

Mid-Nineteenth Century Origins: The Ultimate Boundary Change

We begin our description of Mexican American history, also known as Chicano history, with Mexican independence from Spain in 1821. At about that time, the new government would encourage American immigrants to settle in the Mexican state of Texas to help suppress periodic Indian raids in the remote and sparsely settled region. The central government in Mexico City was unable to fully control Texas from the independence-minded settlers. By 1830, Americans vastly outnumbered Mexicans, and the Mexican government prohibited further American immigration. After a series of battles with Mexican expeditionary militias, the Americans in Texas eventually claimed victory and declared independence from Mexico in 1836. Because the revolt, though led mostly by white American immigrants, had begun as another provincial liberal federalist uprising against Mexico's conservative constitutionalists, many Tejanos, (that is, Texans of Mexican origin), had supported and joined it. The alliance, however, would unravel soon after the American victory. These white Americans gained control and established the independent Republic of Texas, allowing the immigrant-invaders, who were mostly from the American South, to extend their plantation interests.[4]

Texas was annexed to the United States in 1845. The Mexican-American War followed, a result of conflicting claims to the United States-Mexican border, and Americans took over Alta California and New Mexico in 1847.[5] In 1848, the treaty of Guadalupe Hidalgo ended the war, with Mexico ceding California and New Mexico to the United States. Given the earlier loss of Texas, Mexico had thus lost roughly half of its original national territory. For the roughly 100,000 Mexicans remaining on those lands,[6] including those loyal to the victorious Americans, life would be transformed.[7] Although the treaty granted American citizenship and thus de facto white legal status to the original Mexican inhabitants,[8] local jurisdictions and treatment by locals would prevent them from freely exercising full citizenship rights.[9] Over the course of the nineteenth century, they would often be treated as second-class citizens, but social status varied widely by class and place.

The overall perception of Mexican Americans in the mid-nineteenth century was largely based on scientifically endorsed ideas of race. Reginald Horsman shows how American white supremacy and racial thought developed during the nineteenth century in the context of manifest destiny and firmly placed Mexicans among the inferior races to justify its conquest of Mexican lands.[10] In the 1830s and 1840s, many U. S. leaders argued that Mexicans were unable to govern and develop their precious land, and thus Manifest Destiny called for it to be ruled and developed by enterprising and intellectually superior white Americans. Although the United States was eager to annex these territories, they were sanguine about the Mexicans who came with the land. Thus they entered a calculus of how to secure the most Mexican land with the fewest Mexicans on it. A senator from Michigan seemed to speak for the congressional majority when he argued against annexation of more than the sparsely populated northern Mexican territories. He declared, "we do not want the people of Mexico either as citizens or subjects."[11] This sentiment reflected a widespread view that Mexicans as a "partly colored race" were alien, unassimilable, and intellectually inferior.[12]

Mexico's subsequent defeat in the Mexican-American War and their alleged cruelty in the Battle of the Alamo further reinforced the original judgment of Mexican racial inferiority.[13] Throughout the rest of the nineteenth century and into the twentieth, discriminatory social treatment of Mexicans seems to have become a rule in the evolving racial system of the Wild West and the Texan fringes of the South. According to many historians, their subordinate status would create a solidarity and community among Mexicans along with a rigid social boundary—not unlike a caste system—separating them from Anglos.

The history of Mexicans as an ethnic minority in the United States, according to historian Albert Camarillo, "was forged primarily from a set of nineteenth-century experiences."[14] Camarillo chronicles Chicano history in urban areas of southern California, but many of the principal components of this period of Chicano history are similar across the Southwest. Chief among these was American colonization since the 1830s and annexation to the United States from 1845 to 1848, though in Texas this period was preceded by nine years of Republic of Texas independence.[15] Regions differed in the rate at which the white population migrated to the newly conquered territories, from northern California. where Americans, attracted by a the 1849 discovery of gold, soon overwhelmed the native population, to New Mexico, whose large pre-conquest population remained relatively isolated until well into the twentieth century.[16]

In southern California and south and central Texas, urbanization and societal transformation through the immigration of large numbers of Anglos was delayed until the arrival of the railroad in the 1880s.[17] Before that was a period marked by what some have described as the Mexicanization of many Anglos, because Mexicans continued to dominate the Southwest economically and culturally.[18] This involved intermarriage of often impoverished Americans with the numerically dominant Mexicans, including marriage with daughters of the Mexican elite, instantly putting these European Americans at the top of the economic hierarchy. The children of these marriages would often use Spanish as their principal language and Catholicism as their faith, fashioning new identities for the Anglo settlers and their progeny.[19] For a short while, then, Mexican elites and Mexicanized European American new elites together would own the land and control the largely pastoral society.

It would not take long before demography swung in the other direction with a rapid and mass influx of Anglos and the transformation of basic socioeconomic and political structures. They would swiftly transform the economy of the Southwest. The commercialization of land and new trade markets and a shift from a pastoral system to a wage-labor based economy would lead to a new class structure and the end of the Mexican elite. The Mexican property, by far the Mexican elite's greatest asset, was sometimes lost in both fraudulent transactions and the commercialization and capitalization of the formerly pastoral system. Although Mexicans were spread along all classes during the nineteenth century, they tended to be homogenized and racialized by the end of it, concentrated near the bottom of the occupational structure and segregated into urban barrios, perceived as hindrances to the development of the new communities.[20]

Early Twentieth-Century Experiences with Racism

By the turn of the century, egregiously racist practices against Mexican Americans—including lynching, school segregation, and segmented labor markets—had become commonplace. Mexicans who transgressed their place experienced unparalleled levels of white mob violence, often at rates similar or even higher than those blacks experienced. William Carrigan finds that from 1848 to 1879 Mexicans were lynched, often by the Ku Klux Klan, at an astonishing rate of 473 per 100,000.[21] From 1880 to 1930, the rate declined to 27.4 per 100,000 in thirteen states, versus 37.1 for blacks in the ten southern states.[22]

Lasting in some places well into the 1950s, Mexicans in the Southwest were subject to segregation, even though there was no Mexican counterpart to the constitutionally sanctioned separate but equal provision for blacks.[23] School and public facilities segregation in Texas and California and the Southwest states were largely the "the cumulative effect of local administrative policies."[24] Justifications for school segregation ranged from protecting Anglos from the intellectual inferiority and dirtiness of Mexicans to helping Mexicans with language disadvantages and their need to miss classes to work in seasonal employment.[25] Coercive labor systems and segmented labor markets further reinforced policies and practices that subordinated the great majority of Mexican Americans throughout the Southwest.[26]

There were apparently regional differences in the institutions that upheld racial subordination. The Jim Crow system of segregation of the early twentieth century particularly extended to east and central Texas, including San Antonio, which was on the fringe of the American South.[27] Organizations such as the brutal Texas Rangers were probably more involved in racial violence than their counterparts in other states. Also, in 1902, the Texas state legislature authorized poll taxes that prevented many Mexican American Tejanos from voting, not rescinding them with a constitutional amendment until 1964. Such differences between Texas and other Southwest states throughout much of the twentieth century are likely to have had lasting impacts on the social structures and ethnic boundaries between Mexicans and Anglos. In New Mexico, the territory with the largest Mexican American population in the nineteenth century, United States legislators long argued against statehood on the basis of its large numbers of Mexicans and common use of the Spanish language.[28]

Although these experiences suggest that Mexicans were generally treated like blacks, in reality they often experienced an uneven and usually intermediate racialization that often depended—as court rulings have shown—on the time and place[29] or the individual's skin color or class status.[30] In some circumstances and areas, Mexicans and blacks were perceived as "different aspects of the same race problem."[31] In others, however, Mexicans were only gradually racialized, placed below European immigrant groups but often above blacks, Asians, and Indians on the social scale. The bulk of the Texas Mexican population lived in southern Texas and nearby San Antonio, where there were almost no blacks or other nonwhite groups and thus no impediment to a full-blown two-caste system.[32] In nineteenth-century California, Mexican Americans aspired to and sometimes achieved status superior to blacks and Chinese, if inferior to whites.[33] Neil Foley argues that in central Texas in the early twentieth century, white generally meant neither black nor Mexican,[34] though Mexicans were generally perceived as between blacks and whites. He claims that they "walked the color line" and could often escape Jim Crow, if they were educated or "close enough to the white race."[35] On the other hand, Mexicans clearly received inferior treatment in education and elsewhere compared to the Italian, German, Jewish, and other European immigrants commonly found in Los Angeles, San Antonio, and elsewhere in the Southwest.[36] Patricia Limerick writes that western race and ethnic relations made turn of the century urban confrontations between European immigrants and American nativists in the Northeast and Midwest look like family reunions.[37]

Mass Immigration from Mexico: 1910 to 1930

Levels of immigration from Mexico to the new American Southwest of the nineteenth century were relatively low, especially when compared to the large numbers of white Americans who poured into the rapidly developing region. Before 1900, as table 4.1 shows, immigration from Mexico was often not registered because the land border between the United States and Mexico was virtually open. Census data nonetheless suggest that immigrants were a small minority of the population or that residents had not yet acquired a strong sense of where the border was in relation to their birthplace. Data from the 1880 census showed that only a quarter of the 291,000 Mexican-origin persons in the United States were born in what was then Mexico. By 1900, that number had gone up one-third among 400,000 Mexican Americans.[38]

Despite the ease of crossing the border, Mexico's economic growth, coupled with the Southwest's fledgling economy and sparsely populated northern border, made the incentives to emigrate to the United States in the nineteenth century relatively weak. At the same time, many Mexican peasants were tied to haciendas through exploitative labor systems such as debt peonage, though a few escaped to the United States.[39] Temporary

Table 4.1   Mexican Origin Population in, and Legal Mexican Immigration to, United States, 1850 to 2000

Mexican Origin Population		Mexican Immigrants[a]		Immigrants to Residents
Year	Population	Period	Admitted	
1850	81,508	—	—	—
1880	290,642	—	—	—
1900	401,491	1901 to 1910	49,642	12.4%
1910	640,104	1911 to 1920	219,004	34.2
1920	999,535	1921 to 1930	459,287	46.0
1930	1,500,000[b]	1931 to 1940	22,319	1.5
1940	1,567,596	1941 to 1950	60,589	3.9
1950	2,489,477	1951 to 1960	299,811	12.0
1960	4,087,546	1961 to 1970	453,937	11.1
1970	5,641,956	1971 to 1980	640,294	11.3
1980	8,740,439	1981 to 1990	1,655,843	18.9
1990	13,495,938	1991 to 2000	2,249,421	16.7
2000	22,338,000	2001 to 2010[c]	1,790,487	8.0

Source: Gratton and Guttmann (2000); Rumbaut (2006); U.S. Immigration and Naturalization Service (2005); Office of Immigration Statistics (2003).
[a] Immigration statistics not available for Mexicans for 1886 to 1894 and, when available, often did not include land arrivals.
[b] Estimate.
[c] Projection based on immigrant admits in 2001 to 2003 continuing at same rate until 2010.

labor migration across the border also seemed at the time a more common pattern than permanent immigration.[40] Mexico's modernization project, led by President Porfirio Díaz from 1880 to 1910, would displace millions of peasants from their lands as they left to work primarily in the rapidly developing mines and railroad construction within Mexico but that resulted mostly in internal migration. However, by 1907, the bottom had fallen out of the Mexican economy and the Porfirian administration became increasingly unstable. In response, a decade-long Mexican Revolution had begun by 1910.[41]

Also by 1910, the railroads had greatly expanded their Southwest routes and linked them to Mexico's new rail system, which would allow Mexicans deep in the interior to migrate to the United States. The Mexican Revolution and the growing need for cheap labor in American Southwest, especially in California's exploding agricultural sector but also in Texas agriculture and cattle-production, would provoke the immigration of large numbers of Mexicans.[42] Moreover, by 1909, labor recruiting agents had become active in El Paso and other border cities. These agents would solicit and direct the often temporary migrants to distant American cities to feed their growing labor demands in the Southwest. By the late 1910s, immigration had mostly become self-perpetuating.[43] At the same time, Southern and Central Europeans had been flooding into eastern and midwestern cities to meet growing industrial demands there. Relatively few Europeans had settled in the West and Southwest.

In the twenty-year period beginning about 1910, roughly 10 percent of Mexico's population immigrated to the United States. Table 4.1 shows that from 1911 to 1930, nearly 700,000 Mexican immigrants were legally admitted. Motivated by an insatiable appetite for low-skill labor along with xenophobia and nativist fears, both support and restriction of Mexican immigration existed in alternating periods in the early twentieth century. Immigrants admitted to the United States in the first two decades of the twentieth century increased the 1910 resident population by 34.2 percent and the 1920 population by another 46 percent.[44] This gain was particularly large in California, which had a smaller Mexican American population than Texas.[45] In the 1920s, according to José Alvarez,[46] the California Mexican American population gained 20 percent each year from immigration against 7 percent in Texas. At the local level, Los Angeles County and San Antonio each had a Mexican origin population of roughly 30,000 in 1910, which by 1930 had grown to 190,000 in Los Angeles and 82,000 in San Antonio. These numbers in both years represented a large part of the San Antonio population but only a relatively small part of Los Angeles.[47] By the 1920s, Mexican Americans whose ancestors had preceded the large wave of immigrants, had largely intermarried with Mexican immigrants and thus incorporated into the larger Mexican immigrant society,[48] which itself was being Americanized.

During this period of mass immigration, the popular view of Mexican inferiority and their inability to assimilate would come to a head, just as it had done during annexation. Extending into the early 1930s, this view would be shared by at least some of the scientific community.[49] As agribusiness and its allies argued that economic growth required Mexican labor, a group of small farmers, urban workers, eugenicists, and their allies claimed that white Americans would be able to create their own economic development, that the Mexican borders should be closed, and that Mexican workers be repatriated.[50] In the debate over Mexican immigration, economic interests were often pitted against the bleak social consequences of a caste society that many predicted. The growers' desire to maintain high numbers of immigrants tended to win out. Moreover, in their interests as well as those of the restrictionists, Mexicans would be socially segregated and, as much as possible, limited to agricultural labor.[51]

Despite employer demands, United States immigration policy often sought to control Mexican immigration, especially in response to nativist concerns. Restrictionists throughout the United States had been raising alarms about the high rates of immigration since at least 1890, largely on racial grounds. Asians, who largely came to the western half of the United States, were seen as particularly alien and unassimilable,[52] which would lead to laws excluding Asians from immigrating to the United States. Central and Southern Europeans would mostly populate midwestern and eastern American cities. They were also seen to be culturally and racially inferior to Anglo-Saxons and a series of laws would later greatly reduce immigration from southern and central Europe as well. However, Mexicans were hardly affected by any of these laws, as Southwest employers would lobby Congress intensely for the continuance of Mexican immigration.[53] Whereas immigration from several European countries, like Italy, would subside in the mid-1910s with World War I,[54] the first large wave of Mexican immigration in the twentieth century would last until 1929.

The growing thirst for cheap Mexican labor, along with the emergence of discriminatory immigration policies, would further promote the stigmatization of Mexicans. Mae Ngai argues that Mexicans would become fully racialized in the 1920s.[55] Whereas the United States-Mexico border had been quite permeable, the United States began to aggressively police it after the Border Patrol was created in 1924 and, along with the Texas Rangers and other groups, sought to control Mexican immigration, thereby creating both a large illegal alien population and its own so-called racial problem. By 1930, the U.S. Census would create a separate racial category for Mexicans, though the League of United Latin American Citizens and Mexican consulates fought to restore their previous white classification and won.[56] The tension between being socially classified as nonwhite, which most Mexicans seemed to accept,[57] and legal classification as white would become common throughout the twentieth century.

During this period, the Protestant and Catholic Churches invested heavily in Americanizing Mexican immigrants and their families, just as they had done with Europeans on the East Coast.[58] Americanization campaigns sought to instill presumably American values of democracy, hard work, and discipline among Mexican American women and teach them proper hygiene while trying to eradicate their supposedly defective Mexican culture. At the same time, they assumed that Mexicans had limited aspirations and thus were destined to hold lowly positions in American society.[59] Americanizers targeted women in particular because they were thought to be more open to change and would serve as conduits for educating their husbands and children.

The large wave of 1910s and 1920s immigration from Mexico would suddenly end with the Great Depression of 1929. Although most immigration slowed somewhat with the end of employment opportunities, it by no means stopped altogether, perhaps because of family and friendship networks in the United States. Initially, the United States government sometimes also offered social support if not employment. Voluntarily returning to Mexico was not a desirable option because the depression affected Mexico as well, bringing a sharp drop in national income and further delaying recovery from the ten years of Mexican Revolution. Many Mexican immigrants would seek welfare relief in the United States, prompting calls for their repatriation throughout the United States.[60] In response, state agents sent back hundreds of thousands of Mexicans, 60 percent of whom were American-citizen children, through deportation campaigns and subsidized train fares largely borne by the Mexican government and donations from the immigrant community. Despite the mass immigration to the United States from many nations, repatriation would be restricted to Mexicans.

The especially large numbers of repatriations from Los Angeles may not be surprising given that county welfare rolls there increased ten-fold in 1931 alone and the amount of assistance offered per capita amounted to $3.40, compared with other places such as San Antonio's $0.15.[61] Although only 10 percent of welfare recipients in Los Angeles were Mexican (including American citizens), politicians and the media claimed a much higher number, thereby further inflaming anti-Mexican passions. Although records were not kept by either the Mexican or the United States government, Francisco Balderrama and Raymond Rodríguez used government statistics and newspaper accounts to estimate that up to one-third of the Mexican community in the United States had been repatriated in the 1930s, curtailing their socioeconomic development and social acceptance for many years.

Immigration from Mexico would resume in the 1940s as new labor demands to offset the loss of labor to the armed forces and to urban wartime production stimulated calls for new immigration from Mexico. In 1942, the United States and Mexican governments instituted an emergency guest-worker program known as the Bracero Program, which would allow the temporary entry, by contract, of nearly 4 million Mexicans until 1964. During this period, this international agreement allowed agricultural interests to actively recruit labor from deep inside the central-west region of Mexico, because American workers joined the war effort and tended to move to urban areas after they returned.[62] Mexicans had become the preferred source of labor in the highly commercialized agriculture of the Southwest, given that they were considered hard working and their return to Mexico after the harvest season was presumably assured under the Bracero program so that no long-term cost would accrue to American employers. The agricultural labor market and the guest worker program, according to Ngai, worked to "create a kind of imported colonialism, which constructed Mexicans as a foreign race and justified their exclusion from the polity."[63]

Generational Shifts

Such large-scale growth followed by a sudden end to immigration would also create sizable shifts in the internal composition of the Mexican American community, just as it would in the period after 1970. By 1920, half of the Mexican origin population in the United States was born in Mexico,[64] up from about one-third two decades earlier. These shifts would become a dominant theme in issues of identity and politics for Mexican Americans throughout the twentieth century.[65] Anglos rarely seemed to differentiate Mexicans by immigration status, and their treatment of them often targeted Mexicans as a group,[66] as the repatriation and other experiences had demonstrated. Whether born in the United States or in Mexico, all persons of Mexican origin were often considered Mexican and alien.

Conflicts between Mexican immigrants and U.S.-born Mexican Americans were unavoidable. Those born in the United States found themselves either seeking to differentiate themselves from or empathizing with the lower status immigrants. However, the fact that the two groups were often of the same family, often intermarried and shared schools, and together participated in cultural and religious institutions minimized major cleavages and generally led to a shared identity. Moreover, persistent discrimination against the group as a whole had often consolidated a group boundary between the Mexican-origin population against Anglos. Jews and other European groups had been treated as racial others initially but were usually somewhere between whites and Mexican Americans and African Americans. By the mid-twentieth century, the European groups were eventually accepted as fully white and their small numbers in the Southwest, as Anglos.[67] Mexicans never became white because many Americans were concluding that "Mexicans were inferior to even the lowliest Europeans."[68] The very word *Anglo* was used regularly in the nineteenth-century Mexican society of the Southwest to contrast the outsiders from themselves. *Anglos,* which generally became synonymous with white, was the primary contrast to *Mexican*. Certainly, this distinction may have been used as a cultural contrast but in the minds of many, it referred to a racial distinction as well.

Urbanization and Generational Change

By World War II, most of the Mexican American population resided in urban areas.[69] Whereas in 1920 most (55 percent) Mexican immigrants lived in rural areas, only 25 percent of white immigrants did. By 1960, however, the immigrant and U.S.-born Mexican-origin populations were more likely to live in metropolitan areas than the non-Hispanic white population.[70] By 1980, more than 80 percent of Mexican Americans lived in metropolitan areas. Los Angeles and San Antonio continued to have the largest Mexican-origin populations.[71]

The situation of Mexican Americans in urban areas seemed to be somewhat better in major cities during the postwar period. Montejano's study of Texas found that since the 1940s, segregation and repression persisted in rural areas but that a system of patronage and partial integration also developed for Mexican Americans in cities.[72] Many braceros and Mexican Americans from the agricultural migrant stream were attracted to the growing job prospects in defense and other industries in urban areas such as San Antonio and particularly Los Angeles.[73] Although those jobs were probably better than the ones they held before, they were often in the lowest level occupations.

Residentially, rigid segregation persisted in San Antonio and in Los Angeles. In Los Angeles, housing was limited largely to the eastside and a handful of other neighborhoods scattered throughout the county because restrictive covenants and discrimination continued to keep Mexicans out of most Los Angeles neighborhoods.[74] One neighborhood in East Los Angeles, Belvedere, which had the largest concentration of Mexicans in the entire metropolitan area,[75] also "had the distinction of being the worst slum on the Pacific Coast with the highest number of relief cases, delinquencies and other social problems."[76]

With immigration at a low point, growing signs of mobility among some Mexican Americans and the patriotic sacrifice and proud service of several hundred thousand Mexican American soldiers in World War II, expectations of equality and full citizenship began to emerge.[77] Also, a growing but nevertheless small number of U.S.-born Mexican Americans would begin to enter middle class occupations, apparently as the second generation began to numerically dominate the adult population. At the same time, segregation, police harassment, and various racist incidents continued to trouble Mexican American communities.[78]

The war had created labor shortages and military service offered new job opportunities, training, and experience. At the same time, the need for stable relations with Mexico and for Mexican agricultural workers stimulated a drive to reduce discrimination, including formation of the Fair Employment Practices Committee and the Good Neighbor Policy, which sought improvements in relations with "Latin Americans" at home and abroad.[79] Many Mexican Americans felt that it was time to reap their fair share of the benefits of a growing nation, especially given that as many as 500,000 Mexican American soldiers had recently fought and died in its defense.[80] Although Mexican-born residents outnumbered the long-term U.S.-born population of Mexican descent in the 1920s, by the mid-1940s, the proportion of immigrants declined to just above 40 percent, given a second generation well into adulthood and an emerging young third generation, not to mention a small fourth and fifth generation. For sociologist

Figure 4.1   Hispanic Population by Generation, 1950 to 2050

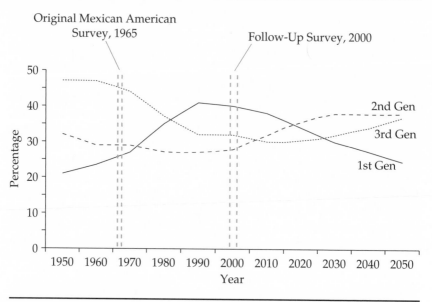

Source: Suro and Passel (2003).

Rodolfo Alvarez,[81] the Mexican American generation had arrived to succeed a Mexican immigrant generation and that demographic shift would produce new assimilationist hopes.[82] The historian Vicki Ruíz, however, contended that such generational distinctions were often ambiguous in practice.[83] Figure 4.1 shows the changing generational composition of the Hispanic population from 1950 to 2050. By the 1950s, nearly half of Hispanics were third generation or more, given that mass immigration from Latin America had ended before 1930. The third generation, however, began to shrink in the 1960s as large-scale Mexican immigration reemerged.

The image of Mexicans and Mexican Americans continued to be poor. The animosity toward Mexicans was apparent in a sensationalist press that reinforced anti-Mexican stereotypes,[84] depicting Mexican American youth as "the enemy within." It became especially heated with the Zoot Suit Riots in 1943, when white sailors systematically and repeatedly attacked Mexican American youth.[85] Negative stereotypes of Mexicans would persist and occasionally enter the public discourse as in Judge Gerald Chargin's 1969 tirade against a juvenile who had pled guilty to incest:

> Mexican people, after 13 years of age, it's perfectly all right to go out and act like an animal . . . You are lower than animals and haven't the right to live in organized society—just miserable, lousy, rotten people.[86]

It was becoming increasingly evident that even as members of a second generation reached adulthood, they would continue to be treated like their despised immigrant parents.

The inferior image of Mexicans was shared among the general public. Sociologist Emory Bogardus's decennial surveys of college students nationwide from 1926 to 1966 found that Mexicans and Mexican Americans consistently occupied the lowest rungs in his "racial distance" rankings.[87] In his study of seven attitudinal items including willingness to have as friends, live in proximity to, or intermarry persons of a particular group, Mexicans and Mexican Americans never scored higher than twenty-first among thirty named groups. In all four surveys in this period, only groups now considered nonwhite fell into the bottom ten and only blacks (referred to as "Negroes") and "Asian Indians" (however that term was interpreted) consistently scored lower. In contrast, Italians, a group considered to have been racialized in the early twentieth century, scored fourteenth in 1926 and by 1966 reached the eighth spot, only behind seven northern and western European groups. In 1966, when immigration was still at a low point, Mexicans had fallen to twenty-eighth.

Emerging Organizational Politics: 1930s to 1950s

With urbanization, the emergence of a second generation well into adulthood and a small but growing middle class, Mexican Americans would begin to organize politically to redress their generally low socioeconomic status. The actions of Mexican American organizations in this period would reveal a tension between assimilation and cultural separateness, a range of opposition and support for immigration, and varying identities as to whether Mexican Americans were white. In this section, we review the struggles of several organizations, which varied considerably among themselves and over their own histories. In response to the local political and race relations context, these organizations tended to be more conservative and accommodating in Texas and more radical in California.

Dating back to the 1920s and extending to the 1960s, the League of United Latin American Citizens (LULAC), led by a growing middle class, sought to politically represent Mexican Americans throughout the Southwest, but especially in Texas.[88] Although other Mexican American organizations would emerge,[89] LULAC was the dominant political entity and sought to represent Mexican Americans as "Americans in politics and philosophy but Mexican in culture and social activity," though the call to remain Mexican seems to not have been shared by all leaders.[90] According to David Gutiérrez, it emphasized assimilationism as a political strategy to achieve full economic incorporation for Mexican Americans, but largely resisted sociocultural assimilation. Gutiérrez notes that in the mid 1920s, LULAC contended that American citizens of Mexican origin were officially a permanent part of American society and therefore "should make every effort to assimilate into the American social and cultural mainstream."[91]

The G.I. Forum was established in 1949 largely by World War II veterans and was also mostly Texas-based. It applied pressure to convince Congress to end the Bracero Program and to instill strict new regulations on future immigration from Mexico. The G.I. Forum promoted the idea that the civil rights of Mexican Americans must be enforced and that the Bracero Program and undocumented immigrants negatively affected their future.[92] In 1947, the Community Service Organization in Los Angeles began with goal of increasing voter registration and the political representation of Mexican Americans in local political bodies. It later broadened to serve a range of community-based interests and needs.

Many of the Mexican American veterans involved in these groups perceived the United States as a democratic society that allowed all citizens to achieve equality and acceptance through electoral politics.[93] The G.I. bill, in particular, with its college benefits, permitted a small Mexican American middle class to emerge. Although veterans who entered college were concerned with individual success,[94] a few took leadership positions in the new Mexican American organizations.[95] Having been influenced by the ideology of patriotic Americanism and anticommunism, such veterans tended to emphasize their Americanness.[96] However, they had also learned that acceptance as white was the surest path to achieving first-class American citizenship. Despite the simultaneous flowering of nationalism in Mexico that glorified racial mixture (mestizaje),[97] these groups promoted the idea that Mexican Americans were a white ethnic group, like Italians or Irish, which allowed them to claim full citizenship rights, such as that which the European groups had achieved. This often meant downplaying their Native American backgrounds and claiming a Spanish or Latin American identity for themselves, despite their mixed racial status.[98] At the same time, they generally distanced themselves from African Americans and their antiracist tactics, which they perceived as anti-integrationist and excessively confrontational. These Mexican American leaders generally thought that if they deemphasized the racism Mexican Americans experienced, they would be better able to deflect anti-Mexican sentiment.

According to these historical accounts, the integrationist sentiment largely reflected a feeling that the Mexican-origin population should set a high priority on its own incorporation into the United States and oppose Mexican immigration, which they argued created unfair economic competition and aggravated stereotypes. Integrationist attitudes were often accompanied by a distancing from Mexico and its people. Others, however, had a strong sense empathy for the poor conditions of recent Mexican immigrants and a shared sense of discrimination that far outweighed the distinctions among them.[99] The passage of the McCarran-Walter Act in 1952 and INS sweeps during Operation Wetback resulted in a shift in the ideological positions of Mexican American organizations regarding Mexican immigrants. For Mexican American organizations generally, the government's treatment of Mexican immigrants would be a catalyst for a broader based civil rights movement that also sought to protect the rights of immigrants.[100] One explanation for this evolution was the realization that the economic, cultural, and political treatment of Mexican Americans and Mexican immigrants differed little.[101]

A left-wing alternative to organizations such as LULAC and the G.I. Forum, the Congress of Spanish Speaking Peoples (El Congreso), was established in 1938 and was boldly opposed to the assimilationist and anti-immigrant proposals of LULAC and similar organizations. This largely Los Angeles-based organization worked closely with trade unions and primarily sought to protect the rights of Mexican workers while proposing bilingual education and strongly denouncing fascism, white supremacy, and racial and gender discrimination.[102] According to Gutiérrez, its "most important contribution was its insistence that all Spanish speaking peoples—citizens and aliens alike—work together to better their conditions as residents of the United States."[103] Often working with El Congreso, individual trade unions in the 1930s and 1940s had little success in organizing Mexican origin workers in Texas but were very successful in southern California.[104]

Educational Segregation

Assimilationist political organizations were limited by their inability to affect discriminatory laws and public policies and so turned to litigation, particularly with regard to educational segregation. Brown vs. the Board of Education ended educational segregation at the federal level in 1954, but the end to legal educational segregation in California and Texas had been decided several years earlier. These cases involved segregation of Mexican American children as early as 1931 in Lemon Grove, California,[105] and statewide cases in both California in 1946 and Texas in 1948.[106] Mexican American leaders identified segregation as the major barrier to school achievement and the social and economic mobility of Mexican American children. Among other things, segregation branded all Mexican American children as inferior and militated against the learning of English and the acquisition of factors conducive to civic participation. Educators went so far as stating that segregation was "pedagogically unsound, socially dangerous and unquestionably un-American."[107] From 1946 to 1957, a series of legal cases granted victories against segregation, though local, state, and federal jurisdictions (including the EEOC-SM:167) often failed to enforce

Table 4.2   Mexican Origin Classmates by Urban Area, 1965[a]

	1930s	1940s	1950s
Los Angeles			
Mostly or all Mexican	84%	84%	83%
All Mexican	48	57	43
San Antonio			
Mostly or all Mexican	91	87	88
All Mexican	66	32	39

Source: Mexican American Study Project.
[a] Based on question: When you were thirteen or fourteen years old, how many of your schoolmates were of Mexican origin? Among those born in Los Angeles or San Antonio or migrated there before age sixteen. Decade refers to when respondent was age thirteen.

the new laws well into the 1960s and after, often using a series of sub-terfuges to avoid integration.[108]

The extent of educational segregation before the 1960s is not well known. Surveys of particular school districts report that 90 percent of these districts in Texas and 85 percent in California were racially segregated.[109] Also, segregation was often limited to elementary school education while nearly all high schools in San Antonio and Los Angeles were mixed.[110] Data from our study permit us to estimate levels of school segregation for the period in Los Angeles County and San Antonio at roughly the middle school level. Based on the 1965 data on original respondents collected by Grebler, Moore, and Guzmán, table 4.2 shows the percent of Mexican Americans in Los Angeles and San Antonio reporting that they attended fully segregated or "Mexican schools" when they were thirteen or four-teen years old. To go back as far as we could, we used the entire original sample and stratified them by age, estimating the decade in which they were that age. In addition, we restricted the sample to those living in Los Angeles or San Antonio at that age based on those who were born in or migrated to Los Angeles or San Antonio before age sixteen.

Table 4.2 shows that 83 or 84 percent of Los Angeles and 87 to 91 per-cent of San Antonio school children had mostly or all Mexican-origin schoolmates from the 1930s to the 1950s. In the 1930s, fully 66 percent of young adolescent San Antonians were in fully segregated classrooms, versus 48 percent of Los Angelenos of the same age, reflecting the rela-tively rigid segregation of Texas cities and the fact that the proportion Mexican was much larger. The extent of segregation in San Antonio subse-quently declines somewhat until the 1940s, and remains flat to at least the 1950s. For Los Angeles, complete segregation is erratic, declining in the 1930s, increasing in the 1940s, and dropping again in the 1950s.[111] On the other hand, 9 percent of San Antonio respondents and 16 percent of Los Angeles respondents reported that a few or none of their classmates were

Mexican in the 1930s, which is inconsistent with the claim of complete or nearly complete Mexican American segregation.[112]

The Civil Rights Era: 1950s to 1970s

The early civil rights victories against educational segregation for Mexican Americans compared with African Americans may have came about because of the intermediate racialization of the former, which allowed defense arguments that Mexican Americans were white.[113] Such a strategy was not surprising, given that full citizenship in the United States was contingent on being white and the collective naturalization of Mexicans in the Southwest under the Treaty of Guadalupe Hidalgo in 1848 had defined them as white under the law.[114] California, however, extended voting only to white-looking Mexican males in 1849 and in 1935 declared that Mexicans were to be treated like Indians in terms of citizenship.[115] Nonetheless, Mexican Americans actively sought to use a whiteness defense in immigration and civil rights cases. They eventually switched, however, to equal protection clauses as the Civil Rights Act became consolidated and Mexican Americans could gain protected status.[116]

Instructively but ironically, a similar point was made by the plaintiff in *Hernández v. Texas* in 1954 alleging that Mexican Americans were systematically excluded from juries in Jackson County, Texas. County officials, however, would argue that because Mexicans were considered white and the juries were entirely white, then Mexicans were neither excluded nor entitled to the equal protection clause of the Fourteenth Amendment.[117] The Texas Supreme Court agreed with Jackson County but the case was overturned by the United States Supreme Court, which extended equal protection to Mexican Americans where they were subject to local discrimination.[118] The written opinion of Chief Justice Warren cited the Jim Crow restrictions on Mexican Americans and the inferiority with which they were perceived as clear evidence that, socially, they occupied a distinct classification and subordinate status from whites.[119]

Although Mexican American leaders had been in an assimilationist mode since World War II, if not earlier, a new generation of activists began to organize and assert their identity, much as blacks did in the civil rights movement at about the same time.[120] As the 1950s came to an end and the black civil rights movement gained national attention, many Mexican Americans began to feel that the organizations of the 1950s were not pressing hard enough to acquire civil rights for Mexicans.[121] As a result, Mexican American organizations altered their political tactics away from the assimilationism of the 1950s and toward the radical tactics of El Congreso. Some leaders argued for more aggressive organizing, a stronger assertion of Mexican identity, and becoming an interest group.[122] Emerging groups such as the Mexican American Political Association (MAPA) in California and the Political Association of Spanish Speaking People (PASSO) in Texas and

Arizona[123] sought to empower Mexican Americans by financially contributing to the election of Mexican American candidates, organizing against gerrymandering and poll taxes, and pressuring the Democratic and Republican
parties to include Mexican Americans in leadership positions.[124]

These organizations were largely successful in gaining federal attention regarding the plight of Mexican Americans and extending civil rights
gains to them, even though there was a strong tendency in Washington
to see civil rights issues as affecting only blacks. The leaders of these organizations had forged strong political alliances with Presidents Kennedy
and Johnson, but especially Johnson, who was personally familiar with the
issues facing Mexican Americans, having been the principal of the Mexican
school in Cotulla, Texas.[125] Moreover, by 1963, Henry González of San
Antonio and Edward Roybal of Los Angeles had both become members
of the House of Representatives and they, with Johnson, pushed hard for
civil rights legislation.[126] The 1964 Civil Rights Act and the Voting Rights
Act of 1965, with its extension to linguistic minorities in 1975, reflected
the cumulative work of these formal political efforts and would signal
large changes in opportunities for minorities and in the political structure of many southwestern cities with Mexican American populations.
By 1966, Johnson also had become concerned that the federal Equal
Employment Opportunity Commission (EEOC) had been unresponsive
to Mexican American demands.

With the emergence of the Chicano generation[127] in the 1960s, when the
third generation (or more) constituted nearly half of the Mexican-origin
population (see figure 4.1), a politics of racial affirmation would largely
displace the politics of assimilation. Frustrated with continuing racism
amidst the assimilationist hopes, styles, and political strategies of the existing leadership, and buoyed by the gains of a black civil rights movement,
these new young leaders sought more dramatic changes in the educational and social position of Mexican Americans. Indeed, the term Chicano
emerged as an identity that symbolized cultural and political autonomy
for Mexican Americans rather than assimilation and acceptance as white.[128]
The tensions between the old and new political styles erupted in a 1969
debate between Congressmen Henry González, perhaps the most important Mexican American politician of the time, and José Angel Gutiérrez,
a leading Chicano activist. As historian David Gutiérrez relates:

> Reflecting the views of many others of his generation who had grown up
> believing that Mexican Americans must work within the system to achieve
> social justice, Congressman González lambasted Gutiérrez and other Chicano
> militants. He characterized them as "professional Mexicans" who were
> attempting to "stir up the people by appeals to emotion [and] prejudice to
> become leaders and achieve selfish ends." In González's view the militant's
> emphasis on Chicano ethnic distinctiveness and their espousal of separatist
> racial ideologies represented the "politics of hatred."[129]

Many Mexican American leaders began favoring the strategy of direct confrontation, and formed several more militant organizations, including the Mexican American Youth Organization and the United Mexican American Students,[130] which would be succeeded by the more radically named Movimiento Estudiantil Chicano de Aztlán (MEChA). Two organizations, the United Farm Workers and the Raza Unida Party, became nationally visible as representative of the Chicano civil rights struggle.[131] The range of strategies used during the Chicano movement, from the 1960s to the mid-1970s, reflected the more general era of political activism. These included bombings, Reyes López Tijerina's 1967 courthouse raids and struggle to reclaim former Mexican land in New Mexico, student walkouts, and the 1970 Chicano Moratorium against the Vietnam War.[132] The new leadership sought to inspire a Chicano identity and became increasingly culturally nationalist and disparaging of non-Mexican identifiers such as Latin American or Spanish-speaking. However, whether these views represented those of the new generation generally or only of the leadership is not clear because historical accounts rarely include representative data.[133]

Mexican American leaders long recognized that education was the main obstacle to their economic mobility in American society. LULAC in Texas focused on fighting for bilingual education and against school segregation and discrimination and obtaining quality education for Mexican Americans.[134] By 1968, Chicano activists focused on improving education in Los Angeles and in 1968 students walked out of several Eastside high schools, an act that would be followed in San Antonio and other southwestern cities.[135] Despite several court-ordered rulings in favor of Mexican American civil rights, LULAC and other leaders realized the need for an NAACP-style organization to monitor judicial decisions. By 1970, the Mexican American Legal Defense and Education Fund (MALDEF) was founded. Its litigation strategies would focus on education, particularly desegregation and school financing.[136] MALDEF and other ethnic political organizations, such as the National Association of Latino Elected Officials and the National Council of La Raza, would become mainstays in ensuing decades and would take on such causes as discrimination, immigrant defense, voting rights, and equitable political representation.

The new Chicano politics of cultural nationalism took particularly strong hold in Los Angeles. Meanwhile, Tejanos continued more traditional politics.[137] Poll taxes, inaccessible polls, gerrymandering, and a nonpartisan and general citywide election in San Antonio had made it difficult for Mexican American political mobilization[138] but the national civil rights agenda including the Voting Rights Act and the war on poverty led to a change in the formal political structure. With pressure from a grassroots movement (COPS) and a new reform-minded generation of local businessmen and the mandate of the Voting Rights Act, Mexican Americans would take the reins of local political power.[139] A switch to single member districts had changed the composition of the San Antonio City Council and, by 1981, Henry Cisneros had become the first Mexican American mayor of San Antonio since the nineteenth century.[140] By contrast, Mexican Americans were a small minority in Los Angeles but it was a population that would grow in the following decades. In 2005, the first Mexican American mayor since the nineteenth century was elected.

The New Immigration: 1970s to the Present

The spirit of the civil rights struggle of the 1960s also extended to fundamental changes in immigration policy. The Immigration Act of 1965, also known as the Hart-Celler Act, came at the end of the Bracero Program. Most important, it abolished the previous national-origins quotas in place since 1882 that favored Europe and set preferences that emphasized family reunification and certain professional occupations. The major effect of this law was to greatly increase immigration from the eastern hemisphere, effectively ending the 1882 Chinese Exclusion Act.[141] Three years later, an amendment established a visa limit of 120,000 for the western hemisphere but only in 1978 did another amendment promulgate a fixed, per-nation quota.[142] The 1978 amendment greatly reduced the number of authorized immigrants that could come from Latin America and especially, Mexico.[143] Against the backdrop of high levels of legal migration and relatively porous borders, due largely to continuing employer demand, these immigration laws led to a surge in the flow of undocumented immigrants. In 1986, an amnesty program known as the Immigration Reform and Control Act (IRCA) led to the legalization of many formerly undocumented immigrants.

A new illegal alien problem emerged in the 1990s and came to be associated with Mexicans, its largest component. The reemergence of this large undocumented population would lead to a sharp rise in nativism and xenophobia. In California, a Republican administration and electorate voted in favor of Proposition 187, which denied health and educational benefits to the undocumented. Ironically this would lead to a spike in naturalization rates among legal Mexican residents and the growing size of a Democratic electorate. The politics of immigration became the new focus of Mexican American politics. In 1996, following California's lead, the federal government passed the Personal Responsibility Act (PRA) to limit noncitizen access to public welfare benefits and the Illegal Immigration Reform and Individual Responsibility Act (IIRIRA), which further strengthened border enforcement and expedited the deportation process while establishing some exceptions to the PRA.

After 2001, anti-immigrant groups began rallying thousands of protestors about border takeovers as undocumented immigrants began to cross the border in large numbers in remote areas like Arizona, as the traditional urban gateways had been largely sealed off with the 1996 reforms.[144] The new security concerns about foreign terrorists increased popular support for this new movement. By 2006, hundreds of thousands of immigrants and their sympathizers would march in major urban areas of the United States to protest proposed immigration reform. Finally, after much debate in Congress, the legislature agreed to extend the United States-Mexico border wall to cover 700 miles of the border, though it remained deadlocked about further reforms.[145]

With the consolidation of social networks deep into Mexico that emerged from the Bracero Program, and with that country's demographic transition, Mexican immigration would experience a new surge in the 1970s, as would immigration from Asia and other parts of Latin America.[146] However, unusually restrictive visa limits along with the relative ease of crossing the border would turn much Mexican immigration into an illegal alien issue and thus make it particularly problematic in the public eye. Today, the tremendous labor demand for Mexicans and renewed nativism has again rekindled public hysteria against Mexican immigration[147] and especially the undocumented. By 2004, Mexicans numbered more than 6 million[148] of the 12 million undocumented immigrants in the United States.[149]

A growing immigrant generation has thus arisen again, overtaking what appeared to be a consolidating third generation (see figure 4.1). An approximation of the hiatus in immigration among European immigrants was short lived and not to be repeated for Mexicans. Table 4.1 shows that persons of Mexican origin had numbered 22.3 million by 2000, four times their population in 1960.[150] This large-scale immigration would again change the nature of the Mexican American community, just as it did in the 1910s and 1920s.[151] As figure 4.1 shows, though immigrants were only 20 percent of all Mexican Americans in the 1950s, by 1990, they were more than 40 percent. During the same period, the third generation plus (at least grandchildren of immigrants), had declined from nearly 50 to about 30 percent.

The relative size of the Mexican American population and its immigrant component are strikingly different in Los Angeles and San Antonio. The Hispanic origin population in Los Angeles County has grown from 9 percent of 6 million in 1960 to 46 percent of 9.5 million in 2000. San Antonio's Mexican-origin population, on the other, has been consistently large—41 percent of 600,000 in 1960 and 58 percent of 1.1 million in 2000. Because of its economic dynamism, immigration has been higher in Los Angeles than San Antonio since World War II. The presence of the immigrant community in Los Angeles in more recent years has greatly changed the nature of the Mexican-origin population there. At the same

Table 4.3   **Characteristics by Urban Area, 1965**

	Los Angeles	San Antonio
Own television	96%	89%
Own telephone	76	60
With private toilet	95	89
With hot water	99	79
Have $500 or more in savings	32	14
Monthly income at primary job (mean)	$439	$251
Monthly income at all jobs (mean)	$677	$260
Earn less than $3,000 a year	13%	40%
Home value (mean)	$16,283	$4,902
Speak only English to children	31%	10%
Frequently attend church	41	62

Source: Mexican American Study Project.

time, San Antonio has seen relatively little immigration in the last fifty years. In 1970, only 9 percent of Mexican Americans in San Antonio were immigrants. By 1990, only 13 percent were. The comparable figures for the same years in Los Angeles County were 25 and 47 percent.

Changing Los Angeles and San Antonio Economies

In 1965, Los Angeles and San Antonio offered quite distinct opportunities for Mexican Americans though that difference would change by the end of the twentieth century. The industrial and occupational structures of San Antonio in the 1960s, along with its segregationist and clientelist politics, clearly afforded fewer opportunities to Mexican Americans than the more economically dynamic and modern Los Angeles did. This is apparent in the data that Grebler, Moore, and Guzmán collected.

We analyzed data from both waves and present basic economic and social indicators in table 4.3. San Antonians were markedly less likely to own televisions and telephones or live in houses with a toilet or hot water. Although roughly 40 percent of San Antonio's Mexicans earned less than $3,000 annually, only about 13 percent of Angelenos did. Costs of living in the two cities at the time, interestingly, were similar. Mexican American homes in 1965 already were worth three times as much in Los Angeles. Most notably, though, Angelenos also seemed to be much more acculturated on language and religiosity as a much larger percentage of them spoke only English at home and they less frequently attended religious services.

Largely coinciding with changing patterns of immigration, major changes have also occurred in the structure of the United States' economy since the mid-1970s. With the end of segregation and the most egregious systems of racism, including the near exclusion of Mexicans from particular occupations and industries, the fortunes of Mexican Americans became increasingly tied to local labor market opportunities. By the 1960s, some Mexican Americans, in Los Angeles especially, seemed to be securing skilled blue-collar jobs.[152] However, these emerging industrial opportunities slowed with major economic changes occurring soon after.

An industrial restructuring of the American economy in the 1970s and 1980s led to the diminishing importance of the manufacturing sector and the highly paid and unionized working class jobs associated with it. Industrial restructuring was particularly noticeable in eastern and midwestern cities but was similarly intense in Los Angeles, noted for being "the most industrialized city west of the Mississippi."[153] San Antonio, by contrast, had little industry and almost no unionization but did have a significant military sector, which contributed to the particularly low status of its working class and mostly Mexican-origin population. However, the end of the cold war in the early 1990s led to sharp reductions in the few good jobs the San Antonio military offered and to the near disappearance of the aerospace industry in Los Angeles, which had been the area's largest employer. As we will show, income inequality clearly increased in Los Angeles's restructured economy and started out higher but increased less in San Antonio.

The election of Henry Cisneros as mayor of San Antonio in 1981 signaled the beginning of its transformation from a racially segregated society based on services to one of the leading Sunbelt cities, even though the new business elite had begun to modernize San Antonio in the early 1970s.[154] Cisneros, with strong backing from these young local businessmen, pursued "unlimited economic development and growth as a way to insure the economic health of the city."[155] Certainly, Mexican Americans would benefit in some respects from this new growth though the mostly Anglo Northside benefited more.[156] The fact that Mexican Americans had elected one of their own as mayor and would hold a large number of city council seats at the same time that ethnic inequalities intensified created what Rudy Rosales has called the "illusion of inclusion."

Urban Industrial Restructuring

San Antonio and Los Angeles were very different places in the 1960s in terms of economic development. There has been a convergence, if not a switch, in the decade that followed, as industrial restructuring led to a decrease in well-paid working class jobs and thus even greater income inequality in Los Angeles. Relatively high levels of income inequality, largely along ethnic lines, have characterized San Antonio throughout its history. Specifically, figure 4.2 shows that the Gini index of income

Figure 4.2   Gini Index[a] and Income per Capita[b] by Urban Area[c], 1970 to 2000

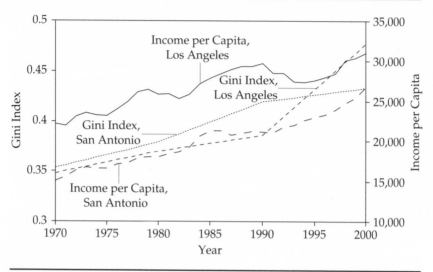

Source: Authors' tabulations from decennial censuses 1970 to 2000; Bureau of Economic Analysis (2005).
[a] Gini index calculated with personal income data from census data.
[b] Income per capita based on personal income divided by population size; calculated by Bureau of Economic Analysis; and adjusted to 2000 dollars.
[c] Data for Los Angeles and Bexar Counties.

inequality increased in both Los Angeles and San Antonio since 1970, just as it did throughout the United States. The growing inequality mirrored the structural transformations from heavy manufacturing and highly paid and unionized blue-collar jobs and toward a service and light manufacturing economy characterized by both a growing number of high paying white-collar work and low paying manual jobs with little job security. Although inequality in the two urban areas was similar from 1970 to 1980, it grew more in San Antonio in the 1980s. However, by the 1990s, inequality shot up in Los Angeles but remained nearly flat in San Antonio, eventually resulting in greater income inequality in Los Angeles.

Nationally, industrial jobs declined numerically from the 1970s forward as the United States faced growing competition from foreign industries; concomitantly, the service sector grew. As a result, average incomes declined as the number of middle-income blue-collar jobs dropped, leading to a growing hourglass shape to the economy. Blue-collar jobs at the time had afforded relatively high pay and internal career mobility for the largely unionized workforce. The new jobs in the low-wage industries tended to be low paying, low skilled, relatively unstable, and nonunionized. At the same time, high-end services, with a highly paid college-educated workforce, especially in the entertainment industry, continued to expand.

These structural changes were especially apparent in the rust belt cities of the East and Midwest but were also important in Los Angeles, which had the largest industrial base west of the Mississippi.[157] Thierry Noyelle and Thomas Stanback characterized Los Angeles in 1980 as a "national modal city," the leading aerospace center, the third largest automobile center, and a diversified service economy.[158] From the 1930s until the 1970s, these and related industries, including tire and steel production, provided the Los Angeles working class with one of the highest living standards in the United States. Although the beneficiaries of these industrial jobs were disproportionately white,[159] some benefits seemed to accrue to the Mexican American population. Mexican Americans began to move out of the inner city and enter the lower middle class by the 1950s. Their suburbanization, however, was largely restricted to particular cities and away from the white working class suburbs that surrounded the booming industrial plants.[160]

Beginning in the late 1970s, jobs in the Los Angeles automobile industry greatly declined. This was compounded by the rapid loss of aerospace jobs in the late 1980s with the end of the cold war. Los Angeles would rebuild its industrial base but with light industries—such as food processing, furniture, garment, and low-end service sectors—characterized by lower wages and dominated by the rapidly growing immigrant workforce.[161] Certainly, some highly paid sectors would remain and be dominated by natives of the United States, including entertainment, a downsized aerospace industry, and a growing professional service economy. Most notably though, a social and ethnic polarization would become increasingly apparent. Most industrial jobs became low paying and dominated by Mexican and Central American immigrants even as the primarily white professional class greatly benefited from Los Angeles's rising status as a global capitalist city. With the decline of industrial and aerospace sectors, many of the formerly well-paid workers moved out of Los Angeles entirely.[162] The city's economic restructuring was accompanied by an ethnic restructuring with the out-migration of working class whites and the immigration of Latin American and Asian immigrants.

Our other study site, San Antonio, was characterized by Noyelle and Stanback as a military specialized center that depended on the flow of federal funds.[163] San Antonio experienced rapid industrial development in the 1920s and 1930s, becoming Texas's largest city.[164] After World War II, the military became dominant industry. During the 1940s, local leaders had lobbied aggressively to bring military expenditures and jobs to the area[165] but rebuffed capitalist industries that might also bring unionization and progressive worker politics.[166] By boosting the military, tourism, and services, high-paying blue-collar jobs in San Antonio were kept to a minimum and were certainly less common than in the rest of the country, which would reinforce the area's deep racial and ethnic divides. At the same time, the dominant regime—predominantly white and closely tied to local business interests—that had long controlled San Antonio politics and impeded economic development would survive into the 1970s.[167]

Reflecting on her impressions of the time, Joan Moore, a member of the original study group, felt that discrimination in the 1960s was much more intense in San Antonio than in Los Angeles because schools, and businesses on the main street, were severely segregated. Poll taxes were not yet outlawed, and much of the housing stock was dilapidated and without urban services. Moreover, Texas welfare provisions were race conscious and official statistics used a Latin American race designation.[168]

In the 1990s, at least a decade after Mexican Americans had transformed local politics in San Antonio, signs of economic development began to emerge. No longer ruled by a small white elite that sought to control all commerce and industry while "keeping Mexicans down," a strategy occasionally articulated by San Antonian leaders, San Antonio would begin to recuperate by the 1990s.[169] Kelly Air Base and other military installations closed, and local leaders took advantage of the opportunity to diversify the San Antonio economy. Today, military and government sectors constitute about one-fifth of the economy. One-third now consists of targeted industries including aerospace, biotechnology and health care, information technology, telecommunications and tourism. The City of San Antonio's website touts that biotechnology and health care alone had an "economic impact of 11.9 billion dollars" in 2002.[170]

Figure 4.2 also shows the trend in per capita income. Higher throughout the past four decades in Los Angeles, it has begun to converge with that in San Antonio. Income in both urban areas steadily increased in both areas between 1960 and 1990. In 1991, though, it began to decline in Los Angeles as it continued to rise in San Antonio. By 1997, the gap was less than $5,000. By 2000, San Antonio incomes were about 15 percent less than those in Los Angeles, a marked change from thirty years earlier, when they were 40 percent less.

The convergence of Los Angeles and San Antonio is also apparent in terms of poverty. Los Angeles now has a higher poverty rate than San Antonio. From 1990–2000, the Los Angeles poverty rate increased from 18.9 to 22.1 percent; it declined by more than 5 percentage points in San Antonio, from 22.6 to 17.3 percent. Jargowsky's calculation of poverty concentration show that only 5 percent of Angelenos lived in high poverty census tracts in 1970 compared to 43 percent of San Antonians.[171] By 2000, poverty concentration increased more than three-fold to 17 percent for Los Angeles and has fallen dramatically to 9 percent in San Antonio. While much of this is surely due to the comparative nature of economic development in the two cities, much is also due to the higher concentration of Mexican immigrants in Los Angeles who often work full time but earn poverty-level wages.

Discussion

Based on the study of Mexican Americans residing in the United States before 1965, we contend that the Mexican American experience is profoundly distinct from that of other ethnic groups in the United States. It requires a reassessment of the theoretical models that explain their current status. Chicano historians argue that Mexican immigrants have arrived in the United States to find a societal template of racial domination that had its own institutions and both informal and formal rules and attitudes about the proper place of Mexicans, a Southwest legacy since the 1830s. Clearly, successive waves of immigrants would transform the racial order, as would a changing American society. However, the continuous immigration of a low-skill workforce to meet employer demands and fill undesirable jobs in the labor markets of the Southwest only reinforced the low status of Mexicans in the United States. On the other hand, an emerging middle class descended from these immigrants and occasional periods of political activism has altered mainstream perceptions and contested mainstream norms about race and the place of Mexican Americans. Nonetheless, one might imagine that even successful Mexican Americans cannot easily escape a history of race-based segregation and violence.

"Living in the shadow of the Alamo," which historian David Montejano and anthropologist Richard Flores describe as an enduring myth, is not merely an issue of collective memory. It also symbolizes the continuing significance of the idea of Mexican race in several ways. It captures a system of ethnic or racial difference in which Mexicans are initially a barbarous enemy but later become incorporated as a racialized source of cheap labor that is ensured by a system of control and separation from whites. These ideas have impeded social interaction with whites and thus undermine assimilation for those of Mexican origin generally. A racial hierarchy, often hidden in discourse and popular thought, has emerged in which Mexicans are classified as separate and inferior; it perpetuates their treatment as subordinates and lowers the self-esteem and aspirations of group members. At the same time, some Mexican Americans have risen to middle class status, intermarry, and even hold assimilationist dreams.

The Mexican category has been an enduring, though changing, one in the Southwest, just as black and white have been throughout the United States. There has long been an assumption among many scholars, including those who study immigration, that the black-white divide is deeply embedded in American society and overrides all other racial divides. To the extent that scholars recognize that any other divide exists, it is often seen in contrast to the long-standing and especially rigid black-white one. However, in places such as south Texas and arguably San Antonio where there have been few blacks or other racial-ethnic groups, Mexicans have clearly occupied the bottom of a two-caste system.[172] Where other non-white groups have lived in significant numbers, Mexicans have often occupied an intermediate status between whites and blacks as in Central Texas, between whites and Indians in New Mexico and Arizona, and between whites and Chinese in nineteenth-century California.[173] However, as a group, they never seem to have been able to get on the white mainstream track, especially in the socioeconomic sense. This is despite the social boundaries and distance that Mexican Americans have sought to maintain from African Americans while often seeking to break down boundaries with Anglos, at times even struggling to be accepted as white. Distinct racial projects of immigrants bringing separate identities, whites seeking to racialize Mexican Americans as nonwhite and some Mexican Americans identifying as white, all interact to create a distinct racial identity for Mexican Americans.

The history of Mexican Americans now is well documented, at least through the 1960s. But perhaps there has been a break in Chicano history since the 1960s. Has the significance of being Mexican in the United States changed in recent decades? Have Mexican Americans broken the negative weight of segregation, coercive labor systems, poll taxes, and lynchings that characterized much of their pre-1960s history? Several analysts have claimed that race has declined in significance over this time.[174] Wilson has announced the declining significance of race in the modern industrial period with the simultaneous importance of class for African Americans. He asserts that a new system of production, with changing policies and laws of the State, have reshaped race relations. But did race actually decline in importance for Mexican Americans since about World War II or the civil rights movement in the 1960s? Has it disappeared, as Linda Chávez and Peter Skerry suggest, especially with civil rights reforms? Have Mexican Americans of the third or fourth generation finally and more fully assimilated? To be sure, discrimination is not likely to have disappeared, even if legal or official discrimination has declined. However, continuing immigration, persistently poor Mexico, and the politics around issues of ethnicity may have reinforced ethnicity and an enduring racial stigma.

Clearly, historical studies often are not sociological. They often focus on the actions and thoughts of leaders who tend to be the most visible, most literate, and the most political. There continues to be little information on the behaviors and feelings of the vast majority of the population, since sources (such as past censuses) which might well revise the historical record have not been fully tapped. Moreover, though historians have described the manifestations of a system of racial domination, the complete set of mechanisms that presumably impede assimilation and mobility is less clear. We hope to provide a better understanding of that process as well as a more representative account of history in the past forty years, based on a random sample of Mexican Americans in their two most important metropolitan areas. The historical accounts we summarize in this chapter have provided the background for understanding the social context in which those of Mexican origin have been received and in which they have sought to integrate.

Finally, we have found surprisingly little analytical attention to generational distinctions in the historical literature. This may be due to both the tendency to homogenize and the lack of evidence. The dominance of an internal colonialism or race perspective, tends to treat everyone of Mexican origin in the United States the same. We believe the group's experience is far more complicated. Also, the historical evidence often does not allow generational distinctions. From reading that history, one gets the impression that a Mexican is a Mexican, no matter how long their family has been in the United States. The end result is a homogenization of the Mexican experience, instead of a multiple generational approach. If Mexicans repeat the experience of Europeans, then we may understand their low status as a transitional phenomenon of the immigrant generation and perhaps their children. For example, when major newspapers report on the large number of Hispanics in the primary schools of California or Texas and their small numbers in the university, they generally fail to distinguish whether these children are immigrants or the children of immigrants or children of U.S.-born parents.

The historical record thus far shows that the Mexican ethnic experience is quite different from the European. Skeptics may argue that this may be at least partly due to the failure to disentangle Mexican immigrant and U.S.-born Mexican American experiences, for a task that is easy for Europeans given that they have had little immigration since the 1920s. Our evidence, to which we now turn, disentangles four generations-since-immigration from two historical generations. We will show that generational progress for Mexican Americans has been quite unlike the European counterpart.

= Chapter 5 =

Education

Today, according to most public opinion polls, education ranks as the most important issue facing Latinos.[1] Despite sixty years of political and legal battles to improve the education of Mexican Americans, they continue to have the lowest average education levels and the highest high school dropout rates among major ethnic and racial groups in the United States.[2] These inequalities generate other social and economic inequalities between them and European Americans throughout their adult lives. However, leading analysts, apparently believing in the universality of assimilation, argue that this is the result of a large first- and second-generation population still adjusting to American society.[3] Although the traditional model generally predicts assimilation within three generations, these and other scholars predict that Mexican Americans will have the same levels of education and socioeconomic status as the dominant non-Hispanic white population by the fourth generation.[4] George Borjas, in particular, argues that Mexican Americans are especially slow to assimilate because the immigrant generation has had especially low levels of education and other forms of human capital compared with other immigrant groups.[5]

However, most social scientists who have closely examined schooling data for Mexican Americans over generations since the immigration of their ancestors have shown that their educational attainment improves from immigrant parents to their children but stalls between the second and third generations, even though the parents of the third generation have significantly more education and understanding of the educational system to pass on to their children than their own immigrant parents had.[6] This pattern is often theorized as reflecting optimism among immigrants, in which the relatively ambitious immigrant parents, who themselves suffered from low education and skills, strive for the American dream. Thus, they drive themselves and their children to do well in school, whereas second generation parents perceive greater limits to their own and their children's success.[7] Others contend that the second generation's schooling advantage derives from their resistance to assimilation and their ability to mobilize ethnicity as a positive resource to escape the disadvantages wrought on them by public schools.[8] For example, James Vigil found an ethnic resurgence or Mexicanization process among mostly, but not exclusively, second-generation Mexican American high school students in Los Angeles, which resulted in their greater self-confidence in the classroom.[9] By contrast, the third generation no longer benefits from immigrant optimism and the cultural protections against discrimination offered by the second generation's immigrant family.

Despite the apparently strong quantitative evidence showing a lack of Mexican American educational assimilation so far, at least two studies claim that the pessimistic conclusions of halted progress for Mexican Americans are based on faulty or inadequate data. Mexican schooling performance, they argue, converges with that of non-Hispanic whites over the generations, albeit at a slower rate. First, James Smith contends that previous conclusions are deceiving because using generation-since-immigration with a single cross-sectional data set does not capture actual generational change—that is, from parents to children.[10] Using a historical series of data sets to approximate parent-to-child generations, Smith finds persistent gains into the third generation, though the gap with non-Hispanic whites does not disappear. Second, Alba and Tariq Islam, reflecting Alba and Nee's optimism, argue that the low educational attainment observed for Mexican Americans may be an artifact of how data are collected.[11] They claim that more successful Mexican Americans might be opting out of the Mexican category—thus identifying in other ethnic categories—by the third generation. As a result, the average educational levels for the group are underestimated. Individuals whose parents may have intermarried, Alba and Islam maintain, which is part of the intergenerational assimilation process, may be particularly likely to opt out.

Available representative data sets do not permit tests of assimilation by the fourth or perhaps the fifth generation because there is no way to distinguish more than three generations-since-immigration. In this chapter, we reexamine this debate with the Mexican American Study Project data, which we believe overcome the deficiencies that have hamstrung previous studies. We show actual intergenerational changes rather than the synthetic changes common to cross-sectional data sources. The sample was drawn based on the reported ethnicity of the parents and thus precluded opting out by children. We also disaggregated the sample into a fourth and an incipient fifth generation. We show that despite improvements, the hypothesis of educational assimilation for Mexican Americans is still not borne out.

A Portrait of Educational Inequality

To put Mexican American education in context, we first examine official census data for major racial and ethnic groups, regionally and locally. The Mexican-origin population in 1970 is identified only for the five-state Southwest region (Arizona, California, Colorado, New Mexico, and Texas), where the vast majority (about 90 percent) of Mexican Americans lived.[12] Despite much settlement by Mexican immigrants elsewhere in the United States in recent years, a substantial majority remain in the Southwest.[13] For comparability with our data, we analyzed census data for Los Angeles and San Antonio at roughly the same ages of respondents in our study. Specifically, table 5.1 shows education indicators for 1970 and 2000 among U.S.-born Mexican Americans, whites, African Americans, and Asian Americans for the five southwestern states as well as Los Angeles and San Antonio. We focus on those age eighteen to fifty-four in the 1970 census and thirty-five to fifty-four in 2000 because these ages roughly match the ages of our original 1965 adult sample and the 2000 child sample, respectively. We calculate the schooling deficit between the average Mexican Americans in our sample and average non-Hispanic whites in the census, and we present these later.

Table 5.1 clearly shows that Mexican American educational levels lag behind all other major race-ethnic groups in the Southwest, Los Angeles and San Antonio. Because the data are just for those born in the United States, we are certain that virtually everyone in the sample was educated in the United States. Educational attainment of Mexican Americans fell behind whites and Asians by about two years and behind African Americans by about one year in 1970 and 2000. High school graduation rates and college completion rates also were lowest for Mexican Americans in both periods. This gap remained from 1970 to 2000, despite the fact that schooling improved for all groups. More than 90 percent of whites and Asians reported completing high school, compared to 84 percent of African Americans and only 74 percent of Mexican Americans. By 2000, fully 35 percent of whites in the Southwest,[14] and 54 percent of Asians,[15] completed college compared to about 17 percent of blacks and 13 percent of Mexican Americans. Regarding place differences, schooling outcomes for Mexican Americans tended to be substantially better in Los Angeles than San Antonio in 1970 but by 2000 were more comparable. The fact that education levels for Mexican Americans were slightly better in the urban areas of Los Angeles and San Antonio than for the region overall is probably why our sample has somewhat higher educational attainment than found in other sources. Whereas our sample was entirely urban in 1965, only 65 percent of Mexican Americans overall actually lived in urban areas. Thus our sample somewhat overestimates Mexican American educational attainment; nonetheless, it provides the best available data for showing and understanding longitudinal and intergenerational relationships with education.

Educational Change Across the Generations

As we have seen, the Mexican-origin population has the lowest educational achievement rates of all racial-ethnic groups. Because this might be interpreted as an immigration effect where years of schooling in another

Table 5.1 Years of Education and Graduation Rates by Race, 1970 and 2000[a]

	1970[b]			2000[c]		
	Southwest States[d]	Los Angeles	San Antonio	Southwest States[d]	Los Angeles	San Antonio
Years of education						
Mexican Americans	9.7	10.7	9.0	12.3	12.6	12.5
Non-Hispanic whites	12.3	12.6	12.3	14.1	14.2	14.2
Blacks	10.9	11.4	11.0	13.2	13.4	13.5
Asians	—	—	—	14.7	14.6	14.7
High school graduate						
Mexican Americans	44%	51%	37%	74%	76%	77%
Non-Hispanic whites	75	79	74	90	94	95
Blacks	54	63	57	84	84	89
Asians	—	—	—	95	95	93
College graduate[e]						
Mexican Americans	3	4	2	13	13	14
Non-Hispanic whites	15	16	15	35	40	39
Blacks	5	5	4	17	19	21
Asians	—	—	—	54	56	52

Source: Authors' tabulations from decennial censuses, 1970 and 2000.

[a] Among U.S. born.

[b] 1970 figures among age eighteen to fifty-four.

[c] 2000 figures among age thirty-five to fifty-four.

[d] Five southwest states: California, Arizona, Colorado, New Mexico, and Texas.

[e] 1970 college graduation figures among age twenty-five to fifty-four.

country are not compatible, we excluded immigrants from the results in table 5.1. Low education might be readily justified by an assimilation hypothesis that because many Mexican Americans grew up in immigrant households with poorly educated parents, their own levels of education would logically be lower than non-Hispanic whites or blacks, the vast majority of whom are third generation or later. To explore this possibility, we examine schooling attainment across generation-since-immigration.

Table 5.2 breaks down education into three levels of schooling completed by generation-since-immigration. We show educational outcomes for original respondents in 1965[16] and 2000 because some respondents may have completed further education in the intervening years. The first row shows that the years of education for original respondents range from 6.8 years to 9.5 years in 1965 but thirty-five years later, their education had improved, on average, by about .6 years for the immigrants, .8 for the second generation, and .9 for the third generation. The second row and third row also show sizable gains in the percentage that finished either high school or college. For the first and second generation, college graduation rates tripled, perhaps reflecting the onset of affirmative action.

Table 5.2 also shows that years of schooling for the children sample had greatly improved from that of the original respondents. Although only 16 to 35 percent of the original respondents reported completing high school, 73 to 87 percent of their children did. Among the original respondents, years of education and high school graduation rates show constant improvement from one generation to the next. College completion rates, on the other hand, do not vary much by generation-since-immigration for original respondents. For their children, all of whom are U.S.-born and educated, there are no clear trends, as shown in table 5.2. Years of education decreases from 13.1 to 12.4 from the second to the fourth generation-since-immigration. High school completion is similar among all three generations-since-immigration, and college completion is noticeably lower for the fourth generation (6 percent) though it is not appreciably different between the second (13 percent) and the third (14 percent) generations. However, as shown in table 5.1, college completion rates among whites had increased to 35 percent in this time period. Sadly and directly in contradistinction to assimilation theory, the fourth generation differs the most from whites, with a college completion rate of only 6 percent.

Based on 1998 and 2000 national household surveys, Reynolds Farley and Richard Alba provided generational comparisons among various national origin groups.[17] We reproduce their illustration as figure 5.1. It shows that Mexican-origin persons have among the lowest educational levels of any group; for example, only 1 percent received master's or doctoral degrees among the first- and second-generation. Similarly, only 2 to 3 percent of Puerto Ricans hold higher degrees. Second-generation Central Americans (primarily Salvadoran and Guatemalan) and Caribbean

Table 5.2   Years of Education and Graduation Rates by Generation-Since-Immigration, 1965 and 2000

	Original Respondents, 1965[a]			Original Respondents, 2000			Children		
	Gen. 1	Gen. 2	Gen. 3	Gen. 1	Gen. 2	Gen. 3	Gen. 2	Gen. 3	Gen. 4+
Years of education	6.8	9.2	9.5	7.4	10.0	10.4	13.1	13.1	12.4
High school graduate	16%	32%	35%	30%	48%	57%	84%	87%	73%
College graduate[b]	2	2	4	7	6	5	13	14	6

Source: Mexican American Study Project.
[a] 1965 figures among age eighteen and older.
[b] 1965 college graduation figures among age twenty-five and older.

Figure 5.1   Educational Attainment by Generation and Origin, 1998 and 2000

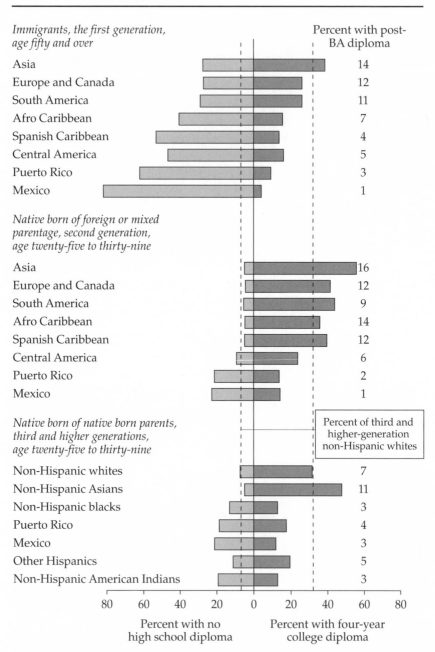

Source: Farley and Alba (2002).

Figure 5.2   Years of Education by Generation-Since-Immigration, 1965 and 2000

Generation-Since-Immigration	Parents of Original Respondents	Original Respondents	Children of Original Respondents
1	4.1	7.4	———
2	6.1	10.0	13.1
3	———	10.4	13.1
4+	———	———	12.4
Years Attended School	1900s to 1930s	1930s to 1950s	1950s to 1980s
Non-Hispanic Whites	9.5	12.5	14.2

Source: Mexican American Study Project.

Americans (from the West Indian islands and Haiti) do considerably better. By the third generation, Mexican Americans have the lowest rate at 3 percent, together with African Americans and American Indians.

Figure 5.2 shows generational changes for Mexican-origin persons over the span of the twentieth century. In addition to the original respondents and their children, we show educational attainment for the parents of original respondents. The parents were educated mostly in the 1900s to 1930s, the original respondents were schooled from the 1930s to 1950s, and their children were educated from the 1950s to the 1980s. At the same time, we present results for three generations-since-immigration within each of these cohorts. Taken together, figure 5.2 shows educational progress among the three cohorts descended from immigrants during three periods in which they entered the United States. For example, the first cohort begins with the immigrant or first generation, which was educated between 1900 and 1930, followed (to the right and down one) by their second-generation children educated between 1930 and 1950, and then their third-generation grandchildren. The second cohort begins with the second generation (or more) since immigration that was schooled at the beginning of the twentieth century, followed by their third-generation children and then their fourth-generation grandchildren. This cohort is especially likely to include descendants of the Mexican population who resided in the former Mexican territories ceded to the United States in 1848.

Overall, both cohorts reveal substantial improvements in education over succeeding generations. Immigrant grandparents, schooled in the earliest period had an average of 4.1 years of schooling. Their U.S.-born children more than doubled these levels to 10.0 years. Finally, their third-generation grandchildren tripled the initial educational levels to 13.1 years. Seen in this way, schooling improved greatly across the generations over the twentieth century. The second cohort shows a similar pattern: the second generation grandparents had 6.1 years of education, followed by 10.4 years among their third generation children, and 12.4 years among their fourth generation grandchildren.

However, despite several decades of struggle to improve the poor state of education and a century-long effort to achieve equality for Mexican Americans, the gap between whites and Mexican Americans persists (the average educational level for non-Hispanic whites is on the bottom line of figure 5.2). The dramatic result is that poor education persists for the fourth generation, which may be the first generation not exposed to immigrant relatives, whose ancestral ties to Mexico are predominantly through their great-grandparents or great-great-grandparents, whom they are unlikely to have met. Despite the optimistic expectations of economists, such as James Smith and George Borjas, and assimilation scholars, such as Richard Alba and Victor Nee, assimilation is very limited, even by the fourth generation. To make matters worse, the expectation that educational attainment improves across generations is turned on its head for the children of the original respondents. Figure 5.2 shows that the fourth generation has fewer years of average schooling than the second or the third generation.

For the original respondents, there is a large gain from the immigrants, most of whom were probably educated in Mexico, to the second generation. The third generation, with 10.4 years of schooling, does slightly better than the second generation. Mexican Americans continue to have lower high school graduation rates than any other major ethnic group in the United States. Figure 5.3 shows that only a minority of original respondents, who were mostly schooled between the 1930s and 1950s,

Figure 5.3   High School Graduation by Generation-Since-Immigration,
               1965 and 2000

Generation-Since-Immigration	Original Respondents	Children of Original Respondents	Grandchildren of Original Respondents[a]
1	30%	—	—
2	48%	84%	—
3	57%	87%	85%
4	—	73%	84%
5+	—	—	81%
Years Attended School	1930s to 1950s	1950s to 1980s	1980s to 1990s

Source: Mexican American Study Project.
[a] As reported by children, among grandchildren age twenty and older.

completed high school, whereas around 80 percent of all children did.[18] Understandably, the graduation rate is especially low for immigrants given that they often completed their educations in Mexico, where high school completion is less common. Only 30 percent of immigrant original respondents completed high school, whereas 48 and 57 percent (respectively) of their second- and third-generation counterparts did, suggesting a smooth generational improvement for those schooled from the 1930s to the 1950s. Thus, though improvements from parents to children in graduation from high school, especially for immigrants, are clear, they are less so for the children of the third generation.

Table 5.3   Graduation Rates and Relative Odds by
             Generation-Since-Immigration, 1965 and 2000

	Original Respondents, 1965			Children		
	Gen. 1	Gen. 2	Gen. 3	Gen. 2	Gen. 3	Gen. 4+
High school graduate						
Mexican Americans	16%	32%	35%	84%	87%	73%
Non-Hispanic whites	75	75	75	90	90	90
Relative odds Mexican to white[a]	0.06	0.14	0.16	0.58	0.74	0.30
College graduate						
Mexican Americans	2%	2%	4%	13%	14%	6%
Non-Hispanic whites	15	15	15	35	35	35
Relative odds Mexican to white[a]	0.12	0.12	0.24	0.28	0.30	0.12

Source: Mexican American Study Project; authors' tabulations from decennial censuses, 1970 and 2000.
[a] Odds for Mexican Americans are p/(1-p) and similarly for non-Hispanic whites. Relative odds are odds for Mexican Americans divided by odds for non-Hispanic whites.

Our data also allowed us to investigate the educational achievement of the grandchildren of the original respondents, enabling us to distinguish a fifth generation-since-immigration. We did not directly interview the children of the child sample, but instead asked the children of the original respondents about their own children's education level. Because many of these children were not yet adults and thus had not completed their education, we limited our investigation to high school graduation rates for those twenty years old and older. Figure 5.3 shows that these grandchildren of the original respondents, who are third to fifth generation, seemed to be doing no better than their parents. By this time, the third, fourth, and fifth generation were performing equally, with no significant differences among them. In the third generation, 85 percent had graduated from high school, versus 84 percent of the fourth generation and 81 percent of the fifth generation.[19]

To demonstrate the gap in educational achievement between Mexican Americans and whites, we computed odds ratios. These are based on data from table 5.1 for whites and table 5.2 for Mexican Americans, and are presented in table 5.3. We calculate the odds that both groups graduated from high school (by dividing the proportion that graduated by the proportion that did not graduate or p/1-p). We then divide the odds for Mexican Americans by the odds for whites to yield odds ratios (also referred to as relative odds). These are presented on the third and sixth rows of table 5.3. Odds ratios have desirable mathematical properties for measuring

Figure 5.4   Relative Odds Ratios of Mexican Americans to Non-Hispanic
Whites, 1965 and 2000

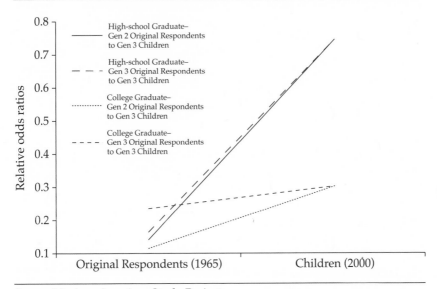

Source: Mexican American Study Project.

inequality because they are not affected, as other indicators of inequality are,
by the size of the gap or the specific point at which the gap is measured.

An odds ratio of .06 for high school graduates among first-generation
respondents in 1965, for example, indicates that the odds that a Mexican
immigrant graduated from high school is about 6 percent (.06) of the odds
that a white graduated. Table 5.3 shows that the odds ratios of graduating
from high school vis-à-vis a non-Hispanic white American are lower among
immigrants than those born in the United States, as expected. The ratios
increase with generation-since-immigration, except in the case of fourth-
generation children, who have lower odds ratios than both second- and
third-generation children. The odds ratios for children are greater than those
of the original respondents, indicating a shrinking racial gap in educational
attainment from the original respondents in 1965 to their children in 2000.

Improvement rates of high school graduation are greater than those for
college graduation. The bold lines in figure 5.4 illustrate the gap between
Mexicans and non-Hispanic whites for high school and college completion
from the second-generation original respondents to their third-generation
children, using the odds ratios. The dotted lines show the same gap for the
third-generation respondents, connected to the third-generation children,
which one could argue is a fairer comparison. Despite three decades of
university-based affirmative action, college education relative to whites
has improved from 12 percent odds in the second generation in 1965 to

30 percent odds for their third-generation children. For other comparable generations, there has been an even smaller change. The odds ratios of college graduation rose from 24 percent for third-generation original respondents to only 30 percent for the third-generation children. For high school graduation, improvements were much better, reflecting a greater universalization of high school graduation, though even then substantial inequalities remain. The odds of high school graduation improved from 14 percent of white odds for second-generation original respondents to 74 percent for their third-generation children in 2000 and from 16 to 74 percent among third generation original respondents and children.

Explaining Educational Disadvantage

Although the gap between the schooling of Mexican Americans and non-Hispanic whites has been closing throughout the past fifty years or so, the gap is still substantial. Many have assumed that educational inequalities are attributable to the disadvantages of poor immigrant households, but the data here show that schooling outcomes stubbornly continue at low rates even into the fourth or fifth generation. The statistics presented thus far show that the educational progress of Mexican Americans does not improve over the generations. At best, given the statistical margin of error, our data show no improvement in education over the generation-since-immigration and in some cases even suggest a decline.

How then can we account for the persistent educational disadvantage of Mexican Americans? Because we have wide variation in educational outcomes—this is by no means a uniformly disadvantaged population—we can use our data to explore what accounts for the high education of some but low education of others. Several theories about ethnic disadvantage, and Mexican American schooling disadvantages in particular, have been explicated and many can be tested with our data. These include the classical assimilation theory, human capital and status attainment theories, segregation theories, industrialization theories, cultural deficit theory, and finally, racialization and racial discrimination. We thus derive hypotheses from these theories to explain variation in educational outcomes among Mexican Americans.

Parental Status and Resources

In the sociological literature, it has become nearly axiomatic that parents with more education tend to raise children who repeat the pattern. Certainly, parents have long sought to transmit any advantages they have to their children. More educated parents are more likely to have higher incomes and be able to afford better schooling for their children—whether parochial or private schooling or housing where public schools are better.

Table 5.4   Intergenerational Educational Mobility by Race, 1988[a]

Respondent's Education	Father's Education		
	Less than High School Graduate	High School Graduate and Some College	College Graduate
Mexican Americans			
Less than high school graduate	41%	35%	—[b]
High school graduate and some college	53	62	—[b]
College graduate	6	3	—[b]
Non-Hispanic white			
Less than high school graduate	19	6	2
High school graduate and some college	68	68	41
College graduate	13	27	57
Blacks			
Less than high school graduate	28	11	4
High school graduate and some college	61	72	60
College graduate	11	17	36

Source: Authors' tabulations from National Survey of Households and Families, 1988.
[a] Among respondents age twenty-five and older and U.S.-born.
[b] Only six respondents among Mexican American with college-educated parents.

They have the knowledge and the time to read frequently to their children and expose them to other cultural advantages. They have higher educational expectations and are role models for their children. They are more likely to know the pathways to educational success, can better navigate complex school systems, and manage their education in numerous other ways.[20] The positive effect of parental education on children's education is thus not surprising.

The conceptual origin of this view is status attainment theory, which has become a mainstay of American sociology. The first stage of this model posits that educational or status attainment of any kind is largely transmitted from parents to children.[21] The model also recognizes that the rate of transmission may vary by race and ethnicity and other factors, such as generation-since-immigration.[22] Modern assimilation theory[23] draws largely from the status attainment model in that it predicts that the children of immigrants with high levels of education will assimilate faster than those whose parents have less education, though it also expects that for most descendants of less educated immigrants, education will improve in the second generation and again in the third.

Table 5.4 shows that among the U.S.-born population, whites transmit their education intergenerationally most efficiently, followed by blacks and then Mexican Americans. Specifically, table 5.4 shows intergenerational educational completion rates for U.S.-born Mexican Americans, whites, and blacks using national data from the 1988 National Survey of Families and Households (NSFH). The columns of the table show the father's level of education and the rows show their children's education. The relation between parents and children is not a perfect one given that some parents with little education have children with high education and vice versa. However, the main tendency is unmistakable. For all race and generation groups in the three panels, the trend is for children of more highly educated parents to have higher educations themselves. However, the degree to which parents transmit their education to their children clearly varies by race and ethnicity. Mexican-origin children are more likely than whites or blacks to not complete high school if their parents did not. According to the NSFH, 41 percent of the children of Mexican-origin parents who did not complete high school had children who also did not, compared to only 19 percent of whites and 28 percent of blacks. Among parents who graduated from high school but did not complete college, 35 percent of Mexican American children did not complete high school compared to 6 percent of whites and 11 percent of blacks. Unfortunately, the sample of Mexican Americans with college-educated parents is too small for analysis.

Because U.S.-born Mexican Americans are much more likely than blacks or whites to have parents who are immigrants, one might attribute their especially low levels of education to their poorly educated immigrant parents. We use our sample to show differences in educational mobility by generation-since-immigration. Table 5.5 presents this analysis. We see few, if any, real differences in educational mobility between the second and third generations. In our sample, 18 and 24 percent of children of high school dropouts also did not finish high school in the second and third plus generations. By contrast, 12 percent of children of high school dropouts in the second generation and 6 percent in the third generation completed college. That is, the second generation is only slightly better off than the third in their ability to turn around the educational disadvantages of their parents. Only 10 percent of both the second-generation and third-generation children of high school graduates dropped out of high school. At the other end, 20 percent of the third-generation children of high school graduates completed college versus 10 percent of second-generation children.

Tables 5.4 and 5.5 showed the effect of father's education. Parental status, however, usually includes other factors, including mother's education, income, homeownership, and family size. The first column of table 5.6 shows that years of schooling were clearly greater among those whose parents had more education and higher income or who owned their home. Those with fewer siblings also had more education. The second column of table 5.6, shows the relationship between parental status-resources and

Table 5.5   Intergenerational Educational Mobility by Generation-Since-Immigration, 2000

	Father's Education		
Child's Education	Less than High School Graduate	High School Graduate and Some College	College Graduate
Generation 2			
Less than high school graduate	18%	10%	—[a]
High school graduate and some college	70	79	—[a]
College graduate	12	10	—[a]
Generation 3+			
Less than high school graduate	24	10	0
High school graduate and some college	71	70	81
College graduate	6	20	18

Source: Mexican American Study Project.
[a] Only nine respondents among generation 2 with college-educated parents.

Table 5.6   Parental Status and Resources and Years of Education, 2000

	Years of Education	Relationship with Education[a]
Father's education		
Nine or less years	12.4	0.10***
More than nine years	13.5	
Mother's education		
Nine or less years	12.5	0.08***
More than nine years	13.4	
Parents' income		
$6,000 or less	12.5	0.06*
More than $6,000	13.4	
Parent was homeowner		
Renter	12.5	0.32†
Owner	13.3	
Number of siblings		
One to three siblings	13.5	−0.08*
More than three siblings	12.7	

Source: Mexican American Study Project.
[a] Linear regression run. Unstandardized coefficients presented. Child sample analyzed. Adjusted for sibling clustering. Father's education, mother's education, parents' income, and number of siblings entered as continuous variables in regression model. See appendix B, table B.3 for full model.
†$p<.10$, *$p<.05$, ***$p<.001$

education based on the multivariate statistical model in which we have simultaneously controlled for other variables. We find that all five of the indicators for parental resources are significantly related to educational attainment. Both father's and mother's education as well as family income have independent and positive effects on education. Homeownership has a marginal effect but, like the parental education and income variables, owning a home does mean more education for children. Lastly, the number of siblings is also significantly related to educational level but the coefficient is negative, as we would expect. Larger families require that family resources be shared across a larger number of persons and therefore are fewer on a per child basis. Thus, larger families imply less education for the next generation when family resources are similar.

Cultural Deficits

The research on Latino education today focuses on the children of the post-1970 wave of immigration. That is understandable given that that population accounts for much of the increase of school age populations in traditional immigration states like California, Texas, and Illinois and even in new destination states like Georgia and North Carolina. At the same time, the Mexican American descendants of older immigrant waves are still a large component of the population, though not they are not demographically growing at the same rate. Findings from research that centers on the children of immigrants is often generalized to the Latino population in general, which we find troubling. The issues faced by the second or 1.5 generation are often quite different from those faced by Latino children of U.S.-born parents.

A central finding in the research on education of the 1.5 and second generation is the inability of parents to communicate in English with teachers and administrators.[24] In a particularly prominent piece, Barbara Schneider, Sylvia Martínez, and Ann Owens concluded that limited English proficiency and low educational attainment of parents were primary reasons for the achievement gap among Hispanic children. It is not surprising to find that the ethnographic studies on which these conclusions were based focused largely on the educational experience of recent immigrants and their children. More to the point, Portes and Rumbaut studied children who immigrated with their parents or who were U.S.-born children of immigrants. They concluded that because the parents were not proficient in English, they were unable to communicate with their children or their educators, and that therefore school failure was attributable primarily to a dissonant acculturation among Mexicans.[25] However, the failure of continuing educational advancement from the second to the third generation suggests limits to this explanation. U.S.-born parents were virtually all proficient in English but their third-generation children did as poorly if

Table 5.7   Cultural Deficits and Years of Education, 2000

	Years of Education	Relationship with Education[a]
Parent is Spanish monolingual		
Not Spanish monolingual	13.0	−0.18
Spanish monolingual	12.6	
Parent spoke Spanish to child		
Did not speak Spanish to child	13.0	0.20
Spoke Spanish to child	12.8	
Parent's college aspirations for children		
Had less than college aspirations	12.7	0.04
Had college aspirations	13.3	

Source: Mexican American Study Project.
[a] Linear regression run. Unstandardized coefficients presented. Child sample analyzed. Adjusted for sibling clustering. See appendix B, table B.3 for full model.

not worse than those of second-generation children. Portes and Rumbaut also contended that the lack of bilingualism among the third generation-since-immigration may be a further language disadvantage, which they claimed reduces cognitive abilities overall and lowers the self-esteem of Mexican Americans.

We test these hypotheses using two variables: whether parents were Spanish monolingual and whether children were bilingual while growing up. Although our sample is primarily U.S.-born, there were Spanish monolingual immigrant parents in our study. The children of Spanish monolinguals had 12.6 years of schooling in contrast to 13.0 for the children of those who knew English, whether bilingual or monolingual. Children who grew up hearing Spanish had 13.0 years of education and those who did not had 12.8 years. However, once we control for other key factors, such as generation-since-immigration and parental status, there are no statistically significant relationships between language and educational outcomes, as the second column of table 5.7 reveals.

A common conception is that the low education of Mexican Americans is due to their parents' low expectations or aspirations. However, Schneider and her colleagues, Portes and Rumbaut, and others recognize that one of the few advantages of Mexican-origin parents is their high educational aspirations and expectations.[26] Based on our data, 65 percent of the parents reported in 1965 that they would have liked their children to graduate from college. Thus, we test whether having these aspirations has any effect on the eventual educational attainment of their children. The children whose parents wanted them to finish college appear to have somewhat higher educational outcomes—13.3 years of schooling for those who had these

Table 5.8   Social Capital and Years of Education, 2000

	Years of Education	Relationship with Education[a]
Child's exposure to professionals		
Did not know professionals	12.7	0.23**
Knew professionals	13.3	
Parent attended church weekly		
Did not attend church weekly	12.6	0.45*
Attended church weekly	13.3	
Parent communicated with school		
Did not communicate	12.7	0.36*
Communicated with school	13.1	
Parent is non-Hispanic		
Hispanic	12.9	0.21
Not Hispanic	13.4	

Source: Mexican American Study Project.
[a] Linear regression run. Unstandardized coefficients presented. Child sample analyzed. Adjusted for sibling clustering. See appendix B, table B.3 for full model.
*p<.05, **p<.01

higher aspirations compared to 12.7 to those who did not (see table 5.7). However, this relationship is not statistically significant in the multivariate analysis. We suggest that higher educational aspirations are related to parent's own level of schooling, which washes out the parental aspirations variable in the multivariate analysis. Parents with higher educational aspirations for their children did not have children who go on to have higher educations, once we control for other factors.

Social Capital

Social capital as we use it refers roughly to the advantages that some individuals have because of their or their family's location in, or relation to, social networks.[27] Although definitions of social capital are varied, they generally refer to the idea that who one knows is beneficial to getting ahead. In our study, our social capital indicators reflect whether respondents were exposed to professionals while growing up, whether they attended church weekly, whether parents communicated with the school, and whether a parent was not Hispanic. The bivariate and multivariate results in table 5.8 indicate that our first indicator of social capital is strongly and positively related to children's educational outcomes. Children who knew "doctors, lawyers or teachers," as we asked in the survey, ended up with more education. We suspect that such persons provided the child with both knowledge and appreciation of the role of education in becoming a professional. Because we control for parental status, the importance of knowing professionals thus cannot simply be attributed to parents' higher status in itself.

Religiosity, or whether parents attended church weekly, is a social capital variable because it indicates institutional or social closure. Theoretically, religious communities are often very close and foster frequent social ties. Participation in them gives one access to these ties and thus to social capital.[28] We find that children growing up in a family where the parents attended church frequently had more years of schooling and this relationship was significant in the multivariate analysis after controlling for other factors, as table 5.8 shows. Whether parents communicated with teachers or other staff at their child's school was also related to the respondents' education. These children had 13.1 years of education, versus 12.7 for those whose parents did not communicate, and this relationship was statistically significant when we control for other factors in the multivariate analysis. The three indicators of social capital we have described so far were all important predictors of Mexican American education.

The last indicator of social capital, whether one parent was not Hispanic, was not related to education in the multivariate analysis. We think of this variable as a social capital variable because it may provide children with access to the networks of other ethnic groups, particularly those of non-Hispanic whites, who are mostly of higher status. In the bivariate analysis, the 9 percent of children with a non-Hispanic parent had a half-year of education more than those with two Hispanic parents, but this effect was largely washed out by the introduction of parental status variables. Since non-Hispanic parents also tend to have more education, this may explain why their children had higher education.

Educational Segregation

Today, levels of educational segregation for Mexican Americans and other Latinos continue to be high, even though forced segregation of students by race has been nearly eliminated.[29] Residential segregation is growing among Latinos, however, due to immigration.[30] The spatial version of assimilation theory contends that as the descendants of immigrants increase their incomes relative to their parents, they are able to afford housing in more expensive and usually more integrated neighborhoods, which provide better schools.[31] In other words, education is lower for the children of immigrants because immigrant parents, who tend to have lower educational levels and incomes, are especially likely to live in segregated neighborhoods. Second- and third-generation households, who presumably residentially assimilate and live in integrated

Table 5.9   **Residential and Educational Segregation
and Years of Education, 2000**

	Years of Education	Relationship with Education[a]
Residential segregation (census)		
Proportion Hispanic in neighborhood, 1965		
0 to .2	13.4	−0.24
.2 to .4	13.0	
.4 to .6	12.9	
.6 to .8	13.0	
.8 to 1.0	12.5	
Residential segregation (self reported)		
Mexican composition of neighborhood		
None or few	13.1	−0.13†
Half	12.9	
Most	13.3	
All	12.5	
Education segregation(self reported)		
Mexican composition of high school		
None or few	13.2	0.03
Half	12.7	
Most	13.1	
All	12.8	

Source: Mexican American Study Project.
[a] Linear regression run. Unstandardized coefficients presented. Child sample analyzed. Adjusted for sibling clustering. Measures of residential and educational segregation included in separate regression models and entered as continuous variables. See appendix B, table B.3 for full model.
†p<.10

neighborhoods, thus should attend more integrated schools and see their children's education improve.

The view that segregation continues to drive the inferior education of Latino and African American children remains popular today. Gary Orfield and Jonathon Kozol, perhaps the two most well-known advocates of this view, have focused much attention on the role of segregation as the major contributor to the lowly state of minority education.[32] They argue that segregated schools have lower levels of funding, less experienced teachers, and poorer facilities in comparison with mostly white schools. Moreover, students in such schools are exposed to more violence.[33]

We measure segregation in table 5.9 as the presence of other Hispanics in the neighborhood or the school. Specifically we use three measures:

actual percentage of Hispanics in the neighborhood they grew up in (based on 1970 census tract information of their neighborhood in 1965); the extent of Mexican-origin neighbors while they were growing up (self-reported by children in 2000); and the extent of Mexican-origin students in their high school (self-reported by children in 2000).

Our bivariate analysis shown in the first column of table 5.9 mildly supports this hypothesis given that Mexican Americans who grew up in ethnically isolated barrios tended to have less education than those raised in more integrated neighborhoods. The three segregation measures show somewhat of a tendency for more segregated schools or neighborhoods to result in lower years of schooling. For example, the top panel of table 5.9 shows that those in the most integrated (least segregated) neighborhoods (0 to 20 percent Hispanic) had an average of 13.4 years of education compared to 12.5 years of education for the most segregated (80 to 100 percent Hispanic). However the three middle categories do not show a completely linear relationship—all have essentially the same years of education. Similar results appear for the extent of segregation that respondents reported for their neighborhood and for their high school. Educational levels tend to be worst in the most segregated environments and best in the least segregated ones, but the middle two categories do not fit a completely linear pattern between the two end categories. The second indicator also captures the neighborhood's racial composition. The trend here is less linear, though those growing up in the most non-Hispanic neighborhoods had a full 0.6 more years of schooling than those in the most segregated. Finally, the third indicator is racial composition of the high school attended. It reveals some relationship between segregation and years of schooling but yields the weakest relationship among the three indicators.

In the second column of table 5.9, we test the strength of these relationships in the multivariate statistical analysis to see whether segregation matters once the other variables are controlled. The results show almost no relationship between segregation and years of education. Self-reported neighborhood segregation has a statistically marginal effect in the negative direction, as some would expect, but the other two variables are unrelated to segregation. Thus, though segregated schools may be inferior schools,[34] segregation itself does not seem to explain why some students complete less schooling than others. Our results suggest that students with similar socioeconomic characteristics perform equally in terms of completed years, whether or not they went to a segregated school. Apparently, students of lower socioeconomic origin who are more likely to attend segregated schools do worse mostly because of their social status, not because of the school's level of segregation, a finding consistent with that of Pat Antonio Goldsmith.[35] Therefore, our findings suggest that school segregation has no independent effect on educational attainment.

Industrial Structure

We are also interested in how the urban-industrial context affects educational outcomes. In particular, we explore whether Los Angeles' developed industrial structure before 1980 favored the educational outcomes of Mexican American children. The heavy industrialization in eastern and midwestern cities at the time of the mass European immigration, and for several decades thereafter, is believed to have helped their descendants assimilate. According to the leading analysts of immigrant incorporation, that industrial structure allowed less educated immigrants and their children to work their way up to well-paid and secure jobs and eventually propelled them and their children to mostly secure middle class jobs and successful integration in American society.[36] By contrast, they argue that the descendants of today's less educated immigrants will have more trouble assimilating because they are precluded from that pathway, if only because those jobs have nearly disappeared in the United States.

However, the kinds of industrial jobs available in midwestern and eastern cities were also common in Los Angeles in 1965. Theoretically, they therefore should have improved the educational outcomes of Mexican Americans growing up at the time. Although the educational mechanisms of this argument are not fully worked out, it would seem that the argument suggests that because immigrants, and especially the second generation, were able to get well-paid and secure manual jobs, they were able to move out of the inner city to areas with better schools or to afford parochial or private schooling and eventually college for their children. Also, local jurisdictions with heavy industry could presumably better finance public schools. For those reasons, much of the third generation was able to secure professional occupations. Thus, we hypothesize that Mexican Americans in industrially favored Los Angeles had greater educational opportunities than in San Antonio, everything else being equal. Also, parents who worked in manufacturing especially should have been able to provide better education to their children under this theory. However, these hypotheses are not supported by our data. Table 5.10 shows that neither urban area nor working in manufacturing was related to educational attainment in the regression analysis. Differences in the bivariate analysis are both small and not significant. The lack of an industrial effect may be attributable to either the exclusion of Mexican Americans from well-paid jobs in industry or to the lack of an industrial effect on assimilation overall.

Table 5.10   Industrial Structure and Years of Education, 2000

	Years of Education	Relationship with Education[a]
Urban area		
Los Angeles	13.0	0.07
San Antonio	12.7	
Head held manufacturing job in 1965[a]		
Not in manufacturing	12.9	−0.26
Worked in manufacturing	13.1	

Source: Mexican American Study Project.
[a] Linear regression run. Unstandardized coefficients presented. Child sample analyzed. Adjusted for sibling clustering. See appendix B, table B.3 for full model.

Institutional

Coleman and others have long argued that Catholic schools provide superior education in part because they have higher expectations for all students and create a more disciplinary climate, which promotes better student behavior.[37] These findings of better educational outcomes for Catholic schools are based mostly on quantitative evidence in the 1980s using national data sets. These studies also conclude that Catholic schools place a greater emphasis on core academic subjects, require more homework, enable a common set of values based on religious beliefs, create a greater sense of community due to smaller school size, and allow for greater teacher and counselor involvement. More importantly, Thomas Hoffer, Andrew Greeley, and James Coleman found that achievement differences among whites, blacks, and Hispanics were smaller in Catholic schools than public ones and that racial differences were especially small by the senior year.[38] At least one study noted the especially positive effect of Catholic school for Hispanics.[39] Several qualitative studies show that African Americans also benefit from a Catholic school education.[40]

We also find that attending Catholic schools had a very strong effect on the education of children, as table 5.11 reveals. Specifically, the 12 percent of the child sample who began their high school educations in Catholic or private schools (89 percent of these were Catholic) eventually completed close to two (1.7) more years of school than those who began high school in public school. In the multivariate analysis, those attending Catholic schools have roughly one more year of schooling than their public school counterparts (see table 5.11). Thus, the very large bivariate difference, while partly explained by the controls such as parental status, appears to be mostly from actual differences between Catholic and public schools.

This finding is consistent with the substantial body of research showing a Catholic–private school bonus, despite extensive methodological debates

Table 5.11   Institutional Structure and Years of Education, 2000

	Years of Education	Relationship with Education[a]
Catholic or private high school		
Public	12.8	0.97***
Catholic or private	14.5	

Source: Mexican American Study Project.
[a] Linear regression run. Unstandardized coefficients presented. Child sample analyzed. Adjusted for sibling clustering. See appendix B, table B.3 for full model.
***p<.001

about selectivity.[41] In particular, much of that research has been challenged by the argument that Catholic and private schools pick the best and most motivated students and particularly those whose parents can afford to pay. Enrollment in a Catholic school probably also reflects the willingness of some parents to sacrifice limited incomes to attend these schools.

Recent research, however, which carefully controls for selectivity, supports the contention of better outcomes overall for Catholic school students,[42] especially for minority and inner-city children who often live where public school education is poor.[43] Our findings also show that a substantial Catholic–private school bonus seems to persist beyond parental financial or other types of advantages since we control for a host of parental socio-economic status and family resource characteristics. Unfortunately, Mexican Americans have not had nearly as much access to Catholic education that Irish and Italian immigrants and their descendants had, which was largely responsible for those groups' mobility.[44]

Skin Color, Gender, and Age

Table 5.12 shows that there are no real differences in educational attainment related to skin color, gender, and age in the bivariate analysis. Except for marginally significant differences by gender, there are no differences in the regression analysis either. The results for gender suggest that Mexican American women have slightly less education than men. Jean Phinney and Juana Flores argue that such differences reflect parental expectations that boys succeed in mainstream society and girls are socialized for more domestic tasks.[45] We also expected that years of education would have improved over the twenty-year age range among the children in our sample. However, we find no such difference.

Despite previous findings showing that darker skin color predicts lower education levels among Mexican Americans,[46] our findings in table 5.12 show that those with lighter skin color did no better than their counterparts. There is also no skin color effect when we examine skin color as a

Table 5.12   Individual Characteristics and Years of Education, 2000

	Years of Education	Relationship with Education[a]
Skin color		
Lighter	12.8	0.07
Darker	13.0	
Age		
Age forty or younger	13.0	0.00
Older than forty years old	12.9	
Gender		
Male	13.0	−0.26†
Female	12.8	

Source: Mexican American Study Project.
[a] Linear regression run. Unstandardized coefficients presented. Child sample analyzed. Adjusted for sibling clustering. Age included as a continuous variable in regression model. See appendix B, table B.3 for full model.
†$p<.10$

continuum—that is using five or seven categories (analysis not shown). This may reflect a changing effect of skin color, which has been observed for African Americans,[47] or perhaps an effect of place. In places where Mexican Americans comprise a large proportion of the population, like Los Angeles or San Antonio, Mexican children in schools may be readily identified on the basis of other characteristics, such as surname or peer associations, so that skin color is only a secondary marker of race or ethnicity.

Generation-Since-Immigration

We now come back to generation-since-immigration, our main independent variable of concern. The bivariate results we presented in table 5.2 show increases in education from the first generation to their children. There are few gains from the second to the third generation across family generations or generation-since-immigration, though the fourth generation had notably lower years of education than the other U.S.-born. The bivariate results in the first column of table 5.13 reflect this pattern for the child sample. However, as the multivariate analysis thus far has revealed, such results may be due to the effect of other variables that may be similarly correlated with years of education. We thus examine the independent effects of generation-since-immigration among the children, as we did for other factors.

We further disaggregate our sample into five generation-since-immigration (1.5, 2, 2.5, 3 and 4), which we define on the basis of the place of birth or generation of both parents. The creation of this variable is described in chapter 3 (see table 3.10). Because the experience of the

Table 5.13   Generation-Since-Immigration and Years of Education, 2000

	Years of Education	Relationship with Education[a]
Generation-since-immigration		
1.5	13.3	1.46**
2	13.1	0.94**
2.5	13.2	0.40†
3 (reference)	13.0	
4+	12.5	−0.08

Source: Mexican American Study Project.
[a] Linear regression run. Unstandardized coefficients presented. Child sample analyzed. Adjusted for sibling clustering. See appendix B, table B.3 for full model.
†p<.10, **p<.01

second generation may be quite heterogeneous, we further divide it into three groups: the 1.5 generation, which refers to persons who are immigrants but immigrated with their parents when they were children; the second generation, which we define for the regression analysis (in this and all subsequent chapters) as the U.S.-born children of two immigrant parents; and the 2.5 generation, which is also U.S.-born with only one immigrant parent. The 1.5 generation were children at the time of immigration, who finished who schooling in the United States.

We present the regression coefficients in the second column of table 5.13 and they show the additional years of schooling that children from generations 1.5, two, 2.5, and four have in comparison to those from generation three. The coefficients reveal quite striking results for generation-since-immigration, when all other variables are controlled. There is a progressive decline in years of education for each subsequent generation-since-immigration in the multivariate analysis. Immigrant children who came to the United States at a young age with their parents, the so-called 1.5 generation, have the highest levels of schooling, once all the other variables are controlled. They have about a half-year greater schooling than the second generation, who have a half-year more schooling than the 2.5 generation, who in turn have a half-year more schooling than the third generation. The third and fourth generations have the least schooling and there is no difference between them. In terms of statistical significance, the 1.5 and the second generation are significantly better educated than the third generation at the .05 level, the 2.5 generation is marginally better educated than the third at a marginally significant level (.10) and there are no statistically significant differences between the third and fourth generations.[48] Moreover, the generational differences in the multivariate analysis (column two) are actually greater than in the bivariate analysis (column one). Therefore, controlling for various alternative explanations actually increases differences by generation.[49] Thus, our results show that educational attainment worsens in each subsequent generation until at least the third generation-since-immigration, clearly suggesting a linear and downward pattern of assimilation!

Racialization and Discrimination

In their benchmark analysis, Alba and Nee theorized that all groups, except African Americans, will assimilate into an American mainstream.[50] Thus they sought explanations other than race for the lack of assimilation among Mexican Americans. In our study, we have sought to control for these nonracial factors, which include class origins, segregation, their presumed low levels of social and cultural capital, and growing up in an underdeveloped economic area. Despite controls for all of the commonly raised and nonracial speculations about why a Mexican American disadvantage persists, our evidence shows no educational assimilation. Indeed, the third and fourth generation do worst of all, suggesting downward assimilation in education. The question remains as to why Mexican Americans are unable to achieve the kind of educational equality that European immigrants and their descendants were able to achieve. Having exhausted major explanations, race or racialization thus emerges as a key suspect. A direct test of the racialization hypotheses, though, is not possible with our data. However, if none of the other hypotheses can explain why later generations do increasingly worse, then such an explanation remains quite viable.

Practices leading to racialization include direct discrimination by educators, structural or institutional discrimination in education, and issues of self-perception—all which derive from ideas about race. Although discrimination is often conceived of as the direct intentional act of a particular person,[51] the concept of racialization is broader. It refers to the ways in which particular individuals are sorted into the social hierarchy based on the meanings that members of society give to presumed physical and cultural characteristics. Through a variety of ways, ideas about race, and the relative worth of European- and Mexican-origin persons specifically lead to advantages for the former and disadvantages for the latter. For example, ideas about Mexicans as inferior leads to discrimination in the form of educators deciding to track individuals into less challenging curriculums on the basis of their race[52] and holding Mexican-origin students to lower academic and social standards.[53] Teachers often invest more in non-Hispanic white and Asian students, whom they expect to be more successful.[54] Mexican American students also are often made to feel uncomfortable and out of place by their non-Hispanic peers and school personnel.[55] Racialization also leads to more diffuse or structural forms of discrimination, including patterns of school financing and decisions by more senior teachers to move to schools in which whites are a majority, which leads to racially differentiated school quality. Although it may be as harmful, structural discrimination is often not considered discrimination in the narrow sense because it is difficult to pin on a single person.

Racialization and direct and structural discrimination also lead to differences in self-perception, which in turn affect educational success. The ethnographic studies of Ogbu and others[56] claim that a peer group culture in high school treats academic success among blacks and Mexican Americans as "acting white," thereby pressuring minority students away from educational pursuits. However, several statistical and ethnographic studies find no support for this contention.[57] Rather, Roland Fryer finds that high achieving minority students, especially Hispanics, are less popular in integrated schools while there was no such effect in segregated schools. Fryer theorizes that more successful minority students in integrated schools have more contact with other groups, thus threatening established ethnic boundaries that low achieving groups maintain from dominant group members.[58] This they do by withdrawing popularity from the most successful co-ethnics, which weakens their response to academic challenges.

The signals and racial stereotypes that educators and society in general send to students affect the extent to which they will engage and persist in school.[59] Racial stereotypes produce a positive self-identity for white and Asian students but a negative one for blacks and Latinos, which affects school success.[60] Students often evaluate their chances of success in light of their perceived role in society. Racialized self-perceptions among Mexican American students generally endure into the third and fourth generation, though positive self-concepts and distancing from negative stereotyping may allow some to defy the odds and do well academically.[61] This seems to be especially likely for the second generation, in which immigrant parents tend to be more optimistic about life in the United States and transmit these values to their children. In some cases, immigrants may also be better at mobilizing supportive ethnic ties to engage schools in the interest of advantages for their children.[62]

Several analysts have attributed downward mobility between the second and third generation to a weakening of immigrant drive and optimism.[63] Matute-Bianchi finds that Mexican immigrant or Mexican-oriented students, though they have more Mexican cultural traits, also have more respect for school culture than the more acculturated but often rebellious Chicano students.[64] Self-perceptions regarding their abilities at school are often higher among immigrants whose parents have instilled in them more optimism for success in the United States.

An alternative or supplemental explanation is that each level of education is worth more in terms of human and social capital for Mexican immigrant parents than for American parents. For example, an immigrant parent with nine years of schooling has an education that is above average in Mexico, which may signify relatively high social status, and implies social and cultural capital. This compares to U.S.-born parents with the same nine years of schooling, which often signifies relatively poor schooling and low social capital in the United States.

Conclusions

Rather than improvements in education in subsequent generations-since-immigration, as assimilation theory predicts, we find quite the opposite. Large gains from immigrant parents to their children aside, Mexican American schooling remained fairly flat in succeeding generations-since-immigration. Assuming equally resourced children, education actually worsened. Greater parental education, household income, social and cultural capital, and fewer children all contribute to more schooling. However, when these factors are held constant, the highest levels of schooling are for those who immigrated as children but were educated in the United States and the lowest for the grandchildren and great-grandchildren of immigrants. The third and fourth generation did worse than the 1.5 or the second generation. Moreover, our study shows similarly poor educational outcomes for the fifth generation so far, that is, the adult children of the fourth-generation children. America's public schools have failed most Mexican Americans, contrary to what they did for European Americans. Instead, our research supports the claims of many educators that public school failure for Mexican Americans derives from a racialized system that stigmatizes Mexican American children in various ways. Racialization through schooling seems to help cement their low status in American society.

Our findings are consistent with the theory of status attainment, in which parents' education and income are the best predictors of their child's education. Mexican American children with more educated parents do better than those whose parents have less education. The payoff to any educational advantages their parents may have is lower for Mexican Americans than it is for both whites and blacks. Moreover, our findings demonstrated that segregation itself bears little relation to educational attainment, once factors such as parental education are held constant. In other words, parental resources mostly shape children's levels of education and the neighborhoods in which they can afford to live. Thus, our evidence suggests that reducing segregation, by itself, will have little effect on the poor educational outcomes of Mexican Americans.

Although status attainment is consistent with assimilation theory, in that children's status depends on parents' status, assimilation theory goes a step further by expecting consecutive and cumulative gains to status over generations-since-immigration. In other words, with assimilation theory, two conditions must be met: those with higher status inherit higher status from the previous generation and status is increased with successive generation-since-immigration. For the Mexican case, the first condition is met but not the second. Status attainment is important, but when it comes to generation-since-immigration, status gains passed down from parents are stalled or even reversed by the third and subsequent generations. Our evidence thus strongly supports research claiming that racial stereotyping and discrimination have largely contributed to enduring Mexican American disadvantage.

We also find that Catholic schools have a beneficial effect on Mexican Americans. Even when a host of other variables that contribute to education are held equal, including parental resources and aspirations, having begun high school in a Catholic or other private school contributes more than a full year of additional education for Mexican Americans—an amount that would largely overcome their educational deficit relative to other Americans. Certainly, one can point to a few public schools that also do well, but these are exceptions. The higher expectations of the Catholic schools themselves, among other things, provides advantages to students in those schools. Could it be that Catholic schools have disrupted the racialization process? There is some evidence of this based on the universally high expectations of these schools and the more personalized and small community identity that such schools often provide, perhaps decreasing racial and ethnic stereotyping and divisions. Whether or not this is true is not well resolved but there may be lessons here for public education.

To end this chapter on a more positive note, if we look at education outcomes for the group over time rather than by generation-since-immigration, Mexican Americans have seen educational progress over the course of the twentieth century. This has not been so much across generation-since-immigration but rather a slow historical trend of gradually reducing, rather than eliminating, the educational gap. A slowly declining gap over time is attributable in part to civil rights gains for minorities, including policies to improve equity in public spending for schools and the end of de jure segregation. These have contributed to educational gains for a considerable number of Mexican Americans. On the other hand, continuously high dropout rates for Mexican-origin children suggests that reversals of this improving long-term trend are also possible.

The question that remains is how do low educational outcomes affect other outcomes for Mexican Americans, particularly in the economic arena? We turn to these questions in chapter 6. The low status we find among Mexican Americans of later generations occurs at the same time that they also experience diminishing attachment to Mexican culture, Spanish language, and Catholicism, as we will show in later chapters. The cultural protections these may provide seem to wear off for most Mexican Americans by the third or fourth generation. Unlike European Americans, education gets worse as culture wears off—a potentially explosive combination.

= Chapter 6 =

Economic Status

No other issue regarding racial and ethnic divisions in the United States is as troubling as the lack of economic incorporation of some groups, most notably African Americans. The persistently low occupational level, income, and accumulated wealth of minorities demonstrate the limits of the equal opportunity principle and the universality of the American dream. Evidence based on national statistics show that Mexican Americans, like Puerto Ricans and African Americans, have persistently low socioeconomic status even among the third generation.[1] Since at least the 1970s, many scholars have argued that racial discrimination in labor and housing markets, inferior and segregated education, and tracking into manual jobs has primarily blocked the mobility of Mexican Americans.[2] In contrast, studies of earlier European immigrant groups suggest that the more important and most impressive gains were made by the second generation, with continuing economic and social gains by the third generation.[3] Both individual and labor market explanations have been used to describe differences in the nature of European American and Mexican American incorporation experiences. In this chapter, we investigate the socioeconomic outcomes of Mexican Americans and whether economic status improves with generational status.

Several leading scholars expect the eventual, though relatively slow, assimilation of Mexican Americans by the fourth generation because of the very low human capital of their immigrant forebears, which puts their descendants at an educational and economic disadvantage.[4] We showed in the previous chapter that Mexican Americans have especially low levels of education, well into the fourth generation, and that education does not steadily improve over the generations. According to human capital and status attainment theories, low educational status is the main reason for low job status, though racial discrimination in the labor market may also affect economic status. The payoff to education, also known as income returns to levels of education, has generally been shown to be similar between Mexican Americans and European Americans, but lower for African Americans. The inference, therefore, is that Mexican Americans' occupational status is primarily due to low education, not to labor market discrimination.[5]

The first stage of the status attainment model posits that characteristics of the family of origin are particularly important for understanding one's economic position.[6] Status attainment describes the process by which parents transmit their social standing to their children, primarily through the children's education. In the second stage, child's education and other human capital characteristics predict their subsequent position in the labor market, particularly their first job. We showed in the previous chapter that indicators of the family's social class—especially parents' education and family income—significantly predict the educational status of the children of the original respondents. In this chapter, we examine the extent to which education, parental capital, and other factors predict occupational and income status and the accumulation of wealth and homeownership.

Opportunities in the labor market largely determine how significantly ethnic groups will assimilate economically beyond individual gains in human capital and status. The incorporation of the descendants of European immigrants seems to have depended largely on expansive industrial labor markets, which offered an abundance of relatively well-paid employment to even low human capital workers.[7] The two original locations of the Mexican American Study Project, Los Angeles and San Antonio, had different economic structures in the 1960s and thus provided distinct opportunities to Mexican American workers. Furthermore, each underwent different kinds of changes in subsequent years. Los Angeles was heavily industrialized and unionized in the 1960s but lost much of its industrial base after that, akin to the experiences of large eastern and midwestern cities. As discussed in chapter 4, Mexican Americans were concentrated in these declining industries.[8] San Antonio, on the other hand, was less industrial, with more jobs in tourism, government, and the military in the 1960s. There has been less change in the industrial composition in San Antonio since the 1960s, though the closing of military bases, which had offered some of the most desirable blue-collar jobs in the area, has diminished its importance as an employer. Thus, we examine whether the socioeconomic outcomes of Mexican Americans differs by urban area.

Gender is well documented as an important issue in understanding the economic position of individuals (which is not as well documented for most of the other indicators we used in this book). Women tend to have lower wages, lower incomes, considerable occupational segregation, and less wealth than men.[9] Of course, race-ethnicity interacts with gender in important ways, so that women of color—such as Mexican American and African American women—have especially low status,[10] all of which argues that an analysis of economic characteristics needs to be done separately by gender. Although our focus is primarily on comparisons by generation and urban area throughout this book, we recognize that there may be important differences by gender. Thus, we also did the bivariate analyses by gender, though we do not present these, and we included gender as independent variable in our regression analysis. Of the four socioeconomic indicators we examine in the multivariate analysis, we find that gender is significant in only one case. Women earn significantly less than men, as has been well documented in the literature.

Industrial Change

Demographically, much of the mostly white and highly paid working class migrated out of the Los Angeles region by the mid-1990s and immigrants began to fill the new low-end jobs.[11] W. J. Wilson argues that the growing labor market polarization increased joblessness among native black men or locked them into low-status jobs, with little opportunity for mobility. Similar arguments have been made for U.S.-born Mexican Americans, whose opportunities in secure working class jobs decreased.[12] Immigration analysts such as Portes and his colleagues and Perlmann and Waldinger argue that many children of immigrants today, unlike their predecessors, will similarly be locked into low-level jobs in the new economy and many will share the multigenerational low status fate of African Americans. The comparative study of widely distinct industrial structures in our urban sites thus allows us to examine the effects of industrial change. This is due, in part, to the increasing educational demands of jobs at the same time that Mexican Americans have, as we showed in chapter 5, relatively low levels of education.

The changes brought about by industrial restructuring also had greater effects on Los Angeles' Mexican Americans. Table 6.1 presents the industrial distributions for original respondent heads in 1965 and 2000 and for their children.[13] In 1965, just over half (51 percent) of the original respondent heads worked in manufacturing, whereas only 16 percent of their children did. In contrast, only 21 percent of San Antonians worked in manufacturing in 1965 compared to 11 percent of their children in 2000. Fully 62 percent of the Los Angeles Mexican Americans employed in manufacturing were in the durable goods sector, precisely those heavy industries that offered relatively well paying jobs. By 2000, 36 percent of the original respondents in Los Angeles and 10 percent in San Antonio held manufacturing jobs.

The second row from the bottom of table 6.1 shows that in 1965 twice as many San Antonio Mexican Americans worked in professional services or public administration (17 percent) as did those in Los Angeles (8 percent). Moreover, only 2 percent of Angelenos had military jobs compared to 16 percent of San Antonians. Therefore, fully one-third (33 percent) of San Antonians were concentrated in industries primarily in the public or government domain. By 2000, original respondents in San Antonio continued to be more concentrated in public administration and military

Table 6.1   Industry[a] by Urban Area, 1965 and 2000[b]

	Original Respondents, 1965		Original Respondents, 2000		Children	
	Los Angeles	San Antonio	Los Angeles	San Antonio	Los Angeles	San Antonio
Manufacturing	51%	21%	36%	10%	16%	11%
Construction	10	8	13	11	8	4
Transportation, communications, utilities	9	9	10	9	9	6
Trade	13	14	14	19	17	16
Business and financial services	2	5	6	8	14	21
Personal services	4	10	5	7	4	7
Public administration and professional services	8	17	16	22	31	33
Military	2	16	0	15	1	1

Source: Mexican American Study Project.
[a] Current or last job.
[b] Among original respondent heads of households in 1965 and children of heads.

Table 6.2   Personal Income[a] by Race, 1970 and 2000[b]

	Male		Female	
	1970[c]	2000	1970[c]	2000
Mexican Americans				
Five southwest states	29,121	25,887	17,003	20,358
Los Angeles	34,010	32,631	20,224	26,109
San Antonio	25,253	23,406	15,903	23,406
Non-Hispanic whites				
Five southwest states	43,310	54,025	21,957	35,175
Los Angeles	47,730	65,784	24,628	45,300
San Antonio	38,198	49,794	20,718	31,302
Blacks				
Five southwest states	27,144	33,290	16,971	27,916
Los Angeles	31,153	37,266	20,511	32,441
San Antonio	21,961	30,771	15,557	26,122
Asians				
Five southwest states	—	48,623	—	34,977
Los Angeles	—	50,637	—	39,678
San Antonio	—	49,161	—	30,117

Source: Authors' tabulations of decennial censuses 1970 and 2000.
[a] Personal income includes earnings, as well as business income, interest, dividends, pensions, and government assistance.
[b] Among age eighteen and fifty-four and full time workers and U.S. born.
[c] 1970 figures adjusted to 2000 dollars.

jobs. For the children, however, dependence on government jobs had equalized in the two urban areas. Most strikingly, military employment in San Antonio decreased from 16 percent for original respondents to 1 percent among the children.

Earnings and Income

Grebler and his colleagues documented that personal income levels[14] for Mexican Americans were significantly lower than among non-Hispanic whites—a gap of 57 percent—in the five southwestern states.[15] The gap was also greater in Texas than in California—79 percent and 50 percent respectively. Grebler also showed that Mexicans had slightly higher income than nonwhites, which at the time of the original study was almost entirely African American. Data presented in table 6.2 show that income inequality between Mexican Americans and whites worsened from 1970 levels.

To get a sense of how racial-ethnic groups have fared economically over time, table 6.2 uses 1970 and 2000 census data to calculate average personal income for full-time male and female U.S.-born Mexican origin workers and compares them to U.S.-born whites and blacks. For the five southwestern states in 1970, Mexican-origin men had an average income well below that of whites but slightly higher than that of African Americans. In the intervening years, income for Mexican American men declined in real dollars whereas that of whites, and to some extent blacks, increased, relegating Mexicans to the bottom of the income distribution. The same pattern held for Los Angeles and San Antonio. The income inequality between Mexican Americans and other Americans worsened in most cases between 1970 and 2000. Our figures are for the U.S.-born so that the effect of low immigrant wages, especially among the Mexican-origin population, is removed. Although one might argue that U.S.-born Mexican Americans have lower incomes because they are more likely than whites or blacks to be children of immigrants (second generation), our study (and other evidence) does not support this hypothesis. As we show later in this chapter, there are no significant differences between the second and the third generation or more in terms of income. We thus believe the figures for table 6.2 are directly comparable to those for whites and blacks. On the other hand, Mexican American income on table 6.2 may be somewhat depressed because of a younger age structure.

Although members in all three groups saw their income increase over the next thirty years, the income of Mexican American men increased the least and was at the bottom in 2000. The income of Mexican American men actually decreased as the incomes of their white counterparts sharply increased. Some of this may be due to an increasingly polarized economic structure in which Mexican American men tended to be in jobs in the low end of the income structure, where real wages declined, whereas non-Hispanic whites rode the increases for those at the upper ends of the new economy.[16] By 2000, Mexican American full-time male workers had less than half the income of Anglos in the five southwestern states and in both urban areas.[17]

All racial-ethnic groups of women had somewhat similar low personal income levels in 1970. Mexican American women were at the bottom of the income distribution, near blacks. Although all three racial-ethnic groups saw their income increase over the next thirty years, the increases were clearly greater for white and black women than for Mexican Americans, making the racial-ethnic gap greater. By 2000, U.S.-born Mexican American women had the lowest income of the major racial-ethnic groups. From 1970 to 2000, Mexican American women increased their income from an especially low point in both urban areas, but not as much as white women. White women increased their income by 60 percent and black women by 64 percent, but Mexican American women by only 20 percent.

Table 6.3 focuses on personal earnings, family income, and poverty status among our sample. The first row shows that average personal earnings

Table 6.3   Earnings and Income by Generation-Since-Immigration, 1965 and 2000

	Original Respondents, 1965[a]			Original Respondents, 2000			Children		
	Gen. 1	Gen. 2	Gen. 3	Gen. 1	Gen. 2	Gen. 3	Gen. 2	Gen. 3	Gen. 4+
Personal earnings[b]	$25,556	$29,243	$29,319	$25,923	$29,748	$29,151	$36,343	$37,615	$30,559
Family income[c]	$32,404	$35,654	$35,537	$25,445	$28,442	$28,952	$53,174	$53,634	$43,891
Below poverty[d]	25%	20%	20%	38%	37%	38%	17%	14%	21%
High family income[e]	11	13	12	10	14	16	47	47	36

Source: Mexican American Study Project.
[a] 1965 figures adjusted to 2000 dollars.
[b] Personal earnings includes wages and business income; among workers.
[c] Family income based on husband's and wife's income and includes personal income, interest, dividends, pensions, and government assistance.
[d] Below poverty based on family income using government thresholds (based on family size and composition).
[e] High family income more than $50,000 in 2000 dollars.

remained nearly static between 1965 and 2000 for original respondents in their current or most recent job or jobs. Earnings increased appreciably from parents to children in all generations-since-immigration, though there was some variation. Comparing original respondents to their children, earnings rose by nearly $10,000 from the immigrant respondents to their children, by about $8,000 from the second-generation original respondents to their children, and by only $1,000 from the third generation to their fourth-generation children. All of these figures are in constant dollars, adjusted to year 2000 values. Overall improvements for Mexican Americans in that period thus mostly benefited those closest to the immigration experience. Among subsequent generations, the second and third had similar earnings, and were somewhat higher than those of the fourth generation, though as we will show later in this chapter, income and earnings for the fourth generation do not differ significantly from those of the second and third generations, once the appropriate factors are controlled.

Family income is the amount of money received by respondents and spouses from all sources—including earnings, pensions, government awards, interest, and the like. Family income fell between 1965 and 2000 for original respondents. Perhaps this is because original respondents are more likely to be retired (approximately 40 percent of original respondents are retired by 2000). Family income rose substantially from the original respondents to children, reflecting both higher individual earnings and the trend toward both spouses being in the labor force, compared to a more common single-earner family in the 1960s.

The percentage of persons in poverty, which reflects family income and the number of persons in the family, increased over the life course of the original respondents and declined substantially for their children. Whereas 25 percent of the immigrants were poor in 1965, 38 percent were by 2000. For the second and third generations, poverty nearly doubled from 20 percent in 1965 to 37 to 38 percent in 2000. Again, this increase in poverty (or decline in income) among original respondents seems largely attributable to their transition into retirement. For the children of the original respondents, poverty decreased significantly and ranged from 14 to 21 percent. However, poverty tends to increase with generation-since-immigration rather than decrease. For fourth generation Mexican Americans, roughly one-fifth (21 percent) of our sample is poor and nearly two-fifths (38 percent) of their third generation parents are also poor. In a wealthy country like the United States, a large number of Mexican Americans thus experience generations of exclusion.

At the high end of the income scale, we found no variation by generation for original respondents in 1965. The percentage with relatively high incomes—more than $50,000 measured in 2000 dollars—did not increase between 1965 and 2000, though there was a modest increase with generational status in 2000. Sixteen percent of the third generation-since-immigration are in that category, compared to 10 percent of the first. However, nearly half of their children were likely to have high family incomes. At the same time, only 36 percent of the fourth generation earned $50,000 or more, compared to 47 percent among the second and third generations. As we noted earlier, children tended to be in families with two employed persons, making family income higher than it was for the original respondents. More important, the $50,000 standard was a relatively high income in 1965 but is no longer. However, it does reveal that living standards increased substantially but probably not as much as for the general population, as table 6.1 suggests.

Table 6.4 shows the same earnings, income, and poverty indicators separately for Los Angeles and San Antonio. It reveals the very large differences between the two urban areas for the original respondents, especially in the earlier period. In 1965, fully 41 percent of those in San Antonio lived in poverty, versus only 12 percent in Los Angeles. Similarly, incomes and earnings were more than 50 percent higher in Los Angeles in 1965. However, all indicators show a trend toward convergence of the two urban areas by 2000, especially among children. Personal earnings, for example, were only about 15 percent higher in Los Angeles, which probably amounts to less than the difference in costs of living between the two urban areas. The poverty rate fell from 41 percent for parents to 19 percent for children in San Antonio. It was 15 percent for children in Los Angeles, slightly higher than of the 12 percent for their parents thirty-five years earlier. However, the poverty rate for the original respondents increased from 12 to 34 percent in Los Angeles and from 41 to 53 percent in San Antonio. In contrast to the decreasing poverty for their children, this may reflect the higher poverty often found for the elderly. Nevertheless, that more than half of the original sample in San Antonio was poor in 2000 does reflect the extremely low status of this population.

Occupation

Grebler and colleagues demonstrated the low occupational status of the Mexican-origin population in the Southwest. In 1960, only 8 percent of the Spanish-surname population held professional or managerial jobs, versus 28 percent of non-Hispanic whites and 9 percent of nonwhites.[18] Also, 64 percent of the Spanish-surname population (and a similar percentage of nonwhites—65 percent) held low-skill manual jobs, versus 32 percent of whites. Grebler and his colleagues also documented a somewhat better occupational distribution for women than men—for instance, only 16 percent of Mexican American men but 36 percent of Mexican American women held white-collar jobs. This was attributable to women being more likely to work in clerical and sales jobs, which were

Table 6.4   Earnings and Income by Urban Area, 1965 and 2000

	Original Respondents, 1965[a]		Original Respondents, 2000		Children	
	Los Angeles	San Antonio	Los Angeles	San Antonio	Los Angeles	San Antonio
Personal earnings[b]	$31,355	$20,411	$31,252	$22,056	$37,463	$32,595
Family income[c]	$38,566	$24,873	$30,484	$22,593	$54,730	$45,145
Poverty[d]	12%	41%	34%	53%	15%	19%
High family income[e]	15	3	15	11	48	38

Source: Mexican American Study Project.
[a] 1965 figures adjusted to 2000 dollars.
[b] Personal earnings includes wages and business income; among workers.
[c] Family income based on husband's and wife's income and includes personal income, interest, dividends, pensions, and government assistance.
[d] Below poverty based on family income using government thresholds (based on family size and composition).
[e] High family income more than $50,000 in 2000 dollars.

included in the white-collar category, rather than their being in professional or managerial positions.

Table 6.5 reports the occupational distribution of original respondents and their children in both 1965 and 2000, all by generation-since-immigration. The breakdown by five major occupational groups suggests substantial mobility out of blue-collar jobs and into white-collar occupations from the original respondents in 1965 to their children in 2000. This may be related to overall changes in the occupational structure of the United States since the 1960s and the decreasing education and earnings of lower white-collar occupations, making these jobs equivalent in status to some blue-collar jobs in the past. This may also be due to general occupational mobility that occurs throughout the life course and to affirmative action programs since 1965. This may also be the result of the large waves of Mexican immigrants who have arrived since 1965, taking low wages and the blue-collar jobs previously held by older immigrants and U.S.-born Mexican Americans; at the same time, creating opportunities in higher level occupations, including jobs as bilingual supervisors and personnel officers.[19]

Occupational gains are most apparent from original respondents to their children, where occupational status increased appreciably in all generations-since-immigration. More than half of children, versus 18 to 27 percent of their parents, held white-collar jobs. The most common professional occupations for the children were as managers of various types of businesses—including education, service organizations, food service, real estate, and marketing. About half of them worked in the private sector and a quarter in the public sector, and the remainder were self-employed. Other common professional occupations were teachers, especially at the elementary school level, and social workers. These jobs largely reflect a step out of the working class. Similarly, original respondents in the broad professional-managerial category were more likely to be managers than any other occupation. In the technical-administrative field, the most common occupations for the adult children were as supervisors of sales persons, secretaries, and bookkeepers. Similarly, the original respondents were most frequently supervisors of sales persons, secretaries, and teacher aides.

In 2000, the child generation was more concentrated in service occupations (10 to 17 percent) than the original respondents in 1965 (4 to 12 percent). Among children in the service category, the most common categories were police officer and other law enforcement occupations. Janitors, cleaners, and maids were also common service occupations, as were nurse's aides and orderlies. Similarly, the original respondents were janitors, cleaners, nurse's aides, and orderlies. At the same time, there has been a massive shift of Mexican Americans out of blue-collar jobs, which were mostly in manufacturing and construction. Only 22 to 34 percent of the children's generation worked in such jobs, versus 60 to 77 percent of the

Table 6.5 Occupational Distribution and Occupational Index by Generation-Since-Immigration, 1965 and 2000

	Original Respondents, 1965			Original Respondents, 2000			Children		
	Gen. 1	Gen. 2	Gen. 3	Gen. 1	Gen. 2	Gen. 3	Gen. 2	Gen. 3	Gen. 4+
Occupational distribution									
Professional or manager	8%	10%	7%	12%	14%	16%	28%	26%	18%
Technical or administrative	10	15	20	21	26	27	38	35	32
Total white collar	18	25	27	33	40	43	66	60	50
Service	5	12	4	13	19	19	12	10	17
Production or repair	20	24	28	19	16	17	10	16	20
Operatives or laborer	57	40	42	35	24	21	12	14	14
Total blue collar	77	64	60	54	40	38	22	30	34
Mean occupational index[a]	28.5	29.9	30.5	28.0	30.2	31.5	36.4	36.1	32.1

Source: Mexican American Study Project.
[a] Occupational index ranges from zero to one-hundred and a composite of education and wages for workers in detailed occupational categories calculated separately for men and women.

parents'. In the immigrant generation, 77 percent held these jobs but only 22 percent of their second-generation children did. Approximately one-quarter of original respondents held production-repair occupations in 1965, while 10 to 20 percent of the children did so. Among children in the production-repair category, the most common occupations were automobile mechanic, concrete finishers, and supervisors of production work. The original respondents in this occupational category were supervisors of construction and supervisors of production work. Around half of original respondents were in operator-laborer occupations in 1965, while 12 to 14 percent of the children were. Last, among children in the operator-laborer category, the most common occupation was truck driver. The original respondents were typically truck drivers and sewing machine operators.

Regarding the occupational distribution by generation-since-immigration, the greatest concentration in 1965 appeared to be in the operator-laborer category, in which fully 57 percent of immigrants were employed, versus only about 40 and 42 percent of the second and third generation, respectively. The U.S.-born second and third generation were more likely to be employed in the more skilled trades involving production and repair. A roughly constant 7 to 10 percent of first-, second-, and third-generation original respondents were in professional and managerial jobs and there was an increase in technical-administrative workers by generation-since-immigration. Although certainly more prestigious than most blue-collar jobs, these tend to be among the lowest-level white-collar occupations. There was a shift to white-collar jobs from 1965 to 2000 for all generations-since-immigration.

From the original respondents to the child generation, the greatest gains were from immigrants to their second-generation children. Although the original respondents who were immigrants were the least likely to be in white collar occupations, the second-generation children had the most. Fully 66 percent of the second-generation children, versus only 18 percent of their parents in 1965 and 33 percent in 2000, were in the white collar occupational categories. Like education and income, though, the weakest gains occurred from the third to fourth generation. For example, representation in professional and managerial occupations approximately doubled for the second- and third-generation children compared to the original respondents in 2000, but went from 16 percent for the original respondents to only 18 percent for the fourth generation. We return to this topic later in the chapter. Fourth-generation children in our sample did not fare nearly as well in professional occupations as those of the second and third generation-since-immigration.

The last row of table 6.5 reports the mean occupational index of original respondents and children in both 1965 and 2000, all by generation-since-immigration. The mean occupational index ranks detailed occupations according to their average educations and income separately for married women,[20] and we apply this score to the detailed occupation of each of

Table 6.6   Government Worker, Self-Employment, and Union Status by Urban Area, 2000

	Original Respondents		Children	
	Los Angeles	San Antonio	Los Angeles	San Antonio
Government worker	20%	33%	19%	27%
Self employed	14	17	21	9
Union member	41	13	23	12

Source: Mexican American Study Project.

our respondents. These results make it quite apparent that intergenerational occupational status has improved from the original respondents to their children. This reflects a long-term change in occupations for the United States overall. We note that the occupational index of the original respondents remained almost exactly the same between 1965 and 2000, suggesting almost no occupational mobility during the careers of original respondents, though intergenerational occupational mobility was considerable.

Additional characteristics—such as government employment, self-employment, and union membership—tell us about the quality of respondent jobs. However, such characteristics may vary widely between California and Texas because of the very different labor markets and legal environments of the two locations. We present data on these characteristics by urban area in table 6.6. Just as Grebler and his colleagues showed that Mexican Americans in Texas in 1965 were more likely to hold government jobs than those in California, we find that both original respondents and their children in San Antonio were also more likely to work in or recently hold government jobs in 2000.[21] Self-employment was relatively low for original respondents in both Los Angeles (17 percent) and San Antonio (14 percent), and was lower still for their children. Last, we observe that fully 41 percent of original respondents in Los Angeles but only 13 percent of those raised in San Antonio were union members. This is consistent with the fact that Texas is a right-to-work state.[22] For the children, the percentages of unionized workers in our sample fell in Los Angeles, reflecting both a national and local decline in union membership and a movement to white-collar jobs, where unions tend to be less prevalent.[23] In San Antonio, rates of unionization remained the same for both original respondents and their children.

Homeownership and Wealth

Recent studies have shown that whereas the average incomes of African Americans are less than those for whites, differences in wealth are huge.[24] Oliver and Shapiro, for example, show that median income among African

Americans ($15,630) is less than two-thirds that of whites ($25,384). Black median net worth—the sum of all assets minus debts—is only $3,700, a meager 8 percent of white net worth ($43,800).[25] Differences in wealth thus reveal a significant racial inequality not apparent in income figures. By far, the largest amount of wealth for middle class Americans is in home equity: fully 66 percent of white households and 42 percent of African American households have equity in their home.[26] Moreover, the dollar amounts in black home equity are far less ($31,000 versus $45,000).[27] The large differences between black and white wealth can be largely attributed to housing discrimination. Blacks have had far less access to housing mortgage loans than whites. When they did get them, they were confined to buying homes in black neighborhoods where the price of housing, and thus the amount of equity accumulated, grew at a lower rate than in white neighborhoods.[28] Because wealth can be transmitted intergenerationally, unlike income, whites have had tremendous resource advantages over blacks, even when their family incomes are similar.

Similar to what has been documented for African Americans, Grebler and his colleagues found lower rates of homeownership among those of Mexican origin. For the residents of metropolitan areas in the entire southwest region, 63 percent of whites owned homes in 1960 but only 53 percent of the Spanish-surname did.[29] We show homeownership on table 6.7. The children in 2000 were as likely to own their own home as the original respondents in 1965.[30] In 1965, 54 percent of the first generation, 55 percent of the second generation, and 47 percent of the third generation were homeowners. Of course, many of these homes are quite modest even when owned, reflecting the high poverty rates of San Antonio in the 1960s.

In our study, wealth data were not collected for the original respondents in 1965, thus precluding direct comparisons with their children in 2000. We collected more extensive wealth information in the 2000 survey for both original respondents and children. Because wealth accumulates over age, the wealth of the now mostly senior original respondents in 2000 cannot be fairly compared to that of their children. In any case, the figures are instructive. Given that the large majority of wealth is in home ownership, we present the proportion of respondents owning one or at least two homes in table 6.7. For the original respondents, the percentage owning a home is high. By 2000, nearly three-quarters of the first- and second-generation respondents own their own homes and nearly one-quarter of the original respondents in all generations own a second one. Among children, less than 60 percent (and only 49 percent of the fourth generation) own a home, but only 10 to 14 percent own a second home.

Wealth is indicated by net worth, which is equity in all homes owned (0 for nonowners) plus financial assets (usually savings) minus financial

Table 6.7   Homeownership and Wealth by Generation-Since-Immigration, 1965 and 2000

| | Original Respondents, 1965 | | | Original Respondents, 2000 | | | Children | | |
	Gen. 1	Gen. 2	Gen. 3	Gen. 1	Gen. 2	Gen. 3	Gen. 2	Gen. 3	Gen. 4+
Owns own home	54%	55%	47%	73%	73%	65%	59%	58%	49%
Owns more than one home	—[a]	—[a]	—[a]	22	22	23	14	12	10
Net worth[b]	—[a]	—[a]	—[a]	$131,122	$111,582	$132,478	$48,424	$44,617	$38,364

Source: Mexican American Study Project.
[a] Data not collected in 1965 survey.
[b] Net worth based on equity in home(s) and financial assets minus debts.

debts (usually for credit cards). We did not include the value of cars, which may add net worth but is typically a very small amount (6 percent).[31] The last row of table 6.7 shows that original respondents in Los Angeles, who by 2000 were all older than fifty-two, had accumulated well over $100,000 in personal wealth. By contrast, children, who did not have as much time to accumulate wealth, had an average net worth of less than $50,000 in all generations. There is no linear pattern or significant difference by generation-since-immigration among the original respondents. For children, net worth was greatest among the second generation and decreased in each subsequent generation.

Finally, table 6.8 shows that homeownership was much higher in San Antonio than in Los Angeles. This was true in the 1960s and in 2000. This urban difference is passed on to the children. Urban differences in homeownership are most likely due to the greater affordability of housing in San Antonio. Despite high rates of poverty in San Antonio in the 1960s, many Mexican Americans owned quite substandard homes. On the other hand, because real estate values are much greater in Los Angeles, wealth in Los Angeles is considerably higher among both original respondents and their children. Wealth is especially high for original respondents because homes in the Los Angeles region have greatly increased in value over the course of their lives.

Factors Affecting Socioeconomic Status

So far, we have presented several indicators of socioeconomic status. We have focused on differences in generation-since-immigration and for each urban area. However, there are several potential predictors of socioeconomic status among Mexican Americans, most important of which is education. We use regression statistical analyses to examine how these factors, including parental socioeconomic characteristics, parental household characteristics, residence and other respondent characteristics such as age and skin color, might each independently contribute to understanding differences in socioeconomic status among the Mexican American population. The independent variables were summarized in chapter 3 and are similar to those used for predicting years of schooling in chapter 5. We present the most important results for this analysis in table 6.9.

The most powerful effect we find is that education affects every indicator of socioeconomic status. No other variable in our model has such a consistent effect. More education clearly means higher socioeconomic status on all four indicators. For every additional year of education, occupational status increases by 3 points on a 100-point scale (first column). Moreover, every year of education significantly increases earnings by about $4,000 (second column), family income by more than $6,000 (third column), and net worth by about $9,000 (fourth column). Although

Table 6.8   Homeownership and Wealth by Urban Area, 1965 and 2000

	Original Respondents, 1965		Original Respondents, 2000		Children	
	Los Angeles	San Antonio	Los Angeles	San Antonio	Los Angeles	San Antonio
Owns own home	43%	65%	69%	77%	53%	64%
Owns more than one home	—[a]	—[a]	22	26	13	15
Net worth[b]	—[a]	—[a]	$141,302	$72,694	$51,711	$40,269

Source: Mexican American Study Project.
[a] Data not collected in 1965 survey.
[b] Net worth based on equity in home(s) and financial assets minus debts.

Table 6.9   **Key Determinants of Socioeconomic Status, 2000**[a]

	Occupational Status	Earnings (Dollars)	Income (Dollars)	Net Worth (Dollars)
Generation-since-immigration (ref: 3)				
1.5	0.57	−354	5,900	11,779
2	0.30	−4,418	−2,584	13,372
2.5	−0.76	−2,324	−630	342
4+	−1.16	−3,663	−777	782
Education	2.99***	4,043***	6,177***	8,977***
Telephone interview (2000)		7,479**	7,816*	25,650*
Work experience[b]		240*		
Age[b]				2,917***
Female		−1,2895***		

Source: Mexican American Study Project.
[a] Only significant or substantive variables presented. Linear regression run. Unstandardized coefficients presented. Child sample analyzed. Adjusted for sibling clustering. See appendix B, table B.4 for full model.
[b] Age and work experience not included in model together because highly correlated.
* p<.05, **p<.01, ***p<.001

parents' education, income, and homeownership had a highly significant effect on education, these variables do not directly affect socioeconomic status.[32] Instead, family background affects socioeconomic status through the child's education, which fits well within the status attainment model.

Despite our expectations, variables such as living in San Antonio or Los Angeles and the extent of ethnic isolation (proportion Hispanics in neighborhood) had no effect on socioeconomic status (as shown in the full model in table B.4 in appendix B). Those who completed the interview by telephone, however, had significantly higher earnings, incomes, and net worth. This effect is partly residential because many of the telephone interviews were with respondents who had moved away from either the Los Angeles or the San Antonio area, though in some cases we simply could not arrange in-person interviews for those who had not moved. Thus, these results suggest that Mexican Americans who left Los Angeles or San Antonio were able to secure higher earnings, income, and wealth.

Interestingly, generation-since-immigration is not significantly related to socioeconomic status. The prediction posed by assimilation theory that socioeconomic status should increase with generational status was not supported by our regression, just as it had not been shown in the descriptive tables. There seems, however, to be minor though not significant or consistent effects suggesting slight downward assimilation on occupation and earnings beyond the schooling effects. Most of the coefficients for the 1.5 generation are positive but not significant. Most effects for the fourth generation are actually negative, though again not significant. By far the largest effect of generation-since-immigration on socioeconomic status, however, is on levels of education, which in turn strongly affect socioeconomic status.

Finally, the expected gender and work experience–age effects arose, as they generally do in such models of economic status. Respondents with more work experience have higher earnings, and older respondents are more likely to own a home and to have greater net worth. Women had lower earnings than men, by nearly $13,000 dollars per year in 2000 dollars, despite similar occupational status. As expected, their increased net worth was similar to that of men because we examined this for husband and wives combined.[33]

Signs of an Underclass: Gangs

The presence of gangs was not uncommon for the children of the European immigrants in the 1920s. By the third generation, however, in concert with little immigration, these had virtually disappeared.[34] On the other hand, gangs have been a common feature of the black underclass throughout the twentieth century with their large-scale migration from the South to urban areas. Moreover, nowhere are gangs as apparent as among the Mexican-origin population in the barrios of southwestern cities, particularly in southern California.[35] Whether or not gangs are, as they were among European immigrants, a feature of only the second generation or later generations as well, as in the case of African Americans, is not well known. Tony Waters found that the second generation is the most susceptible to street socialization and gangs.[36] For this reason, we included several items in our survey to examine gang membership.

The first item asked respondents whether they were familiar with the cholo (gang) lifestyle, to which the majority in all generations, except for the first-generation immigrants, answered affirmatively.[37] Table 6.10 shows that the children reported higher participation in the gang lifestyle. This is not surprising given that gangs became especially prevalent in the 1950s (in Los Angeles) and expanded since then.[38] Also, confirming that gangs are clearly an American phenomenon. U.S.-born Mexican Americans were widely familiar with the gang lifestyle, but immigrants were less likely to be.[39] Interestingly, familiarity with the gang lifestyle increases in each subsequent generation-since-immigration for the original respondents. For the child generation, the children of immigrants were most familiar with gangs (77 percent) but familiarity remained quite strong (65 percent) among the third and fourth generation.

Table 6.10   Gang Knowledge and Involvement by Generation-Since-Immigration, 2000

	Original Respondents			Children		
	Gen. 1	Gen. 2	Gen. 3	Gen. 2	Gen. 3	Gen. 4+
Know about gang lifestyle	38%	55%	61%	77%	65%	65%
Family member involved in gang lifestyle	4	9	14	24	22	26
Respondent involved in gang lifestyle	3	6	6	12	14	10
Interviewer report of gang lifestyle	0	2	3	4	8	6

Source: Mexican American Study Project.

Similarly, involvement in gangs was greatest among the U.S.-born and persisted, if not actually increased, well into the fourth generation. Among the original respondents, the greatest percentage having a family member involved in the gang lifestyle was among the third generation (14 percent). Among the child generation, the fourth generation was the most involved (26 percent). We reach similar conclusions regarding whether the respondent was involved in the gang lifestyle. The later generations are the most involved, but their participation is not significantly different from the second and third generations. Finally, interviewers were given some training in being attentive to gang tattoos, clothing, and posture that might suggest involvement in gangs or the gang lifestyle. We recognize substantial subjectivity on this measure. Our interviewing staff found that none of the immigrant generation showed any signs of gang affiliation and that only 2 to 3 percent among the second and third generation of the original respondents did. For the children's generation, interviewers identified 4 percent of the second generation-since-immigration as gang-affiliated and 6 to 8 percent of the third and fourth generation.

Conclusions

Our findings show a consistent lack of economic progress across generations-since-immigration. Among the child sample, there is no economic assimilation, while there are indications of slight economic assimilation for the original respondents. Indeed, our statistical analysis shows that generation-since-immigration has no significant effects on any of the leading socioeconomic indicators for the child sample, once other variables, especially education, are considered. Indeed, education is the only variable to consistently explain variation in the socioeconomic status of Mexican Americans. We showed that years of schooling has strong significant and positive effects on occupational status, earnings, income, and wealth, independent of a host of other variables. Low education thus determines the economic exclusion of many Mexican Americans, a condition which often persists over generations. Even if returns to schooling in the labor market is similar to that for whites as much previous research has found, this is of little consolation to Mexican Americans, whose schooling tends to be lower. The die for the social disadvantage of Mexican Americans is cast during their educational process, which ultimately determines their position in the American social structure. Although the average socioeconomic status of the Mexican Americans is lower than that of the European American population we also found that there is a fairly wide distribution around the mean. At the top, more than 40 percent of Mexican American families earned more than $50,000 annually in 2000, which is a sharp improvement over their parents' income. However, their parents tended to have greater wealth, which they mostly gained from home equity, especially if they owned homes in Los Angeles.

On the other hand, nearly one-fifth of the younger sample and two-fifths of their parents were in poverty in 2000. For the child sample, their rates of poverty actually decreased a bit for Los Angeles although they greatly decreased in San Antonio. Moreover, a considerable number of the children sample admitted to having been involved in street gangs. Economic exclusion did not improve much overall from 1965 to 2000.

We showed that income inequality has risen since 1970 in San Antonio and especially Los Angeles.[40] The particular labor markets of Los Angeles and San Antonio that differed so dramatically in the 1960s may now have converged in being equally difficult places for less-educated workers to get ahead. These labor markets created more technical middle class occupational opportunities but at the same time expanded low-paying if white-collar jobs. Of course, immigrants are always more likely to be in the lowest level jobs. That said, many Mexican Americans are only slightly better off. On the other hand, the growing presence of immigrants, especially in Los Angeles, may also have improved the economic opportunities for Mexican Americans, who then fill positions as their supervisors, or they more generally benefited from the expanded economy, though these jobs often do not provide the incomes or security that middle class work had in the past.

Our data strongly suggest that underlying the increasing income inequality was an industrial restructuring that replaced manufacturing jobs in Los Angeles and military jobs in San Antonio with a growing private service sector in both places. The restructuring was particularly adverse for Mexican Americans in Los Angeles. It appeared to offer higher status and even higher real incomes through growing white-collar employment but earnings relative to Anglos arguably put Mexican Americans at a growing disadvantage. Any optimism that Grebler, Moore, and Guzmán had about economic equality and the future economic prospects of Mexican Americans in the 1960s has been blunted by conditions in the thirty years since their initial study.[41] Although Mexican Americans were able to leave the egregiously racist systems that kept them behind, especially in San Antonio, economic changes since then, along with the persistently poor state of public education, have kept them toward the bottom, as equal opportunities continue to elude them.

= Chapter 7 =

Interethnic Relations

Residential segregation and intermarriage have become primary indicators of the extent of social distance between race and ethnic groups. High levels of residential segregation and low levels of intermarriage mean that boundaries between groups are rigid, implying social isolation as well as high intragroup social cohesion. Under the traditional assimilation theory, residential segregation declines and intermarriage increases over time or over generations-since-immigration, a pattern commonly supported in empirically based studies.[1] In Gordon's formulation, the development of such primary group affiliations between ethnic groups, which he referred to as structural assimilation, "naturally" leads to assimilation on all other dimensions. Lower residential segregation and greater intermarriage are signs of greater acceptance and are expected to lead to interethnic interaction on many other levels, further breaking down ethnic or racial boundaries.

For Mexican Americans, and Latinos generally, residential segregation and intermarriage with whites has been moderate. Segregation is higher than the low (though highly fluid) level between white ethnics and WASPs, on the one hand, but lower than the near-apartheid separation between whites and African Americans, on the other. Residential segregation between Latinos and whites has increased since 1970, but this appears driven by immigration, in that places with high proportions of Latino immigrants are the most segregated.[2] Intermarriage between Mexican Americans and whites increased steadily from the 1950s to 1980.[3]

Based on the 1965 survey, Grebler, Moore, and Guzmán note:

> The options for Mexican Americans for social interaction and personal association with the outgroup have been enlarging over time. Progressive urbanization and movement into middle class status and out of the barrios into less-segregated neighborhoods have been important factors in this process. Also, the younger people seem to have more opportunity for developing relations with the dominant group than the older generation, or they have been more willing to seize the opportunity or both.[4]

Thus, the original survey found incipient social interaction with the dominant European Americans, a growing trend marked by greater exposure among the younger cohorts and growing social mobility. The authors attributed this limited integration to large-scale structural change, particularly in the form of urbanization and growing economic opportunities, though they noticed "reticence" among some Mexican Americans to move toward more integrated settings.

Trends in the social interaction of ethnic groups with dominant group members have been a central concern of American sociology. Since at least the 1930s, sociologists have documented that immigrants generally arrived to ethnic "ports of entry" in urban areas and rarely ventured beyond the ethnic community. The longer they lived in the United States, the more likely they were to increase contacts with non-ethnics, including members of the majority group. For the children and grandchildren of immigrants, interaction with coethnics became the exception as they melded into general American society. At least for the descendants of European immigrants, this has been the common pattern, which social scientists have largely discovered by examining marriage and residential patterns. These social dynamics are often referred to as marital and spatial assimilation.[5]

Available evidence for intermarriage and residential segregation suggests that Mexican immigrants and their descendants follow a similar pattern, though perhaps at a slower rate than other ethnic groups. In places like Los Angeles in 2000 and San Antonio in 1970 and 2000, greater delays might be expected, given the large size of the Mexican origin population in both places. Because Mexican Americans are such a large population in the two urban areas, their exposure to non-Hispanics may be especially limited, which further limits the formation of interethnic friendships and intermarriage. A large portion of each metropolitan area is composed of barrios (neighborhoods) that are mostly Mexican or Hispanic. Even with socioeconomic mobility and movement to suburbs, in both metro areas, many Mexican Americans often remain residentially segregated, and may be the majority in even lower middle class suburbs.

Segregation and limited intermarriage are the result of both the relative size of the group, social preferences and behavioral patterns of majority and minority group members. The relative size of groups limits the opportunities for interaction between two groups. For example, Mexican Americans in the 1960s were about half of the population in San Antonio but only 10 percent in Los Angeles. That may largely explain why San Antonio Mexican Americans intermarried less often and were more residentially isolated. Also, ethnic group members may decide to "be among their own" as they seek to live near ethnic institutions such as the church or ethnic grocery stores and close to other people who share the same language and culture. This is especially likely to be true among the immigrant generation but may also occur among those born in the United States. Third, economic status also limits where one can buy in the real estate market and affects whom one marries. Fourth, a wide range of discriminatory housing and real estate practices may limit where particular ethnic groups reside.[6] Last, prevailing racial attitudes and stereotypes among dominant group members may prescribe limited contact among racial or ethnic groups, which includes housing discrimination and taboos against intermarriage.

In this chapter, we examine residential segregation, intermarriage, and interethnic friendships among Mexican American parents and children across four generations-since-immigration. We also investigate the attitudes that our respondents hold regarding other groups. In particular, frequent social interaction with other persons who share the same language, identity, and culture is likely to reinforce ethnic behaviors and identities. Such interaction clearly occurs within the family as through intermarriage, but it may also exist in the public world, particularly in one's neighborhood, workplace, or in friendships generally.

A strong sense of identity and speaking Spanish regularly are more likely if one's friends, neighbors, and coworkers are of the same ethnic group. At the other extreme, Mexican Americans, or any other ethnics, isolated in a place where no one else speaks Spanish, would have less opportunity to speak Spanish or celebrate their culture. Moreover, interaction primarily with the dominant or other ethnic group is likely to dilute one's sense of ethnicity and perhaps strengthen one's American identity. On the other hand, arguments have been made that such interaction may reinforce the need to express ethnic identity.[7] At the same time that interaction shapes culture and identity, these also shape interaction—for example, those with strong identities and cultural affinities to the ethnic group may choose to marry a co-ethnic spouse and remain in a segregated neighborhood, even when the conditions allow for the opposite outcome.

Intermarriage and residential segregation are considered group indicators of the extent of assimilation. Specifically, they may be the most obvious indicators that ethnic boundaries are being broken down. If a large number of persons intermarry or live near non-Hispanic whites, then ethnic boundaries have softened. Throughout the past half century or more, sociologists have closely monitored indexes of intermarriage and residential segregation to investigate the extent to which groups are segregated from mainstream society and to detect trends over time. A high level of black-white residential segregation and a very low level of intermarriage between blacks and whites[8] reveal the extremely high and persistent segregation in American society. By contrast, levels of intermarriage were fairly low and residential segregation relatively high for most European immigrants when they first settled in the United States in significant numbers. With each passing generation, however, those numbers declined so that by the third generation, there was virtually no segregation among the various European-origin groups and between the dominant Americans of British or English descent.[9]

According to a spatial version of assimilation theory, immigrants and their descendants will integrate spatially with the dominant group and thus increasingly interact with, share the values of, and eventually identify with the dominant group.[10] Residential assimilation, according to its classic variant, is facilitated by achieving middle class success in the labor market. Alba similarly claims that the declining salience of ethnicity among European ethnic groups is related to the decline of white ethnic neighborhoods.[11]

Historical Trends in Segregation

The patterns of residential segregation for Mexican Americans in cities of the Southwest have their origins in the early twentieth century and, in some cases, the nineteenth century.[12] Mexicans lived in the towns of Los Angeles and San Antonio long before Anglo Americans arrived and continued to live near the old town plazas well after they became minorities. As successive waves of immigrants arrived from Mexico or migrated from rural areas or other cities, they would settle in the original sites or would begin new settlements in places that were often designated as Mexican towns. These were often properties that had little value or that served as labor camps for a particular industry. For many decades, a combination of class, ethnicity, and racial restrictions against living in many white neighborhoods would channel the Mexican-origin population into these barrios.

In the twentieth century, before the 1960s, legal and informal restrictions against purchasing or renting homes in particular neighborhoods were often raised for Mexican Americans in both California and Texas. These segregatory practices extended beyond residence and most notoriously to public schools and public facilities more generally. A high degree of educational segregation largely accompanied housing patterns but was also the result of administrative sorting of white and Mexican students into good and bad schools, respectively. Whether a consequence of residential segregation or of direct discrimination, school segregation would have a devastating effect on Mexican Americans throughout much of the twentieth century.[13]

Since the 1950s, social scientists have calculated overall measures of residential segregation by race and ethnicity, based on the census tract information from the decennial censuses. Table 7.1 presents two types of indexes that represent the extent of segregation between Hispanics and non-Hispanic whites. The traditional measure of segregation is the dissimilarity index. It represents the extent to which two populations are

Table 7.1   **Residential Segregation Between Hispanics and Non-Hispanic Whites, 1960 to 2000**

	1960[a]	1970[b]	1980[c]	1990[d]	2000[d]
Dissimilarity index					
Los Angeles	57	47	57[c]	61	63
San Antonio	64	59	57	54	51
Isolation index[e]					
Los Angeles	—	38	55	71	78
San Antonio	—	68	68	69	70

Source: Grebler, Moore and Guzmán (1970); Massey and Denton (1987); Iceland, Weinberg, and Steinmetz (2002).
[a] 1960 data from Grebler, Moore and Guzmán (1970).
[b] 1970 data from Massey and Denton (1987).
[c] 1980 data from Massey and Denton (1987) and Iceland, Weinberg, and Steinmetz (2002).
[d] 1990 and 2000 data from Iceland, Weinberg, and Steinmetz (2002).
[e] Massey and Denton (1987) and Iceland, Weinberg, and Steinmetz (2002) indexes for isolation differ. Massey and Denton report an isolation index of 50 for Los Angeles and 67 for San Antonio while Iceland, Weinberg, and Steinmetz report 60 and 70 for respective urban areas. Midpoint used.

evenly represented across an urban neighborhoods in respect to each other. It is easily interpretable because the value represents the minimum percentage of each of the compared groups, such as Hispanics and non-Hispanic whites, that would have to exchange residences so that each census tract had the same racial composition as the entire metropolitan area. Thus, the value is completely independent of an urban area's racial composition. The number varies from 0, which represents complete integration, to 100, which represents complete segregation. Neighborhoods, for the purposes of these indexes, are represented by census tracts, which average about 5,000 people in the U.S. Census. Low levels of segregation characterize the descendants of Europeans[14] and high levels characterize African Americans.[15]

The results for dissimilarity show that values for Hispanic-white segregation (Hispanics in Los Angeles and San Antonio are primarily Mexican Americans) vary from 47 to 64. These numbers put Mexican American segregation at the moderate level, though sometimes approaching the extreme.[16] Most interesting are the trends from 1960 to 2000, which are very nearly diametrically opposed in the two urban areas. Los Angeles' segregation increased each decade, with the exception of 1970, whereas San Antonio's decreased. San Antonio segregation in 1960 looks like Los Angeles segregation in 2000. Although we would expect a decrease in segregation since 1960 in response to increasing protections against discrimination in housing and greater mobility afforded to Mexican Americans since then, we find the peculiar opposite trend in Los Angeles, likely a result of large-scale Mexican immigration to the area since the 1970s. Massey and Denton found that the relative size of immigrant populations was directly correlated with levels of Hispanic-white segregation across urban areas in 1980 and our findings over time reveal a similar pattern.[17] Although it looked as if Mexican Americans began to integrate with Anglos in the 1960s, massive immigration reversed this pattern. Immigrants tend to settle in particular neighborhoods, presumably for cultural and economic reasons, and their numbers in Los Angeles began to dominate even among the Mexican American population there.

The bottom panel of table 7.1 shows the isolation measure, another easily interpretable index of segregation, albeit one that captures a different dimension. Whereas dissimilarity measured evenness of distribution in the urban area overall, isolation captured the individual experience of segregation. Specifically, the isolation index refers to the probability that an average Mexican American also lives in the same neighborhood or census tract as another. Isolation is greatly affected, as would be expected, by an area's racial composition. For example, Mexican Americans living in San Antonio can be expected to be much more isolated or living among themselves than those living in a place such as Dayton, Ohio, simply because of the size of the city's Mexican American population.

Table 7.1 shows Mexican American isolation varying from a low of thirty-eight in 1970 to a high of seventy-eight, both in Los Angeles. These numbers again reflect the strong effect of immigration in increasing the size of the Hispanic population. In Los Angeles, the residential isolation of the Mexican origin population skyrocketed in the thirty years from 1970 to 2000. A value of seventy-eight means that the average person of Hispanic origin in Los Angeles, the large majority of which is Mexican, lived in a census tract that was 78 percent Hispanic. This compares to the 1970 figure in which most of the average Mexican American's neighbors were Anglos. By contrast, more than two-thirds of the neighbors of the average Mexican American in San Antonio were coethnics, and that number increased only slightly in subsequent years. Increasing isolation in Los Angeles is hardly surprising given that the Mexican population grew from about 10 percent to nearly 40 percent of the total local population by 2000. By contrast, isolation remained flat in San Antonio through the forty-year period even though the Mexican population grew significantly.

This population growth seemed offset by the decreasing rigidity of residential boundaries as measured by the dissimilarity index. Between 1960 and 1970, residential dissimilarity, the extent to which race groups are unevenly distributed across census tracts, decreased as legal housing exclusions against Mexicans ended. The decrease in San Antonio reflects the erosion of discriminatory housing practices and perhaps the greater economic status of Mexican Americans. It continued to decrease in San

Table 7.2   Place of Residence by Urban Area, 2000

	Los Angeles	San Antonio
Original respondents		
Los Angeles County or San Antonio City	73%	96%
In other part of urban area[a]	12	3
In other part of same state (California or Texas)	7	1
In other part of West and Southwest	8	0
In other part of United States	0	0
Total	100	100
Children		
Los Angeles County or San Antonio City	61	81
In other part of urban area[a]	16	9
In other part of same state (California or Texas)	10	6
In other part of West and Southwest	10	3
In other part of United States	2	2
Total	100	100

Source: Mexican American Study Project.
[a] In Los Angeles, San Bernardino, Riverside, Orange, and Ventura Counties; in San Antonio, within thirty-five mile radius of San Antonio.

Antonio until 2000, but rose in Los Angeles over the same period. Places with more immigrants had greater segregation gains because immigrants seek out ethnic neighborhoods to facilitate settlement and are limited by their lower incomes from moving into integrated neighborhoods.[18] This was surely the case for Los Angeles, which had a much higher rate of immigration than San Antonio.

Of course, these changes are for the overall population of whites and Hispanics. Segregation in each census is not calculated for the same population, even though the internal compositions of these populations may have changed. Most notably, the generational composition of the Mexican-origin population shifted greatly in Los Angeles from 1970 to 2000 with immigration. We cannot control this with the available census data. Our data, however, unlike that based on the census, allow analysis of segregation by generation, which we do in the following section.

Where They Live Now

Our original sample was of residents in Los Angeles County and San Antonio City in 1965, many of whom continued to reside there in 2000 though some had moved out. Before trying to understand urban segregation in the two cities or among the respondents, we investigate the extent of dispersion outside of the two urban areas. Table 7.2 displays our results. The extent to which original respondents and their children migrated out of Los Angeles and San Antonio varies widely between the two urban areas. Moreover, some moved far beyond their limits.

Among the original respondents, 73 percent of the original respondents continued to live in Los Angeles County but fully 96 percent still lived in San Antonio City. Of those who left Los Angeles County, the largest number (12 percent) moved to other counties in the five-county greater Los Angeles metropolitan area, 7 percent moved outside but remained in California, and the remaining 8 percent moved to other states in the Southwest or West. For the 4 percent who left San Antonio, most remained within thirty-five miles around the city. For both the Los Angeles and San Antonio samples, virtually no one moved outside of the West and Southwest.

Only 61 percent of the children in the Los Angeles sample and 81 percent in the San Antonio sample stayed in the original sampled urban area. Fewer than half of those who left stayed in the original metropolitan area. A large number moved to other places in the West and Southwest. For the Los Angeles sample, almost half (10 of 22 percent) of those stayed in California. Of the San Antonio sample, slightly more than half (6 of 11 percent) of those leaving stayed in Texas. Unlike their parents, 2 percent of the children ventured into new regions of the United States. These include states such as New York, Maryland, North Carolina, Tennessee, Virginia, and West Virginia. As we showed in chapter 3, the movers were much more likely to be interviewed by telephone and in the regressions throughout the chapters the independent variable phone interview largely stands as a proxy for those who left.

Segregation by Generation-Since-Immigration

The composition of the average census tract for our sample by generation is shown in table 7.3. The top panel demonstrates how our sample is distributed across neighborhoods with varying percent Hispanic, the middle panel shows the average racial composition of their neighborhood, and the bottom panel shows the percentage immigrant. These numbers include those who left Los Angeles and San Antonio, as do the rest of the analysis. The top panel of table 7.3 reveals several important findings. First was a general trend of increasing residential integration and thus decreasing segregation by generation-since-immigration for both the original respondents and their children. For example, the first row shows that 25 percent of the first generation of original respondents in 1965 resided in the most integrated neighborhoods (less than 25 percent Hispanic) and that 32 percent of the third generation did. Similarly, in 2000, first-generation original respondents were less likely than the third-generation, and their second-generation children were less likely than fourth-generation to live in the most integrated neighborhoods.

Table 7.3   Racial and Immigrant Composition of Neighborhood[a] by Generation-Since-Immigration, 1965 and 2000

	Original Respondents, 1965			Original Respondents, 2000			Children		
	Gen. 1	Gen. 2	Gen. 3	Gen. 1	Gen. 2	Gen. 3	Gen. 2	Gen. 3	Gen. 4+
Hispanic origin[b]									
0 to 24.9 percent	25%	23%	32%	9%	11%	18%	21%	24%	36%
25 to 49.9 percent	16	28	29	22	24	30	25	31	25
50 to 74.9 percent	36	22	19	17	17	15	26	20	18
75 to 100 percent	23	27	19	52	47	37	28	25	20
Racial composition[c]									
Hispanic	54	52	43	68	64	55	53	50	44
Non-Hispanic white	36	42	50	21	23	30	31	36	39
Black	7	4	4	2	3	4	5	4	5
Other or Asian[d]	3	3	3	7	8	9	8	8	9
Immigrant[c]	16	15	13	32	28	26	25	23	21

Source: Mexican American Study Project; authors' tabulations of decennial censuses, 1970 and 2000.
[a] Census tract.
[b] Percent in each category.
[c] Average percent for group.
[d] Other in 1970 and Asian in 2000.

The second important finding is that residential integration decreased, or, to put it another way, that isolation increased between the 1960s and 2000 for the original respondents. Of first-generation original respondents, 25 percent lived in the most integrated neighborhoods in 1965, but by 2000 only 9 percent did. The same holds for the other generation groups. Similarly, only 23 percent of first generation original respondents lived in the most segregated neighborhoods in 1965 (75 percent or more Hispanic), which we can safely call barrios, but by 2000, 52 percent did.

The third but related finding is that the children of the original respondents lived in neighborhoods that were even more Hispanic than the ones they grew up in. For example, whereas 23 percent of immigrants lived in barrios in 1965, fully 28 percent of their second-generation children did in 2000. The pattern is similar for integrated neighborhoods. Some 25 percent of immigrants lived in the most integrated neighborhoods in 1965 but only 21 percent of their children did in 2000. Findings for second- and third-generation respondents compared to their third- and fourth-generation children reveal similar findings—of roughly no change at the extremes of most and least segregated. From this perspective of historical or family generation, which is the appropriate one for understanding actual inter-generational changes, there was virtually no spatial assimilation for Mexican Americans. In fact, this could be interpreted as dis-assimilation. As adults, the children lived in neighborhoods with as many or even more coethnics than where they grew up as part of their parents' household. This is particularly remarkable considering that some Mexican Americans have moved out of Los Angeles and San Antonio altogether.

The middle panel of table 7.3 reveals which other ethnic groups lived in the neighborhoods with our respondents. The first row mirrors findings from the top panel and shows that the average percentage of Hispanics in the person's neighborhood declines by generation-since-immigration. In other words, residential isolation for Mexican Americans diminished over generation-since-immigration, as the assimilation theory would predict, though the pace appeared to be slow. Among the original respondents in 2000, for example, the average third-generation Mexican American lived in a neighborhood that was mostly (55 percent) Hispanic. This compares to 68 percent of the first generation and 64 percent of the second generation. However, from 1965 to 2000, the average percentage Hispanic shows an increase in segregation for the original respondents. For children, there was little change in the residential composition of where they grew up compared to where they live now, although there were fewer Anglos and more Asians in 2000.

The middle panel shows that most of the non-Hispanic neighbors are white in both 1965 and 2000. Moreover, the presence of whites declined in this time period. Third-generation original respondents, for example, lived in neighborhoods that were, on average, 50 percent non-Hispanic white in 1965 but 30 percent white in 2000. On the other hand, the percentage of whites increases with each succeeding generation for both original respondents and children, while all generations-since-immigration lived near similar proportions of blacks and Asians. We suspect that integration with whites is mostly a result of the greater likelihood, with each succeeding generation-since-immigration, of moving out of the Los Angeles or San Antonio area altogether.

The bottom row shows that the average percentage of immigrants increased from 1965 to 2000 for both the original respondents and their children, reflecting the surge in post-1970 wave of new immigration. For the original respondents, the percentage of neighbors who were immigrants roughly doubled between 1965 and 2000. For their children, the percentage immigrant in their neighborhoods increased considerably. Of course, this included Asians immigrants, though Hispanic immigrants were likely to dominate. Immigration has clearly changed the residential experiences of later generations of Mexican Americans from 1965 to 2000 by re-Mexicanizing many of their neighborhoods but also increasing Asian composition.

Overall, our findings of no significant spatial assimilation may reflect that in Los Angeles there were simply many more segregated neighborhoods in 2000 than in 1965 and far fewer neighborhoods that are less than 25 percent Hispanic. Analysts may want to control for local circumstances, but the urban ecology shapes the neighborhood experience as actually lived and this has important social consequences.

We suspected that a significant amount of integration in 1965 was a Los Angeles effect and that in San Antonio at the time there was much higher segregation. As we can see from table 7.4, this was indeed the case. Respondents in Los Angeles in 1965 were most likely to live in moderately integrated communities (25 to 50 percent Hispanic) and those in San Antonio were most likely to live in moderately segregated communities (50 to 75 percent Hispanic). Similarly, the average percentage Hispanic in Los Angeles neighborhoods was lower (49 percent) than in San Antonio (56 percent). Respondents in Los Angeles and San Antonio lived in communities with the same percentage of blacks (6 percent) but Los Angeles had a higher percentage of other racial-ethnic groups. Also, Los Angeles communities had more immigrants in the 1960s.

By 2000, we find that original respondents in San Antonio end up in communities that are overwhelmingly Hispanic—74 percent lived in communities that were 75 to 100 percent Hispanic and only 1 percent in communities that were 0 to 25 percent Hispanic. In Los Angeles communities, on the other hand, the average percentage of immigrants was higher— 33 percent. The percentage Hispanic and Asian in Los Angeles has also increased since the 1960s—also indicating more immigrants. Even if Angelenos remained in the same neighborhood that was likely to be inte-

Table 7.4 Racial and Immigrant Composition of Neighborhood[a] by Urban Area, 1965 and 2000

	Original Respondents, 1965		Original Respondents, 2000		Children	
	Los Angeles	San Antonio	Los Angeles	San Antonio	Los Angeles	San Antonio
Hispanic origin[b]						
0 to 24.9 percent	25%	27%	17%	1%	31%	12%
25 to 49.9 percent	29	14	30	7	31	19
50 to 74.9 percent	20	34	18	17	20	23
75 to 100 percent	26	25	35	74	17	46
Racial composition[c]						
Hispanic	49	56	56	82	43	65
Non-Hispanic white	41	38	27	14	38	28
Black	6	6	3	2	5	4
Other or Asian[d]	5	0	11	1	11	1
Immigrant[c]	19	7	33	16	27	12

Source: Mexican American Study Project; authors' tabulations of decennial censuses, 1970 and 2000.
[a] Census tract.
[b] Percent in each category.
[c] Average percent for group.
[d] Other in 1970 and Asian in 2000.

Table 7.5   Key Determinants of Hispanic Neighborhood, 2000[a]

	Hispanic Neighborhood
Generation-since-immigration (ref: 3)	
1.5	−1.59
2	−3.14
2.5	−0.06
4+	−3.50
Education	−2.64***
San Antonio (1965)	14.26***
Proportion Hispanic in neighborhood (1965)	11.55**
Telephone interview (2000)	−14.13***
Any children under eighteen in household	−3.98†

Source: Mexican American Study Project.
[a]Only significant variables or substantive variables presented. Linear regression run. Unstandardized coefficients presented. Child sample analyzed. Adjusted for sibling clustering. See appendix B, table B.5 for full model.
†p<.10, **p<.01, ***p<.001

grated in 1965, it would almost certainly become more Hispanic by 2000 because of immigration. An equally likely scenario is that many Mexican Americans moved out from the barrio to more integrated suburbs or neighborhoods, though these also became increasingly Hispanic or immigrant.

The children from Los Angeles are likely to live in communities ethnically similar to those where they grew up. For instance, the average percentage Hispanic for Los Angeles respondents in 1965 was 49 percent. For their children, though there were more immigrants, it was 43 percent. The percentage white and percentage black remained relatively similar for the Los Angeles children, though the percentage of Asians more than doubled. For San Antonians, the presence of Anglo neighbors declined from 38 to 28 percent.

Factors Affecting Residential Segregation

As with the other chapters, here we examine the independent effects of generation-since-immigration and other variables on residential segregation through a multivariate analysis. Residential segregation is a continuous dependent variable represented by the percent Hispanic in one's neighborhood (that is, roughly speaking, the extent of residential isolation). We therefore run a linear regression and present the coefficients for the statistically significant effects in table 7.5.

The results for residential segregation reveal that generation-since-immigration has no statistically significant effect, after controlling for a series of other variables. Instead, the largest effects on the residential segregation of children are education and the characteristics of the neighborhood in which they grew up. A regression coefficient of −2.64 for education means that every additional year of education roughly translated into living in a neighborhood that was two and one-half percentage points less Hispanic. Education, the dimension in which Mexican Americans are most likely to suffer the effects of American racialization, also limits their ability to move out of the barrio, which in turn further reduces other types of assimilation.

A regression coefficient of 14.26 for San Antonio means that growing up in San Antonio leads, on average, to living as an adult in a neighborhood that is about 14 percentage points more Hispanic than it is for those growing up in Los Angeles in similar conditions. Also, the percentage Hispanic in one's neighborhood when growing up is apparently reproduced in adulthood. Respondents who lived in Hispanic neighborhoods in 1965 are more likely to live in Hispanic neighborhoods later, net of all other effects. This may have to do with a tendency to live close to parents[19] or where one grew up or perhaps to the fact that homes in barrios have accumulated less equity, which thus limits residential mobility for children. Respondents who were interviewed by telephone lived in neighborhoods about 14 percent less Hispanic than those interviewed in person. We treat this as a residential characteristic because telephone interviews were especially likely when the respondent moved out of the greater San Antonio or Los Angeles area. Last, having young children in the home made it somewhat less likely that the respondent lived in a neighborhood with more Hispanics, suggesting that such families make a greater effort to live in more integrated neighborhoods, where schools may be better.

Social Contact and Friendships

While contact across ethnic groups is often within neighborhoods, people also traverse the neighborhood boundary for work or for other reasons. Thus, residence solely does not circumscribe social relations. For this reason, we asked our respondents how much contact they have with other racial-ethnic groups and with particular groups of Hispanics. Table 7.6 shows the extent to which they claimed to have significant contact with other groups.

As expected, the large majority (71 to 83 percent) of our respondents had substantial contact with other Mexican Americans. For the most part, declines across generations were small. Contact with Mexican immigrants and with other Hispanics, though, decreases across generations-since-immigration for both parents and children. Just over half of the original respondents (53 percent) in the first generation, all of whom have lived in the United States for at least thirty-five years, had significant contact with Mexican immigrants. By the third generation, only 37 percent of the original respondents do. For our children sample, 56 percent of the

Table 7.6   Contact with Various Racial, Ethnic, or Immigration Groups by Generation-Since-Immigration, 2000[a]

	Original Respondents			Children		
	Gen. 1	Gen. 2	Gen. 3	Gen. 2	Gen. 3	Gen. 4+
Mexican Americans	77%	77%	71%	83%	82%	78%
Mexican immigrants	53	41	37	56	37	29
Other Hispanics	37	21	21	33	26	16
Anglos or whites	35	56	64	75	74	73
Blacks	11	15	17	31	26	21
Asians	6	9	8	26	20	16

Source: Mexican American Study Project.
[a] Based on question: How much contact do you have with [particular group]? Would you say none at all, a little, some, or a lot? Report "a lot" of contact.

second generation had much contact with Mexican immigrants, versus only 29 percent of their fourth-generation counterparts. We find similar levels of contact with other Hispanics—37 percent of first-generation original respondents versus 21 percent of the third generation, and 33 percent of second-generation children versus 16 percent of the fourth generation.

For the original respondents in 2000, contact across generations-since-immigration with whites and blacks increased. The original respondent sample shows the traditional assimilation pattern of growing contact with the dominant group, which is consistent with the findings for neighborhoods (shown in table 7.3). Original respondent immigrants have relatively little contact with African Americans and Asians, but it increases with generation-since-immigration, though it also reflects the greater likelihood of traversing residential boundaries, particularly for the U.S.-born. Moreover, they are age fifty to eighty-five by the time of the second survey and thus may be more likely to participate in senior activities that span neighborhoods and are more integrated.

For the children, the extent of contact with non-Hispanic whites is nearly at the level of contact for Mexican Americans. Although many of the children of the original respondents continue to live in mostly Hispanic neighborhoods, they nevertheless have substantial contact with Anglos. Moreover, this contact is essentially the same across generation-since-immigration. On the other hand, contact with blacks and Asians for the children decreases across generation-since-immigration, which may partly reflect the out-migration of the children from Los Angeles and San Antonio.

Because we suspect that the pattern of contact with other groups has much to do with the local racial composition of Los Angeles compared to San Antonio, we explore similar data by urban area. Table 7.7 shows that those living in San Antonio in 1965 and 1966 continued to have more con-

Table 7.7   Contact with Various Racial, Ethnic, or Immigrant Groups
by Urban Area, 2000[a]

	Original Respondents		Children	
	Los Angeles	San Antonio	Los Angeles	San Antonio
Mexican Americans	72%	83%	76%	87%
Mexican immigrants	45	39	47	32
Other Hispanics	30	11	31	18
Anglos or whites	53	52	74	77
Blacks	13	17	26	30
Asians	10	5	24	13

Source: Mexican American Study Project.
[a] Based on question: How much contact do you have with [particular group]? Would you say none at all, a little, some, or a lot? Report "a lot" of contact.

tact with other Mexican Americans than Angelenos did. This largely mirrors the racial composition of the two cities and, for the U.S.-born Mexican American population, also reflects greater residential isolation in San Antonio. On the other hand, those who grew up in Los Angeles continued to have more contact with Mexican immigrants, non-Mexican Hispanics, and Asians, again reflecting urban compositional differences and especially the greater influence of mass immigration from throughout Latin America and Asia on Los Angeles since 1965. Contact with blacks was nearly the same for those growing up in each urban area.

Although the extent of contact may reflect daily interactions, it says little about the meaning or strength of these relationships. Contact may range from colleagues to clients to friends. Table 7.8 provides information on the extent to which the friends of our respondents are of Mexican origin. This question was asked in the original survey in 1965 and asked again in 2000. It generally shows a diversification of friendships over time for the original respondents and by generation-since-immigration for all respondents in both survey years. The first row shows the percent with no or few friends of Mexican origin and overall it shows a fairly constant pattern of assimilation. In 1965, 8 percent of immigrants and 17 percent of the third-generation original respondents had no or few Mexican origin friends. By 2000, these proportions had increased to 18 and 26 percent. At the same time, just over half of the immigrants (54 percent) had only Mexican friends but by 2000 only 27 percent did. For the third generation of original respondents, there was virtually no change in the roughly 20 percent who had only Mexican-origin friends during the thirty-five years, though by 2000 more than that had none or few.

The long-term assimilation pattern suggests gradual assimilation, but even by the fourth generation, signs of ethnic persistence in friendships

Table 7.8   Mexican Origin Friends and Attend Latino Church by Generation-Since-Immigration, 1965 and 2000

	Original Respondents, 1965			Original Respondents, 2000			Children, 2000		
	Gen. 1	Gen. 2	Gen. 3	Gen. 1	Gen. 2	Gen. 3	Gen. 2	Gen. 3	Gen. 4+
Have Mexican friends									
None or few	8%	13%	17%	18%	26%	26%	25%	33%	33%
Half	—a	—a	—a	12	22	23	26	23	24
Most	38	55	63	42	30	30	29	31	29
All	54	31	19	27	22	20	20	13	14
Mostly Latino congregation	87	80	71	45	39	23	39	30	31

Source: Mexican American Study Project.
a Category not used in 1965 questionnaire.

continued. Fully 43 percent of the fourth-generation children claimed friends who were all or mostly of Mexican origin. At the other extreme, 33 percent had none or few, which suggests a slow but constant assimilation.

The bottom row of table 7.8 shows the proportion of our respondents who regularly attended a church with a predominantly Latino congregation. This information was collected in both surveys. Whereas a large majority (71 to 87 percent) of Mexican Americans in 1965 attended churches only with mostly Hispanic congregations, only a minority of original respondents (23 to 45 percent) and their children (30 to 39 percent) continued to do so by 2000. Interestingly, churches seem to have integrated though neighborhoods did not. These data for the proportion attending Latino churches shows an assimilatory trend over generation-since-immigration for both the original respondents and children. More notable, though, is the strong secular trend from 1965 to 2000 toward integration in the churches Mexican Americans attended. This may be due, as we show in the next chapter, to changes in religious preferences among the children.

Intermarriage

Another indicator often used to gauge the rigidity of social boundaries between Mexican Americans and whites is intermarriage. Intermarriage suggests a willingness by two ethnically or racially distinct persons to cross racial or ethnic boundaries. Clearly, cases abound of romantic love not held back by social convention. But they are less likely to occur when social taboos are strong. Marriage in such circumstances is even less likely. Historical trends showing increasing rates of intermarriage across ethnic groups suggest a softening of ethnic boundaries. Frequent intermarriage would invite questions as to whether ethnicity is even important for either group. On the other hand, persistently low rates of intermarriage are likely to indicate rigid ethnic boundaries.

Edward Murguía, compiling the findings of several studies of intermarriage involving Mexican Americans, found substantial variation over time and across places.[20] In San Antonio, only 5 percent of Mexican Americans in 1930 were intermarried, but by 1960,[21] that rate had climbed to 11 percent. The San Antonio rate rose from 11 percent to 16 percent in 1970.[22] In Los Angeles, intermarriage was 9 percent in the late 1920s[23] but had shot up to 25 percent in 1963.[24] Still other places, including those in New Mexico and Arizona, had rates that also increased over time although they varied by the proportion of Mexican Americans in the population. An ethnic group's presence in an urban area is key to intermarriage because it affects the chances of meeting a potential spouse that is or is not of the same ethnicity. In other words, one's chances of intermarriage are greater in places where there are many more persons from other groups.

Table 7.9   **Intermarriage by Generation-Since-Immigration, 2000[a]**

	Original Respondents			Children		
	Gen. 1	Gen. 2	Gen. 3	Gen. 2	Gen. 3	Gen. 4+
Intermarried	10%	15%	17%	18%	32%	38%
Anglo or white or other[b]	9	15	16	16	30	36
Black	0	0	0	0	0	0
Asian	1	0	1	2	1	2
Married to Hispanic	90	85	83	82	68	62
Mexican immigrant	46	17	10	23	10	3
Mexican, U.S. born	41	65	67	53	51	54
Other Hispanic immigrant	3	1	1	3	0	0
Other Hispanic, U.S. born	1	2	6	3	6	5

Source: Mexican American Study Project.
[a] Based on questions: Is your spouse (or last spouse): a Mexican origin person, a Hispanic that is not of Mexican origin, Anglo, black, Asian or other?; followed by: Is your spouse (or last spouse) an immigrant?
[b] Nearly all of "other" appear to be non-Hispanic white but were not identified in that category probably because Anglo used as response category.

The level of exposure to other groups is known in the intermarriage literature as propinquity.

Intermarriage rates are often based on the most recent marriages from marriage vital records and thus provide useful time series for understanding changing ethnic boundaries. They also permit making distinctions by age and gender. However, they are unable to indicate differences in other variables such as generation-since-immigration. According to assimilation theory, intermarriage should increase as persons of a particular ethnic ancestry are further removed from their immigrant ancestors. We calculate the amount to which our sample was intermarried based on the current or most recent marriages for those who ever married. Table 7.9 presents the race-ethnicity-immigration characteristics of the respondents' current or most recent spouse in 2000 for the original respondents and their children.

Table 7.9 shows that extent of intermarriage increases over generation-since-immigration. If we consider intermarriage as marriage to a non-Hispanic, only 10 percent of the immigrant original respondents were intermarried, versus 17 percent of the third generation, and 15 percent of the second generation. Among the child sample, 18 percent of the second generation, 32 percent of the third generation, and 38 percent of the fourth generation were married to a non-Hispanic. Intermarriage thus increased with generation-since-immigration but rose sharply from the original respondents to their children. Intermarriage almost doubled from immigrants to their children (from 10 to 18 percent) and more than doubled from the second-generation original respondents to their children (15 to 32 percent). Where 17 percent of third-generation original respondents intermarried, fully 38 percent of their children did. Intermarriage clearly increased from parents to children but residential segregation remained fairly constant. This probably reflects the fact that younger cohorts were increasingly likely to find marriage partners beyond their neighborhoods.

Nearly all of the 10 to 17 percent intermarried among the original respondents had married with non-Hispanic whites. Very few, if any, marry blacks or Asians. Among the children, the large majority of those who out-marry also married non-Hispanic whites. Marriage with non-Hispanic whites is partly explained by the amount of exposure they have to this group. The rarity of intermarriage with blacks, however, belies the thesis of residential propinquity. We suspect that the reason is that negatives attitudes about blacks, rather than simply the extent of social exposure to them, explain the lack of intermarriage. We explore that possibility later in this chapter.

Our U.S.-born respondents tended to marry other Hispanics that were also U.S.-born. Even among the immigrants, fully 41 percent married a U.S.-born Mexican. Another 46 percent married an immigrant. Because many immigrants might have married before immigrating and were likely to have had only this one marriage, we would expect a relatively large number to have been married to another immigrant. However, our sample includes immigrants who arrived in 1966 or before, when there were relatively few immigrants and when young adult Mexican immigrants were largely single males.

Perhaps more than any other variable, residential propinquity explains why rates of intermarriage vary and which groups intermarry.[25] The fairly low rate of intermarriage for Mexican Americans in places like Los Angeles and San Antonio may be because they comprise such a large proportion of the local population there and thus have relatively little exposure to other groups. Certainly, marriage may occur between persons who live in different regions of the country or of the world. Usually, however, people marry others in close proximity. Table 7.10 shows the extent of intermarriage in Los Angeles and San Antonio and reveals differences that largely reflect local racial composition. Only 5 percent of the original respondents in San Antonio are intermarried whereas 17 percent in Los Angeles are, which is not surprising given that San Antonio has long had a much larger Mexican population. However, despite the Mexican populations in the two cities equalized, the differences in intermarriage rates

Table 7.10   Intermarriage by Urban Area, 2000[a]

	Original Respondents		Children	
	Los Angeles	San Antonio	Los Angeles	San Antonio
Intermarried	17%	5%	37%	13%
Anglo or white or other[b]	16	5	35	12
Black	0	0	0	1
Asian	1	0	2	0
Married to Hispanic	83	95	63	87
Mexican immigrant	26	13	13	10
Mexican, U.S. born	53	76	43	73
Other Hispanic immigrant	1	1	1	0
Other Hispanic, U.S. born	2	5	5	4

Source: Mexican American Study Project.
[a] Based on questions: Is your spouse (or last spouse): a Mexican origin person, a Hispanic that is not of Mexican origin, Anglo, black, Asian or other?; followed by: Is your spouse (or last spouse) an immigrant?
[b] Nearly all of "other" appear to be non-Hispanic white but were not identified in that category probably because Anglo used as response category.

widened. Among the child sample in San Antonio, only 13 percent inter-marry but in Los Angeles, fully 37 percent do. Some of this might be explained by the fact that the marriages took place when social composition in the two cities was still quite different.

Table 7.10 also shows that Angelenos are somewhat more likely to marry Mexican immigrants. The difference is small, however, 13 versus 10 percent, and thus the figures do not come close to reflecting Los Angeles's much larger Mexican immigrant population. The big difference, though, is in marriage to Anglos. Among the children, fully 35 percent marry non-Hispanic whites in Los Angeles but only 12 percent in San Antonio. Given the Mexican proportion of the Los Angeles population in 2000, part of this might be explained by marriages having taken place in the 1980s or earlier, when there were fewer Mexican immigrants, the large majority of whom did not yet have adult children.

All this said, we remain somewhat skeptical of the common argument that intermarriage presents the truest or the ultimate sign of assimilation. In places like Los Angeles and San Antonio, where Mexican Americans make up a large part if not the majority of the population, high inter-marriage rates do not generally mean assimilation. In such contexts, sometimes the non-Mexican partner, who is generally white, may become

Table 7.11   Key Determinants of Married to a Hispanic, 2000[a]

	Married to a Hispanic
Generation-since-immigration (ref: 3)	
1.5	0.84
2	1.39
2.5	1.22
4+	1.11
Education	0.80***
Parent is non-Hispanic	0.19***
San Antonio (1965)	2.55*
Proportion Hispanic in neighborhood (1965)	3.02***
Telephone interview (2000)	0.53**
First marriage	5.17***
Age at first marriage	0.92***

Source: Mexican American Study Project.
[a] Only significant variables or substantive variables presented. Logistic regression run. Adjusted odds ratios presented. Child sample analyzed. Adjusted for sibling clustering. See appendix B, table B.6 for full model.
*p<.05, **p<.01, ***p<.001

integrated into Mexican American families. More importantly, most of the population does not intermarry. Even if there are significant rates of intermarriage, however, the progeny of such intermarriages will often assume a Mexican or Mexican American identity, as we will show in chapter 9. A related issue is the extent to which the children of such intermarriages are identifiable as Mexicans. The point for this chapter, though, has merely been the extent of contact that Mexican origin persons have with others.

Factors Affecting Intermarriage

We ran a logistic regression to examine which factors influence whether respondents married another Hispanic and present the results on table 7.11. Rather than regression coefficients, we present the more readily interpretable odds ratios for intermarriage. Like residential segregation, intermarriage is not significantly related to generation-since-immigration. Instead, the chances of marrying another Hispanic are more strongly related to the urban ecology of one's neighborhood of upbringing. Since the odds ratios for urban area and Hispanic neighborhood are greater than 1, this indicates that San Antonians and those growing up in more Hispanic neighborhoods are more likely to marry other Hispanics. On the other hand, those interviewed by telephone (generally those who moved out of the area) were significantly less likely to marry other Hispanics. These factors are all indicative of residence and reveal how residential propinquity or spatial nearness is closely tied to finding one's spouse.

Like the finding for segregation, education is also highly correlated with marrying a Hispanic in which more educated respondents are less likely to marry another Hispanic. The disproportionate number of Mexican Americans with low levels of education thus means that a relatively low number will intermarry. Again, the apparent racialization in education leads to low intermarriage, which stalls marital assimilation. Low education probably leads to being in more segregated areas and working among coethnics, which reduces exposure to potential marital partners of another ethnicity.

Having a non-Hispanic parent meant a much smaller chance of marrying a Hispanic: those with a non-Hispanic parent had less than one-fifth (.19) the odds of those with two Hispanic parents to marry another Hispanic. Being the product of an intermarriage thus very strongly predicts that the children will also marry a non-Hispanic. The control variables of whether this was a first marriage and the age at marriage were strong, as expected. Those married for the first time and who married younger were more likely to marry other Hispanics than those married at an older age or a second time.

Racial Attitudes

Feelings or attitudes about other groups might also explain the extent of intermarriage between groups. Such racial attitudes could explain the lack of intermarriage between Mexican Americans and blacks. We asked the respondents in 2000 if they would object to their children marrying persons with particular immigration characteristics. We asked a similar question in reference to marriage with whites and blacks. We show our findings on table 7.12.

In 1965, a large majority of the original respondents felt that marriage to blacks was "distasteful" (83 to 91 percent) and this percentage increased with generation-since-immigration. Much of this anti-black statement may be due to much racial turmoil nationally, including the Watts Riots in 1966, which disrupted the interviewing process in Los Angeles. By contrast, only a small minority (12 to 13 percent) found marriage to Anglos distasteful. By 2000, a far smaller proportion, though just over half of the population (51 to 57 percent) voiced at least some objection to marriage by their children with an African American. This suggests that antiblack attitudes have softened, though some analysts would argue that it is the expression of such attitudes that has become more socially unacceptable, not the attitudes themselves.[26] The findings for intermarriage in which both the parent and children generations almost never married blacks

Table 7.12 Object to Children Marrying Other Racial or Ethnic or Immigrant Groups by Generation-Since-Immigration, 1965 and 2000

	Original Respondents, 1965[a]			Original Respondents, 2000[b]			Children, 2000[b]		
	Gen. 1	Gen. 2	Gen. 3	Gen. 1	Gen. 2	Gen. 3	Gen. 2	Gen. 3	Gen. 4+
Anglos or white	12%	13%	13%	19%	14%	13%	20%	15%	13%
Asian	—[c]	—[c]	—[c]	41	40	32	45	36	37
Black	83	88	91	51	52	57	54	50	46
Mexican American	—[c]	—[c]	—[c]	3	1	1	2	4	9
Mexican immigrant	—[c]	—[c]	—[c]	7	18	21	15	25	25
Other Hispanic	—[c]	—[c]	—[c]	—[d]	—[d]	—[d]	20	17	23

Source: Mexican American Study Project.
[a] Report find marriage "distasteful."
[b] Report object "somewhat," "strongly," or "very strongly."
[c] Question not asked in 1965.
[d] Question not asked of original respondents in 2000 interview.

Table 7.13   **Object to Sending Children to Schools with Other Racial or Ethnic or Immigrant Groups by Generation-Since-Immigration, 2000[a]**

	Original Respondents			Children		
	Gen. 1	Gen. 2	Gen. 3	Gen. 2	Gen. 3	Gen. 4+
Anglos or white	9%	10%	5%	14%	12%	7%
Asian	12	21	13	22	26	21
Black	21	32	21	38	32	27
Mexican American	9	5	5	5	9	10
Mexican immigrant	10	17	17	16	24	23
Other Hispanic	—[b]	—[b]	—[b]	12	17	13

Source: Mexican American Study Project.
[a] Report object somewhat, strongly, or very strongly.
[b] Question not asked of original respondents in 2000.

suggests that social distance between Mexican Americans and blacks belie any claim that racial attitudes have improved. On the other hand, the antiblack attitudes are still considerably greater than antiwhite attitudes, which hovered around the 12 to 19 percent range in 1965 and in 2000. Thus, any voiced opposition to marriage is very low for whites but remains considerable when it comes to blacks.

These figures also reveal the extent to which Mexican Americans have historically distanced themselves from African Americans. Although leading "whiteness" scholars have argued that European immigrants and their descendants—especially Jews, the Irish, and Italians—became accepted as white, mostly because they were able to distance themselves from blacks and cope with their own low social status by seeing themselves as hardworking and morally superior to the negative caricatures of blacks.[27] However, the same does not appear to have allowed Mexican Americans to become white. In both 1965 and 2000, our data show that Mexican Americans created social boundaries from blacks while they were closest to whites, both in intermarriage and in racial attitudes.

In 2000, we also asked about objection to marriages with Mexican immigrants, U.S.-born Mexican Americans, other Hispanics, and Asians. Table 7.12 shows almost no opposition to marriage with other Mexican Americans, despite the surprising 9 percent of fourth-generation respondents. Opposition to marriage with Mexican immigrants was in most cases greater than opposition to marriage with Anglos. Opposition to marriage with blacks ranged from 46 to 54 percent, and opposition to marriage with Asians was also large—between 36 and 45 percent.

We also asked in the 2000 questionnaire about opposition to attending schools attended primarily by one or another of these groups. Table 7.13

shows that on this dimension, racial attitudes involving one's children are clearly looser than in intermarriage. The racial hierarchy remains much like that of intermarriage, where schools dominated by Mexican Americans are most preferred (only 5 to 9 percent oppose) and those dominated by blacks are the least preferred, in which 21 to 32 percent oppose. In the middle are schools dominated by Asians and at the higher end those of whites. Surprisingly, the child sample was more opposed to attending predominantly Asian or black schools than their parents. This might have been due to how salient the issue was to them, given that their own children were likely to be school age. Patterns across generation-since-immigration were usually inconsistent except that opposition to attendance in predominantly white or Asian schools seemed to soften and opposition to schools with Mexican immigrants seemed to harden as Mexican Americans became further removed from immigrant ancestors.

Conclusions

We have shown that the social interaction of Mexican Americans with European Americans usually increases with generation-since-immigration, which suggests an assimilation trajectory. On the other hand, residential and marital assimilation is slow. The persistence of mostly coethnics as neighbors and a preference for endogamy reveals much ethnic retention. Assimilation in terms of social exposure is so slow that even in the fourth generation most Mexican Americans continue to have Mexican-origin spouses, live in mostly Mexican neighborhoods, and have mostly Mexican-origin friends, though they report considerable social contact with others, especially Anglos.

Tolerance for members of other groups seems to largely reflect such interaction. Mexican Americans reported (as expected) the least social distance between themselves and other Mexican Americans, followed by similarly low to moderate resistance to Mexican immigrants, other Hispanics, and non-Hispanics. In fact, the social distance from Anglos notably declined with generation-since-immigration for the child generation, so that the fourth generation reported almost no objection to marriage or school integration with non-Hispanic whites. On the other hand, objections to marital or school relations with Asians and especially African Americans were considerably greater, though not as great as those reported by their parents in the 1960s.

Historically speaking, the extent of residential segregation the children experienced as adults in 2000 is much the same as, and in some cases more than, what they grew up with, as measured in 1965. The Los Angeles case, in particular, shows that that spatial mobility from parents to children over that period was offset by the large number of new immigrants. Although many Mexican Americans had moved to more integrated neighborhoods, those new neighborhoods tended to have growing numbers of Hispanics, especially immigrants. The surge of immigration to Los Angeles in the late twentieth century increased the ethnic isolation of Mexican Americans there and reduced their contact with other groups. Rates of segregation in 2000 were thus somewhat greater than those when they were growing up in 1965.

The extent of residential segregation affected the extent of intermarriage, ethnicity of friends and colleagues, and overall contact with other groups. This is apparent in urban differences, which we measured as the percentage Hispanic in the neighborhood and by Los Angeles–San Antonio differences. In this study, the large proportion of Mexican Americans in San Antonio limited social interaction with other groups more than in Los Angeles. Mexican-origin San Antonians have thus historically been more isolated among themselves, where they constituted roughly half of the population in both 1965 and 2000. On the other hand, rates of intermarriage were higher in Los Angeles than in San Antonio, which may reflect greater residential and occupational integration at younger ages. San Antonians, for example, continued to be less likely than Angelenos to intermarry. Contact with other groups and rates of intermarriage for our child sample roughly doubled compared to those for their parents, despite stable or growing segregation. This may be due to a growing acceptance of intermarriage and growing social interaction beyond one's neighborhood. Moreover, we find greater ethnic retention in San Antonio in terms of out-migration. Only about one-tenth of the San Antonio-raised sample compared to one-fifth of Angelenos left the area, which usually means migrating to a place that has fewer Mexican Americans, further enhancing interaction outside the group.

Our regression analysis revealed the dominant effect of greater education in increasing intermarriage and residential integration. In this analysis, generation-since-immigration had no independent effect. Apparently, it was mostly education that accounted for differences in Mexican Americans' social interaction with other groups. Thus we find that the low education of Mexican Americans perpetuates social isolation, thereby constraining assimilation. Low levels of education keep a large segment of the Mexican American population confined to barrios and limit their exposure to persons of other ethnicities, which in turn limits their opportunities for intermarriage, perhaps the ultimate test of real social interaction. Lower levels of education decrease the chances of moving out of a segregated neighborhood or the metropolitan area altogether. Further, as we showed in the previous chapter, low education limits mobility more than anything else, further precluding exposure to other groups.

= Chapter 8 =

Culture and Language

Mexican Americans are often believed to share particular cultural attributes associated with Mexican culture, such as the Spanish language, Catholicism, and pronatalist and patriarchal family orientations. These and other attributes are not only used to describe their culture, but also considered traits that distinguish Mexican Americans from other groups. Cultural differences in themselves do not, social scientists believe, define ethnic boundaries, but the traits clearly strengthen ethnic differences by making the boundaries "quasi-natural and self-evident."[1] Speaking Spanish, for example, marks one's ethnicity and may also strengthen one's ethnic identity. The extent to which such cultural markers persist over generations thus may signify the extent to which ethnic groups remain viable.

However, the assimilation perspective argues that cultural differences more than other differences of ethnicity are sure and especially quick to erode over time or over generations-since-immigration. This dimension is known as acculturation. For Gordon[2] and Park[3] before him, assimilation was mostly about acculturation, which each found to increase across generations-since-immigration. Gordon argued that though American society was largely pluralist on several dimensions and assimilation was often slow, it resembled a melting pot in terms of culture. Contrary to this, Huntington[4] warned recently that because Mexican Americans are resistant to assimilation, they could divide the United States into two languages and cultures and form their own political and linguistic enclaves, which he contends has occurred in Los Angeles and Miami. For him, retaining Spanish across generations, not learning English, makes Hispanics a threat to national unity. As we will show in subsequent chapters, this alarmist position is ill founded. For one, Mexican Americans, including Spanish speakers, are at least as patriotic to the United States as non-Hispanic white Americans.[5]

We expect that as Mexican immigrants spend more time in the United States, and as their descendants are increasingly distant from the immigrant generation, they are less likely to hold the cultural attributes of their

185

immigrant ancestors. Acculturation is likely to occur despite the dire pre-dictions of nativists such as Huntington. What is less clear is the pace of this change, which factors are responsible for cultural loss, what extent parental culture is transmitted to children, and whether recognizable cultural traits remain by the fourth generation. Gans's concept of symbolic ethnicity emphasizes that many third- or fourth-generation descendants of European immigrants may proudly proclaim their ethnicity but have little or no knowledge of their ethnic language or culture.[6] Mary Waters similarly argues that descendants of European immigrants can choose when to become ethnic or simply American mostly because they are essentially indistinguishable from native white Americans and their cul-tural ties to the ethnic culture have nearly disappeared.[7]

Ethnographic studies of the 1950s and 1960s portrayed Mexican Americans as living in an isolated peasant-like culture only gradually shifting toward Americanization.[8] In their chapter "The Tenacity of Ethnic Cultures," Grebler, Moore, and Guzmán found that the culture of urban Mexican Americans in the 1960s was quite different from that described by those earlier ethnographies.[9] They concluded that the Mexican American population ranged from "quite a few typical Americans" to "not very many who could be said to have a distinctive culture."[10] They found that the ethnic values, attitudes, and beliefs thought to hinder achievement were far less prevalent among randomly selected urban Mexican Americans than the previous studies on rural areas had suggested. On the other hand, they discovered an ethnic distinctiveness based on strong Spanish language and Catholic religious loyalty, which distinguished Mexican Americans from European-origin ethnic groups.

Language

Language is the most notable of cultural indicators. In the United States, despite a growing emphasis on multiculturalism, English is perhaps the most important marker of national identity and social inclusion. Even though English has never been the official language in the United States, many Americans understand that it is and that English-language fluency and an American accent delimits who is American. Those that do not speak English with near native fluency are excluded not only from sharing in com-munication with the mainstream but also from institutions that determine success, including primary labor markets and higher education. Moreover, English monolingual Americans often discriminate against those who speak another language, particularly those languages that are at all socially stig-matized as being associated with low class or perhaps rural status, even if people of high status are speaking it.[11] The mere act of speaking Spanish in public may exacerbate ethnic conflict and tension. Thus languages and the people who speak them are stratified in the minds of many Americans.

Scholars have noted how culture is constructed and constantly modified by people talking to each other, in which the language of that interaction is fundamental.[12] Communities generally have a language in common and linguistic distinctions often delimit important social boundaries. The use of a language other than English gives individuals access to an ethnic community and circumscribes members of the ethnic group, who share in a form of communication generally impenetrable by others and often the basis of shared identity.[13] Henry Hale argues that "communications barriers such as those represented by language differences will make it more likely that individuals find the boundary meaningful and will use the corresponding linguistic markers to make cognitive sense of the social world and reduce uncertainty."[14] Spanish in the United States, perhaps like other ethnic mother tongues, also signifies informality and intimacy to members of the ethnic group.[15]

The traditional straight-line linguistic theory of assimilation expects a nearly complete shift to monolingual English usage by the third generation, a pattern observed for most European groups in the United States.[16] Immigrants are generally most comfortable with and sometimes limited to speaking in their native tongue. This includes conversation with their children, the second generation, who learn English in schools and are socialized with peers in English. According to this perspective, the second generation's mother tongue skills are generally limited to what they learn from their parents, making them more comfortable with English. Sometimes they are monolingual English speakers, in those cases when parents know English and make little effort to teach the children their heritage language. In turn, many of the second generation are thus unable to teach their third-generation children the ethnic language. When they do speak the ethnic language, they generally make little effort to teach it to their children because they no longer perceive any benefits in doing so. Thus, according to the traditional assimilation model, the transition to English is virtually complete by the third generation.

Although the available evidence suggests that mother tongue knowledge in the United States clearly declines over generations-since-immigration, the pace of mother tongue loss is not universal and is sometimes but not always associated with economic gain.[17] Spanish-language maintenance, generally known as bilingualism, is known to be particularly high among Mexican Americans.[18] Among European and Asian origin groups, on the other hand, English monolingualism is widespread by the second generation[19] Nativists have raised concerns about the potential divisiveness of ethnic language retention and especially its use in public, even though they may recognize that English is universally learned by the second generation.[20]

Despite the traditional discouraging of mother tongue preservation in the United States, fluent bilingualism has several obvious advantages over exclusive use of English. Research evidence shows that bilingualism may be a positive force in cognitive ability, educational success,[21] and economic incorporation.[22] Portes and Rumbaut note how some immigrant parents in advantaged ethnic communities are able to communicate with children in their mother tongue, creating positive intergenerational bonds that allow them to successfully navigate the school systems and deal with discrimination.[23] For Portes and Rumbaut, though, Mexican Americans do not follow this path but rather another of "downward assimilation," in which the loss of Spanish leads to intergenerational dissonance and especially poor educational outcomes.[24] Through case studies of single sites, Matute-Bianchi and others have found that bilingual students generally fare better than speakers of only Spanish or only English.[25] In the long run, as Portes and Alex Stepick have shown, the economic success of Cuban Miami is in danger because many Cuban Americans are unable to communicate with the Latin American and Spanish-speaking clientele who have become such a staple of the ethnic economy's success.[26] Additionally in many other countries, bilingualism or multilingualism is common and valued.

Especially high Spanish retention for later-generation Mexican Americans and Hispanics generally is thought to be related to various factors, including the large size of the group, its geographic isolation, low rates of intermarriage, and growing availability through the media.[27] For the current generation, there has been an emphasis on the effect on Spanish-language retention of continuing mass immigration and the emergence of transnational communities.[28] Linton emphasizes that the Hispanic civil rights agenda since the 1960s, especially the Voting Rights Act and the Bilingual Education Act, was largely about preserving and valuing the Spanish language in the face of factors that work against bilingualism. These include the fact that many immigrant parents do not pass their language on to children for fear of discrimination, the lack of Spanish-language schools, the exclusiveness of English usage in most schools, and the growing English-language mass media.[29]

English Ability: Complete Acquisition by the Second Generation

According to Frank Bean and Gillian Stevens, many assimilationist theorists view English gain as a zero sum game or as the flip side to Spanish loss.[30] Our data will show that English is universally acquired by the second generation, but that Spanish is maintained by a significant portion of the U.S.-born population. Indeed, bilingualism is common and Spanish monolingualism is rare and virtually nonexistent for U.S.-born Hispanics. Before exploring Spanish language ability across generations, we investigate English fluency.

In our survey, roughly half of all immigrants among the original respondents reported that they are able to understand, speak, or read

Table 8.1   English Language Proficiency by
             Generation-Since-Immigration, 2000

	Original Respondents		
	Gen. 1	Gen. 2	Gen. 3
English well or very well			
Understand	51%	93%	96%
Speak	49	92	96
Read	47	85	92
Write	33	82	90
Average proficiency[a]	3.4	5.2	5.4
Los Angeles[a]	3.5	5.3	5.5
San Antonio[a]	3.0	4.9	5.2

Source: Mexican American Study Project.
[a] Response categories range from (1) not at all to (5) very well and (6) English monolingual.

English well or very well in 2000, as the first column of table 8.1 shows. By the second generation, more than 90 percent are. Thus, in the 1960s, the transition to English was almost complete for the children of immigrants. By the third generation, 96 percent are able to understand or speak English fluently, and more than 90 percent can read and write in English. The final three rows of table 8.1 summarize levels of English proficiency across generations-since-immigration, for the original respondents and separately for Los Angeles and San Antonio. This scale is an average of responses from "not at all" (coded as 1) to "very well" (coded as 5) and English monolinguals (coded as 6) to four questions regarding understanding, speaking, reading, and writing the language. English ability increases sharply from immigrants to their children and then levels off in the third generation for the original respondents. The generational pattern is similar for Los Angeles and San Antonio, though English fluency is somewhat greater in Los Angeles. These results are only for the parental generation, which was mostly raised in the 1930s, 1940s, and 1950s when many Mexican Americans had relatively little contact with American institutions, including schools.

For the child generation raised in the 1950s, 1960s, and 1970s, English proficiency is universal for the U.S.-born. All of the children completed the 2000 interview in English. That is, 100 percent of the children respondents were at least able to understand English well, which is not surprising as most of the literature has shown.

Persistence of Spanish over Time

The important issue in the intergenerational transfer of linguistic ability among Mexican Americans, then, is the extent to which Spanish is

Table 8.2   Spanish Language Proficiency by Generation-Since-Immigration, 2000

	Original Respondents[a]			Children[b]		
	Gen. 1	Gen. 2	Gen. 3	Gen. 2	Gen. 3	Gen. 4+
Spanish well to very well						
Understand	98%	89%	82%	89%	57%	46%
Speak	98	87	75	79	40	36
Read	91	42	33	43	19	11
Write	89	39	26	36	11	7
Average proficiency	5.3	3.9	3.5	3.7	2.8	2.3
Los Angeles	5.3	3.9	3.3	3.7	2.6	2.0
San Antonio	5.2	4.1	3.9	3.7	3.2	3.1

Source: Mexican American Study Project.
[a] Response categories range from (1) not at all to (5) very well and (6) Spanish monolingual for original respondents.
[b] Scale range from (1) not at all to (5) very well for children.

retained. English is universally acquired, making it not an issue among the U.S.-born. If Spanish is retained, we can assume that Mexican Americans are bilingual. If not, they are English monolingual. Table 8.2 shows that among the original respondents or the parental generation, a large number of the second and third generation understood and spoke Spanish. Three-quarters or more of the second and third generation could understand or speak Spanish well or very well, though only a third (33 percent) of the third generation could read and about one-quarter (26 percent) could write at that level.

Spanish-language retention into the second generation of the child sample seems to have remained nearly the same as it did for the second generation among original respondents. Fully 89 percent understood Spanish well or very well. However, the extent to which the third generation retained Spanish dropped considerably in comparison to original respondents of the same generation. For example, 82 percent of the third generation among original respondents could understand Spanish, but only 57 percent of the children could. As signs of further erosion, 46 percent of the fourth generation could understand Spanish, compared to 82 percent of their third-generation parents. In terms of speaking, reading, and writing, less than half of third-generation parents passed them on to their children. It seems that while these parents had Spanish-language abilities, the home language was more than likely to have been exclusively English. This suggests that the social context, at home and outside it, in which the third generation was raised was more Spanish-speaking before the 1960s. Nevertheless, the fact that nearly half of today's fourth generation adults

Table 8.3   **English Use with Family by Generation-Since-Immigration, 2000**

	Original Respondents			Children		
	Gen. 1	Gen. 2	Gen. 3	Gen. 2	Gen. 3	Gen. 4+
My parents spoke to me in English[a]	1%	6%	20%	13%	55%	67%
I spoke to my parents in English[a]	0	8	23	21	64	75
I spoke or speak to my children in English[a]	17	57	62	74	82	83
My children spoke or speak to me in English[a]	30	69	74	82	92	94

Source: Mexican American Study Project.
[a] Report speaking "mostly" or "only" English.

understand Spanish defies the three-generation assimilation model and probably far surpasses the experience of any other ethnic group.

The final three rows of table 8.2 summarize levels of proficiency across generations-since-immigration, for the entire sample and separately for Los Angeles and San Antonio. This scale is an average of responses from "not at all" (coded as 1) to "very well" (coded as 5) and Spanish monolingual (coded as 6) to four questions regarding understanding, speaking, reading, and writing the language. Spanish ability sharply declines from nearly universal fluency from immigrants to their children and then drops to a moderate amount in the third generation, at least for the original respondents. The third generation drop-off, though, is much stronger among their children's generation, with continuing erosion into the fourth generation. Although Spanish proficiency is the same for the second generation in the two urban areas, the language is preserved to a greater extent among the third and fourth generation in San Antonio than in Los Angeles. Despite greater societal openness to the use of foreign languages in the United States, Spanish is not being preserved as it used to be, in Los Angeles or San Antonio. The decline of Spanish use among the U.S.-born and its minimal use in Los Angeles contradicts the idea that bilingualism has a greater chance in a society with mass immigration from Mexico. On the other hand, greater Spanish loss is consistent with a hypothesis that social boundaries between Mexican Americans and the mainstream have softened in the post–civil rights era.

Table 8.3 shows English-language use, when the respondents were children and when they had children, based on their recollection. If one looks from top to bottom in each column, table 8.3 shows that English usage clearly increases with each family generation, independent of generations removed from immigration. Parents of the original respondents spoke relatively little English to their children, who were slightly more likely to speak back to them in English. In turn, the children were even more likely to speak to their own children in English and their children spoke the most English back to them.

This is consistent when comparing the original respondents to the child generation. Again, it shows a large change from the parental to children generation in language preference.[31] As children, very few original respondents spoke to their parents in English. Because they were children from the 1930s to the early 1960s, this especially low number suggests that Spanish language use was greater as one goes farther back in history. Even for the third generation, only one-fifth (20 percent) had parents who spoke to them mostly or only in English.[32] For the third generation of the children, this number was 55 percent as reported by the children and 57 percent as reported by their parents. Among these third-generation children, more than four-fifths (82 percent) spoke primarily in English to their own children, who spoke back in English 92 percent of the time. Finally, at the most extreme, 83 percent of fourth-generation child respondents spoke to their children in English and a full 94 percent of the fifth-generation children responded in English. In sum, though few of the immigrants spoke to their children in English, by the fifth generation, few Mexican American children were spoken to, or responded, in Spanish.

Figure 8.1 summarizes the changing extent to which parents spoke English to their children in 1965 and in 2000 for both parental and child generations. During their lifetimes, parents shifted to speaking more English with their adult children than they did when those children were young. This may reflect a growing use of English generally. Similarly, the children themselves were more likely to speak to their own children in English than their parents did at any time. Moreover, figure 8.1 shows that there was a generational shift from the 1960s to the present toward increasing use of English as more parents of the same generation speak to their children in English. For example, only 41 percent of third generation original respondents spoke to their children in English in 1965, but 62 percent did by 2000. However, fully 82 percent of third-generation children (children of the second generation) spoke English to their own children in 2000.

Other Linguistic Characteristics

Other linguistic characteristics provide outward signs of ethnic attachment and thus may heighten social boundaries, distinguishing the bearers of such characteristics as Mexican American or Hispanic. Those characteristics, such as the simultaneous use of both Spanish and English or an accent, may have positive or negative consequences. The extent to which

Figure 8.1   Spoke English to Children by Generation-Since-Immigration, 1965 and 2000[a]

Generation-Since-Immigration	Parents of Original Respondents[b]	Original Respondents		Children of Original Respondents
		1965	2000	2000
1	6%	11%	17%	———
2	20%	31%	57%	74%
3	———	41%	62%	82%
4+	———	———	———	83%

Source: Mexican American Study Project.
[a] Report spoke "mostly" or "only" English.
[b] As reported by original respondents.

Spanish and English are mixed—or, as some call it, "speaking Spanglish" or "code-switching"—may mark one as both Mexican and American or perhaps as neither, depending on the context. A speaker of Spanglish may be perceived as fluent in two languages, which marks them as both American and Mexican, or as unable to fully communicate in either, marking them as not fully American or Mexican. Alternatively, Spanglish speakers may be fluent in one or both languages but code switch as a signal of their Mexican American ethnicity or to signal intimacy, informality, or a common bond with listeners. On the other hand, the consequences may be quite negative. A study by Thomas Purnell, William Idsard, and John Baugh found that landlords consistently failed to return calls about inquiries from potential renters who spoke in Chicano English but regularly returned calls from those who spoke standard English.[33] For this, we asked respondents how often or whether they mixed Spanish and English in the same sentence.

Table 8.4   Language Use by Generation-Since-Immigration, 2000

	Original Respondents			Children		
	Gen. 1	Gen. 2	Gen. 3	Gen. 2	Gen. 3	Gen. 4+
Frequently mix Spanish and English[a]	19%	26%	22%	29%	21%	13%
Used both languages in interview[b]	22	34	25	26	10	5
Spanish accent when speaking English[c]	88	53	48	38	26	24
Answered interview in English[d]	52	88	97	100	100	100

Source: Mexican American Study Project.
[a] Self report of mixing language.
[b] Interviewer report of respondent speaking both languages.
[c] Interviewer report of accented English during interview.
[d] All children answered interview in English.

The first row of table 8.4 shows that 19 to 26 percent of original respondents in the first to third generations report that they sometimes or frequently mix Spanish and English. The second generation was the most likely to code-switch, perhaps reflecting their fluency and greater exposure to both languages. Interestingly, reported mixing of both languages remained high for second- and third-generation children. This may reflect a greater need to communicate in Spanish to a growing immigrant population in the 1990s, accompanied by a growing inability among later generation Mexican Americans to speak fluent Spanish. However, there is a significant drop in Spanglish from the third-generation original respondents to the fourth-generation children. By the fourth generation, only 13 percent of respondents continued to mix the two languages. By that point, most apparently did not know enough Spanish to mix with English.

The second row of table 8.4 reports, according to the interviewer, whether Spanish and English was actually mixed during the interview. Again, the second generation of the original respondents used mixed Spanish and English the most. However, among the children, self-reported Spanglish use and that reported by interviewers differed by generation. Interestingly, interviewers reported use of both languages among 5 to 10 percent of the third- and fourth-generation children, versus 26 percent of the second-generation children and 34 and 25 percent of the second- and third-generation original respondents. This is consistent with the decline in Spanish among third- and fourth-generation children.

On the other hand, the third row shows that interviewers reported that 38 percent of the second generation and 24 to 26 percent of the third and the fourth generation in the child sample continued to have Spanish

Table 8.5   Key Determinants of Spanish Proficiency, 2000[a]

	Spanish Proficiency[b]
Generation-since-immigration (ref: 3)	
1.5	0.73***
2	0.37**
2.5	0.32***
4+	−0.20*
Education	0.09***
Mother's education	−0.02*
Parent spoke Spanish to child	0.88***
Parent is non-Hispanic	−0.30*
San Antonio (1965)	0.36***
Female	0.13*

Source: Mexican American Study Project.
[a] Only significant variables or substantive variables presented. Linear regression run. Unstandardized coefficients presented. Child sample analyzed. Adjusted for sibling clustering. See appendix B, table B.7 for full model.
[b] Based on average proficiency reported on table 8.2.
*p<.05, **p<.01, ***p<.001

accents when speaking English (as perceived by the interviewer). This compares to accented English pronunciation among fully half of the second- and third-generation original respondents. The last row in table 8.4 shows the percentage of respondents interviewed in English. On the one hand, all of the children answered the English questionnaire. On the other, completing the interview among the original respondents varied by generational status—half of first generation original respondents completed our interview in Spanish, but only a handful among the second and third generation did so.

Factors Affecting Spanish Proficiency

To examine which factors affect Spanish proficiency, we conducted a regression analysis. We ran a linear regression, because this is a continuous variable, and present unstandardized coefficients for significant independent variables in table 8.5. Generational status is a significant predictor of Spanish-language proficiency. There is a constant decline across the five generations or subgenerations in Spanish proficiency, suggesting slow but linear language shift. Each generation is less proficient in Spanish than the generation or half-generation before, all at a statistically significant level when compared to the third generation. This mirrors the results of the bivariate analysis: linguistic assimilation occurs independently of all the variables in the models.

A perusal of the other independent variables reveals several interesting findings. More educated children are more likely to know Spanish; however, the bivariate relationship between speaking Spanish and education is not significant (analysis not shown here). Rather, the regression analysis makes the relationship between Spanish proficiency and education stronger and significant. This occurs after we control for the negative relationship between mother's education and Spanish proficiency. In other words, children with less educated parents are more likely to speak Spanish. Once we control for this, however, children with more education themselves have higher Spanish proficiency—possibly indicating that more educated persons are more likely to learn Spanish as part of their schooling.

Additionally, having been spoken to as a child in Spanish is, not surprisingly, an especially strong predictor of Spanish proficiency.[34] Having a non-Hispanic parent meant that one was less likely to be Spanish proficient. San Antonians are clearly more likely to know Spanish, independent of all other effects. This may reflect more rigid ethnic boundaries there, where the worlds of Anglos and Mexicans may be more separated. This is consistent with the prior findings of greater endogamy in marriages and more residential segregation (chapter 7), suggesting more ethnically isolated social relations in San Antonio. Interestingly, the extent of segregation in one's neighborhood when growing up had no effect on Spanish-language proficiency. San Antonio seems to be more of a Spanish-language context than Los Angeles for U.S.-born Mexican Americans. The extent of neighborhood segregation in each places is less important.

Birth Names

In contrast to language use in everyday life is the important and rare event of naming a child. For immigrants and their descendants, first names can be a powerful indicator of cultural assimilation in that they can be used to quantify the competing influences of two cultures. According to assimilation theories and at least three studies, immigrants and their descendants are less likely to choose ethnic names for their children as they become more exposed to their new society.[35] We suspect that for Mexican Americans, a similar process of increasing use of English names occurs over generations along with a loss in Spanish proficiency. However, naming is different in that it does not require a long-term investment, which learning or teaching a language does. Parents can easily give a Spanish name without teaching the child Spanish or being fluent. Naming may capture a parent's feelings or preferences for Spanish or English. Thus, by itself, Spanish naming is more a transfer of symbolic ethnicity than teaching the child to be ethnic. Of course, there may be various reasons for bestowing a Spanish name on a child. Parental choice may range from the belief that an ethnic

**Table 8.6   Spanishness of Birth Names
by Generation-Since-Immigration, 2000**

	Original Respondents			Children		
	Gen. 1	Gen. 2	Gen. 3	Gen. 2	Gen. 3	Gen. 4+
Spanish, not translatable (5)	43%	33%	24%	20%	8%	10%
Spanish, translatable (4)	41	31	29	39	26	16
(Spanish)	(84)	(64)	(53)	(59)	(34)	(26)
Language neutral (3)	10	16	15	15	16	24
English, translatable (2)	5	16	25	22	39	42
English, not translatable (1)	1	4	7	3	11	7
(English)	(6)	(20)	(32)	(25)	(50)	(50)
Total	100	100	100	100	100	100
Average score of Spanishness (1–5)[a]	4.2	3.7	3.4	3.5	2.8	2.8

Source: Mexican American Study Project.
[a] Five categories range scale of (1) English names not translatable into Spanish (Ashley, Bruce), (2) English names translatable (Marie, Michael), (3) language neutral names (Andrea, Daniel), (4) Spanish names translatable (Maria, Miguel), and (5) Spanish names not translatable (Guadalupe).

name will establish a strong ethnic identity in the child to the belief that a non-ethnic name will improve a child's acceptance in the host society. Although parents may choose from a wide variety of names, their choices are in reality shaped by social and cultural influences. Finally, birth names have obvious long-term consequences: as labels, they influence the socialization of children and contribute to the development of personal identities.

In our 2000 survey, we asked both the original respondent and children samples what their name was on their birth certificate. With this information, we coded all of the first names into five categories that seek to capture a continuum of English to Spanish names. The first category represents the most English names and the last represents the most Spanish. Specifically, category 1 refers to English names that are not translatable into Spanish (such as Ashley and Bruce), category 2 includes English names that are translatable (Marie, Michael), category 3 to language neutral names (Daniel, Andrea), category 4 to translatable Spanish names (Maria, Miguel), and category 5 to not translatable Spanish names (Guadalupe). These names were coded 1 to 5 by a panel of bilingual persons.[36]

The first row of table 8.6 shows that, among the original respondents, fully 43 percent of immigrants were given untranslatable Spanish names, versus 33 percent of the second and 24 percent of the third generation. Among their children, fully 20 percent of the second generation received such names, but only 8 percent of the third generation and about the same amount in the fourth generation (10 percent) did. In comparing similar generations-since-immigration between parents and children, table 8.6 reveals a sizable drop over time in parents giving such names.

At the other end of the continuum, only 1 percent of immigrant original respondents had English untranslatable names (1) and fewer than 10 percent of the U.S.-born received them. More common are English names that are translatable into Spanish (2). These account for 16 and 22 percent of names for second-generation respondents, 25 percent of the third-generation original respondents, and 39 to 42 percent of the third- and fourth-generation children. If one adds up all English names (excluding the neutral names), the tendency for assimilation is clear. For the original respondents, such names go from 6 percent in the first generation to 32 percent in the third, and from 25 percent in the second to 50 percent for their children in the fourth generation. Clearly Spanish names (4 and 5) accounted for decreasing percentage of all names over the generations, though 26 percent of the fourth generation continued to have Spanish names. Although the trend is unmistakably toward English, the persistence into the fourth generation of names that have some tie with Spanish language demonstrates the endurance of ethnicity at least at this level.

The final row of table 8.6 shows the average score of how Spanish names were, which is the mean score on the 1 to 5 scale of names, by generation. This summary measure indicates gradual assimilation across generations in naming and shows that the original respondents, born and thus named between 1915 and 1948, were given more Spanish names than their children, who were born between 1946 and 1966. Specifically, the immigrant generation has very Spanish names, and score on average 4.2 out of 5, whereas the second- and third-generation original respondents score 3.7 and 3.4 (shown in the last row of table 8.6). For the children, scores range from 3.5 in the second generation to 2.8 in the fourth, revealing linguistic change but with a slight tilt remaining toward the Spanish side of the names continuum, fully four generations in the United States.

To examine which factors affect naming in Spanish, we conducted a regression analysis on this variable. We ran a linear regression, because this is a continuous variable, and present unstandardized coefficients for significant independent variables in table 8.7. Generational differences in the tendency for naming are significant. Certainly, those born in Mexico (1.5 generation) as well as the second generation and the 2.5 generation were more likely to have Spanish names. Only the third and fourth generation do not differ from each other in this regard. A perusal of the other independent variables reveals several interesting findings. Children of parents with lower education tend to be given Spanish names. Having a

Table 8.7   Key Determinants of Spanish Birth Name, 2000[a]

	Spanish Birth Name[b]
Generation-since-immigration (ref: 3)	
1.5	0.80***
2	0.52**
2.5	0.58***
4+	0.11
Father's education	−0.06***
Mother's education	−0.02*
Parent is non-Hispanic	−0.38*
Parents were married	−0.23†
San Antonio (1965)	0.39**

Source: Mexican American Study Project.
[a] Only significant variables or substantive variables presented. Linear regression run. Unstandardized coefficients presented. Child sample analyzed. Adjusted for sibling clustering. See appendix B, table B.8 for full model.
[b] Education not included in this model.
†p<.10, *p<.05, **p<.01, ***p<.001

non-Hispanic parent meant that one was less likely to be given a Spanish name. San Antonians are clearly more likely to have Spanish names independent of all other effects.

Religion and Religiosity

Aside from language, perhaps the cultural trait most associated with Mexican Americans has been Catholicism, which also serves as a marker distinguishing Mexican Americans from most other ethnic groups. Many of the poorest and most despised Europeans, particularly the Irish, Italians, and Poles, were strongly Catholic. However, their children and grandchildren seem to have moved to a more secular mindset.[37] Whether Mexican Americans similarly choose to "adopt American ideals of individualism" and a quest for prosperity in place of "religious ideals of community," as a recent *New York Times* article put it, is not clear.[38] The data on such a trend is not clear for any group, especially since the U.S. Census has not collected data on religion since 1950. Several national surveys of religion, though, were taken between 1991 and 2004. Catholics have comprised about one-quarter (23 to 26 percent depending on the estimate and the year) of all Americans, and about one-third of American Catholics are Hispanic.[39]

Finke and Stark stress the vitality and growth of Catholicism throughout American history.[40] However, they raise the concern that Catholicism may become like other mainline religions with a declining membership base. They note that Hispanic immigration has not helped Catholic expansion as much as many have expected because many Hispanic immigrants have

Table 8.8   **Religion and Religiosity by Generation-Since-Immigration, 1965 and 2000**

	Original Respondents, 1965			Original Respondents, 2000			Children, 2000		
	Gen. 1	Gen. 2	Gen. 3	Gen. 1	Gen. 2	Gen. 3	Gen. 2	Gen. 3	Gen. 4+
Catholic	91%	90%	86%	81%	82%	84%	72%	67%	58%
Attend church weekly	61	44	49	54	52	47	36	33	25

Source: Mexican American Study Project.

converted to evangelical religions and their children are even more likely to not be Catholic. Noting widely inconsistent estimates of the religious identities of Hispanics among national surveys, Paul Perl, Jennifer Greely, and Mark Gray find several methodological problems with them and argue that the most reliable estimates reveal that about 70 percent of Hispanics are Catholics and another 20 percent are Protestant.[41] Based on these cross-sectional surveys, they further estimate a downward shift in the proportion of U.S.-born Catholic Hispanics from 74 percent in the first to about 50 percent in the third generation. Espinosa and colleagues find a smaller decline from 74 to 62 percent across the three generations.[42] Religion is also related to politics, as 63 percent of Hispanic Protestants voted for Bush, compared to only 31 percent of Hispanic Catholics.[43]

Our data reveal a similar pattern across generations-since-immigration but also show that historical changes may be even more important. Among original respondents in 1965, about 90 percent of Mexican Americans were Catholic, with 91 percent of immigrants being Catholic and only slight religious assimilation in succeeding generations. By 2000, an additional 8 to 10 percent of the original respondents were no longer Catholic in the first and second generation, while there was relatively little decline for the third generation, as table 8.8 demonstrates.

Many fewer children, though, were Catholic. Generational differences had also become large, suggesting the emergence of religious accultura-tion. Among the second generation, only 72 percent were Catholic, versus 90 percent of second-generation original respondents were when they were young. By the fourth generation, only 58 percent were Catholic, though they were generally raised in households where 86 percent of their original-respondent parents were Catholic. Additionally, from 1965 to 2000, there is a sharpening of differences by generation-since-immigration between original respondents and their children for the entire Mexican American population. These results would have been startling to the inves-

Table 8.9   Detailed Religion by Generation-Since-Immigration, 2000

	Original Respondents			Children		
	Gen. 1	Gen. 2	Gen. 3	Gen. 2	Gen. 3	Gen. 4+
Catholic	81%	82%	84%	72%	67%	58%
Non-Catholic	19	18	16	28	33	42
Evangelical or fundamentalist[a]	13	12	12	17	22	26
Other[b]	5	3	3	4	4	7
No religion	2	2	1	8	6	9

Source: Mexican American Study Project.
[a] Also includes non-denominational Christian.
[b] Other includes mainline Protestant, Church of Latter-Day Saints, Jehovah's Witnesses, Jewish, New Age, Native American.

tigators of the original project, who were particularly interested in the role of the Catholic Church. Grebler, Moore, and Guzmán interviewed parish priests and reported that "no pastor interviewed seems to take Protestant proselytizing seriously."[44] The same religious shift among the general American (and Latin American) Catholic and Protestant religions to evangelicalism might have been similarly surprising, however.

To be sure, some Catholics are Catholic in name only. They were baptized as Catholics and may continue to have a Catholic identity, but rarely practice their religion. More generally, however, Hispanics are believed to be religious as well as predominantly Catholic. Table 8.8 demonstrates the extent to which this is true by measuring religiosity and, more specifically, the proportion who attended religious services at least once per week, regardless of their religion. Like the question on religious identity, a question on religiosity was asked in both the 1965 and the 2000 surveys.

Whereas changes in church attendance from 1965 to 2000 were mixed for original respondents, table 8.8 also demonstrates that religiosity dropped across the board from the parents to the children's generation. Only 25 to 36 percent of children among those who declared they belonged to a religion were regular church-goers, versus 44 to 61 percent of their parents. Also, generation-since-immigration differences sharpened for children, which mirrors the intergenerational findings for Catholic affiliation. For example, where 36 percent of the second generation attended church weekly, only 25 percent of the fourth generation did. Among the original respondents, the percent who attended church weekly dropped from the first generation (61 percent) to the second generation (44 percent), but then it leveled off in the third generation (49 percent).

Table 8.9 shows that the decline in the number of Catholics since the 1960s and across generations was due mostly to the countertrend in the growing proportion that joined evangelical or fundamentalist Christian religions. About 12 or 13 percent of the original respondents and 17 to 26 percent of their children claimed such religions in 2000. The greatest indicators of religious assimilation is that 22 percent of the third generation among children, and fully 26 percent of the fourth generation were evangelical or fundamentalist Christians. These shifts clearly reflect the growing importance of these religions among working class white Americans in the Southwest whom many Mexican-Americans marry or live near. Religious assimilation is also demonstrated by a relatively large number of fourth-generation Mexican Americans in other religions or with no religious affiliation whatsoever.

Fertility

The tremendous growth of the Mexican-origin population in the United States throughout the twentieth century is generally attributed to immigration. A large component of that growth, however, is also related to relatively high fertility (or childbirth) by Mexican American women, both immigrant and U.S.-born.[45] For most of the past few decades, Mexican Americans have registered fertility levels between those for Mexico and the United States. These have been among the highest of any major racial-ethnic group in the United States. This is consistent with a large immigrant component of the Mexican-origin population who came from a high fertility country (until recently). However, despite controls for nativity and a host of other possible structural explanations, including age and socioeconomic status, higher Mexican American fertility—in relation to the rest of the American population—persists into the third generation. This has led to a largely accepted explanation that Mexican Americans retain the strong pro-natalist values of Mexican culture.[46] In other words, fertility is directly associated with an assortment of economic and social variables, but at least part of this is due to persistently distinct Mexican American cultural values.[47]

However, a fertility rate of 2.9 in 2000 is now higher than in Mexico, which experienced one of the world's fastest drops in total fertility (an age-standardized number of children per women) from 7.3 in 1960 to 2.4 in 2000.[48] Ironically, Mexico's fertility rate is approaching the United States' rate of 2.4, which declined from its high of 3.8 during the baby boom in the 1950s.[49] The U.S.-born Mexican-origin population has a fertility rate that is lower than immigrants but higher than those of the general United States population.[50] Moreover, Reanne Frank and Patrick Heuveline find more children being born to the third generation at earlier ages and out of wedlock than to immigrants or the general United States population, a pattern similar to that found for African American women. As a result of these findings, they argue that a racialization explanation resulting from a precarious socioeconomic position better explains Mexican American fertility than the cultural argument that Mexicans are pro-natalist in orientation and with time will culturally conform to American childbearing behaviors.

Table 8.10   Children Ever Born and Siblings by Generation-Since-Immigration, 2000

	Original Respondents			Children		
	Gen. 1	Gen. 2	Gen. 3	Gen. 2	Gen. 3	Gen. 4+
Number of children ever born[a]	5.2	4.6	5.0	2.5	2.7	2.5
Number of siblings[b]	6.0	5.6	5.6	5.5	4.3	4.5

Source: Mexican American Study Project.
[a] Women over age forty-five.
[b] All respondents.

Because our sample size is relatively small, especially when the age range was restricted, we were unable to analyze fertility rates in detail. Instead, we examined the number of children ever born in table 8.10, as reported by our female respondents forty-five years old and older, when they had completed virtually all of their childbearing.[51] We found few generational differences in the number of children ever born among either original respondents or children. Immigrant fertility was a little higher than for the second generation among the original respondents, which in turn was lower than it was for the third generation. Among children, fertility was cut by about half of their parents', reflecting the overall national trend from baby boom to baby bust. Moreover, there were no significant differences by generation. The number of children ever born for mothers who had completed their fertility was 2.5 or 2.7 for all the U.S.-born of the children's generation, which includes second, third, and fourth generation-since-immigration and is exactly the same as that for forty- to forty-four-year-old second- and third-generation Mexican Americans based on the 1998 to 2002 Current Population Survey.[52]

We also asked respondents to report the number of brothers and sisters they had, including any who had died. The second row of table 8.10 shows the number of siblings for our respondents, which reflects their parents' fertility experiences, combined with results in the first row, approximates the experiences of three family generations. Fertility declined precipitously across the generations. The original respondents averages about five children, compared to about two and one-half for their children. The number of siblings also reveals relatively high fertility for the original respondents and their parents.[53] Results for number of children among the original respondents and the siblings among the children were consistent and reveal greater fertility for the third generation among original respondents. For generation-since-immigration, sibling results were like those for number of children. In sum, the findings again reveal somewhat greater fertility for immigrants and declining fertility from grandparents to parents to children.

Table 8.11   **Key Determinants of Children Ever Born, 2000**[a]

	Children Ever Born
Generation-since-immigration (ref: 3)	
1.5	−0.24
2	−0.12
2.5	0.16*
4+	0.03
Education	−0.08***
Age	0.01*

Source: Mexican American Study Project.
[a] Only significant variables or substantive variables presented. Poisson regression run. Unstandardized coefficients presented. Child sample analyzed. Adjusted for sibling clustering. See appendix B, table B.9 for full model.
*p<.05, ***p<.001

To examine which factors affect the number of children ever born, we conducted a regression analysis, using a poisson model because this is an ordinal variable. We present unstandardized coefficients for significant independent variables in table 8.11. Generational differences in fertility were not significant with the exception of generation 2.5 having significantly more children than the third generation. The one strong predictor of fertility is education—with more educated women having fewer children. Age was also significant in that older women had more children, which is expected given that childbearing decreased sharply from the 1970s to the 1990s.[54]

Family Values

Pro-natalist values are commonly thought to operate in tandem with traditional family roles. Early research blamed rigid and authoritarian families for the slow socioeconomic progress of Mexicans and Mexican Americans.[55] In particular, male dominance over the family and rigid gender roles were thought to prevent positive personality development and hinder individual achievement and mobility, though they were believed to provide emotional and economic security. In his review of these studies, Alfredo Mirandé did not so much argue that this portrait of Chicano familism was inaccurate as that it had features that have served Mexican Americans well, in large part by providing refuge from oppressive American economic and cultural colonialism.[56] Moreover, such a model could not be generalized to the entire Mexican American population, because Mexican familism had been largely eroded because of acculturation and urbanization.[57] On the other hand, Mirandé argued that the traditional family and familistic values

Table 8.12   Attitudes About Gender and Family by
             Generation-Since-Immigration, 2000[a]

	Original Respondents			Children		
	Gen. 1	Gen. 2	Gen. 3	Gen. 2	Gen. 3	Gen. 4+
Gender						
Women dependent[b]	78%	63%	62%	58%	41%	33%
Men's authority[c]	42	27	21	18	15	8
Family						
Children can disagree[d]	34	37	47	41	45	36
Individual responsibility[e]	38	27	24	20	15	16

Source: Mexican American Study Project.
[a] Report "agree" or "strongly agree."
[b] Item is "Girls should live at home until married."
[c] Item is "Men should have last word."
[d] Item is "It is ok for children to disagree with parents."
[e] Item is "Each person should be responsible for themselves, not rely on family."

have been largely maintained into later generations because of proximity
to Mexico and because they have served to shield children from an oppressive social world.

This celebration of patriarchal values and familism among Mexican
Americans was subsequently criticized by Chicana feminists. Maxine
Baca Zinn and Lea Ybarra were among the first to take Mirandé to task
because he had not adequately considered the structural factors affecting
Mexican American families or the diversity among them.[58] Both argued,
in fact, that Mexican American families were, in some circumstances,
egalitarian. A second generation of Chicana feminists added further complexity to the critique. For example, Patricia Zavella argued that Chicano
families are diverse and frequently patriarchal, but so are Anglo families.[59] Moreover, she heeded scholars to separate ideology from reality:
even though husbands and wives will frequently voice patriarchal views,
the reality is by necessity more complex and sometimes egalitarian. Debates
about the extent of familism and traditional values continue in more recent
research.[60]

To investigate the extent of agreement with traditional family and gender attitudes and whether these persist across time and over generations,
we asked respondents whether they agreed that girls should live at home,
men should have the last word, whether it is acceptable for children to
disagree with parents, and whether individuals should rely on their families. These results are presented in table 8.12. The questions about appropriate gender roles—whether girls should live at home and men should
have the last word—show a familiar pattern: immigrants and original
respondents hold the most traditional gender attitudes. Traditional gender

Table 8.13   Favorite Music by Generation-Since-Immigration, 2000

	Original Respondents			Children		
	Gen. 1	Gen. 2	Gen. 3	Gen. 2	Gen. 3	Gen. 4+
American, black	20%	37%	46%	55%	59%	65%
Chicano (oldies, Tex-Mex, Latin)	3	15	23	27	29	25
Mexican	74	44	29	15	9	9
No preference	3	4	1	3	3	0

Source: Mexican American Study Project.

attitudes lessen with generation-since-immigration and from parents to the children[61]

On the other hand, the results for the other two questions (rows three and four) were unexpected. The third row refers to individualism versus familism, which Huntington, like many before him, believe represents a cultural divide that explains differences in economic success between Mexican Americans and Anglos.[62] Mexicans, these scholars argue, are too family oriented and not individualistic enough, which impedes them from moving up and out of the working class. However, the results show that immigrants are generally the most individualistic and that the parental generation has the highest proportions of persons believing that they should be responsible for themselves (row 4). Apparently, later generations prefer to rely on their families. Thus, these findings show that belief in the value of individualism is stronger for immigrants and the more ethnic parental generation, which is consistent with de la Garza and his colleagues.[63] The individualism of immigrants makes sense if we consider that they were motivated enough to have left their own communities in search of work opportunities hundreds of miles away in a very culturally distinct place.

Music

Finally, we sought to measure the extent to which ethnic popular culture persists across generations, especially given the enduring persistence of U.S.-based Chicano culture and the diffusion of Spanish media throughout much of the Southwest.[64] We asked respondents to name their favorite genre of music in an open-ended question. We coded responses into categories consisting of more than thirty genres including rock and roll, rancheras, Tex-Mex, big band, and jazz. We then created three general categories to capture a continuum of ethnic preferences, which we present in table 8.13. The American–black music category includes such genres as rock, swing, country, soul, and American-English in general. The Mexican category includes banda, cumbia, ranchera, or Mexican-Spanish in general. We also created an intermediate category to capture types of music commonly considered Chicano, which we define as genres developed in the United States and consumed disproportionately, if not produced by, Mexican Americans (or Latinos).[65] These categories are oldies but goodies, Tex-Mex, and Latin.

The first row of table 8.13 shows a clear progression toward English-American music preferences over generations-since-immigration and the third shows the same trend in the opposite direction, away from Mexican music. Also, the change in the acculturation to English-American music is more sudden in the more recent cohort than in the older generation. For example, among the third generation, 59 percent of the child generation prefers English-American music compared to only 46 percent of the parent generation.

On the other hand, preferences for Chicano music grow in each generation in the parent generation, revealing that the increased detachment from Mexican music over generations-since-immigration means both acculturation to American forms but also about as much movement toward U.S. Latino musical forms. Only 3 percent of the first generation prefer either oldies, Tex-Mex, or Latin music, compared to 15 percent of the second generation and 23 percent of the third generation. For the children generation, about one-quarter of the second, third, and fourth generation continue to prefer Chicano music, suggesting that the alternative ethnic form—neither clearly Mexican nor American—retains an important part of cultural identity for a significant part of late-generation Mexican Americans. This finding reflects an enduring attachment into the fourth generation of cultural forms, which are distinctly ethnic but largely performed in English, the dominant language of that generation.

Holidays

Several analysts have shown that the celebration of holidays remains one of the rare manifestations that third- or fourth-generation European American ethnics retain any of their ancestors' traditions.[66] We asked questions about the celebration of holidays and ethnic culture because we were concerned that this might be the only manifestation of fourth-generation ethnic behavior that we could measure, if Mexican Americans were to mimic the case of similarly situated European American ethnics. The evidence from this and the previous chapter show that this is not at all the case. Nevertheless, we present our results. The first two rows of table 8.14 show that a significant number of Mexican Americans celebrate Mexican holidays into later generations, though the proportion and the number of holidays they celebrate decline by generation. Nonetheless, about half (52 percent) of fourth-generation respondents claimed to celebrate at least one Mexican holiday, though only 37 percent of the third generation among the parental generation do. Of course, age may make a difference in celebration. The now mostly senior original respondents may find it inconvenient to actually

Table 8.14   Mexican Holidays, History and Traditions, and Values
              by Generation-Since-Immigration, 2000

	Original Respondents			Children		
	Gen. 1	Gen. 2	Gen. 3	Gen. 2	Gen. 3	Gen. 4+
Celebrate any Mexican holidays	65%	52%	37%	58%	54%	52%
Average number of holidays celebrated	1.4	1.1	0.7	1.3	1.0	0.9
Mexican history and traditions important[a]	88%	86%	81%	98%	89%	93%
Mexican values important[b]	91	85	80	96	87	87

Source: Mexican American Study Project.
[a] Report "important" or "very important" that children learn Mexican history and traditions.
[b] Report "important" or "very important" that children learn Mexican values.

attend such a celebration whereas the generation mostly in their forties and fifties may seek to instill ethnic pride in their children by celebrating an ethnic holiday. Also, these were self-reports based on a general question about whether respondents celebrate Mexican holidays, which they then named.

Perceptions of discrimination and identity differed greatly between Mexican Americans and European ethnics in later generations, but the extent to which they celebrated holidays differed to a lesser extent. Fully 27 percent of European ethnics participated in ethnic festivals or celebrations in the Albany study by Richard Alba.[67] Participation in ethnic holidays, though, requires little knowledge of or investment in one's ethnicity. Observing ethnic celebrations may be similar for both groups, but ethnicity is a different experience altogether for Mexican Americans. For the descendants of Europeans, ethnicity is largely symbolic. For Mexican Americans, it is much more bound up with other life experiences, as this and the following chapters show.

The last two rows of table 8.14 show that at least 80 percent of Mexican Americans in all generations believe that children should learn about Mexican history, tradition, and values. Mexican history and values seem to be cherished among the vast majority of even those Mexican Americans most removed from the immigration experience, at the point that they would like their children to learn about them. These findings, like those showing significant ethnic holiday observance, demonstrate that fourth-generation Mexican Americans at least hold the symbolic ethnicity of later-generation European Americans. However, based on an abundance of other evidence in this book, there can be no doubt that there is more than symbolic ethnicity among later-generation Mexican Americans in terms of both ethnic identity and culture.

Conclusions

Having focused on the structural or socioeconomic aspects of immigrant incorporation in chapters 5 and 6, this chapter emphasizes the cultural and finds distinct dynamics. Whereas evidence of structural or socioeconomic assimilation is weak, evidence of cultural assimilation is strong on some indicators. At the same time, and unlike the European American pattern, ethnic culture among Mexican Americans endures several generations beyond the immigrant generation.

Mexican Americans show clear signs of linguistic and cultural assimilation over generations, though it is gradual. Thus it is not the direction as much as the speed that greatly differentiates the two experiences. European American acculturation was generally complete by the third generation. By then, any sign of ethnicity was almost entirely symbolic. For Mexican Americans, however, there is much more, as the evidence for language makes clear. Nearly all Mexican Americans speak English well in the second generation, but Spanish endures well into the fourth. Fully one-third of fourth-generation respondents report being bilingual in 2000, with continuing Spanish proficiency declining sharply among fifth-generation children.

Less-educated parents are more likely to speak to and teach their children in Spanish. Thus low levels of parental education also strengthen Spanish retention. Children who learn Spanish are more likely to be raised in Spanish-speaking homes, but as they grow up, those who attain higher levels of education are more likely to pick up or improve their Spanish. This may be in response to the substantial demands for Spanish-speaking professionals among a Spanish-speaking community that has grown because of immigration.

Spanish language use and giving children Spanish names are more common in San Antonio than in Los Angeles, even after controlling for a host of other factors thought to influence bilingualism. This occurs independently of the extent of residential isolation, generation-since-immigration, and a host of other variables, and thus suggests distinct local cultures. Linguistic assimilation is more rapid in Los Angeles. San Antonio retains a Spanish-speaking culture that many later-generation Mexican Americans participate in.

Certainly acculturation after five generations-since-immigration suggests slow but certain movement. We find, however, that the erosion of Mexican cultural traits is not only in the passing of time since the immigration experience, but also in the passing of historical time. Spanish fluency among persons of comparable generations-since-immigration is simply less common among Mexican Americans today than it was among those of earlier periods. This is partly attributable to the greater exposure to English through the media and greater social exposure to monolingual English-speaking Americans, from the workplace to intermarriage. Comparisons of Mexicans now to Europeans then, as is commonly done, thus understates the difference in linguistic assimilation. Mexican American cultural and linguistic assimilation was especially slow in the past but has sped up over time. Nonetheless, it remains slower than it was for the descendants of the Europeans. Reasons are likely to include the persistently low education of parents, greater exposure to Spanish afforded by persistent spatial and occupational isolation, and continuing immigration.

The same historical trend is true for several other cultural indicators. Spanish names for children are less common today among persons of comparable generations, as is being Catholic, going to church, high fertility, paternalistic values, and Mexican musical tastes. The Mexican American acculturation experience, not unlike that of ethnic Catholic European groups, is likely to have accompanied general societal shifts, such as a movement away from mainline religions, declining fertility, and increasingly egalitarian values. Ethnic persistence, though, has been greater for Mexican Americans. However, the shift entangles historical time (family generation) and generation-since-immigration in predicting Mexican American acculturation. There was clearly less cultural differentiation within the Mexican American population in the older generation. Declines in Catholic religion and religiosity have been dramatic primarily because nearly everyone was Catholic and most regularly attended church, with relatively little variation by generation-since-immigration. These figures, however, dropped sharply for their children and generation-since-immigration differences became pronounced.

Finally, we find evidence that symbolic ethnicity has actually increased over time. Celebration of Mexican holidays and the value put on Mexican history and values—as opposed to actually learning about them—is as important or more important for the children's generation than for the original respondents. This suggests a search for ethnic roots among the current generation that is often lost in actual cultural practice. This yearning may be the result of the new societal embrace of multiculturalism and the value given to ethnicity. Although multiculturalism is stronger today than it was in the past, it emerges ironically at the same time that actual cultural differences between later-generation Mexican Americans and Anglos have been declining. Civil rights gains and a generally more open society may have worn down rigid racialized boundaries, but at the same time it also seems to have eroded cultural retention among later generations-since-immigration, despite legislative and activists' efforts to maintain cultural diversity. Notwithstanding a growing acceptance of multiculturalism among at least some sectors of American society, acculturation for Mexican Americans is faster today than ever before.

= Chapter 9 =

Ethnic Identity

Modern understandings of ethnicity stress that ethnics or ethnic groups are created when members of society actively erect and sustain social boundaries between themselves and so-called others, often but not always on the basis of perceived cultural differences. Ethnic identities largely reflect societal ascription, though they may also involve personal and political choices.[1] Thus, ethnic identities and the classification of others delimit who is an insider and who is an outsider. The extent to which ethnicity is sustained for the descendants of immigrants largely depends on the extent to which subsequent generations perceive similarly meaningful differences with others and consequently continue to draw boundaries that in turn condition their lives. Fredrik Barth, who laid the basis for modern understandings of ethnicity, accepted that these boundaries could be crossed to some extent, but observed that at some point boundary crossing may become so extensive that the boundary loses its significance.[2]

Assimilation theory predicts the steady loss of ethnic identification with time since immigration, a process that often continues into the second generation and, in a common version of that theory, is complete by the third generation. In other words, the strength of ethnicity rapidly dissipates from immigrants to their children and disappears by the third generation. The sense of a collective we-ness is no longer an issue by the third or fourth generation, according to this theory, thereby diminishing the usefulness of the ethnicity concept in understanding social interaction among the descendants of immigrants. Based on empirical studies, we know this is generally the case for non-Hispanic whites in the United States.[3] By the third generation, these persons identify primarily as Americans, they have little knowledge of their ancestral homeland or culture, they rarely partake in ethnic cultural or social activities, and their ethnic origins have little importance in their everyday lives.[4] According to Gans, any remaining sense of ethnicity usually consists of mere nostalgic fascination with one's past among persons who have secured comfortable positions in the new society, thus symbolic ethnicity comes to predominate.[5] Some social scientists believe that the descendants of the mostly nonwhite post-1965 wave of immigrants are likely to have a similar experience.[6]

Other social scientists, however, argue that racialization continues as a powerful impediment to full assimilation, as it has been for African Americans for many generations.[7] African Americans continue to be seen as the prototypical other in American society and continue to hold strong ethnic or racial identities. The issue of race may be important in understanding whether Mexican American identity endures into later generations. As we showed in chapter 4, the label of nonwhite has been inconsistently applied to Mexicans in the United States. Hispanic Americans have long sought to uphold their Spanish origins as proof of their whiteness, precisely because of their treatment and sometimes official classification as nonwhite, even though particular individuals and sometimes the group were treated as white. Mexican American leaders from time to time used their racial status as a political strategy to gain access to white privilege.[8]

In the absence of systematic data, there is little consensus about the choice or strength of ethnic identity among later generations of Mexican Americans. Persistent physical differences may continue to demarcate most Mexican Americans from the European-origin majority, but the rigid racial boundaries between whites and blacks do not necessarily apply to Mexican Americans. Certainly, we have long been aware of a large and culturally distinct Mexican origin population in the Southwest but these distinctions might merely be due to the large immigrant component that clearly sees itself as foreign or different from typical Americans. Or do such ethnic boundaries and ethnic identities endure into the third or later generations? Is this related to racial differences that persist despite acculturation? We turn to these questions, beginning with the preference for ethnic labels, followed by the salience given to one's ethnicity and then we explore situations or contexts in which ethnic identity is important.

Preferred Ethnic Label

We begin our analysis of ethnic identity by examining how those of Mexican origin identify on a continuum of ethnic terms from Mexican to American. This is complicated by terms like Hispanic and Chicano that do not easily fit on the continuum. Alvarez describes the distinct socialization experiences of three distinct generations of the developing Mexican-origin population.[9] He follows a single multigenerational cohort from immigration in the early twentieth century to the third generation in the early 1970s because he was writing when the second wave of mass immigration from Mexico was only beginning. Alvarez distinguishes Mexicans, who immigrated to the United States in search of material dreams but remained committed to Mexico, from Mexican Americans, largely socialized during

World War II, who were committed to the United States and questioned the ethnic attachment of their immigrant parents. Then, in the politically active late 1960s, he notes the emergence of the Chicano generation, which rejected the acculturating tendencies of their parents and tried to reclaim the ancestral heritage of their grandparents. This heuristic scheme, though overly simplistic in reality, is useful because it reveals variation by generational and historical period, indicates a relation of labels with consciousness and attitudes, and demonstrates the association of particular labels with generational subgroups.

Survey data since then has revealed that the ethnic labels Mexican origin persons choose are varied. Also, their use is complex as they each cut across generational distinctions and other demographic variables. John García, using a 1976 national survey of the population which asked preferred ethnic label, found that 51 percent of Mexican-origin persons chose Mexican American, 21 percent chose Spanish, 4 percent chose Chicano, and 25 percent chose Mexican or Mexicano.[10] Aida Hurtado and Carlos Arce examined responses to "around here, what name is generally used to refer to people of Mexican descent?" in a national survey of Mexican-origin people in 1979.[11] Mexican-Mexicano was the preferred ethnic label among 38 percent of the respondents, and Chicano was the second most popular term at 32 percent. Another 14 percent reported Mexican American. When worded for preferred labels used in the context of family relations, however, the survey provoked a quite different distribution of responses. When asked "what name do you use in your family when referring to persons of Mexican descent," 16 percent chose Mexican American, 10 percent chose Chicano, and 57 percent chose Mexican-Mexicano.

Identification with one or another of these labels may characterize distinct subpopulations with particular mindsets. They may reveal an orientation about their family's past (Mexican, Mexican American, Spanish American), a statement about primary identification with a nation rather than an ethnicity (American and possibly Mexican), or even an assertion or a shared identity with the larger population of Spanish speakers with common origins in Latin America (Latino, Hispanic). Clearly each of these terms may reflect different types of identity orientations, characterizing distinct subgroups of the Mexican-origin population.

Persons identifying under a common label may share collective sentiments or consciousness that distinguishes them from those choosing other labels. Even within the same ethnic group, one may be able to choose among multiple labels, which themselves may reveal internal group differences and important demographic distinctions including time of residence in the United States, region of birth in the United States, or language. In the case of Mexican Americans, one may choose identity as a Mexican American proper, which implies recognition of both country of ancestral origin and country of residence or citizenship. One may also identify with one or the other society. Another alternative is to choose a pan-ethnic identity such as Latino or Hispanic.

However, boundaries among these subgroups are likely to be quite fluid because individuals may claim identities that vary depending on a particular social situation. Nonetheless, responses to the same questionnaire in the same period for all respondents provide a fairly uniform situation in which respondents can choose their preferred ethnic label. We expect that the attitudes and characteristics of individuals in each subgroup might tell us something about what each of these labels imply because they reflect ways in which particular individuals chose to represent themselves.

Finally, the selection of particular categories by institutions such as the U.S. Census is likely to shape preferences for particular labels. The pan-ethnic label of Hispanic, for example, is commonly thought to have gained popularity with its use in the 1980 census. The choice of particular categories to be used in the census often reflects popular labels but it is also a political process reflecting various ethnic and non-ethnic interests. Marketing firms in search of new ethnic markets also have promoted the Hispanic label.[12]

We begin the analysis by showing the preferred ethnic term among our original respondents and their children. In the 1965 survey, the original respondents, when they responded to the English survey, were asked "As we go around talking with people in this community, we find that some prefer to call themselves Spanish-speaking, Latin American, Mexicans, Mexican Americans, or still other terms. How do you prefer to be identified?" The other responses offered by respondents were American, Spanish American, and Spanish descent. These response categories were those most commonly used at the time.

In table 9.1, we present the distribution of preferred ethnic categories. We present the responses under four broad categories of Mexican, Mexican American, pan-ethnic, and American or non-Hispanic. The first column shows that more than a third (37 percent) of original respondents in 1965 identified as either Mexican or Mexicano and a fifth (20 percent) identified as Mexican American. Another third (33 percent) identified under a pan-ethnic term. Only 8 percent identified as American. The frequent use of pan-ethnic terms may seem surprising for 1965, since we often assume these are post-civil rights era inventions. However, the reasons for using pan-ethnic terms may be different from those today. Specifically, 24 percent of the original respondents in 1965 preferred to call themselves Latin American and 9 percent as Spanish or Spanish American. Terms such as Spanish and Latin American were clearly euphemistic substitutes for the racially stigmatized Mexican terms, which in the pre-civil rights era had especially negative connotations. This was especially true in Texas, where most respondents chose to identify as Latin American, as we show below. By contrast, the use of Latino and Hispanic today are government, media,

Table 9.1   Ethnic Identity, 1965 and 2000

	Original Respondents 1965	Original Respondents 2000	Children
Mexican or Mexicano	37%	33%	17%
Mexican American	20	41	44
Mexican American	20	39	38
Chicano		1	3
American Mexican		1	2
Mexican mixed		0	1
Pan-ethnic	33	16	29
Latin American	24	0	0
Spanish or Spanish American	9	4	1
Hispanic		10	25
Latino		2	2
American and other	10	10	10
American	8	9	8
Anglo		0	1
White		0	1
Other	2	1	0

Source: Mexican American Study Project.

and business endorsed categories that bring together the growing diversity among persons of Spanish-speaking origin, though they may also continue to serve as euphemisms for Mexican.

In the 2000 survey, respondents were asked: "People have different ways of thinking about their ethnic background or origins. What about you? How do you think of yourself: What do you consider your ethnic background to be?"

Unlike the question in the 1965 survey, ours is strictly open-ended. That is, we did not provide any response categories but let respondents give their own answers.[13] The open-ended question in 2000 thus allows for more categories of ethnic identification than did the 1965 item, which was only partially open-ended.

The second column of table 9.1 shows that a combined 74 percent of the original respondents preferred one of the categories of Mexican (or Mexicano) and Mexican American in 2000. The original respondents in 2000 are half as likely to use pan-ethnic terms and twice as likely to use Mexican American regardless of their preferences thirty-five years ago. Because the distribution of the 1965 and the 2000 respondents differ greatly, we examine how the 1965 responses changed by 2000 below.

Column three of table 9.1 indicates that the proportion of children identifying as Mexican or Mexicano is less than half (17 percent) that of the original respondents (33 percent), which is not surprising given that the child sample consists of those born or raised in the United States but only two-thirds of the parent generation were. Instead, 25 percent of children were likely to use the pan-ethnic term Hispanic. Pan-ethnic labels have again have become preferred terms for many in the children's generation, though today's Hispanic is arguably much different in meaning than the Latin American used in 1965.

Among the child respondents, the largest number (38 percent) identified as Mexican American. We included three other ethnic labels under Mexican American because these were used infrequently but are similar. For instance, Chicano was used by only 3 percent of the sample, even though it continues to be widely used in political and academic circles. A small percentage used variations on Mexican American, such as American Mexican and Mexican Mixed. Mexican Mixed reflects the reality that some respondents have one non-Mexican parent (which we examine later in this chapter).

American, Anglo, white, and several infrequently used terms comprise the non-Hispanic category. American was preferred by 8 percent of the child respondents. Anglo and white were each used by 1 percent. A handful of respondents chose other terms, including American Indian, human being, and North American. The roughly 10 percent of the population who preferred non-Hispanic terms remained constant from parents to children. Moreover, this would seem to have implications for measuring the size or characteristics of the Mexican American population or the Hispanic population.

In a cross-sectional census or survey, the population of Mexican Americans, Hispanics, or any other ethnic group is captured as such only to the extent that persons identify in them. However, despite having a particular ancestry, respondents may not identify as such. Both Alba and Islam and Brian Duncan, Joseph Hotz, and Stephen Trejo worry that because the more upwardly mobile Mexican origin may opt out of this stigmatized group, that intergenerational estimates of the progress of Mexican Americans are biased downward.[14] Our open-ended question on preferred identity also allows the choice of a non-Hispanic identity. Ours, though, is an improvement over cross-sectional surveys because we included the children in our study since one of their parents had been considered such in 1965. In at least two instances, we recalled child respondents insisting that they were not of Mexican origin, but because one of their parents was in the original sample, we nonetheless interviewed them and consider them of Mexican origin. We consider their responses essential in trying to understand intergenerational change among the Mexican origin population.

In the 1965 survey, respondents were asked an ethnic identity question in Spanish, even in the English questionnaires, with different responses that

Table 9.2   Second Ethnic Identity Question by Language of Interview, 1965[a]

| | Original Respondents | | |
	English Questionnaire	Spanish Questionnaire	All
Mexicano	45%	65%	49%
Mexico Americano	20	15	19
Latino	18	14	17
Hispano	2	1	1
Tejano	2	1	1
Americano	7	2	6
Other	6	2	6
Total	100	100	100
Number of valid responses	637	172	809
Number missing responses	93	291	384

Source: Mexican American Study Project.
[a] Asked in Spanish using different response categories in both English and Spanish questionnaires.

included Mexicano, Mexicano-Americano, Latino, and Hispano. We suspect that the purpose of the Spanish question was to observe whether one's preferred ethnic label in a Spanish-language context might differ from an English one. Table 9.2 compares the responses of those responding to the English interview with the Spanish one. Among those answering the English questionnaire, fully 18 percent of those choosing any term chose Latino and another 2 percent chose Hispano. This also reveals that most Mexican Americans understood Spanish well enough to have answered the question. Moreover, the second column of table 9.2 also shows that for those answering the Spanish questionnaire, in which the same categories were given, 14 percent chose Latino and 1 percent Hispano, though the question was not asked of most 1965 respondents responding in Spanish for reasons unknown to us.

To consider the issue of assimilation being so advanced that some of Mexican-origin may no longer identify as such, we examined the responses of children whose primary ethnic identity was American, Anglo, white, or other. This is an important issue to explore because it addresses a methodological problem, raised by several researchers,[15] that assimilated Mexican Americans might not identity as such and therefore be missed in analyses of ethnic and generational change. As already noted, we found that the large majority of children had identified as Mexican, Mexican American, or Hispanic (which we refer to as a Hispanic identifier) at some point in the survey. Table 9.3 shows that of eighty-five persons whose primary identity is white, American, or other, forty-four also chose a Hispanic identifier as a second ethnic identifier. Among those who did

Table 9.3   Second Ethnic and Racial Identity Among Those Who
             Identified as White, American, or Other, Children, 2000

	Number Out of Previous Category
Identified as White, American, or other	85
Identified as Mexican or Hispanic to second ethnicity question	44
Identified as Mexican or Hispanic racial question	15
Identified as Mexican at least some of the time	13
Did not identify as Mexican or Hispanic	13

Source: Mexican American Study Project.

not, fifteen chose a Hispanic identifier as a racial identifier. Among the remaining respondents, thirteen reported that they think of themselves as Mexicans at least some of the time. The last thirteen respondents report no affinity with being Mexican or Hispanic in our survey. They represent, however, less than 2 percent of the entire sample. Thus, there is a potentially small degree of opting-out of the Mexican or Hispanic category. Our evidence shows that this amount may be minimized, depending on the ethnic questions in the survey, though it may remain a small problem. With our longitudinal study and intergenerational methodology, we believe that we have nearly eliminated this problem.

Ethnic Identity by Urban Area

The use of particular ethnic terms largely depends on the local context, as table 9.4 shows. In Los Angeles in 1965, nearly half of the original respondents identified as Mexican (45 percent) and more than a quarter (26 percent) identified as Mexican American. This contrasts sharply with San Antonio, where fully 59 percent identified as Latin American and only 7 percent identified as Mexican American and 21 percent as Mexican, which is further evidence of the greater racial stigma of the word *Mexican* in San Antonio. On the other hand, Spanish or Spanish American was used by 10 percent in Los Angeles versus 6 percent in San Antonio, but this pales in comparison to the much greater use of the pan-ethnic Latin American used by 59 percent of San Antonians in 1965. Twelve percent in Los Angeles but only 6 percent in San Antonio identified as American or other.

By 2000, the distribution of the preferred terms had somewhat converged between the two cities, though the original respondents in San Antonio continued to prefer pan-ethnic terms, just as Angelenos had a greater preference for Mexican American. In 2000, fully 21 percent of the San

Table 9.4   Ethnic Identity by Urban Area, 1965 and 2000

	Los Angeles	San Antonio
Original respondents, 1965		
Mexican	45%	21%
Mexican American	26	7
Latin American	6	59
Spanish American or Spanish speaking	10	6
American or other	12	6
Original respondents, 2000		
Mexican or Mexicano	38	23
Mexican American	42	39
Latin American or Spanish	3	7
Hispanic	5	18
Latino	2	3
American or other	10	10
Children		
Mexican or Mexicano	22	9
Mexican American (Chicano)	47 (4)	37 (1)
Latin American or Spanish	2	1
Hispanic	14	46
Latino	3	0
American or Other	12	7

Source: Mexican American Study Project.

Antonio respondents interviewed in 1965 used Hispanic or Latino and only 7 percent continued to prefer Latin American or Spanish. For their children, a similar pattern emerges except that fully 46 percent of San Antonians preferred to be called Hispanic, which is nearly equal to the percentage who choose the combined Mexican (9 percent) and Mexican American (37 percent) categories. In Los Angeles, only 19 percent chose a pan-ethnic term, and a full 69 preferred Mexican or Mexican American. These city differences suggest that Mexican, or its derivative Mexican American, continue to be stigmatized in Texas, making it easier to identify as Hispanic.

We also show, in parentheses, the proportion of the children who prefer the term Chicano, which we put under the category Mexican American but which has special significance as a term of political affirmation for some in that generation. Four percent used the term in Los Angeles compared to only 1 percent in San Antonio, which is not surprising given apparently more intense ethnic politics in Los Angeles.[16] Answers to further open-ended questions showed that many more of the children, especially in Los Angeles, occasionally think of themselves as Chicano though they might prefer one of the more standard categories. They reported that the occasions in which they thought of themselves as Chicano were generally in reference to when they were politically active, often as youth in the 1960s and 1970s, in situations where they continue to be involved in political activity, such as in occupational disputes or in social activities related to Chicano culture, including attending Cinco de Mayo celebrations or listening to oldies but goodies.

Ethnic Identity by Generation-Since-Immigration

One might expect that as Mexican Americans move further away from the immigrant experience that they will identify less as Mexican and increasingly as American. Table 9.5 shows that this expectation is correct. Because self-identification may be subject to age effects, we concentrate on original respondents in 1965 compared to their children in 2000 (who would be roughly about the same age). The percentage identifying as Mexican in the first generation declined from 56 percent for the original respondents in 1965 to 28 percent for their children in 2000. Similarly, 30 percent of the second generation in 1965 called themselves Mexican but only 15 percent of their children did. A quarter (27 percent) of the third generation identified as Mexican in 1965, compared to only 10 percent of their children. These data reveal not only a decline in Mexican identity with greater generational distance from immigration but also a secular trend away from self-identity as simply Mexican.

On the American side, the percentages ran in the opposite direction among both parents and children, but were stable from parents to children despite the latter's greater distance from the immigration generation. For example, in 1965 only 4 percent of the first generation identified as American compared with 12 percent of the second generation. However, only 5 percent of their second-generation children identified as American. These breakdowns were similar for all of the other familial and immigration generations. Thus, though there seems to be a trend toward Americanization in identity over generations removed from immigration, it is apparently counteracted by a more general trend away from an American identity on the part of the children. The parents experienced the patriotic national mobilization for World War II. The children experienced the Chicano movement and the consolidation of multiculturalism and a more positively affirmed ethnic identity.

The generational movement from Mexican to American is complicated by the pan-ethnic categories. Almost half (44 percent) of the third generation in 1965 chose Latin American or Spanish and another 19 percent identified as American, a clear majority avoiding either of the Mexican terms. By 2000, children were more likely to choose Mexican American, which remained popular even into the fourth generation, rather than a pan-ethnic label. At least 40 percent of original respondents and children of the third and fourth generation chose Mexican American in 2000 against

Table 9.5   Ethnic Identity by Generation-Since-Immigration, 1965 and 2000

	Original Respondents, 1965			Original Respondents, 2000			Children		
	Gen. 1	Gen. 2	Gen. 3	Gen. 1	Gen. 2	Gen. 3	Gen. 2	Gen. 3	Gen. 4+
Mexican or Mexicano	56%	30%	27%	67%	25%	19%	28%	15%	10%
Mexican American	21	26	10	15	51	43	43	43	44
Pan-ethnic[a]	20	31	44	11	14	26	25	30	33
American or other	4	12	19	7	10	13	5	12	12

Source: Mexican American Study Project.
[a] Pan-ethnic labels primarily Latin American and Spanish in 1965; primarily Hispanic and Latino in 2000.

the 10 percent who chose it in 1965. This change further confirms a general trend in that period away from the pan-ethnic category and toward a more particularistic Mexican American category. This may be a surprising finding for many who believe that pan-ethnic terms were created in the 1970s and that they been increasingly accepted since then.

Among the children, the second generation is almost twice as likely to identify as Mexican than the third or fourth generation but Mexican American does not vary by generation-since-immigration. Rather, identification as Hispanic and other pan-ethnic labels increases in each succeeding generation from 25 percent in the second generation to 33 percent in the fourth. The percentage identifying as American or other steadily increases from the second generation at 5 percent to the fourth generation at 12 percent. This shows identificational assimilation and signals some opting out of the Mexican or Hispanic category. As we showed in table 9.2, however, in response to other questions, most, but not all, consider themselves of Mexican origin.

Prior Literature on Ethnic Identity

Several explanations have been given as to why ethnic identity would persist among Mexican Americans in later generations. Some, like Milton Yinger,[17] argue that as the largest minority group in the Southwest, their regional concentration has isolated them from other groups, thus strengthening their sense of ethnicity. Similarly, William Yancey, Eugene Erickson, and Richard Juliani argue that persistent segregation at the neighborhood level reinforces ethnic identification.[18] Our study is limited to the two cities used in 1965—Los Angeles and San Antonio—both of which are in the largely and historically Mexican Southwest. We show that their populations identified in different ways. San Antonio had a proportionately larger and more segregated Mexican American community. On the other hand, greater Mexican immigration to Los Angeles since the 1965 study has probably served to reinforce or revitalize attachment of the U.S.-born Mexican origin to their native roots. Those more isolated by virtue of residence or family would presumably choose Mexican or Mexican American, whereas those in more integrated settings might be more likely to choose American. On the other hand, those proximate to non-Mexican Hispanics might be more likely to choose Hispanic or Latino.

Ethnic identity and an emphasis on Mexicanness may be strong among Mexican Americans because they continue to be largely working class into the third and fourth generation. Whereas upwardly mobile ethnics may downplay their ethnicity in the interest of mixing freely with diverse groups, disadvantaged persons tend to be more socially isolated. Thus persistently low socioeconomic status and occupational concentration may reinforce ethnic identity.[19] The persistence of working class status may cause ethnic membership to be perceived as a principal determinant of life chances or the way in which group members understand their disadvantage.[20] Also, social and family networks bring together persons of similar ethnicity to create a social context that is both working class and ethnic simultaneously. Thus those who associate more frequently with coethnics may give greater salience to their ethnicity and behave ethnically.

We expect that ethnic markers, such as surname and phenotype, may also be important for understanding ethnic expressions in later generations. Ethnic markers are characteristics that a person cannot easily hide and that signal to the outside world that the person is a member of a particular ethnicity or race. Factors such as surname, phenotype, limited or accented English among others, should thus affect the strength of ethnic identity. Tomás Jiménez found that persons with one Mexican origin parent and one white parent were more likely to identify as Mexican American when their appearance was similar to the Mexican stereotype or when they lived in largely Mexican or Chicano social or neighborhood contexts.[21] Carl Eschbach and Christina Gómez and Hiromi Ono reach similar conclusions regarding how ethnic contexts reinforce ethnicity and both reported some opting out of the Hispanic category altogether, especially among later generations.[22]

Who Chooses Particular Labels

Various factors over the life course may lead individuals to choose a particular ethnic or national identity. Cornell and Hartmann and Yinger, for example, identify occupational and residential concentration among other factors, as shaping ethnic identities.[23] We expect that variables such as socioeconomic status, urban residence and skin color will also affect ethnicity. We hypothesize that less educated persons, those growing up in a more traditional place like San Antonio, and those with darker skin will have stronger ethnic identities. Using a logistic model, we examine factors, independent of each other, that affect the ethnic identification of children in 2000. The results, in table 9.6, show the odds of persons with particular characteristics identifying either as Mexican in the first column, or identifying as American or other (that is, non-Hispanic) in the second column, compared to all other identities.[24]

Generation 1.5 has more than three and a half times (3.54) the odds of identifying as Mexican than generation three. Because they were born in Mexico, it is not surprising that they are more likely to hold on to a Mexican national origin identity. The other generational groups do not differ from the third generation in identifying as Mexican. The second column shows that there are also no significant generational differences in identifying as American.

Those who spoke Spanish as children are more likely to identify as Mexican and less likely to identify as American. It is important to note that

Table 9.6   Key Determinants of Ethnic Identity, 2000[a]

	Mexican	American or Other
Generation-since-immigration (ref: 3)		
1.5	3.54**	0.61
2	1.01	0.54
2.5	0.88	0.60
4+	0.76	1.24
Education	0.99	1.08
Parent spoke Spanish to child	2.65***	0.36*
Parent is non-Hispanic		2.27*
San Antonio (1965)	0.27***	
Proportion Hispanic in neighborhood (1965)		2.66*
Age		1.08**

Source: Mexican American Study Project.
[a] Only significant variables or substantive variables presented. Logistic regression run. Compared to all other ethnic identities. Adjusted odds ratios presented. Child sample analyzed. Adjusted for sibling clustering. See appendix B, tables B.10 and B.11 for full model.
*p<.05, **p<.01, ***p<.001

the language effect is net of generation, thus not attributable simply to the children of immigrants being more or less likely to have these identities. We also expect that parent's ethnicity should affect the children's identification. We find that children who have a non-Hispanic parent are more likely to identify as American or other.[25]

The results in table 9.6 also show that persons raised in more Hispanic neighborhoods are more likely to identify as American or other. The proportion Hispanic in a neighborhood refers to the neighborhood context in which the respondents were raised (based on 1970 census data for the census tract in which their parents were interviewed and where they resided in 1965). Because this finding is counterintuitive, we examined alternative models to learn what might be driving this effect. We get the effect in the multivariate analysis, but not when we examine the effect of proportion Hispanic with no other variables in the analysis. Moreover, we find it primarily with the Los Angeles sample (analysis not shown). This finding may be the result of U.S.-born Mexican Americans making quasi-ethnic distinctions by identifying themselves as American in distinction to immigrants, especially recent arrivals, in neighborhoods where there are few persons of any other ethnicity. The effect may be particularly strong in Los Angeles because the proportion of recent immigrants there is clearly greater than in San Antonio.

Table 9.7   Ethnicity Very Important by Ethnic Identity
and Generation-Since-Immigration, 2000

	Original Respondents			Children		
	Gen. 1	Gen. 2	Gen. 3	Gen. 2	Gen. 3	Gen. 4+
All respondents	76%	64%	65%	73%	63%	55%
By ethnic identity						
Mexican	78	67	73	80	80	74
Mexican American	80	65	68	73	59	47
Pan-Ethnic	79	62	66	72	69	62
Non-Hispanic	51	52	44	—[a]	39	46

Source: Mexican American Study Project.
[a] Only eight second-generation respondents identified as non-Hispanic.

In addition, we find that San Antonio residents are less likely to use the Mexican category than Angelenos, independent of all other effects in the model. This might be due, in part, to the increased immigration in Los Angeles encouraging an identity as Mexican overall, though again, Mexican Americans may be more likely to identify as American in those neighborhoods where there are few non-Mexicans. Among the respondent's individual characteristics, only age affected ethnic identity. Older persons are more likely to identify as American than any other identity. This probably reflects the fact that the younger respondents came of age in the politically turbulent period of the late 1960s and early 1970s.

Salience of Ethnicity

That persons prefer to identify with a particular category may not reflect how important ethnic identity is for them. Thus, we asked respondents about the salience or importance of their ethnic choice. Table 9.7 reports on those who claimed that their ethnic background was very important to them, by generational status. The results indicate that ethnic identity was most salient for the first generation, at 76 percent. The second and third generation original respondents gave it somewhat less importance than first generation but did not differ in the importance they gave to their ethnicity. Among the children, the importance of their ethnicity steadily decreased by generation, from 73 to 55 percent. Next, we examine importance by the four ethnic identity categories. For those identifying as Mexican, ethnicity remained very important across all generations. As we showed previously in table 9.5, the proportion identifying as Mexican decreased in succeeding generations. It may be that the smaller group that continues to identify as Mexican in later generations does so because the ethnic category has significant meaning to them. More than half in almost every category claim that their ethnicity is very important to them, even into the fourth generation. Respondents who are somewhat less likely to say this are those who identify as non-Hispanic (39 percent for the third generation children and 46 percent for the fourth). While almost all of our respondents were likely to view their ethnicity as important, less than 10 percent of third- and fourth-generation European Americans did so in the mid-1980s Albany survey that used the same question.[26]

In a separate open-ended question, we asked respondents to identify what makes their ethnic background important. The most common responses among the original respondents were related to the family and the idea of respect, emphasized by half of the respondents. Respect was the single most common response, followed first by family unity or closeness, and then family values. Another one-third mentioned culture or customs generally, followed by language (Spanish or bilingualism). A small number mentioned religion, music, food, or fiestas. Most of the remainder specified issues such as roots, pride in heritage or ancestors, or "being of the Mexican race." A handful mentioned Mexico or particular persons.

There was a noticeable generational shift in the qualities that the children most valued. In particular, references to respect dropped out. By contrast, the children emphasized culture, heritage, and history more than their parents did. Responses stressing the family, especially its unity, values and traditions, were especially common.

Mexican or American?

Ethnicity for the Mexican origin population in the United States usually involved choosing an identity that was more or less on a continuum between Mexico and the United States, as the results for preferred ethnic label showed. When asked their preferred ethnic identity, most of the U.S.-born did not choose Mexican or American, the unambiguous citizen designations that immigrant ancestors often had to negotiate between. Instead, they usually preferred a hybrid or pan-ethnic category. However, we found—when respondents were separately asked to report the extent to which they think of themselves as Mexican or as American—that the preferred label did not fully tap into self-perceptions of identity in the Mexican to American continuum.

Table 9.8 shows the percentage of respondents by generation who frequently think of themselves as Mexican (row 1), or American (row 2), or both (row 3), or neither (row 4). Furthermore, the table reveals that just over half of immigrants (56 percent) always or frequently think of themselves as Mexican, but that decreasing proportions of the U.S.-born do. By the third generation of the original respondents, this drops to only 11 percent, versus 17 percent among their fourth-generation children. By contrast, the percentage frequently thinking of themselves only as American increases with generation-since-immigration, about half (49 percent) of

Table 9.8   **Think of Self as Mexican and/or American by Generation-Since-Immigration, 2000[a]**

	Original Respondents			Children		
	Gen. 1	Gen. 2	Gen. 3	Gen. 2	Gen. 3	Gen. 4+
Think of self as						
Only Mexican	56%	25%	11%	31%	18%	17%
Only American	20	33	49	27	38	37
Both American and Mexican	18	28	25	30	31	29
Neither American or Mexican	6	14	15	11	13	16

Source: Mexican American Study Project.
[a] Report percent that think of themselves as Mexican or American "frequently" or "always."

the third-generation respondents and 37 percent of their fourth-generation children. Thus, table 9.8 also provides evidence of ethnic resurgence. From the third generation parents to their fourth generation children, there is a slight increase in the proportion feeling Mexican and a noticeable decrease in the proportion thinking of themselves as American. Of course, "frequently think" may mean different things to different people. Thus, one may interpret this table as showing a drop in the sense of feeling only Mexican, an increase in the sense of feeling American, but at the same time that 25 to 31 percent frequently think of themselves as both, across generations.

When asked to identify when they thought of themselves as American, the most common answer among original respondents was that they or their children were born in the United States: "I was born here and I don't know anything else" being a typical answer. The act of voting was mentioned most often, but more general notions of rights and freedoms also came up occasionally. Other less common responses included having "white relatives or friends," "during the Fourth of July," "when cashing social security checks or paying income tax." Responses for children were similar, except that politics came up much more often. Respondents in the younger generation mentioned voting and feeling a need to discuss or defend America more often.

When asked when they thought of themselves as Mexican, respondents most often referred to social gatherings in which they were either a small minority or the large majority. In the first, respondents often mentioned that their appearance made them stand out as Mexican and that sometimes they felt discriminated against because of it. One original respondent told us, for example, "You get this feeling when you go to an upper class store and people tend to ignore you because they think you are in the wrong place." Another said "When people look at me and think I am Mexican

Table 9.9   Key Determinants of Think of Self as Mexican or American, 2000[a]

	Mexican[b]	American[c]
Generation-since-immigration (ref: 3)		
1.5	2.61*	0.33*
2	1.17	1.01
2.5	1.03	0.94
4+	0.72	1.03
Education	0.94	1.11**
Parent spoke Spanish to child	1.87*	0.60*
Parent is non-Hispanic	0.19**	2.02*
San Antonio (1965)	0.34***	1.93**
Skin color	0.95*	

Source: Mexican American Study Project.
[a] Only significant variables or substantive variables presented. Logistic regression run. Adjusted odds ratios presented. Child sample analyzed. Adjusted for sibling clustering. See appendix B, table B.12 for full model.
[b] Think of self as Mexican frequently and not as American.
[c] Think of self as American frequently and not as Mexican.
*p<.05, **p<.01, ***p<.001

and expect me to speak Spanish." The other end of the social gathering spectrum involved a Mexican-origin majority, such as holiday celebrations. One respondent said he felt most Mexican "around a bunch of other Mexicans." The next two most common responses were listening to Mexican music or speaking Spanish, both typical of social gatherings. Other responses were less frequent and included mentions of food and social status. Responses for the parental and child generations were similar, except the child generation was much more likely to mention Mexican immigrant coworkers, needing to translate at work, and interactions with immigrants suggesting that the new immigration had a greater effect in reinforcing ethnicity among the adult children.

We ran two regressions to examine the factors associated with often thinking of oneself as only Mexican or as American. Table 9.9 shows that those who often thought of themselves as Americans were more likely to be more educated. Thus it appears that greater education implies greater attachment to a national identity than an ethnic one. Additionally, we find, as expected, that immigrants were most likely to consider themselves Mexican and least likely to consider themselves American, as were those growing up with speaking Spanish and those with a non-Hispanic parent. Angelenos also differed from San Antonians in thinking of themselves as more Mexican and less American. Last, darker skin respondents were less likely to see themselves as Mexicans. This result is the opposite of what we would expect and is one of the few instances in which skin color had a significant effect on a dependent variable.

Racial Identity

Perhaps the most enduring and problematic social boundary in American society is that based on race. The most apparent in the United States is of course between blacks and whites, but national concern about the Hispanic-white divide is increasing in step with immigration, though the divide has long characterized social relations in the Southwest. Mexicans have long been treated as a separate racial group for as long as they have been in contact with white Americans. As mentioned earlier, however, ethnic leaders have pushed to have Mexican Americans classified as white. Individually, some have seen success in this regard. Certainly, the racial boundary has not usually been as rigid as it has been between blacks and whites, and the treatment of Mexican Americans as nonwhite has varied over time, across the region and for individuals. A common hypothesis is that a racial boundary clearly exists for Mexican immigrants but much less so for their descendants in the United States.

The extent to which ethnic boundaries persist into later generations in the United States depends on the extent to which they are seen as racial. Racial distinctions in later generations persist despite economic status and adopted culture. Race thinking and thus racial boundary making is prevalent among many ordinary Americans but especially likely to be made and reinforced by government institutions. Most notably, the United States government's official classification of Hispanic as a default racial category reinforces the idea of Hispanics as a separate race. The 1930 census classified Mexicans as a separate race, but the strong reaction of the Mexican American community led to the removal of the category from the census, and subsequent censuses classified Mexicans as white. The U.S. Census Bureau has long struggled with how to categorize Mexicans and various other groups. Mirroring a larger societal struggle, census demographers question whether white or a separate category is more appropriate. Since 1970, the compromise has been to create a separate Hispanic question apart from the racial one, leaving Hispanics to decide whether to identify as white, black, or one of the other standard categories.

Under the race question, several response categories are listed in U.S. Census forms. "Other" solicits a write-in response. In 1990, rejecting the standard categories, almost half of Mexican Americans identified as "other" category, and a slight majority as white[27] The lack of a Mexican category and the fact that a majority of Mexican Americans identified as white has been interpreted as meaning that Mexicans are white. However, the fact that so many avoided the easy path of checking the white box, even though their birth certificates were likely to denote them as white, and wrote in a Mexican or similar response suggests that many Mexican Americans understand Mexican as a racial designation. This reflects a common confusion. Mexican Americans have long stressed their whiteness to the extent possible in order to be accepted by American society. At the same time, they have also recognized the common designation and identity as other than white. This was often possible precisely because they could be classified white under certain legal definitions, even if it meant being socially excluded from the white population.

Of course, a clear-cut rule on the "race" of Mexican Americans is impossible because it assumes that race is fixed and that we accept that all people can be racially designated. Racial categories are not determined only by the U.S. Census Bureau and race is not determined by self-identification on official forms. It may vary with circumstances and it is largely determined by social perceptions. Nevertheless, some analysts have accepted the simplistic idea that Hispanics or Mexican Americans are not a race because the census says so or that particular Hispanics can be any race they want to be. Race, however, is far more complex than that. Indeed, it is arguably important today only because of racism and racial discrimination, which help shape where one ultimately ends up in the social structure.[28] In this sense, one's race as determined by others is especially important.

Nevertheless, self-identification using census questions not only reflects how persons are categorized by others but also reveals individual predispositions or preferences. Our survey, in this sense, must rely on self-identification and, at best, gets at the self-perceptions of how individuals are categorized by others. Thus, we first asked in our survey "when forms or the census ask if you are white, black, Asian, American Indian, or other, what do you answer?" As in the official surveys, we purposefully did not include a Mexican American or Hispanic choice but did provide an "other" category. The first row of table 9.10 shows that only from 11 to 38 percent identified as white, lower than national samples using official data. However, this may not be surprising given that the survey questionnaire emphasized ethnic issues throughout, perhaps allowing respondents to overstate racial differences, whereas whiteness might be emphasized when answering an official document.

A higher proportion of the original respondents (26 to 38 percent) identified as white than the younger (11 to 15 percent), suggesting a growing acceptance of nonwhiteness among the younger generation. This probably reflects the greater stigma associated with not being white when the parents were socialized compared to the growing ethnic or racial pride and tolerance for multiracialism common among the younger generation. Also, immigrants (38 percent) were particularly likely to self-identify as white, while there are no notable differences between the second and third generations. Immigrants from Mexico are more likely to be puzzled by American racial classifications, which differ from those in Mexico. Preference for the white category may reflect their own classification on their own immigration or naturalization form and the lack of socialization about race in the United States. The decreasing proportion identifying as

Table 9.10   Racial Identity, Perceived Classification, Stereotyped, and Discrimination by Generation-Since-Immigration, 2000

	Original Respondents			Children		
	Gen. 1	Gen. 2	Gen. 3	Gen. 2	Gen. 3	Gen. 4+
Identify as white in race question	38%	26%	28%	15%	13%	11%
Definitely perceived as Mexican	48	47	39	39	39	38
Are stereotyped by others	34	34	37	59	56	66
Experience discrimination	24	40	38	48	48	46
Perceive "a great deal" of group discrimination	36	38	37	37	35	37

Source: Mexican American Study Project.

white in subsequent generations-since-immigration supports racialization theories.

Perceived Race, Stereotyping, and Discrimination

We also asked our respondents about how others perceived them, which gets at another, perhaps more important, dimension of race, which is generally believed to be based on physical appearance. For blacks, it is based on having at least one drop of African blood. The vast majority of African Americans, however, are identifiable based on physical appearance. Indeed, racial discrimination often depends on one's physical appearance, especially in the important first impressions made by potential employers or in other consequential social interactions. Race is presumably based on physical appearance for Asians also, but the extent of consistency between self-identification and identification by others is less than for African Americans and in the same range as Latinos.[29] Thus, Latinos are distinguished as a separate group to the same extent as Asians. Racial identities generally mirror those made in general society, and individuals are socialized to understand how others categorize them.

The second row of table 9.10 shows the extent to which our respondents believe they are definitely perceived as Mexican by others. About half (48 percent) of the immigrants believe they are and the percentages decline somewhat with each subsequent generation. By the fourth generation, more than a third (38 percent) sense that they are definitely perceived as Mexican. On the other hand, this may be a high standard since "definitely" may mean that others are always able to distinguish them not only from non-Hispanic whites but from other Hispanics and other ethnics, such as Middle Easterners. A finding we do not show here shows that those in San Antonio, populated by just three groups—whites, blacks, and Mexicans—are more likely to view themselves as being perceived as Mexican than in Los Angeles, which is much more diverse. Specifically, 41 percent of San Antonio respondents claimed they were definitely perceived by others as Mexican versus 32 percent in Los Angeles.

The third row of table 9.10 also shows the extent to which respondents feel stereotyped by others or report to have experienced discrimination. Whereas just over a third (34 to 37 percent) of the original respondents felt they were stereotyped, about two thirds (56 to 66 percent) of the children of all generations felt similarly.[30] This compares with about 22 percent of European Americans in the Albany study who reported being stereotyped about their ethnic group. Interestingly, later generations of Mexican Americans felt slightly more stereotyped than earlier generations.

We also asked respondents about discrimination against Mexican Americans as individuals and for the group. The fourth row shows that about 40 percent of U.S.-born original respondents and almost 50 percent of their children claimed to have experienced discrimination because of their ethnic background, versus only 24 percent of immigrants. This compares with only 5 percent in the Albany study of European Americans.[31] The last row reveals the percentage of those who believe there is "a great deal of" discrimination against Mexican Americans as a group—a constant 35 to 38 percent across all generations.

We asked the original respondents and their children to describe the racial or ethnic discrimination they reported. Among the children sample, nearly all of whom are U.S.-born, the most common incidents were being refused service or given slow service in restaurants and stores, being passed up in hiring or promotions, being discriminated against in dating, or being watched closely in stores. Others mention being called derogatory names, though these incidents often occurred while in the military, outside of Los Angeles or San Antonio, and especially in the South. There was less reporting of educational discrimination, which is understandable given that our respondents have been out of school for many years. Some recalled being steered to lower level classes because they were Mexican. The following are typical accounts of discrimination:

> Sometimes when people mistook me for Italian and when they found out that I was Mexican they changed their attitude. I went for a job, for administrative assistant. I showed up, they saw my skin features and they said the job had been filled. In general, when getting service in predominately white establishments the attitude is always subtly discriminatory. There are

so many—how can I say? In the job environment—being Mexican and a female—the expectation that we will do windows for 50 cents. The most damaging is the perception of us in the labor market. . . . At my job, I cannot advance to a higher position due to my ethnic background.

Two years ago, I really didn't see it until it was brought up as a joke— a kid—19 years old—son of a co-worker, high powered, said to me, "Every American should have a Mexican or Black doing their work." This was without realizing that I'm Mexican. In elementary school, I was judged to be dumb. My teacher said it was because I was from Mexico and I am not from Mexico.

The original respondents had similar stories but were also likely to recall both being purposely segregated—in school and in residence—because of their ethnic background and seeing signs that forbade Mexicans from public facilities. Presumably these incidents occurred mostly before the mid-1960s, during the Jim Crow era. For these reasons and because they sensed some claim to whiteness, it is somewhat understandable at to why the original respondents generally avoided identifying as Mexican or Mexican American in 1965.

These questions are all related to racial discrimination in American society and the extent to which this makes any difference to the lives of Mexican Americans or other ethnic groups. Specifically, it examines the extent to which ethnics classify themselves or are classified by others in white or nonwhite categories and, relatedly, whether they perceive individual or group discrimination or stereotyping by others. The fact that Mexican Americans more often see themselves as not white and perceive more discrimination than Europeans is likely to be a consequence of racism. Today, third and fourth generation Mexican Americans perceive more discrimination and identify themselves as nonwhite to a much greater extent than European ethnics of the same generation-since-immigration do.

The greater incidence of racism or perceived racism by Mexican Americans is often believed to be related to skin color, the master marker of racial distinction in the United States. On average, Mexican Americans certainly have darker skin color than European ethnics. On the other hand, there is much variation in the skin color of Mexican Americans, a result of centuries of intermarriage between indigenous peoples and Europeans, mostly Spaniards. Although many Mexican Americans are as dark as some African Americans, others are as light as non-Hispanic whites and often easily pass as such if they do not exhibit other markers of ethnic distinction. Other markers might include other phenotypical features, accent, last name, and height.

Table 9.11 examines the relation of racial identity and perceived classification and discrimination with skin color. The results show a consistent relation between skin color and the race-related questions in which darker

Table 9.11   Racial Identity, Perceived Classification, Stereotyped, and Discrimination by Skin Color, 2000

	Original Respondents			Children		
	Light	Medium	Dark	Light	Medium	Dark
Identify as white in race question	36%	31%	20%	18%	15%	12%
Definitely perceived as Mexican	29	53	57	32	44	53
Stereotyped by others	34	39	33	57	55	65
Experience discrimination	35	36	38	41	48	63
Perceive "a great deal" of group discrimination	37	38	37	37	33	30

Source: Mexican American Study Project.

persons were less likely to identify as white, more likely to be perceived as Mexican, and more likely to experience stereotyping and discrimination. Differences in stereotyping are not well correlated with skin color, perhaps because the question can be interpreted about stereotyping of the group and not the individual respondent. The same goes for group discrimination. For the most part, the correlation is strong and suggests that darker persons were more discriminated against and saw themselves as nonwhite, though the percentage of light-colored Mexican Americans also identifying as nonwhite and perceiving discrimination is substantial as well, certainly greater than for European Americans.

Factors Affecting Racial Identity and Perceived Discrimination

Table 9.12 presents the odds ratios for determinants of whether respondents identified as white and reported experiencing discrimination. We present the coefficients for variables that are statistically significant and for generation-since-immigration and education. Interestingly, column 1 results demonstrate that only one significant variable determined whether respondents identified as white, the comparison of Los Angeles and San Antonio. Mexican Americans who grew up in San Antonio were more than five times as likely to identify as white as their counterparts in Los Angeles. This reveals a regional context of racial identity that is widely differentiated between the two cities and probably between Texas and California. This also reflects a well-accepted understanding that the Chicano political

Table 9.12   Key Determinants of Racial Identity and Discrimination, 2000[a]

	Identify as White	Experienced Discrimination
Generation-since-immigration (ref: 3)		
1.5	0.74	2.28*
2	2.02	0.81
2.5	1.13	1.34
4+	0.92	1.20
Education	1.03	1.14**
San Antonio (1965)	5.60***	
Telephone interview (2000)		0.66*
Skin color		1.24**
Female		0.47***

Source: Mexican American Study Project.
[a] Only significant variables or substantive variables presented. Logistic regression run. Adjusted odds ratios presented. Child sample analyzed. Adjusted for sibling clustering. See appendix B, table B.13 for full model.
*p<.05, **p<.01, ***p<.001

movement of the 1960s, which pursued a racialized identity rather than an assimilationist strategy, as we described in chapter 4, became more entrenched and accepted in Los Angeles than in San Antonio.

Angelenos and San Antonians are equally likely to report experiences of discrimination. Many Mexican Americans, in Texas especially, were conscious of discrimination but were nevertheless more likely to identify as white. The idea of Mexicans as white but distinguished from so-called Anglos, seems to be a locally accepted identity derived from the strategies of Mexican American leaders of claiming whiteness to overcome their race-based exclusion. Reporting a white racial identity for Mexican Americans is not inconsistent with experiencing racial discrimination.

The second column of table 9.12 shows that the 1.5 generation was more likely than the U.S.-born to experience discrimination, even though nearly all of them were at least partially educated and socialized in the United States. This may have to do with language characteristics that further distinguish them from non-Hispanics, including accent and a high comfort level with Spanish. Also, more educated persons are generally more likely to report discrimination. That may reflect that they are more likely to have contact and compete with whites in the labor market or perhaps it reveals a more heightened sense that discrimination limits their opportunities. Respondents interviewed over the telephone were about two-thirds (.66) as likely to report experiences with discrimination. This probably reflects the fact that they had mostly moved out of the Los Angeles or San Antonio area, suggesting that discrimination, or at least the perception of it, against Mexican origin persons in less ethnically concentrated areas was less intense.

Darker persons were more likely to report experiencing discrimination, which may not be surprising, though they were not less likely than lighter persons to identify as white, once all the other variables in the model were controlled. The multivariate results thus suggest that the census classification as white may not reflect actual skin color for Mexican Americans. A similar finding can be found for Puerto Ricans, where classification as white, black, or other correlated poorly with actual skin color.[32] Latinos identify as other, not necessarily because they perceive themselves as not having white skin but often because the census does not provide a category for their national group or for Hispanics in general. For Mexican Americans, concepts of race are often based on national origin.[33]

Finally, females are half as likely as males to perceive discrimination. This may be because males are more likely to be in the labor market competing with whites or because they are more likely to have encounters with the police, where discrimination is often particularly explicit.

Conclusions

In this chapter, we find strong evidence of ethnic persistence across generations. Ethnic identification for Mexican Americans remains strong even into the fourth generation. Mexican, Mexican American, or Hispanic labels are preferred over American by nearly all of our respondents, even into the fourth generation. They also endure well after ethnic cultural characteristics, such as Spanish language or Catholic affiliation, have largely eroded. The immigrant generation clearly prefers the Mexican-Mexicano label whereas nearly half of the respondents of all the U.S.-born generations prefer Mexican American. The pan-ethnic Hispanic or Latino and the American labels were increasingly chosen in each subsequent generation so that by the fourth generation, one-third chose them and about 12 percent identified as American. A mixed ethnic background largely shapes these identities, where having a non-Hispanic parent predicts American identity.

Our evidence shows that ethnicity and racial classification are not fixed, but instead may differ appreciably over time and place. In this study, the choice of ethnic labels changed from 1965 to 2000 and was notably different in Los Angeles and San Antonio. In 1965, Latin American was the preferred ethnic term among Mexican Americans, particularly in San Antonio, where more than half chose it, apparently as a euphemism for the highly stigmatized Mexican. By 2000, Latin American had nearly fallen out of the classification lexicon and the pan-ethnic Latino and Hispanic had emerged. Hispanic was preferred by nearly half of San Antonians, but Mexican or Mexican American continued to be used by about three-quarters of the

Angelenos. Roughly 10 percent of Mexican Americans overall in both urban areas chose American in 1965 and 2000.

When asked the extent to which they felt American or Mexican, the results were more nuanced and followed a pattern of assimilation. Ethnic identity clearly followed the assimilation patter of erosion by generation-since-immigration. The immigrant generation was clearly more likely to think of themselves as Mexican. By the second generation, identities were more balanced. By the fourth generation, though, a much higher proportion thought of themselves as only American. A constant 20 percent of U.S.-born Mexican Americans of all generations thought of themselves as both.

Moreover, those raised in Los Angeles were more likely to think of themselves as only Mexican, whereas San Antonians were more likely to think of themselves as only American, independent of generation-since-immigration and other factors. Education also played a key role in ethnic identity. More highly educated Mexican Americans were clearly more likely to consider themselves only American. Also, identity as American or Mexican depended largely on the extent of Spanish usage in the home, which indicates the importance of cultural background for adult ethnic identity. Those learning Spanish in the home identified more as Mexican and less as American even though such identities did not seem to affect strong patriotism for the group.[34]

The especially slow rate of identificational assimilation seems to be at least partly shaped by racialization experiences. The vast majority of fourth-generation Mexican Americans, like the U.S.-born overall, identified as nonwhite and felt stereotyped as Mexican by others. A large number also believed they were perceived as Mexicans and reported that they were individually discriminated against. We find that strong ethnic and racial identities are also shaped by the ethnic context in which individuals were raised, particularly ethnic residential concentration, whether or not Spanish was spoken, and whether or not the parents were intermarried. All of this suggests that persistent ethnic identity is largely the result of intergenerational transmission in a context that to a substantial degree is ethnically isolated. Furthermore, Mexican immigrants and Mexican Americans with darker skin were more likely to report experiencing racial discrimination, which suggests that such markers enhance racial boundaries.

Chapter 10

Politics

Grebler, Moore, and Guzmán blamed a "history of conflict" for the limited Mexican American political involvement outside of New Mexico and south Texas. "No other ethnic group," they asserted, "has labored under a similar handicap of hostility, mistrust and suspicion as the result of an historic struggle with the dominant society."[1]

This conflict included Mexican American clashes with the Border Patrol and the Texas Rangers, the massive repatriations during the Great Depression, the roundups of undocumented immigrants during Operation Wetback in the 1950s and "humiliating tests of citizenship of people who were required to prove they were not deportable."[2] They also noted the ongoing racial profiling of Mexican Americans and the general association of the era's narcotics problem as a Mexican problem. Furthermore, they also found that the political effectiveness of Mexican Americans had been impeded by "internal disunity, by external restraints imposed through voting laws and procedures and by the gerrymandering of electoral districts."[3] However, Grebler and his colleagues were optimistic, discovering in the 1960s that Mexican Americans were beginning to "influence their environment" through the political process.[4] Grebler and his colleagues attributed this to a population explosion and a new leadership class from the ranks of the growing middle class and the returning veterans from World War II and the Korean War.

Soon after the 1970 publication of *The Mexican American People*, an extension to the 1965 Voting Rights Act in 1975 would remedy many of the constraints that impeded the fair participation of Mexican Americans in the electoral process, especially in the design of electoral districts. Almost immediately after its passage, Mexican Americans would make unprecedented electoral gains throughout the Southwest. The threat of a lawsuit led to a voter initiative to create single-member districts in San Antonio, an increase in minority city council representation, and the possibility of electing politicians dedicated to ethnic neighborhoods and issues.[5] In Los Angeles and throughout California, passage of the Voting Rights Act, along with rapid population growth from immigration, led to more equitable

238

districting and a growing number of Mexican American elected officials. At about the same time, young Mexican Americans would organize a Chicano social movement that aggressively demanded redress for social injustices, created an unprecedented ethnic political consciousness among large sectors of Mexican American society, and sparked its own cultural movement, as discussed in chapter 4.

Today, Mexican American voters (and Hispanic voters overall) have become an important new electorate, in large part a result of massive immigration in the last three decades and subsequent naturalization, which were especially high in the 1990s. Since the 1970s, the upsurge in immigration levels has transformed the political role of Hispanics through-out the United States, particularly in immigrant states such as California, where they are becoming a powerful interest group. The number of Hispanic voters grew from 2 million in 1972 to fully 7.6 million in 2004, which nearly parallels their population growth.[6] Large-scale immigration from Mexico and the subsequent naturalization of many immigrants along with their children reaching voting age would further increase the number of elected officials.[7] Representation by Mexican American elected officials at the federal and state level in the early 1960s was only about 20 percent of what it should have been in Texas and California, given the adult citizen population. Representation shot up to nearly 80 percent by 1980, however.[8] Although the upturn in formal Mexican American politics occurred several years before the 1975 extension,[9] the law would lead to still further gains. By 2005, eight of the top elected offices in Los Angeles were held by Mexican Americans, only one of which had had a Latino incumbent just a few years before.[10]

The political unity of Mexican Americans is another issue of concern. If they are politically divided as Grebler, Moore, and Guzmán claimed, or they have assimilated, voting would make relatively little difference in electoral outcomes and overall public opinion. If the ethnic identities of Mexican Americans remain vigorous into the fourth generation, then we might expect a corresponding ethnic political identity. We thus question whether third and fourth generations share the cohesive political identity of the immigrants and their children.

Although the patriotism and national identity have been questioned by many, including Huntington,[11] academic research shows the opposite. In a careful empirical analysis, Rodolfo de la Garza, Angelo Falcón, and Chris García found that Mexican Americans at all levels of acculturation were at least as likely to endorse values of economic individualism and patriotism as Anglo Americans.[12] Theoretically, though discrimination may impede mobility, national identity and allegiance may be ironically quite strong, as this evidence shows. The claim that that Latin American values are incompatible with economic individualism does not seem to apply, even to immigrants.[13] For Mexican Americans, at least, ethnic identity does not challenge national identity. They are in fact quite compatible.

Theories of Political Incorporation

American politics has had distinctive ethnic overtones for many years. Bell argued that because politics has replaced the market as the chief arena for distribution of societal resources, and because politics recognizes only claims, ethnic group interests have become particularly salient.[14] Struggles for political power among white ethnic groups defined local politics in major cities of the East and Midwest throughout much of the twentieth century. Ethnic leaders have used politics to gain advantages for members of their groups and, in turn, politics has emphasized ethnicity.

Robert Dahl, in his early study of urban politics in New Haven, recognized the importance of ethnic politics and elaborated a multigenerational assimilation theory of political development.[15] He argued that, in the first of three stages of ethnic politics, various waves of immigrants to New Haven—which included Germans, Irish, Russians, and Italians—were almost entirely proletarian at the time of immigration and shortly thereafter. Their class interests were thus fairly homogeneous, but they depended on dominant group members for political influence. In the second stage, many ethnics ascended into the middle class, allowing them to become ethnic leaders. However, because the group's class interests diversified, making class potentially divisive to the ethnic group, the new leaders stressed ethnic solidarity. The final stage is one of widespread assimilation in class, lifestyles, marriage partners, and political ideas, greatly diminishing the ethnic appeal of electoral candidates. For Dahl, writing more than forty years ago, all of the European-origin groups had entered the third stage by 1950. In contrast, blacks entered the second stage only in 1950, even though they began arriving to New Haven well before the white groups and are arguably still in that stage. They have thus proved the exception to Dahl's theory of political assimilation.

In his encyclopedic volume on ethnicity and American politics, Lawrence Fuchs argues that despite the historically disadvantaged status of Mexican Americans, their pattern of political or civic incorporation is similar to that predicted by traditional assimilation theory.[16] Fuchs is optimistic about the political assimilation of Mexican Americans, expecting them to follow the pattern of earlier ethnic groups who, like the Irish, were able to "negotiate, bargain and work within the system,"[17] eventually dominating Boston politics. He claims that

> by the end of the 1980s, there was abundant evidence that Mexican Americans were participating extensively in mainstream American politics. In every city and state where they became active in electoral politics, Mexican

Americans extended their political agenda beyond their first concerns [for example, civil rights, immigration and bilingual education] and elected representatives who entered coalitions with others.[18]

However, though Fuchs touted Mexican American civic incorporation, he seemed to agree that they remain in Dahl's second stage. He also cited evidence that the U.S.-born have strong American political values,[19] suggesting that Mexican Americans, like the European ethnic groups, will complete Dahl's cycle of political assimilation.

If assimilation theories work for Mexican Americans, as they did for Dahl's European immigrants, then Mexican Americans are presented with a political paradox, at least in terms of electoral politics. First, Mexican Americans are different from Dahl's European groups because they are products of successive waves of Mexican immigration throughout the twentieth century. Most of the immigrants are not citizens and are therefore ineligible to vote, just as immigrants were in Dahl's first wave. However, unlike the European immigrants in Dahl's study, who relied on other ethnic groups for political leadership, the Mexican immigrant noncitizens generally depend on Mexican American leaders who are descendants of earlier waves. They often also assume that the later-generation Mexican Americans have ethnic interests similar to their own. However, this is problematic if the later generations' values, ideas, and interests have become more like those of the dominant group, as in Dahl's account of European ethnics.

However, Dahl's theory suggests another possibility: that racialized ethnic groups like African Americans, which have been in the United States for many generations, either do not assimilate or assimilate slowly, and therefore remain in the second stage of ethnic politics. Using Dahl's three stages, the bulk of scholarly specialists on the topic would seem to argue that Mexican Americans are also in the second stage of political incorporation, like blacks in New Haven[20] and throughout the United States.[21] A racialization argument is also consistent with recent empirical findings of growing political socialization between the first and the second generation but receding political incorporation and greater apathy by the third.[22] Later-generation Mexican Americans, largely lacking the ethnic resources and positive outlook of the immigrant community, become apathetic as they perceive a stigmatized status for themselves.

Dahl's theory is largely descriptive and does not directly explain why only blacks remained in the second stage, though he discussed racial discrimination as an enduring, though declining, obstacle to their economic success. Since Dahl, many others have argued that some groups experience discrimination, leading to their greater political solidarity as ethnics. Alejandro Portes and Robert Bach and Rodolfo de la Garza and Louis De Sipio expected that the third and later generations better recognize discrimination than immigrants and their children, and thus react in the form of ethnic politics.[23] De la Garza, Falcón, and García acknowledged cultural and socioeconomic assimilation for Mexican Americans but suggested that acculturation leads to a heightened sense of discrimination, which promotes rather than diminishes ethnic political behaviors.[24] Keefe and Padilla argued that Latino ethnic identity comes primarily from the consciousness-raising of encounters with systems of racism and inequality in American society and consequent political struggles, such as those in favor of affirmative action or against immigration restriction.[25] Similarly, Ian Haney López argued that the young Mexican American activists in the 1960s rejected their parents failed claims to whiteness and middle class American aspirations and therefore became Chicanos as they sought an ethnic or racial path to political mobilization.[26] In a similar vein, Smith argued that though it may seem like separatism for some, ethnics in the United States have long sought to increase group solidarity, organize politically, and build ethnic political institutions as strategies for achieving full participation and incorporation in American society.[27] Separatist inclinations in the short run are meant for political incorporation in the long run.

The separatist argument has been taken up by others to argue that in an era of increasing multiculturalism, Mexican American and other ethnic group leaders are not committed to incorporation but instead seek out policies that advance ethnic interests, including entitlements, and that emphasize group boundaries, such as bilingual education or affirmative action.[28] In particular, they claim that the extension of the Voting Rights Act to Mexican Americans signaled the recognition of the group as requiring special state protections against disadvantages that earlier immigrants were able to overcome on their own. This allowed Mexican American leaders to make political claims as a racial minority, much as blacks do.[29] Huntington went as far as to issue a warning that Mexican Americans were resistant to assimilation, which could divide the United States into two languages and cultures, and establish separate political and linguistic enclaves.[30]

Objectives

Following these general sociological theories about incorporation, we examine the political incorporation of Mexican Americans as a whole, in which politics is part of a system of individual decisions, shaped and constrained by individual and societal characteristics, including the larger ethnic polity. Following our general methodological task in this book, we look at politics across the generations, especially individual level politics, including voting, partisanship and public opinion, which precede and ultimately decide the extent of ethnic leadership. We focus on formal politics, rather than political mobilization, which is important for political identity. Because relatively few persons are political activists, political mobilization is difficult to capture in a population-based survey like this one.[31]

Ultimately, we want to know whether any semblance of ethnic politics remains by the fourth generation. Although many political pundits and ethnic leaders assume a cross-generational Mexican American or Latino political community or voting bloc, there is little evidence that allows us to know for sure. Has political participation and voting behavior increased from 1965 to 2000? How does political participation and voting behavior change over generations? Is political participation and voting behavior related to local context? How do generation, class, geographical location or other variables explain the voting behavior and public opinion of Mexican Americans?

Naturalization by Immigrants

For ethnic groups with a large recent immigrant component, voting strength tends to be low relative to the size of its population because voting requires citizenship. Although Hispanics constituted 12.8 percent of the total United States population in 2000, they made up only 5.5 percent of the voters in the presidential race that year.[32] The recent arrival of many immigrants and the undocumented status of some even long-term residents make many Latinos automatically ineligible.

Voting in the United States requires immigrants to either naturalize or become an American citizen. Among Mexican immigrants, naturalization rates are particularly low, which might be expected given their greater possibility of wanting to return to Mexico and thus their greater hesitation to surrender Mexican citizenship. Thus citizenship rates among Mexican immigrants are also considered low when compared to those for other countries. In the 1990s, for example, only 27 percent of Mexican immigrants who had lived in California for at least ten years had become citizens, versus 40 percent of other Latinos, 57 percent of Koreans, 76 percent of Chinese, and 78 percent of Filipinos.[33] However, there is evidence that naturalization rates increased in the 1990s, apparently in reaction to anti-immigrant hostility during the period and to the growing possibility of dual nationalities.[34]

Our data allow us to examine long term trends in naturalization for Mexican immigrants. Table 10.1 shows the percentage of the immigrant original respondents who had become citizens, first in 1965 and then again in 2000. Among those who immigrated before 1945, 49 percent were citizens by 1965 and 71 percent by 2000. Among the recently immigrated in 1965, only 7 percent were citizens but more than half (57 percent) were by 2000. Nearly three-quarters of those who lived in the United States for at least five years by 1965 had become citizens by 2000. The lower rate of citizenship among those immigrating after 1960 may reflect some selectivity in which they were more likely to have been transient immigrants and never have established firm roots and commitments in the United States.

Table 10.1   Citizenship by Period of Immigration Among Immigrants, 1965 and 2000

	Original Respondents	
	1965	2000
Period of immigration		
Pre-1945	49%	71%
1945 to 1954	24	75
1955 to 1959	10	72
1960 to 1965	7	57
Total	19	70

Source: Mexican American Study Project.

Voter Registration and Turnout

Although citizenship status is an issue for the Mexican-origin population today, our sample was largely born in the United States and those who were not have been United States residents for at least thirty years. Thus ineligibility is not the primary reason for not voting or participating in the political process. Voting in the United States requires two steps for the U.S.-born, registration and actual voting. Table 10.2 shows that among American citizens, non-Hispanic whites have the highest registration and voting rates, followed by blacks, then by Hispanics, and lastly by Asians. These numbers were self-reported by American citizens soon after the elections in 2000. Among adult American citizen Latinos, both voter registration and turnout was low compared to other groups.[35] Some, though not all, of these differences may be explained by differences in age structure and educational levels. Older and more educated people are more likely to register and to vote.

Table 10.3 shows self-reported voting behavior from our data. Specifically, it presents voting registration and voting turnout rates in 1965 and 2000 for original respondents and their children. In surveys of this type, overreporting is the rule, especially if much time has expired between the

Table 10.2   Registered and Voted by Race, 2000[a]

	Registered	Voted
Hispanics	57%	45%
Non-Hispanic whites	72	62
Blacks	67	57
Asians	52	43

Source: U.S. Bureau of the Census (2002).
[a] Among general population of U.S. citizens.

Table 10.3 Registered and Voted in Last Presidential Election by Generation-Since-Immigration, 1965 and 2000[a]

	Original Respondents, 1965			Original Respondents, 2000			Children		
	Gen. 1	Gen. 2	Gen. 3	Gen. 1	Gen. 2	Gen. 3	Gen. 2	Gen. 3	Gen. 4+
Registered	61%	71%	67%	91%	88%	85%	81%	82%	81%
Voted[b]	54	62	57	87	82	78	61	65	59

Source: Mexican American Study Project.

[a] Among citizens.

[b] 1964 presidential election in 1965 survey and 1996 presidential election in 2000 survey.

Table 10.4   **Key Determinants of Voting in 1996 Presidential Election, 2000**[a]

	Voted in 1996
Generation-since-immigration (ref: 3)	
1.5	0.27*
2	0.87
2.5	0.82
4	0.95
Education	1.30***

Source: Mexican American Study Project.
[a] Only significant variables or substantive variables presented. Logistic regression run. Adjusted odds ratios presented. Child sample analyzed. Adjusted for sibling clustering. See appendix B, table B.14 for full model.
*p<.05, ***p<.001

election and the survey. Overreports of registering to vote can be expected given that many Americans consider it their duty and lapses are often unjustifiable. Nonetheless, the figures in table 10.3 are useful in providing relational differences among the generations. In 1965, voter registration was between 61 and 71 percent for all generational groups. It increased between 1965 and 2000, when respondents in all generations reported voter registration rates of greater than 80 percent (actual registration rates in the general population are likely to be in the 60 to 70 percent range). The children of the original respondents were more likely to register to vote than their parents, at roughly the same age, were in 1965. However, by 2000, parents were more likely to register than their children. This might be an age effect because seniors are the most likely age group to vote.[36]

Voting, like registration, is overreported, especially in surveys taken some time after the vote is cast. For example, more than half (54 to 62 percent) of the eligible original respondents reported voting in 1964. However, 78 percent or more reported voting in 1996, but only 59 to 65 percent of the children did. Thus, the elderly original respondents were thus clearly more likely to vote than their children, in both elections. These numbers indicate that 80 to 90 percent reported voting out of those registered to vote. Figures of actual voting do not therefore appear to be as exaggerated as those for registration because data based on exit poll data showed that more than 80 percent of registered Latinos voted in the 1996 election.[37] Among original respondents and children, there is no well-defined generational pattern.

We conducted regression analysis to predict reported voting in the 1996 election. The results in table 10.4 show that the 1.5 generation, those who arrived in the United States as children, was much less likely to vote than the third generation. There are no other significant differences by generation-since-immigration in voting. Each subsequent generation is only slightly less likely to vote than the third generation. The only statistically significant variable is education—the more educated are significantly more likely to vote than the less educated—a finding nearly axiomatic among political scientists. Thus, the persistence of especially low levels of education among Mexican Americans of all generations-since-immigration largely accounts for their low levels of formal political participation in American society.

Los Angeles Versus San Antonio

An important aspect of our study is to return to Grebler, Moore, and Guzmán's emphasis on the importance of local context in understanding Mexican American social outcomes. Local context is clearly important for politics in general and we strongly suspect that it has been so for differentiating the political behavior of Mexican Americans. Grebler, Moore, and Guzmán saw possibilities of political socialization for Mexican Americans when they compared Los Angeles and San Antonio. Los Angeles had clearly higher rates of registration and participation among eligible voters.

In Los Angeles County, the rate of voter registration among our respondents was within the range of norms in the United States, and the actual voting rate was not much below the average. Here, as in other parts of our study, the assimilative potentials in a relatively open milieu are clear.[38] The original authors went on to attribute lower participation rates in San Antonio to greater isolation and poverty and more restrictive voting laws and practices.[39] They also attributed low voter registration in San Antonio to a high number of "recent migrants from rural areas with their limited view of their potential role in political life."[40] Table 10.5 shows the same urban difference that Grebler and his colleagues pointed out. Angelenos were 15 percentage points more likely to register and 18 percentage points more likely to vote. Fully 62 percent of American citizens reported voting in Los Angeles in the 1964 presidential elections, versus only 44 percent in San Antonio. However, the differences between the two urban centers among the original respondents disappeared and in fact reversed by 2000. San Antonians, both original respondents and children, were then more likely to register and actually vote.

Partisanship

Ethnicity and partisanship have been strongly linked in American politics for some groups. For blacks and Jews, even today, political behaviors tend to be liberal with up to 90 percent or more of these groups voting for Democrats. African Americans tend to be strongly Democratic. The rates for Jews, however, have been declining. Mexican Americans are traditional Democrats even though Republicans claim that strong Mexican American

Table 10.5   **Registered and Voted in Last Presidential Election by Urban Area, 1965 and 2000**[a]

	Original Respondents, 1965		Original Respondents, 2000		Children	
	Los Angeles	San Antonio	Los Angeles	San Antonio	Los Angeles	San Antonio
Registered	71%	56%	86%	89%	79%	84%
Voted[b]	62	44	80	83	63	65

Source: Mexican American Study Project.
[a] Among citizens.
[b] 1964 presidential election in 1965 survey and 1996 presidential election in 2000 survey.

family and other values make them self-professed conservative or, as De Sipio calls them, "proto-Republicans."[41] Indeed, Republicans have recently made inroads in capturing the Latino vote. They have shown that the presumed allegiance of Mexican Americans to the Democratic Party is questionable.[42] On the other hand, though Mexican Americans are conservative on moral issues, entrepreneurialism, support for the military, and the death penalty, these issues rank as less important to them than others that make them closer to the Democrats. These include education and social services spending and the appropriate role and scope of the government.[43] Generational differences for Mexican Americans thus capture the extent of stability or malleability of the Mexican American vote.[44]

Table 10.6 shows that fully 69 to 80 percent of the original respondents considered themselves Democrats in 2000 versus only 54 to 62 percent of the children's generation. For the original respondents, the third generation was less Democratic than the other two generations. Among the children,

Table 10.6   **Party Affiliation by Generation-Since-Immigration, 2000**

	Original Respondents			Children		
	Gen. 1	Gen. 2	Gen. 3	Gen. 2	Gen. 3	Gen. 4+
Democrat	78%	80%	69%	56%	54%	62%
Republican	5	6	11	20	16	15
Independent	10	10	12	15	21	14
Other	7	4	8	9	9	9

Source: Mexican American Study Project.

Table 10.7   Party Affiliation by Urban Area, 2000

	Original Respondents		Children	
	Los Angeles	San Antonio	Los Angeles	San Antonio
Democrat	78%	70%	58%	55%
Republican	7	6	18	13
Independent	8	19	15	23
Other	7	5	10	9

Source: Mexican American Study Project.

however, the fourth generation was the most Democratic, but the differences were not large in either cohort. On the other hand, only 5 or 6 percent of the original respondents in the first and second generations—versus 11 percent of the third generation—considered themselves Republican. Most of the non-Democrats considered themselves Independent or third party and generational differences were not significant in either category. Many of the children of the original respondents had become Republicans. Interestingly, it was the second generation that had become the most Republican, the opposite of the pattern for their parents' generation. Fully 20 percent of the second generation among children were Republican and another 24 percent reported being Independent or another party.

Where between 5 and 11 percent of the original respondents considered themselves Republicans in 2000, fully 15 to 20 percent of their children did. From the original respondents to their children, the proportion Republican grew four times between immigrants and their second-generation children, more than two times from the second to the third generation, and almost 50 percent from the third to the fourth generation. We suspect that if we had comparable 1965 data about which party respondents considered themselves, the intergenerational partisan shift would have been even more pronounced. We do have data on voting for president, which suggests great change.

Table 10.7, showing partisan data by urban area, indicates that both original respondents and their children in Los Angeles were more likely to be Democrat than in San Antonio. Yet those in San Antonio were not more likely to be Republican. Rather they described themselves more often as Independents, which may simply indicate dissatisfaction with the political process rather than a particular ideology.

Presidential Voting, 1964 and 2000

Partisanship in actual voting is often quite different from declared partisanship. Many more of both original respondents and children voted

Democratic than said they considered themselves Democrats, for example. Such shifts, however, are often one-time and due to the particular candidates of an election. Table 10.8 shows that the large majority of Mexican Americans of all generations voted for the 1964 and 1996 Democratic presidential candidates, both of whom won. In 1964, 96 percent of immigrants and about 90 percent of the second and third generation in our sample voted for Lyndon Johnson. This compares to a national figure of 90 percent for Mexican Americans.[45] Johnson easily won that election with 63 percent of the popular vote.

Thirty-two years later, Mexican Americans again overwhelmingly supported a Democratic candidate in a far closer election. Bill Clinton won his reelection bid in 1996 with only 49 percent of the popular vote, the remaining 51 percent split between contenders Bob Dole and Ross Perot. Nationally, 72 percent of Latinos voted for Clinton,[46] though the numbers were probably higher for Mexican Americans. Among the original respondents, fully 93 percent of the immigrants in our sample voted for Clinton as did 85 percent of the second generation and 80 percent of the third. The child generation was a bit less enthusiastic about Clinton but large majorities voted for him—74 percent of the fourth generation and slightly greater numbers of the second and third generations.

The number of original respondents and their children who actually voted for Dole, the Republican candidate, was close to the number claiming to be Republican. Only 6 percent of immigrants voted Republican, but fully 18 percent of the fourth-generation children did so. On the other hand, even though many considered themselves Independents and in other parties, very few claim to have voted that way in 1996, even though Independents had a viable candidate.

As happens in the general population, there were also differences in voting by Mexican Americans according to where they lived and, in this case, where they grew up. An overwhelming majority of Mexican Americans in both urban areas voted for Johnson in 1964, but by 2000 regional differences had increased (see table 10.9). In 1996, for example, Angelenos were somewhat more likely to vote for Clinton but the big difference was in support for Dole. Many more of the original respondents and their children voted for Dole in San Antonio than in Los Angeles. Angelenos were at least twice as likely to vote for Perot.

Factors Affecting Voting and Partisanship

Our findings in the descriptive tables thus far suggest that, among the children, there is a significant, if small, movement away from the Democratic Party with generation-since-immigration. How do we explain this? Is it the result of a natural trend toward the American norm, as assimilation theory might predict, or is it indirectly attributable to factors such as upward educational or residential mobility over the generations? Table 10.10 seeks

Table 10.8   Presidential Choice in 1964 and 1996 by Generation-Since-Immigration, 1965 and 2000[a]

	Original Respondents, 1965			Original Respondents, 2000			Children		
	Gen. 1	Gen. 2	Gen. 3	Gen. 1	Gen. 2	Gen. 3	Gen. 2	Gen. 3	Gen. 4+
Democrat[b]	96%	91%	89%	93%	85%	80%	76%	78%	74%
Republican[c]	4	9	11	6	11	17	16	17	18
Independent[d]	—	—	—	1	2	3	5	4	7
Other	—	—	—	0	2	1	4	2	2

Source: Mexican American Study Project.

[a] Among those who voted.
[b] Johnson in 1964 or Clinton in 1996.
[c] Goldwater in 1964 or Dole in 1996.
[d] None in 1964 or Perot in 1996.

Table 10.9   Presidential Choice in 1964 and 1996 by Urban Area, 1965 and 2000[a]

	Original Respondents, 1965		Original Respondents, 2000		Children	
	Los Angeles	San Antonio	Los Angeles	San Antonio	Los Angeles	San Antonio
Democrat[b]	91%	93%	86%	80%	77%	74%
Republican[c]	9	7	10	17	15	23
Independent[d]	—	—	3	1	6	3
Other	—	—	1	2	2	1

Source: Mexican American Study Project.
[a] Among those who voted.
[b] Johnson in 1964 or Clinton in 1996.
[c] Goldwater in 1964 or Dole in 1996.
[d] None in 1964 or Perot in 1996.

Table 10.10   Key Determinants of Voted Republican in 1996 and Identify Republican, 2000[a]

	Voted Republican	Identify Republican
Generation-Since-Immigration (ref: 3)		
1.5	0.96	0.66
2	2.23	3.21*
2.5	1.28	2.07*
4+	1.33	1.18
Education	1.05	1.08
Father's education		1.15**
Parent voted in 1964 (ref: voted Democrat)		
Voted Republican	4.36**	3.95**
Did not vote		0.53*

Source: Mexican American Study Project.
[a] Only significant variables or substantive variables presented. Logistic regression run. Adjusted odds ratios presented. Child sample analyzed. Adjusted for sibling clustering. See appendix B, table B.15 for full model.
*$p < .05$, **$p < .01$

to predict which childhood factors best account for whether Mexican Americans become Republicans or voted for the Republican candidate in 1996. The children of immigrants (generation two and 2.5) were more likely to become Republican than either immigrants who came as children (1.5 generation) or later (third or fourth) generation Mexican Americans. This may be related to the bootstraps philosophy of the Republican party and the large socioeconomic mobility gain for the second generation compared to their immigrant parents. Immigrants, including the 1.5 generation, are likely to be in the party that favors immigration. On the other hand, there were no statistically significant generational differences in actual voting for the Republican candidate, though the coefficients suggest a similar, albeit weaker, generational pattern.

The other important predictor of both voting and identification as Republican is the voting behavior of parents. Children of parents who voted Republican in 1964 were about four times as likely as the children of Democrats to consider themselves and vote Republican. Also, parents who did not vote in 1964 were less likely to have children who become Republicans. By implication, the obverse of this is that parents who voted Democratic were much more likely to have children who were also not Republican, which could mean Democratic or Independent. Whether the parent voted Republican in 1964 also made it much more likely that the individual themselves would vote Republican and identify as such. The results suggest a ratcheting effect in which the switch to being Republican by Mexican American parents creates a Republican familial culture in which their children tend to remain Republican. We thus find that party affiliation is largely an intergenerational affair in which parental or perhaps family politics strongly predicts children's politics, whereas the effect of generation-since-immigration is not linear and sees the most change from the first to the second generation.

Surprisingly, growing up in Los Angeles or San Antonio does not make a difference to partisanship in 2000. Notably, the survey was mostly taken before the 2000 elections that George W. Bush (a Republican from Texas) won. Although parental education usually does not make a difference in predicting voting and party identification, it did in our study. Fathers with more education were more likely to have children who identified with the Republican Party than fathers with less schooling. On the other hand, the individual's education had no effect on how they voted or their party affiliation. Other than parent's voting behavior, characteristics while growing up did a fairly poor job of predicting partisanship as adults, suggesting that few child life experiences are important.[47]

Political Attitudes

Political participation and voting depend on public attitudes, particularly on a small set of issues, which sometimes determine whether Mexican

Americans identify or vote as Democrats, Republicans, or Independents. The extent of ethnic bloc voting would seem to depend largely on the extent of common support for issues related to ethnic group interests. If ethnicity disappears by the third or fourth generation, as assimilation theory would predict, then support for ethnic issues would be undifferentiated from that of the general population. The political positions of Latinos, in general, are known to be different from those of whites and blacks but the extent to which these views are driven by immigrants, and possibly their children, is less known. In other words, the average political attitudes of the group might be distant from those of other groups but for the third and fourth generation there may be little or no distinction.

The issues of immigration, affirmative action, and language policy became flashpoints of ethnic difference in California in the 1990s, when residents voted on several statewide referendums that would deny public services to illegal immigrants (Proposition 187 in 1994), end affirmative action (Proposition 209 in 1996), and cut the state's bilingual education programs (Proposition 227 in 1998). All three passed with widespread support from white voters, who continue to comprise the large majority of California voters. Latino voters, the large majority of whom were Mexican Americans, strongly opposed all three measures. Their influence, however, was relatively weak for the overall vote in 2000 because, despite being 26 percent of the state's adult population, they accounted for only 14 percent of California voters. In contrast, whites were 54 percent of the adult population in 2000 but 70 percent of the voters.[48] The ethnic gap in votes for Propositions 187 and 227 were similar: 63 percent of whites to 23 percent and 24 percent of Latinos, respectively. The difference for Proposition 209, however, was smaller—67 percent of whites to 37 percent of Latinos. That is the story of the overall Latino vote, but it tells us nothing about whether Mexican Americans in later generations hold such contrasting views as Dahl and traditional assimilationists might predict.

Consistent with Dahl's theory of political assimilation, at least one observer believes that racial and ethnic differences are currently diminishing with the assimilation of U.S.-born Latinos.[49] On issues affecting a particular ethnic group, however, it could be that individuals having a shared identity with the victim group may perceive societal injustice toward their group and thus mobilize and form strong ethnic identities in response. The case of United States immigration policy seems apt. One may argue that the United States immigration policy for Mexicans has been particularly unfair. Mexican immigrants have received little government assistance compared to other groups, particularly refugees such as those from Cuba and Vietnam. Moreover, a very large number of Mexican immigrants have been driven into undocumented status by an especially low ceiling placed on the numbers of visas Washington grants to Mexican citizens. Furthermore, Mexicans have been the special targets of antago-

Table 10.11   Immigration Attitudes by Race, 2005

	Non-Hispanic Whites	Blacks	Hispanics
Immigrants hurt economy by reducing wages	52%	66%	27%
United States should make it easier for illegals to become American citizens	19	30	70

Source: Gallup Poll (2005).

nistic nativist policies that seek to curtail or end immigration. Chapter 9 showed that many Mexican-origin persons of all generations perceived discrimination against members of their group.

Immigration Attitudes   Ethnic attitudes about immigration vary widely by race-ethnicity. Hispanics were much more pro-immigrant than whites and African Americans.[50] Based on a nationwide Gallup Poll about immigration, Table 10.11 shows that the majority of non-Hispanic whites (52 percent) and blacks (66 percent) believed that immigrants hurt citizens by driving down wages, but only 27 percent of Hispanics held such an opinion. Similarly, only 19 percent of whites and 30 percent of blacks agreed that the United States should make it easier for illegal immigrants to become American citizens but fully 70 percent of Hispanics did.

But does this mean that all Mexican Americans, regardless of immigration status, hold these attitudes? To what extent are pro-immigration attitudes merely due to self-interested immigrants or perhaps their second-generation children? The failure to disentangle most presentations of immigration attitudes by generation among Hispanics is certainly a problem. One might expect later generations-since-immigration to hold attitudes about immigration similar to those of blacks and whites. This expectation is consistent with assimilation theory. On the other hand, there may be an ethnic bloc that supported immigrants and that kept later-generation Mexican Americans from holding widespread nativist sentiments.

Table 10.12 shows a surprising amount of ethnic cohesion around immigration. It also reveals much less assimilation than assimilation theorists might expect. Third- and fourth-generation voters had remarkably similar preferences as immigrants and thus their attitudes on these contentious issues are quite distinct from those of non-Hispanics. The overall differences between Mexican American or Latino attitudes compared to either whites or blacks on immigration shown in table 10.11 thus seem to hold up regardless of generation-since-immigration. Table 10.12 presents some signs of eroding support for immigration by later-generation Mexican Americans compared to immigrants, but this was not always the case. More important, their opinions were quite strong compared with those

Table 10.12   Immigration Attitudes by Generation-Since-Immigration, 2000

	Original Respondents			Children		
	Gen. 1	Gen. 2	Gen. 3	Gen. 2	Gen. 3	Gen. 4+
Immigration levels						
1. United States should have an open border policy with Mexico	47%	42%	33%	35%	36%	41%
2. United States should allow Mexicans to immigrate to country if they want	72	63	56	50	52	53
3. There are too many immigrants coming into this country	74	77	83	70	73	70
4. There are too many illegal immigrants in this country	82	85	89	73	77	74
Immigration and jobs or citizenship						
5. Mexican immigrants take jobs away from Americans	23	32	33	31	34	39
6. American citizens should be favored for jobs over non-citizens	41	60	71	54	58	53
7. The United States should make it easier for recent Mexican immigrants to become American citizens	75	66	60	69	56	55
Average positive attitudes toward immigration[a]	2.53	2.41	2.67	2.42	2.41	2.44

Source: Mexican American Study Project.

[a] Average of items shown on rows 1 to 7. For items in favor of immigration (rows 1, 2, and 7), response categories range from (1) strongly disagree to (4) strongly agree. For items against immigration (rows 3 to 6), response categories are reversed and range from (1) strongly agree to (4) strongly disagree.

of the dominant group. The common but poorly substantiated (and apparently imagined) claim that Mexican American leadership is out of touch with the Mexican American voting public on such issues was thus clearly exaggerated.[51]

The several questions on immigration in our survey revealed a common pattern. For example, the first row of table 10.12 shows the extent to which respondents agreed that the United States should have an open border policy with Mexico. For the original respondents, nearly half of immigrants (47 percent) agreed compared with 42 percent of the second generation and one-third (33 percent) of the third generation. For the child generation, greater generational distance from immigration meant more favorable positions about an open border. Fully 41 percent of fourth-generation Mexican Americans supported the idea, for example. The biggest difference by generation-since-immigration for original respondents was the question about whether the United States should allow Mexicans to immigrate if they want (row 2). Fully 72 percent of immigrant original respondents agreed with this statement but only 56 percent of the third generation did. For their children, though, there were no differences.

The most contentious question concerned attitudes toward illegal immigration (row 4). More than 80 percent of the original respondents of all generations agreed that there were too many illegal immigrants in the United States. The largest differences are not among the original respondents but between them and their children. Seventy-three percent of the second-generation, 77 percent of the third generation, and 74 percent of the fourth generation agreed that there were too many illegal immigrants. The distinction between feelings about immigrants in general (row 3) and illegal immigrants (row 4) was 6 to 8 percent for the original respondents. This difference was smaller for their children.

Overall opinions on the levels of immigration did not vary for the children's generation as they did for their parents (rows 1 to 4). Generation-since-immigration did not make a difference for the U.S.-born children, suggesting that there is no assimilation on public opinion about immigration as there was for the parent generation.

On the question of immigrant displacement in the labor force (row 5), later generations tend to more strongly agree that immigrants take jobs away from Americans. The percent agreeing, however, was always less than 40 percent. Less than one-quarter (23 percent) of the first generation increased to about one third for the second and third generation of the original respondents (32 and 33 percent respectively). Similar figures held for the child generation, though by the fourth generation those believing in such immigrant displacement increased slightly to 39 percent. This compared to the majority of blacks and whites, as table 10.11 revealed.

On the question of whether American citizens should be favored for jobs over noncitizens (row 6), the percentages clearly increased for each succeeding generation among the original respondents. By the third generation, fully 71 percent agreed. However, for the child generation, there were relatively small generational differences, with all three responses around 55 percent.

The last question on immigration shown in table 10.12 asked the extent to which respondents agree whether the United States should make it easier for recent Mexican immigrants to become American citizens (row 7), which is almost identical to the Gallup Poll survey question shown in table 10.11. The only difference is that the national poll asked about illegal immigrants and our survey asked about recent Mexican immigrants, which might be similarly interpreted. We found that 75 percent of immigrants agreed with that statement but the numbers for the U.S.-born were lower. About two-thirds of the second generation original respondents (66 percent) and 60 percent of the third generation. Among the children, 69 percent of the second generation agree, while 55 to 56 percent of the third and fourth generations do. This compares with about 70 percent of all Hispanics in the Gallup Poll, which puts our sample in the ballpark of the national sample. This is realistic, if we consider that the proportion of immigrants in the national sample is likely to be greater than ours. Most important, the finding that the majority of even third- and fourth-generation Mexican Americans would support such immigration policies contrasts sharply with much lower percentages of blacks (30 percent) and especially non-Hispanic whites (19 percent).

Only one attitudinal question about immigration was asked in the original survey. We repeated the question in 2000, whether respondents agree that Mexicans should be able to immigrate to the United States if they want (row 2). The results are shown in figure 10.1. Because we have already discussed findings from the 2000 survey, we focus here on the 1965 findings and how they differ. The main difference is that original respondents seem to have relaxed their restrictionist opinions over the thirty-five years. For instance, half of the second generation agreed that the United States should allow Mexicans to immigrate in 1965 and almost two-thirds did by 2000. The first and third generations showed similar increased support for immigration.

To recap, the children of the original respondents were less tolerant of unrestricted immigration. Just over half of all their children agreed that Mexicans should be able to immigrate if they want. There were no generational differences. On issues of immigration, there does not seem to be an overall assimilation pattern in which opinions in favor of immigrants diminish over generations but rather they continue to be notably different from those of the general American population. More important, even among the fourth generation, such attitudes suggest ethnic persistence in which their attitudes contrast sharply with those of the general white population.

Figure 10.1   Agree that Mexicans Should be Able to Immigrate, 1965 and 2000

Generation-Since-Immigration	Original Respondents		Children of Original Respondents
	1965	2000	2000
1	62%	72%	———
2	50%	63%	53%
3	43%	56%	54%
4+	———	———	53%

Source: Mexican American Study Project.

Regression Analysis of Immigration Attitudes   Last we examine what best predicts having positive attitudes toward immigration (using the composite measure of attitudes in the last row on table 10.12). This is shown on table 10.13. Not surprisingly, immigrants (generation 1.5) have significantly more positive attitudes toward immigration than other generations. This may reflect the fact that the less educated are more likely to directly compete with immigrants in the labor market and thus would probably be inclined to want greater restrictions on immigration. Similarly, competition for housing and schools from immigrants may be seen as negatively affecting cost and quality of housing and education. More educated Mexican Americans also have significantly more positive attitudes than the less educated. The children of homeowners had less positive attitudes—this could be an effect of feeling that increased immigration negatively affects neighborhoods and consequently home values. Apparently, this is a sentiment passed on from parents to children. Children growing up in San Antonio had less positive attitudes toward immigration, which probably reflects less exposure to immigration. Interestingly, women also had less positive attitudes.

Table 10.13   Key Determinants of Positive Attitudes Toward Immigration, 2000[a]

	Positive Attitudes Toward Immigration[b]
Generation-since-immigration (ref: 3)	
1.5	0.17*
2	0.03
2.5	−0.03
4+	−0.03
Education	0.03***
Parent was homeowner	−0.10*
San Antonio (1965)	−0.10*
Female	−0.08*

Source: Mexican American Study Project.
[a] Only significant variables or substantive variables presented. Linear regression run. Unstandardized coefficients presented. Child sample analyzed. Adjusted for sibling clustering. See appendix B, table B.16 for full model.
[b] Based on average attitudes reported in last row of table 10.12.
*p<.05, ***p<.001

Affirmative Action Attitudes   We asked one question about affirmative action in our survey (table 10.14). We found strong support in all generations of Mexican Americans, but immigrants were the most supportive. There is no strong trend toward assimilation after that. The lack of a clear pattern, however, may not be surprising given that affirmative action, unlike immigration, is likely to affect all generations similarly. Among the general population, Hispanics support for affirmative action (69 percent) is considerably more than that of non-Hispanic whites (44 percent), and similar to that of blacks (64 percent).

Language Attitudes   Finally, we asked several attitudinal questions in relation to the use of Spanish or English and bilingualism. Table 10.15 shows that, for the most part, attitudes about language use do not clearly follow distinctions by generation-since-immigration. It does demonstrate, however, that the child cohort has more relaxed attitudes about whether Spanish or English should be used. On all language items, whether pro-Spanish or pro-English, sentiments were always stronger in the parent generation, suggesting simultaneous feelings of both ethnic distinctiveness and Americanness among that generation. In only one question did generation-since-immigration matter for both parents and children in any consistent way. Agreement with whether everyone should know English (row 4) increased with each succeeding generation-since-immigration in

Table 10.14   Affirmative Action Attitudes by Generation-Since-Immigration and Race, 2000 and 2001

	Original Respondents, 2000		
	Gen. 1	Gen. 2	Gen. 3
Affirmative action is a good thing for persons of Mexican origin	85%	78%	80%

	Children, 2000		
	Gen. 2	Gen. 3	Gen. 4+
Affirmative action is a good thing for persons of Mexican origin	80%	73%	75%

	General Population, 2001		
	Whites	Blacks	Hispanics
Support affirmative action for racial minorities	44%	64%	69%

Source: Mexican American Study Project; Gallup Poll (2001).

both samples. For the parent generation only, feelings that the local population should learn Spanish (row 5) tended to erode over succeeding generations-since-immigration. Nearly half (48 percent) of immigrants in the original sample believed that all residents in Los Angeles or San Antonio, regardless of ancestry, should learn Spanish versus only one-third (33 percent) of the third generation.

Conclusions

Our evidence shows that though the participation of Mexican Americans in formal politics has been increasing through voting registration, participation continues to be low compared to whites and African Americans. We find no evidence of any patterned change with generation-since-immigration. We do, however, find that participation in the electoral process increased sharply from 1965 to 2000, especially in San Antonio. The weight of poll taxes in Texas and other factors that had discouraged Mexican Americans from voting have since been largely lifted, extending political citizenship to Mexican Americans on a wide basis. The low overall rates of voter registration and participation among the Mexican American population are partly driven by the immigrant generation, many of whom are not citizens and thus cannot vote. Among our surviving immigrant original respondents of the 1965 sample, fully 70 percent had become citizens by 2000. However, among U.S.-born Mexican Americans, voting registration and participation continues to be lower than for other whites, which is

Table 10.15 Language Attitudes by Generation-Since-Immigration, 2000

	Original Respondents			Children		
	Gen. 1	Gen. 2	Gen. 3	Gen. 2	Gen. 3	Gen. 4+
Language						
1. Spanish should only be spoken at home	13%	10%	11%	4%	2%	6%
2. Citizens who do not read English should not vote	41	43	36	16	24	28
3. All residents of Los Angeles or San Antonio regardless of ancestry should learn Spanish	48	41	33	35	28	37
4. Everyone in California or Texas should know English	79	82	91	62	65	79
5. Hispanics should know English and Spanish	94	90	91	88	78	82
6. Hispanic children should learn both languages	97	90	88	91	82	88

Source: Mexican American Study Project.

largely attributable to low levels of formal education. Participation and registration is also lower than for blacks, but this is probably attributable to lower levels of voter mobilization, a factor we cannot measure.

In 1965, the Mexican American electorate was almost entirely Democrat. That proportion had noticeably declined a generation later in 2000, when nearly one-fifth of the children sample self-reported as Independent and a similar number identified as Republican. In terms of actual voting in 1996, about three-quarters voted for the victorious Democratic candidate (Clinton) and most of the remainder voted Republican, especially in San Antonio. Like the shift from 1965 to 2000, the earlier generation of original respondents showed signs of political assimilation by becoming less Democrat in terms of generation-since-immigration. Yet, even by the third or fourth generation, at least three-quarters of Mexican Americans continued to vote Democratic in 1996. Indeed, our statistical analysis revealed that parent's partisanship was clearly transmitted to their children.

On political attitudes about ethnically related issues such as immigration, affirmative action, and bilingual education, we found evidence of an ethnic community of interests and little that indicated assimilation, either historically or by generation-since-immigration. Historically, our data suggest increasing tolerance for immigration among Mexican Americans of all generations-since-immigration. Even into the fourth generation, Mexican Americans strongly supported immigration, affirmative action, and bilingualism. Our statistical analysis of attitudes about immigration suggests that less educated Mexican Americans were more anti-immigrant, suggesting that they were more likely to perceive immigrants as a threat. Immigration, to the extent that it has a negative effect on less skilled Americans, is likely to affect less educated Mexican Americans more than any other sector of the population.

This chapter revealed an ethnic politics among Mexican Americans that endured well into the fourth generation. Although there is a gradual trend toward political behavior and attitudes of the general American population, the fourth generation continued to vote and hold attitudes on ethnic issues more like immigrants than non-Hispanic Americans. They are predominantly Democratic and pro-immigration across generations. This largely common community of interest seems to reflect persistent ethnic identities shaped by persistent ethnic behaviors. The Mexican Americans in our sample were engaged in American politics and their political behavior on particular issues seemed to reflect their attempts to challenge their group's marginalization in American society.

═ Chapter 11 ═

Conclusions

The Mexican American experience requires that we look beyond the traditional assimilation versus race theories that have been based almost entirely on the European American and African American experiences. The well-known assimilation story, in its classic and modern forms, has been the dominant theory for explaining immigrant integration and was derived from the experiences of European immigrants to the United States and their descendants. Even though many of them occupied the bottom rungs of the American class structure when they arrived, their children and grandchildren successfully rode the mobility escalator to middle class status, stopped speaking their native languages, and thoroughly mixed with the general white population, including the descendants of other recent European immigrants. Overall, they would no longer be differentiated from other Americans, and were hardly ethnic by the third generation. We find that is not at all the story for Mexican Americans, whose ancestors immigrated during the same period as the Europeans and in some cases were natives of what was then Mexico but is now the United States.

For third- and fourth-generation Mexican Americans, we find that ethnic boundaries are much more than merely symbolic, which they are for later-generation European Americans. Mexican American ethnicity continues to influence their language, who they choose as friends and marriage partners, where they live, how they see themselves, and how they vote. Unfortunately, it also shapes their class position. However, the slow acculturation and persistent low status of Mexican Americans is also clearly not the rigid caste-like type predicted by the internal colonial model or by theories predicated on the African American example. Mexican Americans intermarry much more than do blacks, live in less segregated areas, and face less labor market discrimination, which suggests a path also different from that of African Americans. In this sense, racial boundaries for Mexican Americans are clearly less rigid than for African Americans, despite even worse schooling.

Using state-of-the-art social science methods, we have followed the intergenerational experience of Mexican origin adults in 1965 to their children as adults in 2000. As far as we know, this research design is unique and for many reasons it is the most appropriate for addressing the actual intergenerational integration of immigrants and their descendants. Among its advantages, it permits the investigation of real intergenerational change by seeing how events occurring during childhood or a generation ago are related to adult outcomes and by matching parents to their actual children rather than relying on proxies.

We have shown that the experience of assimilation, where it occurred, was far slower than it was for European Americans. The erosion of ethnic boundaries over generations between Mexicans and Anglos, the defining feature of assimilation in our view, is most apparent in the linguistic realm. Although English proficiency is virtually universal for the U.S.-born today, Spanish fluency is not. There is a gradual weaning away from Spanish so that by the fourth generation (or more), only one-third of the child sample is able to speak Spanish and fully 94 percent speak mostly or only English to their fifth-generation children at home.

However, there is a surprising amount of ethnic persistence into the fourth generation regarding identities, voting behaviors, and some cultural practices. Among fourth-generation Mexican Americans, most live in majority Hispanic neighborhoods, most marry other Hispanics, most frequently think of themselves as Mexican, and most agree that the United States should allow Mexicans to immigrate to the United States if they want to. Although intermarriage with other groups tends to grow with each generation, it is so slow so that even by the fourth generation, nearly two-thirds are still married to other Hispanics. Their identity change is far from complete in the third or even fourth generation and their politics continue to be on the left of the spectrum and to strongly support ethnic issues. All of these sharpen racial and cultural boundaries between Mexican Americans and Anglos, which in turn further restricts their assimilation. Although they may have lost some ethnic cultural attributes like language, most fourth-generation Mexican Americans in our study experience a world largely shaped by their race and ethnicity.

In education, which best determines life chances in the United States, assimilation is interrupted by the second generation and stagnates thereafter. Considering the education of parents, it can even be characterized as backwards. Mexican Americans, three or four generations removed from their immigrant ancestors, are less likely than the Mexican American second generation of similar characteristics to have completed either high school or college. Mexican Americans also have lower levels of schooling than any other major racial-ethnic group. Because education helps propel individuals toward assimilation on most other dimensions, a lack of educational progress thus limits Mexican American assimilation overall. In terms of adult socioeconomic status, there are no differences by generation-since-immigration. While the children of U.S.-born parents (third generation-since-immigration or more) benefit from having parents with higher levels of schooling than Mexican-born parents, the children of Mexican immigrants (second generation-since-immigration) seem to benefit from greater optimism about life in the United States and seem to have higher human and social capital for the same years of schooling.

We extended the scope of previous investigations by introducing a long dureé, multigenerational perspective that covers much of the twentieth century, by examining variation within Mexicans and, by investigating a fuller range of dimensions in which integration may occur. Moreover, we disentangle the generally intertwined dimensions of generation-since-immigration from historical or family generation, which has confounded previous studies of immigrant integration. For example, we find backward assimilation in education from the perspective of generation-since-immigration, but from the perspective of historical or family generation, we find gradual educational assimilation over the course of the twentieth century. The former supports the ideas of segmented assimilation theory[1] while the latter suggests a slow but constant assimilation over the course of the twentieth century though one that is far from complete even after four or five generations.

Generation-Since-Immigration

From the perspective of generation-since-immigration, we find slow assimilation on most dimensions but stalled or reversed on education. Linguistic assimilation toward English monolingualism is constant and occurs more rapidly than on any other dimension though it was clearly slower than for other ethnic groups.[2] Despite linguistic assimilation, though, other behaviors and ethnic identities suggest strong attachment to the ethnic group and they often remain even for those who are four generations removed from immigration. Marriage within the group, residential segregation, ethnic identity, and support for pro-ethnic group social policies persisted well into the fourth generation, though their strength tends to slightly erode with each generation-since-immigration. This is in marked contrast to European Americans, whose assimilation on most dimensions was rapid and complete by the third generation. Most notably, though, levels of education peak among the children of immigrants and worsen for the third and fourth generation. Education, the most important variable determining adult socioeconomic status, bucks the path expected by assimilation theory. It is affected by generation-since-immigration but in a way that runs contrary to traditional assimilation theory, and the experiences of long-settled European immigrant groups in the United States.

Generation-since-immigration simulates the "intergenerational experience" of an ethnic group at one point in time, though this experience actually occurs over time, by definition. One advantage of such a simulation is that data are more easily available cross-sectionally. A more important one, however, is that it allows one to keep the historical context constant. Thus, the second-generation respondents are not the children of the immigrant respondents, at least not those who are of comparable ages. Rather, they are children of immigrants a historical generation earlier and may have had characteristics that were quite different from the immigrant generation at the same timepoint.

The multivariate statistical analyses we present throughout the chapters permit us to simulate the independent effects of generation-since-immigration on Mexican Americans of similar backgrounds—including parents' education, urban background, age, gender, and skin color. After we statistically controlled for other variables thought to affect the assimilation outcomes of interest, only education and language were independently related to generation-since-immigration, which we present in figure 11.1. Other variables—including occupation, income, wealth, homeownership, segregation, intermarriage, racial identification as white, and experience with discrimination—were not, though there may have been indications of a relationship in the bivariate analysis. Figure 11.1 shows that third and fourth generations did statistically worse in schooling than immigrants who came as children or the children of immigrants. The collective second generation (generations 1.5 and two) completed decidedly more education than their parents, while further educational gains were aborted for the third and fourth generations. Second-generation Mexicans, compared to their immigrant parents, seemed to assimilate at least as rapidly as second-generation Italians and other European groups.[3] For the third generation, however, educational assimilation abruptly halted and even slightly reversed. Unlike European ethnics, whose status continued to rise into the third generation, low levels of schooling kept Mexican Americans concentrated in working class or low-level white-collar occupations well into the third and fourth generation.

Why then did education fall for Mexican Americans from the second to the third generation? We controlled for all hypothesized nonracial causes but the negative trajectory of generation-since-immigration only sharpened. The leading explanation for why the second generation did better is that a more optimistic disposition among immigrants and their families cushioned them from the full effects of racialization. Immigrant parents and their immigrant children, often believing in the American dream, probably perceive the advantages of a better life in the United States, whereas U.S.-born parents do not have that reference but instead an Americanized image of their proper place.[4] Their acculturation is not only one of losing ethnic cultural traits but probably also of acquiring a strong

Figure 11.1   Educational and Linguistic Incorporation by Generation-Since-Immigration, 2000[a]

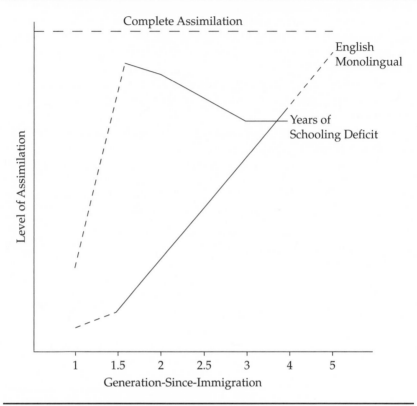

Source: Mexican American Study Project.
[a] From multivariate analysis among children.

sense of the American racial hierarchy. Our analysis shows that the low levels of education of later generations are unlikely to be attributable to the alleged cultural deficiencies sometimes used to explain low education for immigrant children, such as poor ability in English or the lack of discipline or knowledge of American schools.

Figure 11.1 also shows a quite different pattern for language. Specifically, it reveals a slow but certain linear trend toward universal English monolingualism, which is consistent with reaching full assimilation on the linguistic dimension. Mexican Americans retain Spanish more than other groups but do not keep it indefinitely. In the American context, the eventual loss of the ethnic language of immigrant ancestors is considered normal and even desirable, though bilingualism is common and often perceived as indispensable in other societies. Virtually all other groups in United

States lost their ethnic-origin languages within two or three generations. Even though bilingual education is favored by most Mexican Americans of all generations, Spanish fluency is close to extinct by the fifth generation. More than any other dimension, language can be expected to exhibit a linear assimilatory path because of a ratcheting effect. Because ethnic languages are learned mostly at home, once the previous generation is no longer fluent, the children miss the best opportunity to learn the language. Thus, the percentage of those who can speak an ethnic language can only get smaller from generation to generation, unless a compelling reason drives large numbers to learn it later in life.

The Historical Perspective

Our study demonstrates the importance of separating two very different generational processes of immigrant and ethnic group integration previously seen as a single process or, at best, consistent processes. A historical or family generation perspective yields distinct results from those based on generation-since-immigration. Specifically, our analysis of changes from the original respondents in 1965 to their children in 2000 suggests considerable assimilation over that period. From 1965 to 2000, assimilation for Mexican Americans was probably faster that it has ever been, on many dimensions. We find a slow but constant assimilation of Mexican Americans in education over historical time as the gap between levels of schooling between Mexican Americans and Anglos slowly decreased over the course of the twentieth century. Various other types of ethnic boundaries also softened. For example, English monolingualism and intermarriage rapidly increased, probably the results of overall changes in American society, such as the spread of English-language media, the growing participation of women in the labor market, and greater universalism in education. This is broadly consistent with predictions of assimilation[5] but the slowness of change suggests that optimism regarding improvements in the group's status is unwarranted.

We present the findings for some of our key indicators in figure 11.2. The figure mostly suggests a slow historical trajectory from 1965 to 2000 toward assimilation and the erosion of ethnic boundaries. Specifically, the bold lines in figure 11.2 show the real intergenerational changes from the second generation in 1965 to their third-generation children in 2000. Given that one may expect signs of assimilation for subsequent generations despite the historical context, we also plotted a dotted line to show the difference between the third generation in 1965 and in 2000. Although the trends may be sharper when comparing second- to third-generation changes, the dotted lines connecting third generations reveal that these trends are nonetheless affected by the historical context.

Figure 11.2 (panel a) shows that the college completion gap with white Americans gradually decreased, though it remained substantial. Based on

Figure 11.2   Intergenerational Patterns of Incorporation for Mexican Americans, 1965 to 2000

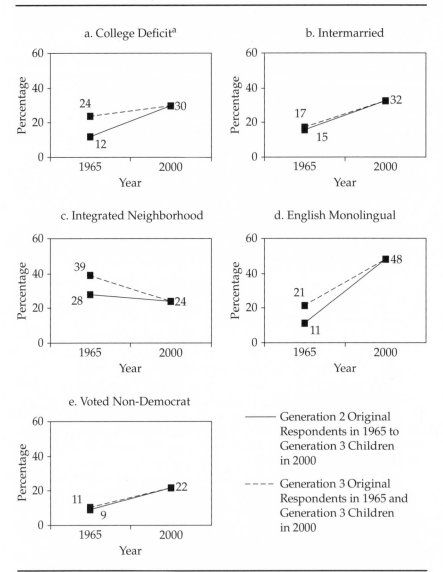

Source: Mexican American Study Project.
[a] Odds of completing college for Mexican Americans compared to non-Hispanic whites.

the college completion rates we calculated in chapter 5, we show that by 2000, third-generation Mexican Americans in our child sample were about 30 percent as likely as non-Hispanics to have completed college. This compares to just over 10 percent for their second-generation parents (original respondents) and less than 25 percent among the third-generation original respondents. Given the affirmative action policies of universities to accept more Mexican Americans, their intentions seem to have helped but nonetheless fallen short. Although the proportion of Mexican Americans graduating from college increased, they continued to lag far behind the also large increases in college completion among the general population. Critics might argue that downward assimilation from the second to the third generation in the cross-sectional analysis might be explained by relatively high selectivity of pre-1965 immigrants. The historical data, however, show that real educational progress among the descendants of an even earlier immigration moved forward only at a crawl.

Most Mexican Americans age thirty-five to fifty-four in 2000 were high school graduates with no or some college, a large improvement over the previous generation's high school completion. Nevertheless, the persistence of high school dropout rates of 15 to 25 percent over generations-since-immigration is a cause for concern. Such high rates appear to persist for recent graduates in very recent cohorts.[6] The persistence of gang membership among many later-generation Mexican Americans also raises concerns about the formation of a multiple generation Mexican American underclass. States like California and Texas have class systems with bottoms already occupied mostly by those of Mexican origin, including many U.S.-born. Given that the white working class is more likely to move up and that it is increasingly moving to states away from those where Hispanics and blacks are concentrated,[7] the danger of a largely Hispanic working class becoming an underclass is real if not for robust labor markets.

Figure 11.2 (panel d) also shows decline in Spanish language ability, or linguistic assimilation. A shift to English monolingualism was particularly strong from 1965 to 2000. Whereas only a little over 10 percent of the second generation in 1965 were English monolinguals, nearly 50 percent of their third generation children were. The dotted lines for language show that there have been sharp declines in Spanish language fluency among later-generation Mexican Americans. Whereas 80 percent of third-generation Mexican Americans spoke some Spanish in 1965, only about half of the third generation children did so in 2000.

Similarly, intermarriage increased substantially from about 15 percent for both the second- and third-generation original respondents to 30 percent for the third-generation children (panel b of figure 11.2). The percentage not voting for the Democratic candidate for President increased from about 10 percent for both generations in the 1964 election to about 20 percent in 1996 (panel e of figure 11.2). Also, though not shown, the increase in the number of non-Catholics from 10 percent in 1965 to about 40 percent in 2000 demonstrates sharp religious assimilation to the mostly working class fundamentalist and evangelical religions.

Contrary to the assimilation direction of other dimensions, levels of residential isolation for Mexican Americans increased from 1965 to 2000. Almost a quarter of second-generation original respondents lived in a neighborhood in which Hispanics were a small minority in 1965, and about the same percentage of their third-generation children did so in 2000. This contrasts with the 32 percent of third-generation respondents who lived in such neighborhoods in 1965. As we showed in chapter 7, this was largely due to the resurgence of immigration from Latin America, which increased the percentage of Hispanics in neighborhoods throughout the Southwest. Therefore, even though some of our respondents may have moved to more integrated and higher status neighborhoods in, say, 1980, the neighborhoods were likely to become increasingly Hispanic because of immigration after that time. These changes in the ethnic composition of the neighborhood are thus likely to have altered the ethnic experience of Mexican Americans and their children in 2000 with respect to the average experiences of Mexican Americans in the 1960s. We expect that rates of intermarriage for later-generation Mexican Americans will remain stable or even decrease for the next generation, because childhood segregation shapes the extent of intermarriage, as our results showed.

There was no information on race in the 1965 survey. However, we can speculate that identification as white declined between 1965 and 2000, even though racial boundaries became more fluid. Many of Mexican origin, especially in Texas, sought to avoid a Mexican identity in the 1940s and 1950s because of its extreme racial stigma. Years later, though, being Mexican, Mexican American, or even Chicano came to be proudly accepted with the social justice and often nationalist social movements of the 1960s.[8] Although the original respondents were not asked their race in the 1965 survey, the sample was selected from the 1960 census population of "white persons of Spanish surname," a proxy for Mexican Americans in the Southwest. Certainly, Mexican Americans were generally not considered white, as historic evidence shows,[9] but were usually labeled as such in official documents by 1965. Most of our respondents did not identify as white in our 2000 survey and nearly half of Mexican Americans also did not in the 2000 U.S. Census. Moreover, we found a smaller number of the children sample identifying as white compared to their parents, which also suggests that Mexican Americans are increasingly likely to see themselves as nonwhite.

However, most boundaries between later-generation Mexican Americans and whites seem to soften from 1965 to 2000. The 1960s marked a period of major legislation and policy changes in favor of civil rights and the end of egregious racism and segregation in the American Southwest, which was largely directed at Mexican Americans. Up to that time, racial boundaries in such areas as housing, employment, and even romance were often cast in law or policy, sometimes heavily policed, formally and informally, and generally accepted as natural. A slowly declining educational gap over time may be partly attributable to civil rights gains for minorities, including affirmative action in universities, policies to improve equity in public spending for schools, and the end of de jure segregation, though a persistent gap, in light of these changes, remains worrisome. Assimilation over time is also probably related to growing universalism through structural and political change, which largely resulted from the earlier civil rights struggles of Mexican Americans and other minorities. However, a surge in immigration helped increase residential isolation, which may lead to lower intermarriage rates for Mexican Americans in the future. Additionally, and contrary to the assimilation thesis, the Chicano nationalist movement helped shape more racialized and nonwhite identities.

In sum, historical change for equivalent generations-since-immigration among Mexican Americans shows assimilation but one much slower than for European Americans. The assimilation of European Americans involved a historical and political process of their becoming or being accepted as white in the first half of the twentieth century,[10] rather than merely a process of integration thought to naturally occur over generations-since-immigration. That magic historical moment of incorporation did not happen for Mexican Americans. Widespread participation in international wars[11] and unionization in Los Angeles did not help them like it helped European Americans. Indeed, they were mostly excluded from this process as they were perceived as insufficiently American or white, and historically, they were subject to a comprehensive system of racial domination, unlike any experienced by European Americans.[12] By the 1960s, when third-generation European Americans had become nearly fully incorporated, third-generation Mexican Americans had not. By 2000, they still had not. Although ethnic boundaries with whites became more fluid and their situation improved from 1965 to 2000, Mexican Americans were still far from assimilated and definitely had not become accepted as white. For a process of assimilation to occur for them, a new and more inclusive historical context must emerge. Without such a change, assimilation is not likely.

Variation Among Mexican Americans

We have sought to overcome a general tendency in the literature to emphasize differences between ethnic groups and downplay the substantial diversity within groups. Certainly some Mexican Americans have been able to penetrate racial or ethnic boundaries and move into the mainstream more easily than others. A few may even assimilate to a point where their ethnicity makes little or no difference. Richard Alba and

Victor Nee and Portes and Rumbaut note that particular variables may hasten or impede assimilation, but tend to assign such variables wholesale to one or another ethnic group.[13] Instead, we found wide variation in the extent of assimilation among the Mexican American population, despite their generation. For example, those who attained relatively high levels of education, those growing up in more integrated neighborhoods, especially in Los Angeles, and those with parents of mixed ethnic origin assimilate more easily. Although group-level experiences largely predict individual experiences of integration, individuals within the group may also be subject to a wide range of contextual and social forces.

Some U.S.-born Mexican Americans become solidly middle class and occasionally even very successful in their field. Such persons tended to have grown up in households where parents had relatively high levels of schooling and greater economic and social resources. Those who attended Catholic schools also tend to be better educated and thus have greater life chances than those who attended public schools. At the same time, these more economically successful individuals are especially likely to have integrated into the American mainstream and have cultural or linguistic attributes that are decidedly mainstream American. A disproportionate number, though, continue to occupy the lower ranks of the American class structure. Certainly, later-generation Mexican Americans and European Americans overlap in their class distributions. The difference is that the bulk of Mexican Americans are in lower class sectors, but only a relatively small part of the European American population is similarly positioned.

Education as the Linchpin of Slow Assimilation

More than any other variable, education accounts for the slow assimilation of Mexican Americans on most social dimensions. Throughout this book, our statistical models have shown that the low education levels of Mexican Americans have impeded most other types of assimilation, thus reinforcing a range of ethnic boundaries between them and white Americans. Mexican Americans with low levels of schooling tend to have lower income, wealth, and occupational status, which limit their ability to move out of the barrio. Their limited schooling locks many of them into a future of low socioeconomic status. A disproportionate segment of the Mexican American population is thus subordinated in the youthful process of educational and human capital formation.[14] Low levels of education also predict lower rates of intermarriage, a weaker American identity, and lower likelihood of registering to vote and voting. Just as segregation has been described as the linchpin of the African American experience,[15] low education is the linchpin of the ethnic persistence of Mexican Americans.

We illustrate the difference that one's level of schooling makes on these and other indicators for the children sample in figure 11.3. We present differences in the extent of integration along seven indicators by three

Figure 11.3   Assimilation and Education Among Children, 2000

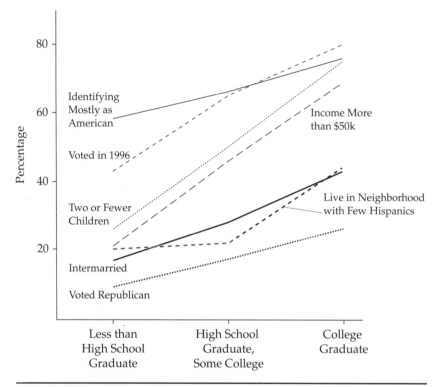

Source: Mexican American Study Project.

levels of schooling: less than high school, high school graduates with no or some college, and college graduates. Figure 11.3 demonstrates that assimilation on each dimension increased with the level of schooling.[16] It shows, for example, that Mexican Americans with higher levels of education are more likely to have an American than an ethnic identity and are more likely to vote, suggesting greater integration in the American polity. Relatedly, they are also more likely to vote Republican, suggesting that they are less committed to the usual party of the ethnic group. Their level of education makes a notable difference in socioeconomic status (percentage with incomes greater than $50,000)[17] and exposure to other groups (percentage living in a neighborhood with 25 percent or fewer Hispanics and percentage intermarried). Finally, they also have lower fertility (percentage with two or fewer children), itself an important determinant of the educational level of the next generation.

These patterns are similar for the original respondent generation, though the rates are often lower. We show these results in figure 11.4. For example, only about 5 percent of high school dropouts among the original respon-

Figure 11.4   Assimilation and Education Among Original Respondents, 2000

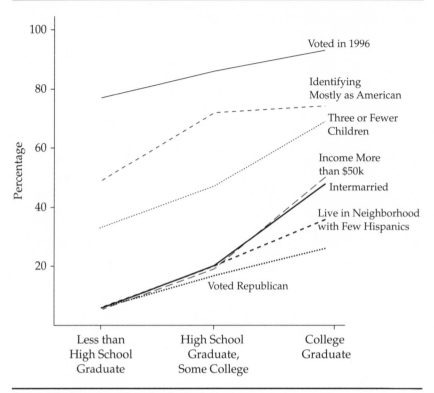

Source: Mexican American Study Project.

dents intermarried, versus more than 40 percent of college graduates. This compares with their children's generation, in which about 15 percent of high school dropouts intermarried and nearly 40 percent of college graduates did. Thus, at the less-educated end, rates of intermarriage increased about three times. At the other, though, intermarriage rates have surprisingly remained stable from 1965 to 2000. To take two more examples, less-educated people in 1964 were much less likely to vote than in 1996 but were also much more likely to live in integrated neighborhoods in 1964 than in 1996.[18] The most important point of figures 11.3 and 11.4, though, is to show that assimilation is consistently related to education for two distinct generations of Mexican Americans and the persistence of educational disadvantage largely predicts the group's slow or halted assimilation.

Race, ethnicity, and class are thus deeply intertwined for Mexican Americans. Low levels of education puts them largely in working class sectors (including low-level white-collar jobs) and the ethnic boundaries of later generations are especially strong for the working class. Since low education tends to be transmitted across generations, this segment of the Mexican American population is likely to remain working class and especially immersed in ethnic culture for several generations. For the middle class, however, ethnic boundaries are relatively light. Thus, class defines race and ethnic experiences to a large extent.

Other Factors Affecting Mexican American Integration

We also discuss how urban context, parental status, gender, intermarriage, and skin color also help shape Mexican American integration. These variables influence individual prospects for assimilation and the way Mexican Americans experience race and ethnicity. We begin with an analysis of urban context at the metropolitan and at the neighborhood level.

The Urban Context

Our sample consists of Mexican Americans growing up in Los Angeles County and San Antonio City in the 1960s. These two areas represented the largest concentrations of Mexican Americans at the time and often represented quite distinct socioeconomic, political, and cultural experiences. Based on select indicators such as education and income, the average outcome for Mexican Americans in general seems to lie between the two. More important, these two areas illustrate how urban contexts can shape the experience of ethnicity in the United States. Local political and economic histories have varied substantially and left their mark on how race and ethnicity have been experienced.

The specific differences in our study between Los Angeles and San Antonio continue to be quite striking even after controlling for many other respondent characteristics, including the extent of residential segregation and human capital. The context of much of the Southwest is bicultural but this is especially true in San Antonio. More third- and fourth-generation Mexican Americans raised in San Antonio are proficient in Spanish than in Los Angeles, revealing the importance of the particular local context in which ethnicity is sustained. Spanish language dies earlier in Los Angeles but such acculturation does not affect socioeconomic assimilation. Mexican Americans are similarly disadvantaged in both cities, though San Antonians were clearly worse off at the time of the original study (1960s). Despite this, they became similar socioeconomically to their counterparts in Los Angeles by 2000.

Mexican Americans are more Mexican in lifestyle and behaviors in San Antonio but are more Democratic and politically liberal in Los Angeles. Besides being more likely to speak Spanish, San Antonians are more likely than Angelenos both to marry and live near other Mexican-origin persons and to remain in the area they grew up in. On the other hand, despite a history of greater racialized oppression, Mexican Americans growing up in San Antonio are much more likely to identify as white. They are also more likely to identify as Hispanic and to vote Republican, reflecting the more conservative and assimilationist political strategies that Mexican American leaders pursued in Texas.

Such differences between the two places may also be related to more traditional Anglo-Mexican relations in San Antonio. Such relations probably derive from Mexican San Antonio's recent emergence from a deeply racialized system. Racialization for Mexican Americans in San Antonio until well into the 1960s included widespread segregation, poverty, and social isolation as well as a related tradition of patronage in politics and paternalism. Thus, when our child respondents were growing up, racial boundaries between Anglos and Mexicans were much more rigid in San Antonio than in Los Angeles. These boundaries sealed off much of the Mexican American community, thus promoting ethnic culture and possibly traditional ways of thinking and deference in an especially hierarchical society. At the same time, Mexican American San Antonians were more likely to identify as white, in that nearly Southern city, where clear distinctions from blacks were socially and politically valued. In contrast, racial boundaries and relations were more fluid in the more cosmopolitan and integrated Los Angeles of the 1960s, where legal segregation and explicit racism had become less common. Assertions of an explicitly nonwhite racial identity also emerged by the late 1960s, especially in Los Angeles, which provided fertile ground for progressive political activism.

A changing industrial structure and the opportunities for mobility that it affords have been commonly used to explain why European immigrants succeeded and why the descendants of immigrants today will have a harder time moving into the middle class.[19] Under the pre-1970s industrial structure, manual jobs paid well, were unionized, had long-term security, and provided opportunities for career mobility. Because of this, we would expect that the children of Mexican American Angelenos would do better than those of San Antonians, given that Los Angeles had a large industrial base much like East Coast American cities[20] and San Antonio did not. Mexican Americans in Los Angeles in the original sample had better economic opportunities, indicated by their concentration in manufacturing jobs and their higher incomes. In addition, the profitable industrial composition of Los Angeles likely contributed to better schools in the region overall. However, we found no evidence that Mexican American children growing up in Los Angeles did better socioeconomically than in San Antonio, nor did we find that children of parents working in industrial manufacturing did better educationally. Apparently, the advantages of a traditional manufacturing economy did not extend to the Mexican American population. Relatedly, the availability of manufacturing jobs also did not help the next generation of Mexican Americans in Los Angeles to secure more professional and high status occupations than their San Antonio counterparts.

A major point of the industrial restructuring argument is that the less educated had better labor market opportunities under the old industrial structure and that by the third generation, schooling had often become high enough for such individuals to enter secure professional occupations. That favorable economic structure is often used to argue how immigrants were able to move up the occupational ladder in two or three generations-since-immigration. However, the educational and socioeconomic status of the original respondents and their children were similar in Los Angeles and San Antonio, despite the greater economic opportunities in the "most industrialized city west of the Mississippi."[21] Moreover, the pattern of third-generation decline or maintenance of status was also similar in both cities. Apparently, the more robust Los Angeles economy seemed to make little difference, probably because Mexican Americans were generally excluded from many industrial occupations and neighborhoods. Moreover, educational opportunities were far from evenly distributed. European immigrants and their descendants, by contrast, seemed to benefit from industrialization because they could be fully integrated in industrial employment. This is not to deny that even relatively poor manufacturing jobs could have provided greater mobility and wages but that these apparently lower middle class jobs cited by Grebler, Moore, and Guzmán as evidence of an emerging Mexican American middle class could also be found in San Antonio's large government and military sector.

Neighborhood segregation also affected the assimilation prospects of some Mexican Americans. Our sample in Los Angeles had neighborhood experiences varying from nearly complete segregation to those where they were a small minority whereas the San Antonio sample tended to grow up in more segregated areas. Those in more segregated neighborhoods clearly have lower educational outcomes than those in more integrated neighborhoods, but educational levels for those in integrated schools and neighborhoods also fell below those of whites. However, controls for parental socioeconomic status reveal that segregation itself had almost no independent effect on schooling. Rather, it was the lower parental education and their consequently low financial resources that often limited Mexican-origin persons to segregated neighborhoods and schools.[22]

Growing up in a segregated or ethnically concentrated neighborhood heightens other dimensions of the ethnic boundary. Mexican Americans raised in barrios were more likely to marry Hispanics and more likely to live in segregated neighborhoods themselves, even after controlling for socioeconomic and other factors. Ethnic culture and identity are shaped by the extent to which one lives in an ethnic context. Thus the slow assimilation of Mexican Americans was partly attributable to their uniquely large size and demographic concentration, both in 1965 and 2000. However, greater spatial isolation was also attributable to their low levels of education, which is a better predictor of the lack of assimilation overall.

Parental Socioeconomic Status

As the large sociological literature on status attainment repeatedly confirms, a primary determinant of one's status in American society is the status of parents. Our findings show that this is no different for the Mexican American population. The most educated and the most successful Mexican Americans tended to have parents with relatively high levels of schooling. Similarly, parental income and whether parents were homeowners also affected the education of children. In turn, such parent resources may facilitate assimilation and reduce the negative effects of racialization. However, the ability of subsequent generations to convert or improve on the education of their parents seems to be worse for Mexican Americans than for other major racial-ethnic groups. Compared to African Americans, Mexican Americans certainly have higher returns to human capital in the labor market but they also have lower educational returns to the education of their parents.

The assimilation literature takes status attainment a step further and predicts upward economic mobility from low status immigrant to U.S.-born generations, at least until ethnic groups reach the overall status of the mainstream. For the descendants of European immigrants, human capital deficits were generally overcome by the third generation. Their returns to parental human capital are relatively high and thus they are especially likely to overcome the educational deficiencies of earlier generations. The Mexican American case, however, differs because there were only modest gains, at best, after the second generation. The lack of educational and economic mobility across generations reinforces other ethnic boundaries. Given an intergenerational transfer of lower status, less educated parents also tend to have children who are less likely to culturally, residentially, and maritally assimilate. The disproportionately low education of the children further limits their societal integration as adults.

Gender

Gender is not a central factor in assimilation theory yet we find that it matters for some dimensions we studied. As has been well documented previously, we found lower earnings for women. This was, however, not coupled with disadvantages along other economic indicators. For example, women had similar occupational status to that of men. This suggests that Mexican American women were in jobs that might be considered women's work—jobs of a similar status to those of men but which tended to pay less. Moreover, we found that women did not have lower family income or net worth. This was attributable to their being married and being part of a two-earner household. Women also had somewhat less education than men. Our respondents were in their late thirties or older and thus educated by the late 1980s—a period during which men continued to do better educationally.[23] These results for socioeconomic status, though, tend to hold for the general population in the United States and Mexico and thus say little about how integration varies by gender.

Our findings on how women differed from men in their ethnic behaviors, attitudes, and culture are more revealing. For instance, Mexican American women had significantly higher Spanish proficiency than men, indicating slower linguistic assimilation. This might be attributable to women having closer relationships with family and therefore learning Spanish within the home context. We also found that Mexican American women reported less discrimination. This might be indicative of the experiences of nonwhite men in society today—where they are more likely to be penalized in the educational, labor market, and criminal justice system.[24] Compared to other ethnic groups, Mexican American women had especially high fertility even among the third and fourth generation. Mexican immigrants generally held traditional gender attitudes but became more egalitarian as generations further removed from the immigration generation. On the other hand, Mexican American men and women did not differ on most ethnic behaviors and attitudes. Women were not more likely to intermarry and did not differ in ethnic or racial identification.

Intermarriage

Intermarriage itself is an indicator of assimilation, particularly at the aggregate group level. Greater intermarriage implies that ethnic boundaries are relatively fluid or more easily crossed. Moderate rates of intermarriage for Mexican Americans suggest that they were accepted well enough by at least some of the white population. However, intermarriage often has limited effects on the individuals who intermarry, because factors such as language, identities, and politics are often consolidated by the time of marriage. More than likely, intermarriage is selective of those who are already more assimilated. We found, though, that intermarriage was particularly powerful for Mexican Americans in its effect on the children of intermarried couples. The 9 percent of children with a non-Hispanic parent were less likely to know Spanish, were more likely to intermarry themselves, identified less with their Mexican origin, and were more likely to call themselves Americans. Such children were often perceived as and understood themselves as less Mexican. In some cases they do not identify as Mexican origin at all, although we found very few such cases. We should note that the proportion of this group has roughly doubled in the past decade[25] compared to our children cohort, which was born from 1946 to 1966.

For our study, we generated a representative sample of all the children of the original respondents, regardless of whether or not they identified as Mexican origin, Hispanic, or the like. Official surveys like the Census are unable to identify such cases as part of the Mexican origin population and thus studies on Mexican Americans that use this data miss such individuals. However, such cases should be included to more accurately examine the nature or extent of intergenerational change. One might argue that we might miss such cases if persons in the 1965 sample screening did not similarly identify as Mexican or Spanish origin in 1965, but we consider this a relatively minor problem in a study such as ours. We have no doubt that the progeny of one or two generations of intermarriage sometimes may not identify as or be seen as a Mexican American, especially if they no longer live in places like San Antonio or Los Angeles or do not bear markers such as a Spanish surname. There simply is nothing like the unusual hypodescent (one-drop) rule for Mexican Americans, as there is for African Americans. Persons with small amounts of Mexican ancestry, unless they tend to identify as Mexican American, simply are not Mexican American. Why should they be if they don't consider themselves as such and society doesn't either? Such amalgamation may mean full assimilation but that is of little consequence or consolation to those who remain Mexican American. Once enough markers of Mexicanness or nonwhiteness have been removed through mixture with whites, complete assimilation might become possible, though some children of mixed unions will surely continue to identify and be identified as Mexican American, to varying degrees.[26]

Skin Color

Given that skin color seems to be the primary marker of race in the United States, and that the Mexican-origin population runs the gamut from light and seemingly European to dark and seemingly indigenous, we expected that it would predict differences in many of our outcomes. One might, for example, expect that persons that physically appear as nonwhite or closer to the Mexican stereotype would be most discriminated and therefore suffer greater disadvantage. However, aside from reported discrimination and the extent to which one thinks of oneself as Mexican, we found no differences by color among the children of the original respondents, even though color affected education and income among a national sample for an earlier period.[27] We speculate that the lack of a skin color effect on variables such as occupation and education might be due to more generalized Mexican-origin stigma based on a variety of markers in Los Angeles and San Antonio, in contrast to less ethnic places, where it is easier to pass into the white category if one is light enough. That many or most Mexican Americans are perceived as nonwhite could negatively affect the entire group by further racializing them. Individual Mexican Americans who do not meet the physical stereotypes, though, may also be identified as such through other characteristics such as names, language or accent, friendships or where they reside. While first impressions based on physical appearance may be especially important in other social arenas like racial profiling by police or in getting a job, other criteria may be as important in education, where social categorization is likely to be better, though perhaps not well, informed.

Skin color may also be more important nationally because Mexicans are less visible in many places other than in San Antonio or Los Angeles, and thus may be less threatening to whites. It is also possible that color today is less important than in the past. A study of African Americans found that younger cohorts raised in the post–civil rights era are unaffected by skin tone variation, unlike older African Americans.[28] The same may be true for Mexican Americans. In the future, though, as Mexican immigration increasingly involves indigenous and indigenous looking persons, skin tone may come to have a more prominent role in Mexican American integration, although it is far from being the only determinant in racialization.

Revisiting Assimilation and Racialization

As we indicated in the first two chapters, there are two broad theories that have been used to explain the integration trajectories of particular ethnic groups in the United States. These are, generally, theories of assimilation and those of race, both of which are reflected in the subtitle of this book. Specifically, the leading contenders today seeking to explain immigrant and ethnic incorporation are modern assimilation theory as espoused by Alba and Nee and segmented assimilation theory as developed by Portes and his colleagues. To be sure, these theories are much closer to each other than the older assimilation versus race (e.g. internal colonialism) theories that existed before them, thanks largely to increasing empirical evidence indicating that integration may be affected by assimilation, race, and a host of other factors. Both modern assimilation and segmented assimilation theories consider assimilation and race explanations though in different ways and to different degrees. We hope to have provided more evidence to further refine our understanding of ethnic integration, especially for the large Mexican origin population.

We have mentioned our contributions throughout the text, confirming and contesting previous theories including those of standard assimilation and segmented assimilation. We summarize eight of them here. First, we show the important effects of social barriers based on race for Mexican Americans that previous scholars often underestimated (Alba and Nee) or completely disregarded (Huntington). Second, we believe that most theories of integration including those by Portes and his colleagues and by Alba and Nee tend to confuse the effects of historical period with generation-since-immigration, generally slighting the former. We have shown the importance of disentangling these two types of generational comparisons. Third, we have shown that there is wide variation within the group which has been nearly ignored by both schools of thought, probably a consequence of the methodological tack of comparing several groups. Relatedly and fourthly, we demonstrated the sizeable effects of local context in shaping integration outcomes. Fifth, both schools of thought have exaggerated the consistency and uniformity in direction to which assimilation occurs across a wide range of social dimensions. We showed how assimilation, and the lack of it, can occur at quite distinct paces and even in an opposite direction. Sixth, we have also demonstrated how one factor—namely, the absence of educational assimilation—shapes most other types of assimilation, specifically by slowing it and thus fostering ethnic distinctions. Seventh, Portes and his colleagues blame status and linguistic dissonance between immigrant parents and their children as largely responsible for poor educational assimilation but we find that low education persists into the third and fourth generation when such dissonance no longer exists. Finally, we also find problematic any theoretical time frame that assimilation takes more than three generations, which would be needed to explain the Mexican American trajectory. Even if Mexican Americans were to fully assimilate within six or seven generations, how can assimilation theory be the principal explanation of ethnicity? How do we explain ethnic phenomenon, racialization, and periods of ethnic resurgence in the intervening 150 to 200 years?

Our study is designed to directly assess the direction and extent of assimilation as well as the effects of factors like education, urban and demographic context, parental resources and home culture. While we find assimilation in social exposure, politics, identity and especially cultural aspects, such assimilation is slower than has been shown for other groups. However, our evidence does not similarly support assimilation in educational and economic status for Mexican Americans and there is little support for other theories like those based on culture, language or industrialization. Instead, we find corroborating evidence suggesting racialization, which is not surprising give their history as victims of outright racial coercion, segregation, and discrimination. Racialization includes the societal practice of assigning others to a "race", which is generally ranked by characteristics such as intelligence and worth, or placing them in a racial hierarchy even if they are not referred to as a race. Direct proof of racialization and especially discrimination requires different study design from this one, which shows integration trajectories and the measurable factors that influence it.[29]

We have demonstrated that Mexican Americans are disproportionately sorted into the low socioeconomic strata, mostly via the educational system and while they are young. That suggests racialization. Moreover, the failure or insufficiency of other perspectives to account for the low education of Mexican Americans as well as the findings from other studies leads us to support a racialization hypothesis. Certainly, many of our respondents experienced discrimination and were aware of common stereotypes based on popular ideas that Mexican origin persons possess an inferior culture and an inherent unworthiness that keeps them from becoming fully American even when they may no longer bear the cultural characteristics attributed to the group.

Studies find that a range of institutional and interpersonal discrimination and racialization practices limit the educational attainment of Mexican Americans.[30] Institutional discrimination includes the under-financing of public schools which mostly Mexican origin students attend and their avoidance by more experienced teachers as well as tracking these children into low level curriculum in the case of integrated schools. Interpersonal discrimination includes the racially distinct expectations of students by teachers and counselors and the stigmatizing of Mexican Americans as inferior, lazy or less worthy students by society in general. Racialized ideas guide individual interactions, including those between student and teacher/counselor. These interactions may involve direct advice to students about which classes to take or avoid or they may send signals to students that shape personal identities, sense of adequacy and more specifically, may limit self-investment and effort in school.[31] These adverse effects, though, do not deny that some of these students achieve academic success, especially under more favorable learning conditions[32] or when they possess an advantaged self concept.[33]

Toward a Historical-Structural Theory of Mexican Immigration and Mexican American Integration

We have described general patterns for the group as well as intra-group variation and we have suggested how various factors account for the peculiar integration of Mexican Americans. In particular, educational disadvantage persists for several generations-since-immigration and this partly accounts for their slow or uneven assimilation on various dimensions. We have also shown that other crucial determinants explain the low status and ethnic persistence of Mexican Americans including demographic size and concentration, for which we have direct evidence, and racism and nativism, for which we have indirect evidence. Rather than review the list of causes, in this section we propose a heuristic model based on an ultimate single cause to account for the peculiar nature of Mexican American integration into the United States.

We argue that American capitalists' desire to quench its persistent thirst for cheap Mexican labor for a century, which is supported by the American state and enabled by Mexico's proximity and its large labor supply, can largely account for the persistent low status and ethnic retention of Mexican Americans. For an entire century, inexpensive and easily disposable Mexican labor has filled the labor needs of Southwest agriculture as well as those of Southwest urban employers. More recently, the reliance on Mexican labor beyond the Southwest and throughout the United States has grown.[34] Throughout the twentieth century and into the twenty-first, capitalist labor demands have been facilitated by United States immigration policy, which has often treated Mexicans as a special case.[35] This has led to an especially adverse context of reception in comparison to other immigrant groups.[36] The resultant nature of immigration perpetuates the racialization of Mexican American children in school, which slows or halts Mexican American economic, social, identificational and civic assimilation. That historical process has also created a large and concentrated Mexican American population, which is fed by continuing immigration, all of which foster ethnic retention.

In many ways, the integration pattern of Mexican immigrants is thus the consequence of the witting and unwitting actions of the American state coupled with Mexico's own social condition and development needs. Largely through several amnesty programs, Mexicans continue to be the largest legal immigrant group but they have also comprised the majority of undocumented immigrants. By granting the right to live and work in the United States, legal status becomes the ultimate criteria of belonging to the American nation.[37] In contrast, the lack of legal status for many immigrants represents complete national exclusion but permits a cheaper and more disposable labor force to better satisfy employer demands. The fact that the citizens of one country are disproportionately illegal may create ethnic stereotypes and send signals to co-ethnics that they are not fully American, especially since the usual racial-categorical thinking of American society often fails to distinguish between natives and immigrants. Such nativism and stereotyping harms the image of Mexican Americans as Americans by denying them equal education, among other things, and this ultimately heightens racial and ethnic identities.[38]

Perceptions of Mexicans as low status persons and often illegal entrants and Mexico as perpetually impoverished, crime-ridden and dependent on the United States has led to stereotyping of Mexican origin persons generally. With a century of continuous immigration, Mexican Americans of all generations often share residential, marriage and labor markets, which further promotes the stereotypes and racialization of Mexican Americans irrespective of generations-since-immigration. Perceived as foreigners, even Mexican Americans with deep roots in the United States are excluded from enjoying a full American identity. Mexico and its non-emigrant citizens are also perceived as and treated as inferior neighbors. This is as true in public opinion as in economic and political relations. Although Mexico arguably benefits from immigration to the United States, it has, in the words of Mexico's former ambassador to the United Nations Adolfo Aguilar Zinser, simply become Washington's back yard as American interests have often been imposed, especially though a unilateral immigration policy.[39] American nativism is especially aimed against Mexicans, whether they are immigrant or non-immigrant citizens of Mexico. Whether or not it is also directed at U.S.-born Mexican Americans, nevertheless has the effect of limiting the identities of later generation Mexican Americans. It shapes their perceived role in American society and especially affects their educational experience. This persistent foreignness makes the Mexican Americans case different from that of African or European Americans.

The American reliance on Mexican labor has also led to a demographic predominance of Mexicans in the Southwest, especially in cities like Los Angeles and San Antonio. A century of immigration has produced a very large, though multigenerational, population. This is quite unlike the experience of European immigration before, which was nationally and linguistically diverse, and in which migration stopped after one generation, or Asian immigration today, in which no single national or linguistic group has predominated. The large presence of Mexican origin persons, immigrants and U.S.-born, in particular areas may create institutional incentives for mobility into jobs that serve the ethnic population and thus may also lower incentives to move away from these areas. Large numbers of Mexicans have also created both a large demand for Spanish-language media and a wide array of ethnic institutions, as well as allowed for large ethnic neighborhoods where there is often little contact with other groups and much contact between various generations of Mexicans. The moderate segregation and large size of the group means that residence and thus educational and other institutions are often demographically dominated by Mexican origin persons, which may include those of the fourth generation. This allows the top-down policies of state institutions to target particular communities or schools on the basis of Mexican ethnicity. Also, such residential segregation may regenerate ethnic identity for later-generation Mexican Americans and foster endogamous marriages and in-group social relationships.

The geographical concentration and the large size of the group also makes Mexican Americans especially visible, which itself evokes attention to the group and thus the tendency to categorize. The demographic predominance of this single low status and perceptibly foreign group reinforces xenophobic fears among non-Mexicans of labor market substitution, demographic inundation and racial and cultural hybridization[40] Such fears are often directed at U.S.-born Mexican Americans as well. Immigration restrictionists generally believe that immigrants, most notably Mexicans, take jobs away from U.S.-born workers, even though the evidence shows that immigration, legal and illegal, benefit the vast majority of American workers and consumers.[41]

Furthermore, the low status of the immigrant generation throughout the twentieth century was produced originally by the selective needs of

American employers. Since then, a system of cumulative causation and social networks expanded the sources of Mexican immigration and further decreased its selectivity.[42] As a result, immigration from the Mexican middle class is relatively rare, quite unlike immigration from other countries to the United States today.[43] Along with its large size and largely illegal status, the lack of Mexican immigrant selectivity, especially when contrasted to so much middle class immigration among many other national groups that comprise the new immigration population, continues to make the Mexicans case exceptional.[44] This low status contributes to their stigmatization in the educational system and on the American social totem pole generally.

This seems to contrast with the example of Asians today, in which changes in immigration policy since 1965 have been selective of persons with high education and professional occupations. As a result, the success of the Asian second generation today is largely due to their parents' high levels of education and other resources, as the status attainment model predicts. However, not all Asian immigration is of high status. Even though some Asians do not have the high levels of human and social capital associated with many of the immigrants, even those identified as Asian with relatively low human capital benefit from belonging or being ascribed to a successful group. Such benefits include high expectations by educators, employers and other societal members. The obverse would thus seem to hold true for Mexican Americans, in that ascription to a group with little capital or status impedes the progress of even those individuals with relatively high status.

Finally, the century-long reliance on Mexican labor prolonged a nineteenth century racial order in which Mexicans were considered inferior and perceived as outsiders and even enemies of American nationhood.[45] These ideas continue to resonate in the public mind. Although it was nineteenth century or traditional views of Mexicans, driven in part by a legacy of war and conquest, that originally racialized Mexican Americans, stigmatization of Mexican origin persons persists largely because of the enduring American labor need and Mexico's large low-skilled labor supply. The American racial order has changed throughout that time, most notably for Southern and Central European groups,[46] but it has not for Mexican origin persons. Their position in the racial order continues to be near the bottom, which continues to be self-evident, commonsense and natural in many American minds, despite the passing of time and the end of explicit racial policies or laws.

Racial discrimination against Mexicans no longer occurs in the classical sense but by way of a social stigmatization that is entwined in a series of economic, political, and social processes and practices. The idea of race continues to be an important concept among Americans, one in which particular racial categories carry meanings about one's capabilities and worthiness. They also create stereotypes which are used to rank ethnic groups in the American social hierarchy. National opinion research, for example, shows that the American public ranks Hispanics as the second lowest among racial-ethnic groups overall after blacks. A national survey also shows that Hispanics earn the lowest ranking of all groups when they are rated on the basis of poverty, intelligence, and patriotism.[47] These findings extend early findings by Bogardus in which Americans consistently ranked Mexican Americans near the bottom of the social scale from 1936 to 1966.

What Would Happen Without Immigration?

Mexican immigration and Mexican American ethnicity and racialization are intimately intertwined. An important theoretical question becomes "what would happen to Mexican Americans if there had not been the surge of post-1970 immigration?"[48] Can we assume there would have been rapid assimilation instead? Indeed, the assimilation of Italians and other groups is often argued to have been the result of an immigration hiatus soon after the larger waves of immigration.[49] In the case of Mexicans, though, things are not likely to be so simple. This question forces us to think about the processes of both assimilation and racialization. This question, though, is not as straightforward as it seems because immigration is not a static feature of society but rather both a consequence and cause of changes in the economy and politics. An end to immigration would affect assimilation prospects not only directly but also indirectly by causing changes in the structure of the economy and economic opportunity.

One might expect that Mexican Americans would probably assimilate to a greater extent without immigration because opportunities for speaking Spanish, living in barrios, and marrying other persons of Mexican origin would diminish because there would be fewer Mexican immigrants among the population. Moreover, growth in residential segregation in past decades for Mexican Americans has been driven by immigration.[50] Without immigration, Mexican American residential segregation would thus likely decrease, which would in turn trigger other assimilative processes, such as intermarriage and perhaps social and geographic mobility. Also, Mexican American politics and identity, which have jelled largely on issues of immigration, would probably not have formed as strongly as they have. A post–civil rights context, in which segregation and the most egregious of racism have ended, would further stimulate assimilation.

However, the absence of immigration, though it is unlikely to happen anytime soon, does not guarantee assimilation. The example of San Antonio today shows the persistence of racial boundaries despite little immigration to that city since 1929. The state of New Mexico is an even better case in that it has seen even less Mexican immigration since about the same time. There, Mexican Americans continue to be racialized, even with little immigration. An entrenched racialized way of thinking that places Mexicans in the lower rungs of society seems to be at least partly responsible for their persistently low status, though the stigmatized nature of Mexican immigration has maintained or lowered their status.

An end to immigration would require a new source of cheap labor if the American economy is to continue growing as it has. Given American history, that source is unlikely to be shouldered evenly by all Americans. Mexican Americans would be a ready source, especially because they tend to have low levels of education and they populate those regions where low-wage industries are concentrated to benefit from Mexican immigration. The end to immigration could even harden social boundaries for Mexican Americans, because labor market segmentation could increase where the dividing line would be less on immigration status and more on race or ethnicity. This possibility is enhanced given the growing income polarization of urban labor markets. On the other hand, assimilation for Mexican Americans might be especially likely if a large substitute source of cheap labor other than Mexican immigrants could be found or if the American demand for cheap labor could somehow be eliminated.

Policy and the Future

Most of the sociological literature about Mexican Americans focuses on what will happen to the children of the current wave of immigrants.[51] Our study has examined what did happen to the descendants of past waves of Mexican immigrants. This approach has allowed us to examine long-term integration. We believe, however, that the past is critical to informing the future as well. Although there has been a very gradual breaking down of Mexican American ethnic boundaries over the last 100 years, three disturbing trends in recent years might slow or even reverse the prospects for further integration. These are labor market polarization, worsening public education, and the growing size of the undocumented population. The course of labor market polarization is difficult to control, though public policy has shown it is capable of making major changes in education and immigration.

The potential policy levers for improving the integration prospects of Mexican Americans must, then, address education and immigration. Overall, we agree with Portes and Rumbaut that the dominant ideologies that propose either to stop immigration (intransigent nativism) or to force assimilation are short-sighted and unlikely to ever work.[52] Rather, we need to focus on investing in the education of the descendants of Mexican immigrants and on a fair and welcoming immigration policy with respect to Mexico that recognizes American needs for its labor. Not doing so will likely lead to continuously poor economic outcomes for Mexican Americans and their poor integration into American society. Such policies to improve their lot are likely to improve the lives of Americans in general, because Mexican Americans will soon represent most of the lower end work forces in vital states such as Texas and California. The retiring and mostly white baby boomers will also largely depend on the contributions of these mostly Mexican American youth and their low education will translate into lower earnings to support these senior citizens.[53]

Public education is the greatest source of Mexican American exclusion, in that low education impedes their economic prospects. In California, a voter-led initiative in 1979 (Proposition 13) undermined its primary funding source and its quality has deteriorated at the same time that Hispanics have become the largest ethnic population among all public school students.[54] The future of Mexican Americans for at least the next twenty to thirty years depends largely on education today. About half of Mexican origin youth do not complete high school on time, apparently reversing improving trends in recent decades.[55] Although the lack of such an education could be overcome by manual labor jobs that ensured decent pay, stability, and mobility, such jobs are increasingly difficult to find as the divide between bad and good jobs widens. The choice for many U.S.-born Mexican Americans may be restricted to jobs that are not much better than those of their immigrant ancestors. Indeed, even with affirmative action, the large majority of even later-generation Mexican Americans still do not have a college education. This means they will continue to be concentrated in the lower rungs of a widening class divide. We found that the educational situation is as bad if not worse for later-generation Mexican Americans and more recent evidence shows that this pattern continues.[56]

Public schools are the single greatest institutional culprit for the persistent low status of U.S.-born Mexican Americans, although a few do well. Mexican Americans continue to have the lowest levels of education in the country. The public schools that serve Mexican American communities, which are largely in the central cities and in rural areas, are increasingly segregated and have been among this country's worst.[57] For those in integrated schools, schools are often better but educational scholars have found that Mexican-origin students are disproportionately tracked into lower level curricula and made to feel unwanted or uncomfortable in school.[58] Many of these are segregated schools but the problem is not limited to segregated schools. Most of our sample attended integrated schools.

For Mexican Americans to become successful, we need, above all, a Marshall Plan that invests heavily in public school education, addressing the issues that disadvantage students. We need to emphasize educational opportunities, rather than adoption of American values, since Mexican Americans already have these.[59] Sociologist Mary Waters of Harvard

University,[60] studying the integration experiences of the old classic wave of European immigrants and their descendants, found that the Americanization programs were not nearly as important as the enormous economic payoff to immigration that the descendants of European immigration enjoyed. For Mexican Americans, the payoff can only come by giving them the same quality and quantity of education as whites receive. The problem is not the unwillingness of Mexican Americans to adopt American values and culture but the failure of societal institutions, particularly public schools, to successfully integrate them as they did the descendants of European immigrants. Since the 1970s, schooling has become an ever more important predictor of success. A restructured economy has led to increased demand for the college educated and decreased demand for those with a high school education, making this a worrisome fact for the future of most Mexican Americans.

The growing population of undocumented immigrants in recent years, as in previous periods, has again brought the Mexican problem into the center of public debate. Nativists often make Mexicans the scapegoat for many social problems, which further stigmatizes the entire population of Mexican origin. Immigration proposals that seek to criminalize illegal immigration rather than offer paths to legal residency and citizenship also bode ill for the future of Mexican Americans. The illegality of many of today's immigrants is also likely to slow mobility for their children. Moreover, such policies not only harm Mexican Americans but American society in general because they increase the potential for creating a large number of persons without rights and further stigmatize the large population of Mexican Americans.

United States immigration policies have largely sought to control the flows of immigrants, particularly those coming from Mexico. The large size of the undocumented population reflects failed immigration policies and America's contradictory need for low-wage labor at the same time that nativist impulses feel that the border and immigration is out of control. Any attempt to seal off the United States-Mexico border, as some have suggested, represents an anachronism in a globalizing world, especially in a liberal democracy such as the United States. Moreover, this would be a slap at Mexico and the global community as well as a blow to human rights, which the United States claims to fiercely defend. Such an initiative may likely reinforce, rather than improve, the racialized status of Mexican-origin persons in the United States. American dependence on Mexican and Mexican American labor needs to be acknowledged without the common scapegoating of Mexicans as criminal trespassers and Mexican Americans as their unassimilable progeny.

= Appendix A =

Descriptive Statistics

Table A.1   Descriptive Statistics for Dependent Variables in Regression Analysis, 2000[a]

Dependent Variables	Mean	Standard Deviation	Minimum	Maximum	Sample Size	Chapter
Years of education	13.26	2.18	2	17	758	5
Occupational status	36.65	12.98	7	81	723	6
Earnings	$37,001	$26,142	$1,758	$167,962	698	6
Family income	$54,425	$37,301	$0	$171,672	725	6
Net worth	$51,190	$99,570	−$74,000	$1,000,000	700	6
Hispanic in neighborhood (2000)	50.28	29.50	1	98	709	7
Married to Hispanic	0.70	0.46	0	1	660	7
Spanish proficiency	3.04	1.14	1	5	758	8
Spanish birth name	2.98	1.17	1	5	758	8
Children ever born	2.18	1.41	0	8	419	8
Identify as Mexican	0.16	0.37	0	1	758	9
Identify as Mexican American	0.43	0.49	0	1	758	9
Identify as Hispanic or Latino	0.30	0.46	0	1	758	9
Identify as American or other	0.11	0.32	0	1	758	9
Think of self as Mexican frequently	0.19	0.39	0	1	758	9
Think of self as American frequently	0.37	0.48	0	1	758	9
Identify as white	0.15	0.35	0	1	758	9
Experienced discrimination	0.46	0.50	0	1	758	9
Voted in 1996	0.68	0.47	0	1	758	10
Voted Republican	0.18	0.38	0	1	515	10
Identify with Republican party	0.17	0.38	0	1	562	10
Positive attitudes toward immigration	2.42	0.45	1	4	562	10

Source: Mexican American Study Project.

[a] Child sample used in all regression analyses.

Table A.2   Descriptive Statistics for Independent Variables in Regression Analysis, 1965 and 2000

Independent Variables	Mean	Standard Deviation	Minimum	Maximum	Sample Size	Chapter
Generation 1.5	0.05	0.22	0	1	758	All
Generation 2	0.08	0.27	0	1	758	All
Generation 2.5	0.22	0.41	0	1	758	All
Generation 3 (reference category)	0.41	0.49	0	1	758	All
Generation 4	0.24	0.43	0	1	758	All
Father's education	9.36	3.77	0	17	758	All
Mother's education	9.78	3.85	0	17	758	All
Parent's income in thousands (1965)	6.40	3.20	1	20	758	All
Parent was homeowner (1965)	0.61	0.49	0	1	758	All
Number of siblings	3.99	2.37	0	15	758	5
Head held manufacturing job (1965)	0.16	0.37	0	1	758	5
Industry information missing (1965)	0.60	0.49	0	1	758	5
Child exposed to professionals	0.84	1.05	0	3	758	5
Catholic or private high school	0.12	0.33	0	1	758	5
Parent attended church weekly (1965)	0.47	0.50	0	1	758	5
Parent communicated with school (1965)	0.55	0.50	0	1	758	5
Parent had college expectations (1965)	0.67	0.47	0	1	758	5
Parent is Spanish monolingual	0.11	0.31	0	1	758	5
Parent spoke Spanish to child	0.35	0.48	0	1	758	All
Parent is non-Hispanic	0.09	0.29	0	1	758	All
Parents were married (1965)	0.89	0.32	0	1	758	All
San Antonio (1965)	0.38	0.49	0	1	758	All

(Continued)

Table A.2   Descriptive Statistics for Independent Variables in Regression Analysis, 1965 and 2000 (*Continued*)

Independent Variables	Mean	Standard Deviation	Minimum	Maximum	Sample Size	Chapter
Proportion Hispanic in neighborhood (1965)	0.51	0.29	0	1	758	All
Telephone interview (2000)	0.26	0.44	0	1	758	All
Education	13.26	2.18	2	17	758	All
Age	41.83	5.92	32	59	758	All
Female	0.55	0.50	0	1	758	All
Skin color	4.25	1.18	2	7	758	All
Years of work experience	19.52	7.81	0	39	758	6
Number of children under eighteen in household	1.20	1.24	0	6	758	6
First marriage	0.69	0.46	0	1	695	7
Age at first marriage	23.40	5.28	13	50	695	7
Parent voted Republican in 1964 (1965)	0.50	0.50	0	1	758	10
Parent did not vote in 1964 (1965)	0.17	0.37	0	1	758	10

Source: Mexican American Study Project.

= Appendix B =

Multivariate Analyses

Table B.1   Determinants of Locating and Interviewing Original
              Respondents, 2000[a]

	Located	Interviewed
San Antonio	1.05	1.25
Age	0.99	0.99
Male	1.04	0.98
Married	1.51*	1.42*
Born in U.S.	1.34	1.07
English interview	1.39	1.14
Education	1.04	1.03
Income (thousands)	1.05	1.00
Homeowner	3.22***	1.58**
Mean on dependent variable	.789	.573
Pseudo R^2	.099	.025
Log pseudo-likelihood	−554	−794
N	1193	1193

Source: Mexican American Study Project.
[a] Logistic regression run. Adjusted odds ratios presented. Searched sample of
original respondents analyzed. Predictors based on 1965 characteristics.
*p<.05, **p<.01; ***p<.001

Table B.2   Determinants of Selecting and Interviewing Child Respondents, 2000[a]

	Selected	Interviewed
Number of eligible children	0.60***	0.69***
Education	1.02	1.08***
Female	0.96	1.28*
San Antonio	0.78*	0.87
Born in United States	1.17	1.25
Birth year	1.00	1.00
Working	0.86	1.11
Mean on dependent variable	.553	.378
Pseudo R^2	.169	.108
Log pseudo-likelihood	−1161	−1181
N	2019	2019

Source: Mexican American Study Project.
[a] Logistic regression run. Adjusted odds ratios presented. Predictors based on characteristics of children listed on child roster in original respondent questionnaire.
*p<.05, ***p<.001

Table B.3   Determinants of Years of Education, 2000[a]

	Years of Education	
	Unstandardized Coefficient	Robust Standard Errors
Generation-since-immigration (ref: 3)		
1.5	1.46**	0.45
2	0.94**	0.31
2.5	0.40†	0.21
4+	−0.08	0.21
Parental status characteristics		
Father's education	0.10***	0.03
Mother's education	0.08***	0.02
Parents' income (1965)	0.06*	0.03
Parent was homeowner (1965)	0.32†	0.19
Number of siblings	−0.08*	0.03
Head held manufacturing job (1965)	−0.26	0.23
Industry information missing (1965)	−0.45*	0.19
Childhood characteristics		
Child exposed to professionals	0.23**	0.07
Catholic or private high school	0.97***	0.22
Parent attended church weekly (1965)	0.45*	0.17
Parent communicated with school (1965)	0.36*	0.18
Parent had college expectations for children (1965)	0.04	0.17
Parent spoke Spanish to child	0.20	0.21
Parent is Spanish monolingual	−0.18	0.32
Parent is non-Hispanic	0.21	0.30
Parents were married (1965)	−0.10	0.28
Residential characteristics		
San Antonio (1965)	0.07	0.21
Proportion Hispanic in neighborhood (1965)	−0.24	0.28
Telephone interview (2000)	−0.05	0.18
Individual characteristics		
Female	−0.26†	0.15
Skin color	0.07	0.06
Age	0.00	0.02
Intercept	10.69	
R^2	.257	
N	758	

Source: Mexican American Study Project.
[a] Linear regression run. Child sample analyzed. Adjusted for sibling clustering: number of clusters = 482; robust standard errors are calculated.
†p<.10, *p<.05, **p<.01, ***p<.001

Table B.4   Determinants of Socioeconomic Status, 2000[a]

	Occupational Status		Earnings (Dollars)	
	Unstandardized Coefficient	Robust Standard Errors	Unstandardized Coefficient	Robust Standard Errors
Generation-since-immigration (ref: 3)				
1.5	0.57	2.45	–354	4,522
2	0.30	1.77	–4,418	3,788
2.5	–0.76	1.23	–2,324	2,641
4+	–1.16	1.10	–3,641	2,221
Socioeconomic characteristics				
Father's education	0.16	0.13	26	320
Mother's education	0.34**	0.13	712*	295
Parents' income (1965)	0.28	0.17	424	420
Parent was homeowner (1965)	0.74	1.02	204	2,135
Childhood characteristics				
Parent spoke Spanish to child	1.36	1.09	1,809	2,288
Parent is non-Hispanic	2.41	1.76	3,525	4,298
Parents were married (1965)	1.46	1.23	1,946	2,601

Residential characteristics				
San Antonio (1965)	1.57	1.16	−1,053	2,273
Proportion Hispanic in neighborhood (1965)	1.42	1.58	−3,807	3,466
Telephone interview (2000)	1.28	1.02	7,479**	2,483
Human capital				
Education	2.99***	0.22	4,043***	486
Years of work experience[b]	0.09	0.06	240*	120
Age[b]				
Individual characteristics				
Female	1.16	0.81	−12,676***	1,717
Skin color	0.26	0.33	742	685
Intercept	−17.29		−29,402	
R^2	.332		.261	
N	723		698	

(Continued)

Table B.4 Determinants of Socioeconomic Status, 2000ᵃ (Continued)

	Family Income (Dollars)		Net Worth (Dollars)	
	Unstandardized Coefficient	Robust Standard Errors	Unstandardized Coefficient	Robust Standard Errors
Generation-since-immigration (ref: 3)				
1.5	5,900	8,450	11,779	19,448
2	−2,584	5,374	13,372	13,172
2.5	−630	3,853	342	11,571
4+	−777	3,154	782	9,088
Socioeconomic characteristics				
Father's education	−241	482	−622	1,259
Mother's education	695	433	444	1,373
Parents' income (1965)	1,120	614	1,870	1,581
Parent was homeowner (1965)	1,707	3,150	5,395	8,542
Childhood characteristics				
Parent spoke Spanish to child	326	3,389	2,931	7,912
Parent is non-Hispanic	1,442	6,374	15,643	15,862
Parents were married (1965)	4,533	3,777	13,712	10,426

	Model 1		Model 2	
	Coef.	SE	Coef.	SE
Residential characteristics				
San Antonio (1965)	−3,464	3,468	−4,955	10,998
Proportion Hispanic in neighborhood (1965)	−440	5,067	5,029	13,345
Telephone interview (2000)	7,816*	3,477	25,650*	11,054
Human capital				
Education	6,177***	693	8,977***	2,200
Years of work experience[b]				
Age[b]	−2	211	2,917***	707
Individual characteristics				
Female	−2,729	2,518	734	8,044
Skin color	−233	943	2,466	2,300
Intercept	−42,479		−236,561	
R^2	.209		.106	
N	725		700	

Source: Mexican American Study Project.

[a] Linear regression run. Child sample analyzed. Adjusted for sibling clustering: number of clusters = 482; robust standard errors are calculated.

[b] Age and work experience are not included in model together because they are highly correlated.

†p<.10, *p<.05, **p<.01, ***p<.001

Table B.5   Determinants of Hispanic Neighborhood, 2000[a]

	Hispanic Neighborhood	
	Unstandardized Coefficient	Robust Standard Errors
Generation-since-immigration (ref: 3)		
1.5	−1.59	5.33
2	−3.14	4.42
2.5	−0.06	2.68
4+	−3.50	2.64
Socioeconomic characteristics		
Father's education	−0.51	0.34
Mother's education	−0.62*	0.31
Parents' income (1965)	−0.02	0.40
Parent was homeowner (1965)	1.53	2.55
Childhood characteristics		
Parent spoke Spanish to child	1.77	2.64
Parent is non-Hispanic	−5.07	3.31
Parents were married (1965)	3.89	3.53
Residential characteristics		
San Antonio (1965)	14.26***	2.74
Proportion Hispanic in neighborhood (1965)	11.55**	3.78
Telephone interview (2000)	−14.13***	2.46
Human capital		
Education	−2.64***	0.53
Individual characteristics		
Female	−1.59	2.02
Skin color	−0.99	0.88
Age	−0.37	0.20
Any children under eighteen in household	−3.98†	2.09
Intercept	108.13	
R^2	.329	
N	709	

Source: Mexican American Study Project.

[a] Linear regression run. Child sample analyzed. Adjusted for sibling clustering: number of clusters = 482; robust standard errors are calculated.

[b] Age and work experience not included in model together because highly correlated.

†p<.10, *p<.05, **p<.01, ***p<.001

Table B.6   Determinants of Married to a Hispanic, 2000[a]

	Married to a Hispanic
Generation-since-immigration (ref: 3)	
1.5	0.84
2	1.39
2.5	1.22
4+	1.11
Socioeconomic characteristics	
Father's education	0.97
Mother's education	0.95
Parents' income (1965)	1.03
Parent was homeowner (1965)	0.86
Childhood characteristics	
Parent spoke Spanish to child	1.63
Parent is non-Hispanic	0.19***
Parents were married (1965)	0.50
Residential characteristics	
San Antonio (1965)	2.55*
Proportion Hispanic in neighborhood (1965)	3.02***
Telephone interview (2000)	0.53**
Human capital	
Education	0.80***
Individual characteristics	
Female	1.01
Skin color	0.92
Age	1.00
First marriage	5.17***
Age at first marriage	0.92***
Pseudo R^2	.253
Log pseudo-likelihood	−301
N	660

Source: Mexican American Study Project.
[a] Logistic regression run. Adjusted odds ratios presented. Child sample analyzed. Adjusted for sibling clustering: number of clusters = 482; robust standard errors are calculated.
*p<.05, **p<.01, ***p<.001

Table B.7   Determinants of Spanish Proficiency, 2000[a]

	Spanish Proficiency	
	Unstandardized Coefficient	Robust Standard Errors
Generation-since-immigration (ref: 3)		
1.5	0.73***	0.19
2	0.37**	0.16
2.5	0.32***	0.10
4+	−0.20*	0.09
Socioeconomic characteristics		
Father's education	−0.02	0.01
Mother's education	−0.02*	0.01
Parents' income (1965)	0.01	0.01
Parent was homeowner (1965)	0.01	0.08
Childhood characteristics (1965)		
Parent spoke Spanish to child	0.88***	0.10
Parent is non-Hispanic	−0.30*	0.14
Parents were married (1965)	−0.04	0.14
Residential characteristics		
San Antonio (1965)	0.36***	0.10
Proportion Hispanic in neighborhood (1965)	0.20	0.13
Telephone interview (2000)	−0.17†	0.09
Human capital		
Education	0.09***	0.02
Individual characteristics		
Female	0.13*	0.07
Skin color	−0.01	0.03
Age	0.01	0.01
Intercept	1.23	
R²	.405	
N	758	

Source: Mexican American Study Project.
[a] Linear regression run. Child sample analyzed. Adjusted for sibling clustering: number of clusters = 482; robust standard errors are calculated.
†p<.10, *p<.05, **p<.01, ***p<.001

Table B.8   Determinants of Spanish Birth Name, 2000[a]

	Spanish Birth Name	
	Unstandardized Coefficient	Robust Standard Errors
Generation-since-immigration (ref: 3)		
1.5	0.80***	0.17
2	0.52**	0.17
2.5	0.58***	0.12
4+	0.11	0.10
Socioeconomic characteristics		
Father's education	−0.06***	0.01
Mother's education	−0.02*	0.01
Parents' income (1965)	0.01	0.02
Parent was homeowner (1965)	−0.01	0.10
Childhood characteristics		
Parent is non-Hispanic	−0.38*	0.16
Parents were married (1965)	−0.23†	0.12
Residential characteristics		
San Antonio (1965)	0.39**	0.11
Proportion Hispanic in neighborhood (1965)	0.16	0.16
Telephone interview (2000)	0.03	0.10
Individual characteristics		
Female	−0.05	0.08
Skin color	0.01	0.04
Age	0.01	0.01
Intercept	3.17	
R^2	.192	
N	758	

Source: Mexican American Study Project.
[a]Linear regression run. Child sample analyzed. Adjusted for sibling clustering: number of clusters = 482; robust standard errors are calculated.
†p<.10, *p<.05, **p<.01, ***p<.001

Table B.9   Determinants of Children Ever Born, 2000[a]

	Children Ever Born	
	Unstandardized Coefficient	Robust Standard Errors
Generation-since-immigration (ref: 3)		
1.5	−0.24	0.15
2	−0.12	0.14
2.5	0.16*	0.08
4+	0.03	0.07
Socioeconomic characteristics		
Father's education	−0.01	0.01
Mother's education	−0.01	0.01
Parents' income (1965)	−0.01	0.01
Parent was homeowner (1965)	0.09	0.07
Childhood characteristics		
Parent spoke Spanish to child	0.13	0.07
Parent is non-Hispanic	−0.12	0.13
Parents were married (1965)	−0.06	0.08
Residential characteristics		
San Antonio (1965)	0.04	0.08
Proportion Hispanic in neighborhood (1965)	−0.07	0.11
Telephone interview (2000)	0.04	0.08
Human capital		
Education	−0.08***	0.01
Individual characteristics		
Skin color	−0.02	0.03
Age	0.01*	0.01
Intercept	1.55	
N	758	

Source: Mexican American Study Project.
[a] Poisson regression run. Child sample analyzed. Adjusted for sibling clustering: number of clusters = 482; robust standard errors are calculated.
*$p<.05$, ***$p<.001$

Table B.10   Determinants of Ethnic Identity, 2000[a]

	Mexican	American or Other
Generation-since-immigration (ref: 3)		
1.5	3.54**	0.61
2	1.01	0.54
2.5	0.88	0.60
4+	0.76	1.24
Socioeconomic characteristics		
Father's education	0.96	1.03
Mother's education	1.03	1.04
Parents' income (1965)	0.98	0.99
Parent was homeowner (1965)	0.80	1.14
Childhood characteristics		
Parent spoke Spanish to child	2.65***	0.36*
Parent is non-Hispanic	1.38	2.27*
Parents were married (1965)	0.76	2.75†
Residential characteristics		
San Antonio (1965)	0.27***	0.79
Proportion Hispanic in neighborhood (1965)	0.61	2.66*
Telephone interview (2000)	0.78	1.47
Human capital		
Education	0.99	1.08
Individual characteristics		
Female	0.74	1.28
Skin color	1.04	1.09
Age	1.01	1.08**
Pseudo R^2	.122	108
Log Pseudo-Likelihood	−296	−237
N	758	758

Source: Mexican American Study Project.

[a] Logistic regression run. Compared to all other ethnic identities. Adjusted odds ratios presented. Child sample analyzed. Adjusted for sibling clustering: number of clusters = 482; robust standard errors are calculated.

†p<.10, *p<.05, **p<.01, ***p<.001

Table B.11   Determinants of Ethnic Identity, 2000[a]

	Mexican	Hispanic or Latino	American or Other
Generation-since-immigration (ref: 3)			
1.5	4.20**	1.60	1.25
2	0.88	0.74	0.49
2.5	0.81	0.91	0.57†
4+	0.77	0.96	1.11
Socioeconomic characteristics			
Father's education	0.95	0.96	1.01
Mother's education	1.05	1.03	1.06
Parents' income (1965)	0.98	0.99	0.98
Parent was homeowner (1965)	0.92	1.24	1.26
Childhood characteristics			
Parent spoke Spanish to child	2.38**	0.98	0.40*
Parent is non-Hispanic	1.71	1.19	2.54*
Parents were married (1965)	0.86	1.13	2.73†
Residential characteristics			
San Antonio (1965)	0.45**	3.74***	1.16
Proportion Hispanic in neighborhood (1965)	0.76	1.32	2.80*
Telephone interview (2000)	0.89	1.31	1.56
Human capital			
Education	1.00	1.00	1.08
Individual characteristics			
Female	0.79	1.11	1.28
Skin color	1.03	0.96	1.08
Age	1.00	0.96**	1.06*
Pseudo R^2		.104	
Log pseudo-likelihood		−860	
N		758	

Source: Mexican American Study Project.
[a] Multinomial logistic regression run. Compared to Mexican American. Relative risk ratios presented. Child sample analyzed. Adjusted for sibling clustering: number of clusters = 482; robust standard errors are calculated.
†$p<.10$, *$p<.05$, **$p<.01$, ***$p<.001$

Table B.12   Determinants of Think of Self as Mexican or American, 2000[a]

	Mexican[b]	American[c]
Generation-since-immigration (ref: 3)		
1.5	2.61*	0.33*
2	1.17	1.01
2.5	1.03	0.94
4+	0.72	1.03
Socioeconomic characteristics (1965)		
Father's education	1.01	0.99
Mother's education	0.96	1.04
Parents' income (1965)	1.00	0.99
Parent was homeowner (1965)	1.06	1.06
Childhood characteristics		
Parent spoke Spanish to child	1.87*	0.60*
Parent is non-Hispanic	0.19**	2.02*
Parents were married (1965)	0.98	1.20
Residential characteristics		
San Antonio (1965)	0.34***	1.93**
Proportion Hispanic in neighborhood (1965)	0.54†	1.11
Telephone interview (2000)	0.71	0.89
Human capital		
Education	0.94	1.11**
Individual characteristics		
Female	1.38	0.82
Skin color	0.95*	1.10
Age	0.97	1.02
Pseudo R²	.103	.061
Log pseudo–likelihood	−329	−469
N	758	758

Source: Mexican American Study Project.

[a] Logistic regression run. Adjusted odds ratios presented. Child sample analyzed. Adjusted for sibling clustering: number of clusters = 482; robust standard errors are calculated.

[b] Think of self as Mexican frequently and not as American.

[c] Think of self as American frequently and not as Mexican.

†p<.10, *p<.05, **p<.01, ***p<.001

Table B.13   Determinants of Racial Identity and Discrimination, 2000[a]

	Identify as White	Experienced Discrimination
Generation-since-immigration (ref: 3)		
1.5	0.74	2.28*
2	2.02	0.81
2.5	1.13	1.34
4+	0.92	1.20
Socioeconomic characteristics		
Father's education	0.99	1.06*
Mother's education	1.04	0.94*
Parents' income (1965)	1.01	0.99
Parent was homeowner (1965)	1.00	0.89
Childhood characteristics		
Parent spoke Spanish to child	0.68	0.99
Parent is non-Hispanic	1.59	0.96
Parents were married (1965)	1.05	0.77
Residential characteristics		
San Antonio (1965)	5.60***	1.01
Proportion Hispanic in neighborhood (1965)	0.76	1.08
Telephone interview (2000)	0.90	0.66*
Human Capital		
Education	1.03	1.14**
Individual characteristics		
Female	1.50	0.47***
Skin color	0.97	1.24**
Age	1.03	1.01
Pseudo R^2	.107	.070
Log pseudo-likelihood	−282	−486
N	758	758

Source: Mexican American Study Project.
[a] Logistic regression run. Adjusted odds ratios presented. Child sample analyzed. Adjusted for sibling clustering: number of clusters = 482; robust standard errors are calculated.
*p<.05, **p<.01, ***p<.001

Table B.14   Determinants of Voted in 1996 Presidential Elections, 2000[a]

	Voted in 1996
Generation-since-immigration (ref: 3)	
1.5	0.27*
2	0.87
2.5	0.82
4+	0.95
Socioeconomic characteristics	
Father's education	1.00
Mother's education	1.01
Parents' income (1965)	1.02
Parent was homeowner (1965)	0.95
Parental characteristics	
Parent spoke Spanish to child	0.98
Parent is non-Hispanic	1.16
Parents were married (1965)	0.96
Parental prior voting behavior (1965)	
(ref: parent voted Democrat)	
Parent voted Republican in 1964[a]	1.50†
Parent did not vote in 1964[a]	1.48
Residential characteristics	
San Antonio (1965)	1.26
Proportion Hispanic in neighborhood (1965)	0.88
Telephone interview (2000)	1.07
Human capital	
Education	1.30***
Respondent Characteristics	
Female	1.47
Skin color	0.93
Age	1.00
Pseudo R^2	.084
Log pseudo-likelihood	−435
N	758

Source: Mexican American Study Project.
[a] Logistic regression run. Adjusted odds ratios presented. Child sample analyzed. Adjusted for sibling clustering: number of clusters = 482; robust standard errors are calculated.
†p<.10, *p<.05, ***p<.001

Table B.15   Determinants of Voted Republican in 1996
and Identify Republican, 2000[a]

	Voted Republican	Identify Republican
Generation-since-immigration (ref: 3)		
1.5	0.96	0.66
2	2.23	3.21*
2.5	1.28	2.07*
4+	1.33	1.18
Socioeconomic characteristics		
Father's education	1.06	1.15**
Mother's education	1.04	0.97
Parents' income (1965)	0.98	0.95
Parent was homeowner (1965)	0.88	1.02
Parental characteristics		
Parent spoke Spanish to child	1.11	0.80
Parent is non-Hispanic	0.63	0.49
Parents were married (1965)	1.95	2.25
Parental prior voting behavior (1965) (ref: parent voted Democrat)		
Parent voted Republican in 1964[a]	4.36**	3.95**
Parent did not vote in 1964[a]	0.70	0.53*
Residential characteristics		
San Antonio (1965)	1.73†	0.98
Proportion Hispanic in neighborhood (1965)	0.88	0.42†
Human capital		
Education	1.05	1.08
Respondent characteristics		
Female	0.70	0.90
Skin color	0.89	0.86
Age	1.04	0.97
Pseudo R^2	.079	.128
Log Pseudo-Likelihood	−223	−223
N	515	562

Source: Mexican American Study Project.
[a] Logistic regression run. Adjusted odds ratios presented. Child sample analyzed. Adjusted for sibling clustering: number of clusters = 482; robust standard errors are calculated.
†$p<.10$, *$p<.05$, **$p<.01$

Table B.16   Determinants of Positive Attitudes Toward Immigration, 2000[a]

	Positive Attitudes Toward Immigration[b]	
	Unstandardized Coefficient	Robust Standard Errors
Generation-since-immigration (ref: 3)		
1.5	0.17*	0.08
2	0.03	0.08
2.5	−0.03	0.05
4+	−0.03	0.05
Socioeconomic characteristics		
Father's education	0.00	0.01
Mother's education	0.00	0.01
Parents' income (1965)	0.01	0.01
Parent was homeowner (1965)	−0.10*	0.04
Parental characteristics		
Parent spoke Spanish to child	0.01	0.05
Parent is non-Hispanic	0.00	0.06
Parents were married (1965)	0.02	0.06
Residential characteristics		
San Antonio (1965)	−0.10*	0.05
Proportion Hispanic in neighborhood (1965)	0.04	0.07
Human capital		
Education	0.03***	0.01
Respondent characteristics		
Female	−0.08*	0.04
Skin color	−0.03	0.02
Age	0.00	0.00
Constant	2.19	
R^2	.082	
N	562	

Source: Mexican American Study Project.

[a] Linear regression run. Child sample analyzed. Adjusted for sibling clustering: number of clusters = 482; robust standard errors are calculated.

[b] Based on a four-point scale ranging from strong agree to strongly disagree of seven items shown on rows 1 to 7 of table 10.12. Items on rows 3 to 6 reversed to positive direction.

*$p < .05$, ***$p < .001$

$=$ Notes $=$

Foreword

1. This memoir has benefited greatly from comments by Lionel Maldonado, Frank Mittelbach, Alan Moore, Avelardo Valdez, William Vélez, and Diego Vigil. I am grateful to all of them.

2. When we did our study, about 88 percent of the Mexican origin population lived in the five southwestern states of their traditional settlement: Texas, Arizona, California, New Mexico, and Colorado. For these states, the U.S. census was then collecting data on the population under the rubric of "White Persons of Spanish Surname."

3. In addition to the Leo Grebler, Ralph Guzmán, and myself (the three main authors of *The Mexican American People*), seven other scholars made major contributions to that final report of the study. These included Jeffrey Berlant, Thomas Carter, Walter Fogel, Wayne Gordon, Patrick McNamara, Frank Mittelbach, and Sam Surace. In addition, Stanley Plog, Julian Samora, Richard Lamanna, Nancie González, Ray Jessen, Velma Montoya Thompson, Taher Moustafa, Gertrud Weiss, and Clifton Wignall all contributed to the study, either by authoring one of the eleven advance reports issued by the project or by preparing other specialized manuscripts. (The substance of some of these advance reports was included in our final volume, while others found publication in a variety of outlets.) We convened a faculty advisory committee at UCLA, and also enlisted the help of notable community leaders in advisory committees in both Los Angeles and San Antonio.

4. Early in the project, Grebler spoke of the monumental Gunnar Myrdal study of black Americans, *An American Dilemma* (1944) as a model for the Mexican American Study Project. In that study, the Swedish-born Myrdal could draw on the expertise of a large number of mature black social scientists.

5. Note from Telles and Ortiz: In this foreword, Joan Moore uses the term Chicano over Mexican American. While Chicano has also been used to refer to this population, it came into wider use by a small number of politically active Mexican Americans in the late 1960s and continues to be used in certain circles, particularly on some college campuses. As we explain in chapter 1, we use Mexican American because it is much preferred by that population, it captures the expected integration path from Mexican to American which is our focus, and it is consistent with terms used for other ethnic groups, like European Americans.

317

6. Right after the Watts riots a special census was initiated to cover not only Watts, but, after some political pressure, the equally poverty-stricken but then comparatively "quiescent" Mexican American barrios (U.S. Bureau of the Census 1966).

7. Even the term *Mexican American* was avoided: the largest traditional advocacy organization was called the League of United Latin American Citizens, formed in 1929, and Texans' continued preference for euphemism was manifest in their post-World War II Political Association of Spanish Speaking Organizations (PASSO) and American G.I. Forum. California's bolder Mexican American Political Association was formed only in 1958.

8. Though many individual religious worked closely with the Chicano movement, the Catholic church itself was never an institutional base for the movement. There was no Chicano equivalent of the organized power of the black churches.

9. In 1968, before the findings of the study had been published, our data became a resource for one such cause. In March, young Chicano activists had organized "blowouts" at high schools in East Los Angeles to protest poor educational conditions. A grand jury was convened to indict thirteen of these young men on fifteen separate counts of conspiracy to disturb the peace, which ratcheted relatively minor charges into a felony. The attorney for the defendants, Oscar Acosta, challenged the indictments on several grounds, including that the grand jury was unconstitutionally composed because it systematically under-represented Spanish-surnamed persons. He asked our research group to help him. Using MASP data, I testified that the defendants did belong to a distinctive class. Acosta made headlines by subpoenaing all superior court judges to testify about their failure to nominate Mexican Americans to the grand jury. The case is cited extensively because of the first amendment rights that it raised, but not (unfortunately for my story) for its impact on establishing Chicanos as a distinct class of persons (for details, see Acosta 1968 and Haney López 2003).

10. Grebler, Moore, and Guzmán (1970).

11. The federal Bilingual Education Act was passed in 1968.

12. The sociologist Herbert Gans denigrates these efforts as the "Skirmish on Poverty of the 1960s" and (along with others) argues that subsequent federal policy has been, as his title indicates, a *War Against the Poor* (1995).

13. See Perry and Watkins (1977), the semi-popular book that began to make job shifts a national preoccupation.

14. The Border Industrialization Program, initiated in 1965, might be construed as an early, and government-sponsored, form of globalization. Jointly sponsored by the United States and Mexico, this "maquiladora" program permitted U.S.-owned companies to establish assembly plants in border cities of Mexico. The finished goods were returned to the United States with only minimal taxation.

15. Compare Wilson (2005).

16. Compare Moore and Pinderhughes (1993).

17. Grebler, Moore, and Guzmán (1970, 579).

18. Grebler, Moore, and Guzmán (1970, 76).

19. Chinchilla, Hamilton, and Loucky 1993; López, Popkin, and Telles (1996).

20. Compare Ortiz (1996).

21. Amid strident political claims about the economic problems created by undocumented workers, the *Wall Street Journal* (July 8, 2005, p. 1) noted that local businesses were taking profitable advantage of this newly discovered market, and a California think tank found that immigrants produced a "net benefit" for the state.

22. The term *charter member minority* had been used by Everett Hughes to characterize the anomalous position of the French Canadian population. It seemed to apply to the Spanish Americans of New Mexico and southern Colorado, as well, but never gained currency among social scientists. *Internal colonialism* briefly became another term to capture the position of Mexican Americans, along with other minorities.

23. The perception that Mexican Americans are "just" an immigrant population persists. As recently as 2003, the authors of a generally sophisticated analysis of ethnicity commented "[S]ome Latino immigrant groups . . . could also be construed as long-resident domestic minorities that had suffered systematic disadvantage (in the Mexican case, to be sure, this characterization applies strictly to only a small percentage, since the great majority of the group is descended from immigrants who have arrived over the last hundred years)" (Alba and Nee 2003,153). This kind of formulation, which negates the impact of anti-Chicano discrimination "over the last hundred years," was common among East Coast social scientists in the 1960s, and was exactly what our study was designed to combat. After thirty-odd years of Chicano scholarship, the statement demonstrates surprising ignorance about the treatment of Mexican Americans in the Southwest during the twentieth century.

24. This is a reference to the segmented assimilation theory of Portes and Rumbaut (2001). I do not intend to denigrate the theory, which is complex and subtle, but the authors are interested only in immigrant populations, and emphasize downward assimilation as the fate awaiting many Mexican immigrants. They highlight the obstacles facing the population (racial discrimination, bifurcated labor markets, dissonant acculturation, scanty human and social capital). The conclusions of this influential study are often extended to all Mexican Americans, but raise the question addressed in this volume: What about Mexican Americans who have been in the United States for three or more generations?

Chapter 1

1. In terms of policy, the study provided critical data to justify including Mexican Americans in the Civil Rights and Voting Rights Acts and to form civil rights institutions such as the National Council of La Raza and the Mexican American Legal Defense and Educational Fund.

2. Roybal (1966); Moore (1967).

3. Grebler, Moore, and Guzmán (1970, 575); see also Madsen (1964); Rubel (1966); Kluckhohn and Strodtback (1961).

4. The intergenerational success of Italian Americans is well documented (see, for example, Alba 1985).

5. Such as Linda Chávez (1991) and Peter Skerry (1993).

6. See, for example, Acuña (1972); Blauner (1972); Barrera (1979).

7. Wilson (1978).

8. Alba and Nee (2003); Portes and Rumbaut (2001).

9. Only 1 percent of their sample of Mexican-origin persons were found in their other study site, Miami/Ft. Lauderdale.

10. Portes and Rumbaut (2001).

11. Alba and Nee (2003).

12. The 2004 article later (Huntington 2004a) became chapter 9 of his 2004 book. (Huntington 2004b, 145).
13. See, for example, reviews by Massey (2004); Montejano (2004); Telles (2006).
14. In 2006, as this book was nearly finished, along came still another assault, this time from conservative commentator Patrick Buchanan.
15. Alba and Nee (2003).
16. Tremblay and Vézina (2000) contend that 30 years is a good estimate of inter-generational intervals, though it may be over 30 in modern populations.
17. Roediger (2005).
18. For the more than 180 years that the Immigration and Naturalization Service collected immigration data, only Germany has sent more legal immigrants to the United States. That said, Mexican legal immigration is likely to pass Germany within the next ten years if current rates continue. Considering that there was virtually no illegal immigration from Europe during the period of mass immigration and that most illegal immigration in the modern period has been from Mexico, immigrants from Mexico may well outnumber those from Germany. As far as contemporary immigration is concerned, legal Mexican immigration is clearly the largest (U.S. Immigration and Naturalization Service 2005).
19. Ngai (2004); Durand, Telles, and Flashman (2006).
20. This pattern seems to have changed since the 1990s (Massey, Durand, and Malone 2003).
21. Guzmán (2001).
22. Bean and Tienda (1987); Tienda and Mitchell (2006).
23. Our study will show that even into the fourth generation, Mexican or Mexican American remain preferred labels for self-identity, though Hispanic and Latino are also used.
24. Tienda and Mitchell (2006).
25. Alba and Nee (2003).
26. Omi and Winant (1986).
27. Gans (1999); Bonilla-Silva (2003).
28. Telles (2004).
29. Ladányi and Szelényi (2006).
30. Ryang (2000).
31. Fredrickson (2002).
32. Crul and Vermeulen (2003).
33. Cornell and Hartmann (1998).
34. Banton (1977); Barot and Bird (2001); Miles (1989); Small (1994); Winant (1994).
35. Brown et al. (2003); Bonilla-Silva (2003).
36. Omi and Winant (1986); Bonilla-Silva (2003).

Chapter 2

1. Cornell and Hartmann (1998, 9).
2. Neidert and Farley (1985); Bean and Tienda (1987); Chapa (1988).
3. Acuña (1972); Barrera (1979); Blauner (1972); Estrada et al. (1981).
4. Alba (1990).
5. Alba and Nee (2003).

6. Interestingly, early analysts focused on acculturation or integration on cultural dimensions and largely neglected the economic dimension.

7. Psychologists Susan Keefe and Amado Padilla (1987) find relatively low acculturation for Mexican Americans in their study of three California towns.

8. Gans (1979).

9. Comaroff (1991, 663), cited in Cornell and Hartmann (1998, 11).

10. Barth (1969).

11. Frederickson (1997); Cornell and Hartmann (1998); Telles (2004).

12. Alba and Nee (2003, 59).

13. Sanders (2002).

14. Hannaford (1996); Horsman (1981).

15. Menchaca (1993); Gómez (2002).

16. Gutiérrez (1995); Haney López (2003).

17. Barth (1969).

18. Cornell and Hartmann (1998).

19. Jenkins (1997).

20. Lamont and Molnár (2002).

21. Ibid.

22. Ibid.

23. Cornell and Hartmann (1998, 4, 6).

24. Brubaker (2004); Hodson, Sekulic, and Massey (1994); Cornell and Hartmann (1998); Wimmer (2002).

25. Blumer (1965).

26. Cornell and Hartmann (1998); Montejano (1987); Feagin (2006); Mary Waters (1999).

27. Gordon (1964).

28. Ibid., 70

29. Ibid.; Alba and Nee (2003).

30. Mexicans are mentioned in Gordon (1964) in only one sentence on page 108–109. "For somewhat similar reasons [as the Negro], augmented by the language difference, the Spanish speaking people of Mexican origin in the Southwest appear to be developing a middle class out of the second generation rather slowly, an unmistakable sign of the retardation of the assimilation process."

31. Park (1926).

32. Blauner (1972).

33. Gordon (1964).

34. Although Gordon (1964) expected that full assimilation might take up to six generations, a basic three-generation model to full assimilation was widely accepted in areas as diverse as language (Veltman 1983), ethnic identity (Alba 1990), and politics (Dahl 1961).

35. Warner and Srole (1945) were rare exceptions in their pessimism about the assimilation of Mexicans.

36. Alba and Nee (2003, 30).

37. Shibutani and Kwan (1965).

38. Alba and Nee (2003).

39. *Santa Barbara News Press*, Obituary for Tamotsu (Tom) Shibutani, August 13, 2004; UC Berkeley alumni news on Kian Kwan, accessed at http://sociology. berkeley.edu/alumni2/viewbio_querylist.php?ID=214.

40. Grebler, Moore, and Guzmán (1970).
41. Shibutani and Kwan (1965).
42. Park (1926).
43. Interview with Joan Moore, February 28, (2005).
44. Grebler, Moore, and Guzmán (1970).
45. Ibid., 8
46. Grebler, Moore, and Guzmán (1970, 578). This is clearly not the case for the "manito" population of New Mexico and southern Colorado, who have lived in the area in relative isolation since the sixteenth and seventeenth centuries. The 1880 U.S. Census shows that more than half of the native Mexican American population was born in those two relatively small states (Gutmann et al. 2000).
47. Cruse (1967); Blauner (1972).
48. Alba (1985); Sandberg (1974).
49. See Gutiérrez (2005) for a review of the development of internal colonial theory, including common references to this model for African Americans as early as 1962. Hechter's (1975) history of the British expansion into the Celtic fringe may be the most fully developed account. Stone (1979) claims that before these "radical critics who recast it in sociological jargon," the concept can be traced to the 1930s.
50. Blauner (1969, 1972); Hechter (1975, 1985).
51. Blauner (1969, 1972).
52. Blauner (1972).
53. Hechter (1975).
54. Gutiérrez (2005).
55. Acuña (1972).
56. According to Alex Saragoza (1987), Acuña retreated from his wholesale interpretation of the internal colonial model in his 1982 edition, though the victimization (them versus us) character endured.
57. Barrera (1979).
58. Moore (1970).
59. Saragoza (1987).
60. Almaguer (1987); Omi and Winant (1986); Gutiérrez (2005).
61. Gordon (1964); Alba and Nee (2003).
62. Shibutani and Kwan (1965).
63. Gordon (1964).
64. Alba and Nee (2003, 273).
65. Ibid., 12
66. Ibid., 32
67. Ibid., 31
68. Kasinitz (1992); Nagel (1994); Mary Waters (1999); Foner (2000).
69. Alba and Nee (2003, 243, 247).
70. Ibid., 256
71. Alba and Islam (2005).
72. Alba and Nee (2003).
73. Bean and Stevens (2003), who are particularly attentive to the Mexican case, note the importance of separating out economic from sociocultural dimensions

of immigrant integration and how the two can run in opposite and apparently conflicting directions. They argue that the case of African Americans demonstrates sociocultural integration without economic assimilation.

74. Gans (1992).
75. Portes and Zhou (1993).
76. Which was further elaborated by Portes and Rumbaut (2001).
77. For example, Portes and Rumbaut (2001).
78. Ibid.
79. Portes and Rumbaut's (2001) findings are consistent with the Hispanic health paradox that shows that greater time spent in the United States, or acculturation generally, may have adverse outcomes For example, infant mortality and low birth weight are greater for the Hispanic second generation compared to that for immigrants, apparently because of the healthier habits of immigrants including breastfeeding, more wholesome diets and more frequent inoculations and visits to doctors. Similarly, Brian Carl Finch and William Vega (2004) show greater alcohol abuse, substance dependence, depression, and anxiety among U.S.-born Latino schoolchildren than among Latino immigrants. Rumbaut and others claim that assimilation is hazardous to one's health and other socioeconomic indicators, though Alberto Palloni and Elizabeth Arias (2004) show that observed Mexican immigrant advantages in adult mortality are due to migrant selectivity, where the more sickly are more likely to never have immigrated to the United States in the first place or to have returned to Mexico at old age, where they elude U.S. health statistics.
80. Portes and Rumbaut (2001).
81. Portes and Rumbaut (2001, 284) affirm John Ogbu (1978) and Maria Matute-Bianchi (1986). Oppositional identity theorists argue that minority students perceive that their opportunities for social advancement are poor and respond by labeling school success as "acting white." On the other hand, more recent studies based on national samples have failed to find support for the oppositional identity hypothesis (Carter 2005; Downey and Ainsworth-Darnell 2002), though there is some evidence of it in integrated schools (Fryer 2006; Fryer with Torelli 2006).
82. Alba and Nee (2003); Portes and Rumbaut (2001).
83. Portes and Rumbaut (2001); Alba and Nee (2003).
84. Alba and Nee (1997).
85. Rumbaut and Portes (2003, 5).
86. Alba and Nee (2003). The survey was also taken in South Florida, but the Mexican sample is nearly all in San Diego.
87. Alba and Nee (2003); Portes and Rumbaut (2001).
88. Sewell and Hauser (1975); Featherman and Hauser (1978); Blau and Duncan (1978).
89. Borjas (1994); Bean and Stevens (2003); Perlmann (2005).
90. Blau and Duncan (1978).
91. Cordelia Reimers (1985); Borjas (1994); Gratton (2002).
92. Chapa (1988); Smith (2003); Romo and Falbo (1996).
93. Blumer (1958); Bobo and Hutchings (1996); Bobo and Tuan (2006, 32).

94. Omi and Winant (1986).
95. Banton (1977); Miles (1989); Small (1994); Winant (1994).
96. Rumbaut (2006).
97. Lakoff and Johnson (1980).
98. Flores (2002).
99. Surprisingly, political scientists such as Peter Skerry (1990) and John Skrentny (2002, 106) seem to care about biology or official classification. Skerry writes that Hispanics cannot be discriminated against since they are not a race and Skrentny is concerned that Hispanics benefited from affirmative action despite biology never recognizing them as a race!
100. Cornell and Hartmann (1998, 30).
101. Another term, ethnicity, often refers to persons of common ancestry or culture, and in the sociological literature is generally differentiated from race. Nonracialized ethnics are often thought to be the targets of ethnocentrism.
102. Portes and Rumbaut (2001).
103. Waldinger (2003).
104. Ngai (2004).
105. Waldinger (2007a, 139).
106. Jiménez (2005).
107. Massey, Durand, and Malone (2003).
108. Recent U.S. State Department visa bulletins denote a wait time of eight to thirteen years for Mexicans, depending on the visa preference level. However, according to historian Mae Ngai and immigration attorney Daniel Kowalski, the gap between the cutoff date and today's date, as shown on the face of any given month's visa bulletin, is not the true gap. They calculate the true gap by multiplying the stated State Department gap by the rate of advance over the past two years. The rate of advance for Mexican applicants, has been, on average, one week for each month stated on the bulletin (Correspondence with Mae Ngai on March 13 and 14, 2007, based on information she received from Kowalski, the editor-in-chief on Bender's immigration bulletin). Thus, the wait based on recent waiting times may even be more than forty years.
109. Portes and Rumbaut (2001); Ngai (2004).
110. López and Stanton-Salazar (2001).
111. Freeman (2004).
112. Alba and Nee (2003).
113. Alba and Nee (2003); Portes and Rumbaut (2001).
114. Grebler, Moore, and Guzmán (1970); Redfield (1960, 295–96).
115. Redfield (1960); Wirth (1938).
116. Grebler, Moore, and Guzmán (1970). Indeed, they believed that previous research focused on places like towns in South Texas or New Mexico that were even more traditional than San Antonio and tended to neglect the wide diversity of the Mexican American experience, especially at the modern end of the continuum as in Los Angeles.
117. Gans (1962); Fischer et al. (1977).
118. Grebler, Moore, and Guzmán (1970).
119. Ibid., 312.

120. Wilson (1987); Massey and Denton (1993); Brooks-Gunn et al. (1993).
121. Moore and Pinderhughes (1993).
122. We expect the effect of percentage in neighborhood on poverty on many of our outcomes and found no significant effects. We decided not to show these results in the chapters since the lack of such effects would distract from our focus.
123. South, Crowder, and Chávez (2005); Massey (1985).
124. Ibid.; Gordon (1964).
125. Alba (1990).
126. Fully 200,000 Africans entered Mexico in the sixteenth and seventeenth centuries as slaves mostly through the Caribbean port of Veracruz. In 1800, the entire Mexican population numbered 5 million (McCaa 1997). Unlike the Spanish and the indigenous Mexican identity, the African origin has been largely forgotten. On the other hand, except perhaps in the state of Veracruz and a handful of isolated areas in Mexico, African origins are not readily apparent among the Mexican population, as they are throughout the Caribbean and Brazil, where African slaves at one time constituted national majorities.
127. Telles and Murguía (1990); Murguía and Telles (1996).
128. Guillickson (2005); Hochschild, Burch, and Weaver (2006).

Chapter 3

1. Grebler, Moore, and Guzmán (1970, 8).
2. Ibid., 295.
3. These two urban areas seen cover a rough average of the Mexican American population in the 1960s. For example, our most important variable, education, shows that education for Mexican Americans in the five southwestern states is roughly halfway between that in Los Angeles and San Antonio. Other status indicators are likely to be similar. We suspect that socioeconomic outcomes for Mexican Americans are best in low ethnic density urban centers, followed by California cities such as Los Angeles, whereas Texas cities have been less well off, but the large numbers of Mexican Americans in rural areas throughout the Southwest are likely to have fared the worst. Overall, we suspect that assimilation and racialization follows this pattern of success.
4. Grebler, Moore, and Guzmán (1970, 417).
5. In some cases, analysts have sought to lag the years so that the parent generation is captured. While this is an improvement, these are still not their actual parents. At most, one can describe changes on the few variables available with such data but cannot examine how parental characteristics are associated with those of children. In our data set, we can link parents to children.
6. Tremblay and Vézina (2000).
7. Originally, we had planned to complete the interviews by 1997 but we greatly underestimated the time consuming tasks of securing funding and locating respondents.
8. This section reviews some of the major decisions for drawing the 1965 to 1966 sample (for more information, see Grebler, Moore, and Guzmán 1970, appendix H).

9. Grebler, Moore, and Guzmán (1970, 302–5).
10. Ibid.
11. Jessen (1969, 1970).
12. We thank Edward Murguía for assistance in interpreting the changing ethnic geography in San Antonio.
13. For more information, see Ortiz and Ballon (2007).
14. For instance, pre-1950 marriage records or pre-1965 property deed were not computerized.
15. The availability of death certificates helped considerably in being able to locate the family of original respondents who had died. The death certificates list the name and contact information of a family member (as the person who provided information about the deceased).
16. In the San Antonio sample, only one respondent was missing both last name and first name.
17. The survey questionnaires are available at http://www.russellsage.org/publications/books/080117.517606.
18. We also selected some of the interviewees and conducted additional in-depth interviews about twenty families (both original respondents and children) in Los Angeles and another twenty in San Antonio in 2003 and 2004. We intend to publish a more systematic analysis of those data in the future.
19. We examined a wider range of variables from the original survey to examine selectivity. We have listed those where there were large differences in rates of locating and interviewing.
20. We also found that the 1965 characteristics of respondents interviewed in 2000 did not generally differ from those that we located but did not interview. This is consistent with Lin, Schaeffer, and Seltzer's findings that there are few significant differences between those interviewed and those not interviewed (1999). However, similar in our study, Lin and his colleagues reported large differences between those located and those not located.
21. Laurie, Smith, and Scott (1999); Lin, Schaeffer, and Seltzer (1999).
22. Because we sampled from living children, the issue of children dying was mostly irrelevant. Although we did have one case in which the child died between the time we did the interview with the original respondent and the child selection was done; and when we contacted the child to do the interview. We did not select another child to interview.
23. Most recent birthdate compares to the interview date and ensures a random selection of two children out of all eligible children.
24. Dr. Robert Mare also provided assistance in developing the child weights.
25. Alba (1985, 45–46).
26. See the appendix for full regressions.
27. See, for example, Mary Waters (1999) and Portes and Rumbaut (2001).

Chapter 4

1. Romano (1968, 14).
2. There were only a handful of Mexican American academics before 1960. Writing in the 1940s, historian Carlos Castañeda and educator George I. Sánchez were exceptions to the lack of a Mexican American presence at major universities. At the time, both had described a stratified southwestern society

of whites, Mexicans, and blacks, in which Mexicans were perceived as foreigners and nonwhite, even though many were both more native to the U.S. Southwest than whites and officially classified as white (García 1991, 242).

3. Montejano (1987, 260).

4. Ibid.

5. The New Mexico territories encompassed the area between Texas and Alta California, which includes the current states of New Mexico and Arizona and parts of Colorado, Utah, Nevada, and Wyoming (Gómez 2007).

6. Oscar Martínez estimates this population at between 87,000 and 118,000 (1975). Brian Gratton and Myron Guttmann (2000) provide a figure of 81,508, which they claim is only a minimum and that actual numbers are likely to be greater.

7. Based on the declarations of a Mexican senator, Laura Gómez notes: "Some of the Mexican legislators debating ratification after the U.S. Senate's amendments strongly feared that Mexican citizens were doomed to ill treatment by the Americans. 'The North Americans hate us, their orators deprecate us, even in speeches in which they recognize the justice of our cause, and they consider us unable to form a single nation or society with them'."

8. The Naturalization Law of 1790 deemed that only whites could become citizens and thus the naturalization of Mexican Americans in 1848 made them de facto white (Haney López 1996; Takaki 1989). This law would be repealed only in 1952 by the McCarran-Walter Act.

9. Gómez (2007).

10. Horsman (1981).

11. Gutiérrez (1995, 16).

12. Montejano (1987, 181); Gutiérrez (1995, 16).

13. Gutiérrez (1995); Flores (2002).

14. Camarillo (1984, 2).

15. Camarillo (1984); Montejano (1987).

16. The history of Mexicans in New Mexico departs significantly from the rest of the Southwest. Most of the southwest region's pre-1848 population lived in that state, relatively few whites migrated there until well into the twentieth century, political representation by Hispanos has long been at rough parity with the general population, and there has been relatively little ethnic labor market segmentation.

17. Camarillo (1979); Montejano (1987).

18. Almaguer (1994); García (1991).

19. Brown-Coronel (2006).

20. Almaguer (1994); Camarillo (1979, 32).

21. Carrigan (2003).

22. Data for Mexicans are from Carrigan (2003) and included the five southwestern states and Nevada, Nebraska, Oklahoma, Oregon, Kansas, Louisiana, Montana, and Wyoming. Data for blacks are from Tolnay and Beck (1995, as cited in Carrigan 2003). Black lynching rates varied from 11.4 in North Carolina to 52.8 in Mississippi.

23. Montejano (1987, 262).

24. San Miguel (1987, 54).

25. San Miguel (1987); Ruíz (2004). Similar arguments have been made for California, though the involvement of the state may have been less than in

Texas and egregious discrimination may not have endured into the 1960s to the same extent as in Texas. In southern California, one study reported that sixty-four schools in eight counties had Mexican student enrollments of 90 percent or more in 1928 and another reported that 80 percent of school districts with substantial Mexican American enrollment practiced segregation (both studies cited in Sánchez 1993, 258). Alvarez lists sixty-four schools in eight California counties, including several in Los Angeles, that were 90 to 100 percent Mexican (1986). Well-known California judicial cases of segregation involved the districts of Westminster and Lemon Grove.

26. Camarillo (1984); Montejano (1987); Nakano-Glenn (2002).
27. Foley (1997).
28. Gómez (2007).
29. Almaguer (1994); Foley (1997).
30. Menchaca (1993); Haney López (2003).
31. Montejano (1987).
32. Ibid.
33. Camarillo (1984); Almaguer (1994).
34. Foley (1997, 8). On the other hand, Foley argues that in rural areas of central Texas in the 1920s, poor whites were losing their white privileges and became "white trash" (1997, 6).
35. Foley (1997, 41–42).
36. García (1991); Sánchez (1993); Roediger (2005).
37. Limerick (1987).
38. Gratton and Guttmann (2000). Historical demographers Gratton and Guttmann use census data and various adjustment techniques to derive an estimate of 401,000 Mexican Americans in 1900, though based on other information they concede that the 1900 population may have been considerably greater. Martínez estimated a range of 381,000 to 562,000 (1975).
39. Montejano (1987).
40. Sánchez (1993).
41. González and Fernández (2003).
42. Womack (1991); Guttmann et al. (2000); Gutiérrez (1995); González and Fernández (2003).
43. Sánchez (1993).
44. Population gains in the population may also be from fertility and decreasing rates of mortality.
45. Gutiérrez (1995).
46. Alvarez (1983); compare Sánchez (1993, 254).
47. Gutiérrez (1995, 57); García (1991, 29). Gutiérrez notes that these early censuses may have underestimated population by as much as 30 percent (1995). An underestimate is especially likely for 1930 given that the census used a close-ended race question, which captured only "persons born in Mexico or of Mexican parents, who are not definitely white or negro" (Gratton and Guttmann 2000, 138). San Antonio had been Texas's largest city in 1900.
48. Sánchez (1993). Although Chicano historians generally recognize the importance of Mexican immigration on the development of the Mexican American

community, they differ on the importance of the nineteenth century colonization and conquest experience. The earlier generation of historians emphasizes
the nineteenth-century experiences of dispossession, barrioization, racial
violence, and Anglo occupation strongly imply its lasting impacts on Mexican
Americans today. A newer generation, however, points to a discontinuity
between the two centuries and asserts that the twentieth-century Mexican
American experience is fundamentally shaped by twentieth-century immigration; for an overview, see González and Fernández (2003).

49. See, for example, Handman (1930); Allen (1931).
50. Montejano (1987, 182).
51. Ibid.
52. Ngai (2004).
53. Gutiérrez (1995).
54. Perlmann (2005); Alba (1990).
55. Ngai (2004).
56. Ngai (2004); Foley (1997).
57. Foley (1997, 210–11).
58. Ruíz (1998).
59. Sánchez (1993); Ruíz (1998).
60. Balderrama and Rodríguez (1995).
61. Balderrama and Rodríguez (1995, 79–80). García notes how San Antonio
    leaders debated the repatriation of Mexicans though Blackwelder argues that
    there was relatively little repatriation in San Antonio because of continuing
    heavy reliance on cheap Mexican labor (García 1991, 114–6; Blackwelder
    1984, 14).
62. Sociologists Douglas Massey and Jorge Durand argue that the braceros of
    this period would become the seeds of today's largely undocumented mass-
    immigration from Mexico (see, for example, Massey, Durand, and Malone
    2003).
63. Ngai (2004, 95). Interestingly, the Mexican government prevented the Bracero
    Program in Texas until that state guaranteed the end of de facto segregation
    against Mexicans in Texas, which the Texas legislature did on paper with the
    passage of the Caucasian Race Resolution in 1947. Of course, in the Anglo
    mind, Mexicans were rarely, if ever, considered Caucasian though they were
    argued to be in a strict scientific sense (Foley 1997; Guglielmo 2006).
64. Guttmann et al. (2000).
65. Sánchez (1993); Gutiérrez (1995).
66. Arthur Slayden argued "there are probably 250,000 Mexicans in Texas who
    were born in the state but they are [defined as] 'Mexicans' just as all blacks are
    negroes though they may have five generations of American ancestors" (1921,
    124). Many of our respondents reported similar treatment many years later.
67. Roediger (1999); Jacobsen (1998); Guglielmo (2006).
68. Gutiérrez (1995, 53).
69. Camarillo (1984). The 1930 census had shown that 66 percent of Mexicans in
    California, 47 percent in Texas, and lower rates in Arizona lived in cities; by
    1960, when census data on Mexicans again became available, 74 percent
    lived in urban areas (Camarillo 1984; Bean and Tienda 1987).
70. Bean and Tienda (1987).

71. Ibid. Other metropolitan areas would surpass San Antonio after 1980 because of differential rates of immigration.
72. Montejano (1987, 263).
73. Sánchez (1993); Vargas (2005).
74. Vargas (2005, 224); Sánchez (1993); Avila (2004).
75. Sánchez (1993).
76. Vargas (2005, 225).
77. Guglielmo (2006); Rivas-Rodríguez (2005).
78. García (1991); Sánchez (1993). For example, the Sleepy Lagoon case in Los Angeles in 1942 and in Texas, the inability of returning veterans to be buried in cemeteries deemed only for whites.
79. San Miguel (1987); Gutiérrez (1995).
80. Rivas-Rodríguez (2005).
81. Alvarez (1973).
82. García (1991).
83. Ruíz (1998).
84. This anti-Mexican fervor was apparent a year earlier in which press coverage of the so-called Sleepy Lagoon murder case, which resulted in the largest mass conviction in California history and in which police submitted a report to the grand jury that declared Mexicans inherently criminal and biologically prone to violence (Sánchez 1993, 266–7).
85. Sánchez (1993, 266–7).
86. Haney López (2003, 84–85).
87. Bogardus (1967).
88. Griswold del Castillo (1993); García (1991).
89. Other Mexican American organizations, including the Community Service Organization, the American G.I. Forum and the Association of Mexican American Educators, like LULAC, sought to promote economic and political integration and combat persistent discrimination (Allsup 1982; McLemore and Romo 1985; Muñoz 1989). Historian Carlos Muñoz characterizes these organizations as representing "the new professional sector of an emerging Mexican American middle class with a progressive politics in the liberal capitalist tradition" (1989, 43).
90. San Miguel (1987); García (1991).
91. Gutiérrez (1995, 71).
92. Gutiérrez (1995).
93. Muñoz (1989).
94. Navarro (1995).
95. Muñoz (1989).
96. Ibid.
97. Knight (1990); Wimmer (2002).
98. Grebler, Moore, and Guzmán (1970); Muñoz (1989); Guglielmo (2006).
99. Gutiérrez (1995, 70).
100. Ibid.
101. Ibid.
102. Sánchez (1993); Gutiérrez (1995).
103. Gutiérrez (1995, 122).

104. Vargas (2005).
105. Ruíz (2004); Alvarez (1986).
106. Olivas (2006); San Miguel (1987). The 1931 case was *Martínez v. Lemon Grove School District* though it was an isolated case which set no jurisdictional precedent. *Mendez v. Westminster School District* was decided in 1946 in California and upheld by the 9th Circuit Court in 1947 (Ruíz 2004) and the Texas case was *Delgado v. Bastrop Independent School District* (1998).
107. San Miguel (1987, 117).
108. Ibid.
109. Valencia, Menchaca, and Donato (2002).
110. See Naboa (2005) for San Antonio.
111. We do not think these changes are an artifact of the data because we have a random sample with substantial number of cases, at least seventy in each decade and city, suggest robust results with only a small margin of error.
112. San Miguel (1987). Notably, though, some scholars have noted that segregation was the most widespread in the primary grades and so by age thirteen, some students may have begun to attend integrated schools. Only a small minority reported that their schoolmates were all of Mexican ancestry. This is, however, an overly strict standard for segregation because even a rare non-Mexican, including one black or Asian, would preclude this level of segregation. Considering that fewer than 14 percent of all schoolchildren in California were Mexican American, these segregation figures are quite high (Grebler, Moore, and Gusman 1970). Segregation is likely to have been even higher at younger ages because some school districts are known to have segregated only in elementary school (San Miguel 1987).
113. Menchaca (1993); Haney López (2003); Gómez (2002). Indeed, Grebler, Moore, and Guzmán relied on the 1960 census category of "white persons of Spanish surname" to capture the Mexican-origin population for data analysis and as a basis for survey sampling. This compares to the 1930 census, which listed Mexican as a separate racial category. Protests by the Mexican consulate and LULAC, however, insisted on Mexicans as whites. The separate racial designation was rescinded by the 1940 census. Grebler, Moore, and Guzmán note "the statistical identification had run full circle from a subcategory of other races to a subgroup of the white population" (1970, 602).
114. Gómez (2007).
115. Valencia, Menchaca, and Donato (2002).
116. San Miguel (1987); Haney López (2003); Gómez (2007). The judge in *Mendez v. Westminster* ruled against racial segregation for Mexican Americans in California because, according to Ruíz, it violated the equal protection clause and, according to Menchaca, because there was no California law stipulating that Mexicans were Indian (2004). The period from 1949 to 1966 marked the demise of legal segregation. *Brown v. Education* ended legal segregation in public schools in 1954. In 1966, *State of Virginia v. Loving* struck down all laws preventing miscegenation.
117. Olivas (2006); Haney López (2003); Martínez (1997).
118. Martínez (1997).
119. Ibid.

120. Acuña (1972); Alvarez (1973); Gutiérrez (1995).
121. McLemore and Romo (1985).
122. Gutiérrez (1995).
123. McLemore and Romo (1985); Gutiérrez (1995).
124. Gutiérrez (1995).
125. Pycior (1997).
126. Ibid.
127. Alvarez (1973).
128. Foley argues that many if not most Mexican Americans were unlikely to think of themselves as white, especially because they lived in a context in which they were clearly seen as nonwhite (1997, 210–11). Rather, acceptance as white was most likely restricted to the small middle class who used it as a way to promote individual and group acceptance in the white society they sought to penetrate. Certainly, identification as white was likely to fissure on the basis of class, nativity, language, and culture.
129. Gutiérrez (1995, 186). The activities of the Mexican American Political Association (MAPA) also provide an example of the changing nature of culture and nationalism in their political activities. At their first convention in 1960, the participants, mostly middle-class professionals, spoke in both English and Spanish, but some cultural nationalists refused to speak in English. Moreover, the issue of ethnic identity terms was raised. A few people, though the minority, preferred using traditional terms such as *Latin American* and *Spanish-speaking* but Bert Corona, an important MAPA leader, felt that these obscured a Mexican identity (García 1991). Corona supported the term *Mexican American*, with an emphasis on Mexican because he felt that Mexicans should assert themselves rather than using terms that made them more acceptable to whites (García 1991). Another issue raised at the 1960 MAPA convention was about forming coalitions. Some members of MAPA fought for a resolution that would have committed MAPA to create coalitions with other nonwhite minorities such as African Americans, Asian Americans and Native Americans. However, the issue became controversial largely because many participants were not prepared to identify as *nonwhite* and the resolution was therefore dropped, but later readopted (García 1991).
130. McLemore and Romo (1985).
131. The United Farm Workers was a union organization that organized workers of various ethnic groups but most of its leaders and members were of Mexican origin, including its highly visible leader, César Chávez.
132. Acuña (1972); Muñoz (1989).
133. The authors of *The Mexican American People* were not free of this political battle as they were discredited by many Mexican American leaders as assimilationist (Moore 1967).
134. Muñoz (1989); San Miguel (1987).
135. Ibid.
136. A particularly important case was *Rodríguez v. San Antonio Independent School District,* which sought to correct the typically unequal funding of school districts throughout Texas that worked against Mexican American students (San Miguel 1987). Although the district court ruled in favor of Rodríguez

and MALDEF, the U.S. Supreme Court reversed the lower court's decision (Long 1996).

137. Skerry (1993b); Haney López (2003).
138. Muñoz (1989); Rosales (2000).
139. Ibid.
140. Muñoz (1989); Rosales (2000).
141. The Chinese Exclusion Act was actually repealed in 1952 with the Magneson Act, which permitted a visa allotment to Chinese of 105 per year but only with the Hart-Celler were significant numbers of Chinese permitted to legally immigrate to the United States. The Gentlemen's Agreement between the Japanese and U.S. governments in 1907, that similarly ended Japanese immigration, though the agreement ended in 1924. In the nineteenth century, Chinese and Japanese immigrants comprised the vast majority of Asian immigration to the United States.
142. D. Reimers (1985, 87).
143. D. Reimers (1985).
144. Massey, Durand, and Malone (2003).
145. Durand, Telles, and Flashman (2006).
146. Massey, Durand, and Malone (2003).
147. Undocumented Mexican immigrants hail back to the 1940s, when growers sought out the cheap immigrant labor they saw in the braceros but were ineligible to hire through the official program (Ngai 2004, 147–48).
148. Passel (2005).
149. In terms of our study, immigration after 1966 did not affect our 1965 to 1966 sample, but it would renew Mexican culture in the United States, increase Mexican American visibility, and change ethnic politics.
150. Certainly, much of this population growth was the result of relatively high Mexican fertility (Durand, Telles, and Flashman 2006).
151. Although the new immigration would be distinguished by significant settlement in new destinations well outside the Southwest.
152. Grebler, Moore, and Guzmán (1970).
153. Soja (1989).
154. Johnson, Booth, and Harris (1983); Buitron (2004).
155. Buitron (2004); Rosales (2000).
156. Johnson, Booth, and Harris (1983); Rosales (2000); Flores (2002).
157. Soja (1989).
158. Noyelle and Stanback (1984).
159. Avila (2004); Soja (1989); Davis (1990).
160. Avila (2004).
161. Soja (1989).
162. Ellis and Wright (1999).
163. Noyelle and Stanback (1984).
164. García (1991).
165. Johnson, Booth, and Harris (1983).
166. Ibid.
167. Skerry (1993b); Rosales (2000).
168. Interview with Joan Moore, December 2004.
169. Skerry (1993b, 39, 36).

170. City of San Antonio, 2004, "Community Economic Development Profile," accessed at http://www.sanantonio.gov.
171. Jargowsky (1997, 2003).
172. Montejano (1987); García (1991).
173. Foley (1997); Gomez (2002); Almaguer (1994); Ngai (2004).
174. Wilson (1978); Thernstrom and Thernstrom (1997); for Mexican Americans, see Skerry (1993b); Chávez (1991).

Chapter 5

1. De Sipio (2006).
2. Neidert and Farley (1985); Borjas (1994); Trejo (1997); Hauser, Simmons, and Pager (2004).
3. Borjas (1994); Smith (2003); Bean and Stevens (2003).
4. Alba and Nee (2003); Bean and Stevens (2003); Perlmann (2005).
5. Borjas (1994).
6. Featherman and Hauser (1978); Trejo (1997); Bean et al. (1994); Borjas (1994); Wojtkiewicz and Donato (1995); Alba et al. (2004); Duncan, Hotz, and Trejo (2006). Alba et al. (2004, table 4) find improvements between generations two and three using the National Longitudinal Survey of Youth (NLSY) but not the National Education Longitudinal Survey (NELS).
7. Kao and Tienda (1995).
8. Gibson (1988); Vigil (1997); Zhou and Bankston (1998).
9. Vigil (1997).
10. Smith (2003).
11. Alba and Islam (2005).
12. Bean and Tienda (1987).
13. See Durand, Telles, and Flashman (2006).
14. College completion rates are somewhat high for Los Angeles and San Antonio but we suspect that this is due to the in-migration of more educated whites and the out-migration of working class or less educated whites, a trend that is apparent in several metropolitan areas with large or growing minority populations (Frey 1999).
15. There is a large literature on the educational success of Asian Americans. Much of it can be attributed to the U.S. immigration policy. Since 1965, Asian immigrant visas are given primarily to those in professional and technical occupations and for family reunification and thus they rarely enter at the bottom rungs of American society as do Mexican immigrants and several of the European groups that came during the previous large immigration wave. Asian Americans thus receive the great advantages of their parents' higher education, not to mention the higher teacher expectations that go with their generally higher socioeconomic status.
16. Frequently, analyses of educational attainment are calculated for age twenty-five and older to ensure that their education is complete. For years of education or high school graduation, we used age eighteen and older to be comparable with the census data we compiled. There was essentially no difference in our results whether we used an age cutoff of eighteen, twenty, or twenty-five (analysis not shown).

17. Farley and Alba (2002).
18. We estimate high school graduation by using respondents' report about highest degree obtained. Those who report obtaining no degree are considered not high school graduates and those who either earned a high school diploma, obtained a general equivalency diploma, or attended some form of higher education are considered graduates. It is possible that there is some error in this: for instance, someone who drops out of high school but attends a technical or vocation school is classified as a high school graduate according to our definition. One could argue that such a person should not be considered a graduate. Fortunately, only three respondents match this scenario. Our measure of high school graduation is comparable to what is used in the literature to estimate education attainment among particular populations. Measures of how successful institutions (high schools or school districts) are in retaining and graduating students differ from population estimates and are not an appropriate comparison for our purposes.
19. Given that our age cutoff is twenty, it is possible that these percentages could improve. Also, there are cases where adults who did not complete high school obtain a graduate equivalency diploma (GED), which we do not consider a school graduate. However, we do not expect rates at older ages to be much higher. More importantly, figure 5.2 shows that there are no differences between the third, fourth, and fifth generation-since-immigration, suggesting that educational attainment has leveled out by the third generation.
20. Massey et al. (2003).
21. This stage of the model is surprisingly similar in outcomes, though not explanation, as the Marxist oriented reproduction of labor arguments, which explicate that capitalism needs labor power to survive and controls and uses schools for the purpose of educating working-class and minority children to become workers (Willis 1981; Bowles and Gintis 1977).
22. Blau and Duncan (1967); Featherman and Hauser (1978).
23. Alba and Nee (2003).
24. Schneider, Martínez, and Owens (2006); Portes and Rumbaut (2001).
25. Portes and Rumbaut (2001).
26. Schneider, Martínez, and Owens (2006); Portes and Rumbaut (2001).
27. See Portes (1998) for one common definition of the concept.
28. Coleman (1988).
29. Orfield and Yun (1999).
30. Massey and Denton (1987).
31. Massey (1985); South, Crowler, and Chávez (2005).
32. Orfield (1993); Kozol (2005).
33. Orfield (1993); Valencia (2002); Massey et al. (2003).
34. There is also evidence that achievement scores tend to decline with greater segregation (Valencia 2002).
35. Goldsmith (2003).
36. Portes and Rumbaut (2001); Alba and Nee (2003).
37. Coleman, Hoffer, and Kilgore (1982); Hoffer, Greely, and Coleman (1985); Bryk et al. (1984); Bryk, Lee, and Holland (1993).
38. Hoffer, Greeley, and Coleman (1985).
39. Keith and Page (1985).
40. Irvine and Foster (1996)
41. Ibid.; Evans and Schwab (1995); Neal (1997).

42. Evans and Schwab (1995); Neal (1997); Altonji, Elder, and Taber (2005).
43. Neal (1997).
44. López (forthcoming).
45. Phinney and Flores (2002).
46. Murguía and Telles (1996).
47. Gullickson (2005).
48. Differences between subsequent generations from the 1.5 to the third generation all appear to be marginally significant, which nevertheless is remarkable since there is only one half of a generation between them.
49. We suspected that early marriage and short periods between generations might be related to low educational outcomes overall and to the especially low educational outcomes of the fourth generation. To test this, we controlled for mother's age at marriage in additional analyses. We found that mother's age at marriage had no direct effect on educational outcomes nor did it explain the lower education of the fourth generation.
50. Alba and Nee (2003).
51. Mica Pollock (forthcoming) describes how the U.S. Office of Civil Rights and many educators more generally are hesitant to fault discrimination as the underlying cause of harms to minority children, especially in the absence of proof of a discriminatory intent. Despite numerous complaints to the OCR alleging racial discrimination, many debates would ensue among professional staff and other educators about what acts and situations in educational settings the federal government would actually deem discrimination because of race. Such complaints included a Latino father contending that white administrators unfairly assumed his sophomore son was a gang member because he was Latino; a Latina teacher and mother arguing that minority students were ostracized and harassed by white peers and denigrated by white teachers in a rural district; and a Latina mother arguing that her middle-school son was under excessive surveillance by the school's white disciplinary authorities.
52. Valencia (2002); Oakes (2005).
53. Suárez-Orozco (1987); Matute-Bianchi (1986).
54. Valencia (2002).
55. Ibid.; Allen, Solórzano, and Carroll (2002).
56. Ogbu (1978); Matute-Bianchi (1986); Valenzuela (1999).
57. Ainsworth-Darnell and Downey (1998); Cook and Ludwig (1997); Carter (2005).
58. Fryer (2006); Fryer with Torelli (2006).
59. It seems that persistence in school is particular crucial upon taking algebra in high school. Algebra has been found to be a crucial gatekeeper for Latino students, who are often counseled out of that course and thus out of the college track. There is also an effect in which the presence of only a few Latinos in algebra signals to other Latino students that algebra is not for them (Oakes 2005; Gándara 1995).
60. Oyserman et al. (2003); Steele, Spencer, and Aronson (2002).
61. Solórzano (1995); Gándara (1995); Conchas (2006); Oyserman et al. (2003).
62. Stanton-Salazar and Dornbusch (1995); Conchas (2006).
63. Matute-Bianchi (1986); Fernández and Nielson (1986); Suárez-Orozco (1987); Portes and Rumbaut (2001).
64. Matute-Bianchi (1986).

Chapter 6

1. Neidert and Farley (1985); Bean and Tienda (1987); Chapa (1988).
2. Acuña (1972); Barrera (1979); Blauner (1972); Estrada et al. (1981).
3. Alba and Nee (2003).
4. Borjas (1994); Bean and Stevens (2003); Perlmann (2005).
5. C. Reimers (1985); Duncan, Hotz, and Trejo (2006).
6. See, for example, Featherman and Hauser (1978); Blau and Duncan (1967).
7. Perlmann and Waldinger (1997); Alba and Nee (2003).
8. Grebler, Moore, and Guzmán (1970); Ortiz (1996).
9. Blau and Kahn (1997); England (1992); Reskin (1993).
10. Ortiz (1994); Segura (1994).
11. Ellis and Wright (1999).
12. Bean, Telles, and Lowell (1987); Moore and Pinderhughes (1993).
13. In the 1965 survey, the detailed job questions were asked only about the head of household, rather than of the original respondents. Head, for the purposes of the original survey, was defined as the husband in a husband-wife household. When there was one adult in the household—usually a non-married woman—that person was considered the head. The industry figures are therefore restricted to respondents who were heads in 1965 (approximately 85 percent of those with jobs were heads). To make comparisons across time and between original respondents and children, the 2000 original respondent figures are for those who were heads in 1965; the child figures are the offspring of original respondent heads in 1965.
14. Earnings refer to wages obtained from one or more jobs and to income from a business. Income includes earnings as well as other sources of income like interest, dividends, pensions, and government assistance. For working-age adults, income and earnings are very similar (obviously older persons might have very different earnings and income levels). Personal income refers to income for individuals while family income refers to that for family members. In our analysis, family income includes that of husbands and wives (in contrast, the U.S. Census Bureau definition of family income is that of all family members).
15. Grebler, Moore, and Guzmán (1970, 187).
16. Certainly, there was also much change in the population, especially the white population. In 1970, there was a large working class white population. Many, however, migrated out of the area during and after the restructuring, and especially in the 1990s, when the regional aerospace sector collapsed.
17. This could partly be attributable to age if Mexican Americans are more concentrated in the younger portion of our selected age range (eighteen to fifty-four) than in the older portion.
18. Grebler, Moore, and Guzmán (1970, 209).
19. Bean, Telles, and Lowell (1987).
20. Hauser and Warren (1997). These are available in the U.S. censuses of 1970, 1980, and 1990.
21. Grebler, Moore, and Guzmán (1970, 223).
22. Right-to-work laws prohibit requiring union membership or union dues as a condition of employment.

23. Milkman (2006).
24. Oliver and Shapiro (1995); Conley (1999).
25. Oliver and Shapiro (1995, 86).
26. Ibid.; Oliver and Shapiro (1995, 106).
27. Oliver and Shapiro (1995, 106).
28. Oliver and Shapiro (1995); Massey and Denton (1993).
29. Grebler, Moore, and Guzmán (1970, 255).
30. There was actually a slight increase, but the average age of their children in 2000 was also somewhat greater, which may explain the difference.
31. Oliver and Shapiro (1995).
32. We find that the parents' socioeconomic status does have a significant effect on the socioeconomic outcomes when respondent's education is out of the model. This is consistent with the point that the effect of parental status is through the respondent's educational status.
33. We conducted regression analysis for owning a home that we do not present. The results are similar to that of the other socioeconomic indicators we examined. Education has a strong effect as does living in San Antonio, being older, and having more children in the home.
34. Tony Waters (1999).
35. Vigil (1988).
36. Tony Waters (1999).
37. We thank James Diego Vigil, who assisted us in the careful phrasing of these questions and in training of interviewers.
38. Vigil (1988). We conducted logistic regression of gang participation that we do not present here. This analysis shows that three variables determine gang participation: education, being male, and growing up in Los Angeles rather than San Antonio. Generation-since-immigration, however, made no difference in gang membership except that none of the immigrants (1.5 generation) in our sample participated in gangs.
39. Vigil (1988).
40. Tienda (1995).
41. Grebler, Moore, and Guzmán (1970).

Chapter 7

1. Lieberson and Waters (1988); South, Crowder, and Chávez (2005).
2. Massey and Denton (1987).
3. Murguía (1982).
4. Grebler, Moore, and Guzmán (1970, 405).
5. Gordon (1964); Massey (1985); Alba and Nee (2003).
6. Massey and Denton (1993); Avila (2004).
7. Fishman (1977); Valdes (2000).
8. These numbers have varied but they have remained in the extreme range of little interracial interaction (Massey and Denton 1993; Sollors 2000).
9. Lieberson and Waters (1988); Alba (1985).
10. Gordon (1964); Massey (1985); South, Crowder, and Chávez (2005).
11. Alba (1990).
12. Camarillo (1984).
13. San Miguel (1987); González (1990).

14. Lieberson and Waters (1988).
15. Massey and Denton (1987, 1993).
16. This is based on a common rule of thumb that puts levels of the dissimilarity index for African Americans that are 70 or greater as high and levels of 30 or less for white ethnics as low (Massey and Denton 1993).
17. Massey and Denton (1987).
18. Ibid.
19. We suspected that children might be staying in the same neighborhoods as their parents. We created a variable "residing in same census tract in 2000 as in 1965" but unfortunately only twenty respondents did so. This is not surprising when we consider that census tracts are fairly small geographic areas. However, it did not make sense to include this variable in the analysis to distinguish such a small group of respondents. Now it is possible that respondents live in nearby neighborhoods. after all we did find that children are likely to stay in the same city where they grew up, but creating this indicator was not easily done from the census tract information.
20. Murguía (1982).
21. Bean and Bradshaw (1970).
22. Valdez (1983).
23. Panunzio (1942).
24. Grebler, Moore, and Guzmán (1970). The percent intermarried in our 1965 sample is lower probably because it includes marriages since the 1930s and some in Mexico.
25. Blau, Blum, and Schwartz (1982).
26. Bobo and Kluegel (1993).
27. Ignatiev (1996); Roediger (1999); Jacobsen (1998).

Chapter 8

1. Wimmer (2007).
2. Gordon (1964).
3. Park (1930).
4. Huntington (2004b).
5. De la Garza, Falcón, and García (1996).
6. Gans (1979).
7. Waters (1990).
8. Madsen (1964); Rubel (1966).
9. Grebler, Moore, and Guzmán (1970, 420–3).
10. Ibid., 423.
11. Valdes (2000).
12. Fishman (1977); Stevens (1992).
13. Fishman (1977).
14. Hale (2004, 474).
15. Macías (1985); Valdes (2000).
16. Alba et al. (2002).
17. Stevens (1985); Rumbaut, Massey, and Bean (2006).
18. Alba et al. (2002); López (1982); Rumbaut, Massey, and Bean (2006).
19. Rumbaut, Massey, and Bean (2006).
20. See, for example, Huntington (2004b).
21. Buriel and Cardoza (1988); Matute-Bianchi (1986); Portes and Rumbaut (2001).

22. Gibson (1988).
23. Portes and Rumbaut (2001).
24. Ibid.
25. Matute-Bianchi (1986); Gibson (1988).
26. Portes and Stepick (1994).
27. Lieberson (1980); López (1982); Linton (1994); Stevens (1992).
28. López (1982); Linton (1994); Bean and Stevens (2003); Portes and Rumbaut (2001).
29. Linton (1994).
30. Bean and Stevens (2003, 171). Alba and Nee (2003), for example, focused on foreign language use and nearly ignored bilingualism.
31. Indeed, the top right quadrant is very similar to the bottom left quadrant, as they should be.
32. There is not full correspondence with the language they replied in to their parents—a slightly higher proportion of respondents spoke to their parents in English—but the patterns across generations are similar.
33. Purnell, Idsard, and Baugh (1999).
34. Because speaking Spanish as a child has such a strong relationship to Spanish proficiency as an adult, we were concerned that this might influence the effects of other variables (particularly generational status) in the multivariate analysis. We redid the multivariate analysis leaving out Spanish spoken as a child and the effects of other variables were unchanged.
35. Lieberson (2000); Watkins and London (1994); Sue and Telles (2007).
36. For details, see Christina Sue and Edward Telles (2007). The association of particular names with a particular language category (1–5) may have admittedly shifted over time. However, we believe that for the vast majority of names, the categories are the same as those Sue and Telles selected in 2007.
37. Greeley (1971).
38. Rieff (2006).
39. Based on National Survey of Religious Identification conducted in 1990, American Religion Identification Survey conducted in 2001, Gallup Polls conducted between 1992 and 2004, and the Pew Research Council Survey conducted in 2002. All of these data are available online at http://www.adherents.com/rel-USA.html.
40. Finke and Stark (2005).
41. Perl, Greely, and Gray (2004).
42. Espinosa, Elizondo, and Miranda (2003); Hill (2005). Reporting on a survey by the University of Akron using the Fourth National Survey of Religion and Politics by the Pew Charitable Trusts and the Pew Forum on Religion and Public Life.
43. Green et al. (2005).
44. Grebler, Moore, and Guzmán (1970, 470).
45. Bean and Swicegood (1985); Bean and Tienda (1987); Bradshaw and Bean (1973).
46. Rindfuss and Sweet (1977); Bean and Swicegood (1985).
47. Bean and Swicegood (1985).
48. Frank and Heuveline (2005).
49. Population Reference Bureau (2006).

50. Frank and Heuveline (2005); Bean and Swicegood (1985).
51. All of the original respondents are older than forty-five. The children are between thirty-two and fifty-nine.
52. Frank and Heuveline (2005).
53. Fertility for the parents based on number of siblings may, on the one hand, be underestimated because of unreported mortality of some siblings and, on the other hand, be overestimated because of half and non-biological siblings being counted. The end result is that these trends probably offset each other.
54. This is the reason that fertility analysis is generally limited to women older than forty-five. Younger women may not have completed their fertility and consequently have fewer children than older women. In our sample, the number of respondents got relatively small when we restricted the analysis by age as well as gender. We therefore kept all women in the analysis—the youngest women in our sample are thirty-two years old—and controlled for age. We also redid our multivariate analysis for women age thirty-five and older and age forty and older. These results do not differ significantly from the analysis based on all women.
55. Madsen (1964); Rubel (1966).
56. Mirandé (1977).
57. Ibid.
58. Baca Zinn (1980); Ybarra (1982).
59. Zavella (1987).
60. See, for example, Williams (1990); Hondagneu-Sotelo (1994).
61. In multivariate analysis of these variables based on our full model, we find no gender differences in whether girls should live at home but women disagree more that men should have the last word. There were no gender differences in the two items on family relations.
62. Huntington (2004b).
63. De la Garza, Falcón, and García (1996).
64. Ybarra-Frausto (1999).
65. The middle (Chicano) genre can be found in local radio stations throughout the Southwest. Although in English or bilingual (especially in Texas), the audience is clearly targeted largely for Mexican Americans. One gets a strong sense by listening to callers that they are mostly Mexican American, based on their names, accents, and locations from which they are calling. Statistics on this are hard to come by.
66. Alba (1985); Waters (1990); Schultz (1992).
67. Alba (1990).

Chapter 9

1. Nagel (1996); Cornell and Hartmann (1998).
2. Barth (1969).
3. Alba (1990); Lieberson and Waters (1988); Waters (1990). This was in response to Andrew Greeley's pithy observation that the third generation seeks to reclaim what the second generation sought to forget in its attempt to secure the American dream (Greeley 1971).
4. Gans (1979); Waters (1990).
5. Gans (1979).

6. Alba and Nee (2003).
7. Mary Waters (1999); Portes and Rumbaut (2001).
8. Gómez (2002); Gutiérrez (1995).
9. Alvarez (1973).
10. García (1982). For some reason, persons born in New Mexico were more likely to be in the sample, which might explain the high incidence of preferring the label, Other Spanish.
11. Hurtado and Arce (1986, 116).
12. Dávila (2001).
13. On the actual survey instrument, we listed the most common categories based on the literature and preliminary field tests. If respondents provided an answer that was not our list, their response was recorded verbatim in the other categories. In addition, we recorded the order in which respondents provided answers (for example, first response was Mexican, second response was American). Our strategy allowed respondents to provide more than one ethnic response. When they did, we followed up with "Which one ethnic background do you feel closest to?" To come up with a single measure of ethnic identification, we used their response to the first question if they provided one ethnic response and their response to the follow-up if they provided more than one. Among both the original respondent and children samples, almost 75 percent provided only one response, about 20 percent provided two, and only 5 percent provided three or more.
14. Alba and Islam (2005); Duncan, Hotz, and Trejo (2006).
15. See, for example, Alba and Islam (2005); Trejo (1997).
16. Skerry (1993b).
17. Yinger (1985).
18. Yancey, Erickson, and Juliani (1976).
19. Ibid.
20. Ibid.; Alba (1990).
21. Jiménez (2004).
22. Eschbach and Gómez (1998); Ono (2002).
23. Cornell and Hartmann (1998); Yinger (1994).
24. We present the full regression results for these two logistics models in the appendix. In addition, we conduct multinominal regression analysis of ethnic identity, which would be the appropriate statistical procedure given that this is a categorical dependent variable with more than two categories. We also present these results in the appendix. One difference between the logistics and multinominal models is in the reference group. In the logistics model, the reference group is all other identities. In the multinominal analysis, the reference group is Mexican Americans. The multinominal analysis yields essentially the same results as the two logistics models. In other words, the significant predictors of Mexican versus other in the logistics regression are also significant predictors of Mexican versus Mexican American in the multi-nominal analysis. Similarly, the significant predictors of American-other versus all other identities in the logistics analysis are also significant predictors in the multivariate analysis. The results presented in the appendix are relative risk ratios, which are interpreted similarly to odds ratios from a logistics regression with a dichotomous outcome.

25. These are mostly white parents, though a few are African American, Asian American, and American Indian.
26. Alba (1990, 64).
27. Rodríguez (2000). Such classification varies among Hispanic national groups and by generation. For example, Portes and Rumbaut found that while a large majority of Cuban and Nicaraguan parents identified as white, most of their children did not (2001).
28. Jenkins (1997); Cornell and Hartmann (1998); Hirschman (2004).
29. Hahn, Mulinare, and Teutsch (1992).
30. The stereotype question was "sometimes people have ideas about what certain groups are like or what they are supposed to do. Do you ever find that other people expect you to be like or do things that they expect of Mexicans?" The discrimination question was "have you ever been treated unfairly because of your ethnic background?" The response categories for both questions were yes or no.
31. Alba (1990).
32. Lansdale and Oropeza (2002).
33. Rodríguez (2000).
34. De la Garza, Falcón, and García (1996).

Chapter 10

1. Grebler, Moore, and Guzmán (1970, 514).
2. Ibid., 514.
3. Ibid., 569.
4. Ibid., 512.
5. Johnson, Booth, and Harris (1983); Rosales (2000).
6. The number of elected officials increased even though proportional representation decreased. We expect that the decline in representation since 1980 that Rosenfeld reported is largely attributable to the changing immigrant composition of the citizen population, in which immigrant citizens are less likely than the U.S. born to vote (De Sipio 1996) and the concentration of new immigrant citizens in districts that may have gone to Mexican Americans candidates even without their vote.
7. Suro, Fry, and Passell (2005).
8. Rosenfeld (1998). Proportional representation declined to about 50 percent in California in the 1990s but was more stable, between 60 and 80 percent, in Texas from 1980 to the mid-1990s. Representation in Colorado and in Arizona were also at 20 percent or less in the early 1960s but reached parity (100 percent) in the early 1980s, though they have declined since the late 1980s. New Mexico has a unique historical trajectory, in which Mexican American representation was at 80 percent in 1960 and has remained between 80 and 110 percent since then.
9. Rosenfeld (1998).
10. Patrick McGreevy, "Latinos, Flexing Political Muscle, Come of Age in L.A.; A new generation of leaders now debates how to use its power to shape public policy." *Los Angeles Times,* June 27, 2005, section A, 1.

11. Huntington (2004b).
12. De la Garza, Falcón, and García (1996). This is particularly true in recent years, according to De Sipio (2004). Opinion polls conducted over the past decade consistently demonstrate that Hispanics are focused on issues that create opportunities for their economic and social advancement. De Sipio dubs this an "immigrant-settlement agenda" as opposed to the earlier political agenda of civil rights demands. He argues that increased immigration has undercut Latino support for demand-making based on claims of past exclusion and remedial politics (the civil rights agenda) because this notion of past exclusion is not relevant to an increasing share of the Latino population.
13. Caplan (1987, 338).
14. Bell (1976).
15. Dahl (1961).
16. Fuchs (1990).
17. Ibid., 44.
18. Ibid., 266.
19. He cites James Lamare (1982) but fails to note that Lamare finds strong political socialization in the second generation but a decline in political assimilation in the third generation.
20. Dahl (1961).
21. See, for example, de la Garza, Falcón, and García (1996); De Sipio (2006).
22. Kellstedt (1974); Lamare (1982); De Sipio (1999); Chui, Curtis, and Lambert (1991). Chui and her colleagues suggest that heightened political activity might be due to either second-generation optimism or a greater sense of discrimination but have no data to support either hypothesis.
23. Portes and Bach (1985); de la Garza and De Sipio (1999).
24. De la Garza, Falcón, and García (1996).
25. Keefe and Padilla (1987).
26. Haney López (2003).
27. Anthony Smith (1990).
28. Schlesinger (1992); Thernstrom and Thernstrom (1997); Chávez (1991); Skerry (1993b)
29. Skerry (1993a); Thernstrom and Thernstrom (1997).
30. Huntington (2004b).
31. The 1965 data showed that very few Mexican Americans actually participate in ethnic-based political organizations. Only 10 percent or less in Los Angeles or San Antonio belonged to or were very familiar with leading organizations such as the American GI Forum, the Mexican American Political Association, or the Viva Johnson clubs. Most had never heard of these organizations (Grebler, Moore, and Guzmán 1970, 547). The only exception was that 15 percent of San Antonians belonged to or were very familiar with LULAC and only 26 percent had never heard of it. By contrast, only 4 percent of Angelenos had a high level of familiarity with LULAC but fully 86 percent had never heard of it.
32. Suro, Fry, and Passell (2005).
33. Citrin and Highton (2002).
34. De Sipio (2006).
35. De Sipio (1996, 89).

36. For example, our older original respondents were 3 percentage points more likely to register and 4 percentage points more likely to vote when registered compared to their younger counterparts (data not shown).
37. De Sipio (1996).
38. Grebler, Moore, and Guzmán (1970, 570).
39. Ibid., 515 and 564.
40. Ibid., 569.
41. De Sipio (1996, 26).
42. De Sipio (2006); de la Garza and De Sipio (1999).
43. De Sipio (1996).
44. Alvarez and Bedolla (2003).
45. De la Garza and De Sipio (1999, 8).
46. Ibid.
47. One reviewer suggested that religion would be an important predictor of partisanship, but using religion in 1965 or in 2000 in our regression analysis had no statistically significant effects.
48. Citrin and Highton (2002, 17).
49. Rodríguez (1996); compare Hajnal and Baldassare (2001).
50. Institutionally, there is an assumption that the public policy concerns of Mexican Americans are mostly about immigration and, to a lesser extent, civil rights and bilingual education (De Sipio 1996, 44). They are actually wider than that, and thus do not reflect the opinions of the Mexican American electorate. The Mexican American Legal Defense and Educational Fund (MALDEF), for example, emphasizes civil and voting rights, education (initially primary but now higher), workplace rights, and redistricting (De Sipio 1996, 45). To take another example, the National Association of Latino Elected Officials (NALEO) networks, works on naturalization data, and provides leadership support.
51. Chávez (1991); Skerry (1993b); Thernstrom and Thernstrom (1997).

Chapter 11

1. Portes and Zhou (1993); Portes and Rumbaut (2001).
2. Rumbaut, Massey and Bean (2006).
3. Alba (1985); Perlmann (2005).
4. Matute-Bianchi (1986); Kao and Tienda (1995).
5. Alba and Nee (2003).
6. Portes and Rumbaut (2001); Duncan, Hotz, and Trejo (2006).
7. Frey (1999).
8. Haney López (2003).
9. Foley (1997); Menchaca (1993); Montejano (1987).
10. Jacobsen (1998); Roediger (2005).
11. Rivas Rodriguez (2005). We also found that 54 percent of men among original respondents and 21 percent of men among the children were military veterans.
12. Roediger (2005); Ngai (2004); Foley (1997).
13. Alba and Nee (2003); Portes and Rumbaut (2001).
14. The lower rates of education for Mexican Americans than African Americans may be due to the fact that employability in low-skilled work is poorer for blacks, making staying in school a more attractive option.

15. Pettigrew (1979); Massey and Denton (1993).
16. Interestingly, Spanish fluency is an exception. The multivariate analysis presented in chapter 8 shows a significant positive relationship between Spanish proficiency and education. This relationship becomes significant after we control for the negative relationship between parent's education and Spanish proficiency. In other words, children with less-educated parents are more likely to speak Spanish, but once we control for this, children with more education have greater Spanish proficiency.
17. Other indicators of socioeconomic status that are not shown—including wealth, occupational status, and rates of homeownership—are also clearly related to education.
18. This probably reflects a likely marriage market for Mexican Americans who finished college before 1965.
19. See, for example, Perlmann and Waldinger (1997); Perlmann (2005).
20. Soja (1989).
21. Ibid.
22. Quality of schooling may be another matter.
23. In 1976, 46 percent of Hispanics enrolling in college were women. By 2004, 59 percent of Hispanics enrolling in college were women (National Center for Education Statistics 2005).
24. In analysis not shown in this book, we found that women were significantly less likely to be involved in gangs than men were.
25. Tafoya (2002) found that children born to Hispanic mothers and non-Hispanic fathers peaked at about 25 percent of all children born to Hispanic mothers in 1990 but had declined to nearly 20 percent in 2000. This seems to reflect the growing size of the first and second generation young adult population compared to later generations as well as the increasing residential isolation of all generations.
26. Jiménez (2004).
27. Telles and Murguía (1990); Murguía and Telles (1996).
28. Gullickson (2005).
29. See Pager (forthcoming) regarding the difficulty in measuring discrimination and for the few examples of direct measurement.
30. Valencia (2002); Conchas (2006); Vigil (1997).
31. Matute-Bianchi (1996); Valenzuela (1999); Bonilla-Silva (2003).
32. Conchas (2006); Gándara (1995); Valenzuela (1999).
33. Oyserman et al. (2003).
34. Zúñiga and Hernández (2005).
35. Massey, Durand, and Malone (2003).
36. Portes and Rumbaut (2001).
37. Waldinger (2007a).
38. Jiménez (2005).
39. Economic News and Analysis on Mexico (2003).
40. Huntington (2004b); Buchanan (2006).
41. Smith and Edmonston (1998).
42. Massey, Durand and Malone (2003).
43. Feliciano (2005).
44. Perlmann and Waldinger (1997); Feliciano (2005).

45. Horsman (1981); Montejano (1987).
46. Roediger (1999); Jacobsen (1998); Bogardus (1967).
47. Tom Smith (1990).
48. This section was inspired by the comments of Rodolfo de la Garza, who questioned its absence.
49. Alba (1985).
50. Massey and Denton (1987).
51. Perlmann and Waldinger (1997); Portes and Rumbaut (2001); Zhou and Bankston (1998).
52. Portes and Rumbaut (2001).
53. Myers (2007).
54. Many, but not all, of our sample completed their K-12 education before this initiative (Proposition 13) went into effect.
55. Orfield and Yun (1999).
56. Portes and Rumbaut (2001); Duncan, Hotz, and Trejo (2006).
57. Orfield (1993, 2004).
58. Allen, Solórzano, and Carroll (2002); Oakes (2005); Valencia (2002).
59. De la Garza, Falcón, and García (1996).
60. Mary Waters (1999).

═══ References ═══

Acosta, Oscar. 1968. "Challenging Racial Exclusion on the Grand Jury." *The Caveat* 1998(Winter): 7–9.

Acuña, Rodolfo. 1972. *Occupied America: The Chicano's Struggle Toward Liberation.* San Francisco, Calif.: Canfield Press.

Ainsworth-Darnell, James W., and Douglas B. Downey. 1998. "Assessing the Oppositional Culture Explanation for Racial/Ethnic Differences in School Performance." *American Sociological Review* 63(4): 536–53.

Alba, Richard. 1985. *Italian Americans: Into the Twilight of Ethnicity.* Englewood Cliffs, N.J.: Prentice-Hall.

———. 1990. *Ethnic Identity: The Transformation of White America.* New Haven, Conn.: Yale University Press.

Alba, Richard, and Tariq Islam. 2005. "The Case of the Disappearing Mexican Americans: An Ethnic-Identity Mystery." Presented at the Meeting of the Population Association of America. April 2, 2005, Philadelphia, Pa.

Alba, Richard, and Victor Nee. 1997. "Rethinking Assimilation Theory in a New Era of Immigration." *International Migration Review* 31(4): 826–74.

———. 2003. *Remaking the American Mainstream: Assimilation and Contemporary Immigration.* Cambridge, Mass.: Harvard University Press.

Alba, Richard, Dalia Abdel-Hady, Tariqul Islam, and Karen Marotz. 2004. "Downward Assimilation and Mexican Americans: An Examination of Intergenerational Advance and Stagnation in Educational Attainment." Unpublished paper. The Radcliffe Institute for Advanced Study.

Alba, Richard, John Logan, Amy Lutz, and Brian Stults. 2002. "Only English by the Third Generation? Loss and Preservation of the Mother Tongue among the Grandchildren of Contemporary Immigrants." *Demography* 39(3): 467–84.

Allen, Ruth. 1931. "Mexican Peon Women in Texas." *Sociology and Social Research* 16(Nov–Dec): 131–42.

Allen, Walter, Daniel Solórzano, and Grace Carroll. 2002. "Keeping Race in Place: Racial Microaggressions and Campus Racial Climate at the University of California, Berkeley." *Chicano Latino Law Review* 23(Spring): 15–112.

Allsup, Carl. 1982. *The American G.I. Forum: Origins and Evolution.* Austin, Tex.: The University of Texas Press.

Almaguer, Tomás. 1987. "Ideological Distortions in Recent Chicano Historiography: The Internal Model and Chicano Historical Interpretation." *Aztlán: A Journal of Chicano Studies* 18(1): 7–28.

————. 1994. *Racial Fault Lines: The Historical Origins of White Supremacy in California.* Berkeley, Calif.: University of California Press.

Altonji, Joseph G., Todd E. Elder, and Christopher R. Taber. 2005. "Selection on Observed and Unobserved Variables: Assessing the Effectiveness of Catholic Schools." *Journal of Political Economy* 113(1): 151–84.

Alvarez, José Hernández. 1983. "A Demographic Profile of the Mexican Immigration to the United States, 1910–1950." *Journal of the Inter-American Affairs* 8(3): 471–96.

Alvarez, Michael R., and Lisa García Bedolla. 2003. "The Foundations of Latino Voter Partisanship: Evidence from the 2000 Election." *Journal of Politics* 65(1): 31–49.

Alvarez, Robert R., Jr. 1986. "The Lemon Grove Incident: The Nation's First Successful Desegregation Case." *The Journal of San Diego History* 32(2): 116–35.

Alvarez, Rodolfo. 1973. "The Psycho-Historical and Socioeconomic Development of the Chicano Community in the United States." *Social Science Quarterly* 53(4): 920–43.

Avila, Eric. 2004. *Popular Culture in the Age of White Flight: Fear and Fantasy in Suburban Los Angeles.* Berkeley, Calif.: University of California Press.

Baca Zinn, Maxine. 1980. "Employment and Education of Mexican American Women: The Interplay of Modernity and Ethnicity in Eight Families." *Harvard Education Review* 50(1): 47–62.

Balderrama, Francisco E., and Raymond Rodríguez. 1995. *Decade of Betrayal: Mexican Repatriation in the 1930s.* Albuquerque, N.M.: University of New Mexico Press.

Banton, Michael. 1977. *The Idea of Race.* Boulder, Colo.: Westview.

Barot, Rohit, and John Bird. 2001. "Racialization: The Genealogy and Critique of a Concept." *Ethnic and Racial Studies* 24(4): 601–18.

Barrera, Mario. 1979. *Race and Class in the Southwest: A Theory of Racial Inequality.* Notre Dame, Ind.: University of Notre Dame Press.

Barth, Fredrik, editor. 1969. *Ethnic Groups and Boundaries: The Social Organization of Culture Difference.* Boston, Mass.: Little, Brown.

Bean, Frank, and Benjamin S. Bradshaw. 1970. "Intermarriage Between Persons of Spanish and Non-Spanish Surname: Changes from the Mid-Nineteenth to the Mid-Twentieth Century." *Social Science Quarterly* 51(2): 389–95.

Bean, Frank, and Gillian Stevens. 2003. *America's Newcomers and the Dynamics of Diversity.* New York: Russell Sage Foundation.

Bean, Frank, and Gray Swicegood. 1985. *Mexican American Fertility Patterns.* Austin, Tex.: University of Texas Press.

Bean, Frank, and Marta Tienda. 1987. *The Hispanic Population of the United States.* New York: Russell Sage Foundation.

Bean, Frank, Edward Telles, and Lindsay Lowell. 1987. "Undocumented Migration to the United States: Perceptions and Evidence." *Population and Development Review* 13(4): 671–90.

Bean, Frank, George Chapa, Ruth R. Berg, and Kathryn A. Sowards. 1994. "Educational and Sociodemographic Incorporation Among Hispanic Immigrants to the United States." In *Immigration and Ethnicity: The Integration of America's Newest Arrivals,* edited by Barry Edmonston and Jeffrey Passel. Washington: Urban Institute Press.

Bell, Daniel. 1976. *The Coming of Post-Industrial Society: A Venture in Social Forecasting.* New York: Basic Books.

Blackwelder, Julia Kirk. 1984. *Women of the Depression: Caste and Culture in San Antonio, 1929–1939.* College Station, Tex.: Texas A & M University Press.

Blau, Francine and Lawrence Kahn. 1997. "Swimming Upstream: Trends in the Gender Wage Differential in the 1980s." *Journal of Labor Economics* 15(1): 1–42.

Blau, Peter, and Otis Dudley Duncan. 1967. *The American Occupational Structure.* New York: John Wiley & Sons.

———. 1978. *The American Occupational Structure.* New York: Free Press.

Blau, Peter, Terry C. Blum, and Joseph E. Schwartz. 1982. "Heterogeneity and Intermarriage." *American Sociological Review* 47(5): 45–62.

Blauner, Robert. 1969. "Internal Colonialism and Ghetto Revolt." *Social Problems* 16(4): 393–408.

———. 1972. *Racial Oppression in America.* New York: Harper & Row.

Blumer, Herbert. 1958. "Race Prejudice as a Sense of Group Position." *Pacific Sociological Review* 1(1): 3–7.

———. 1965. "Industrialization and Race Relations." In *Industrialization and Race Relations,* edited by Guy Hunter. Oxford: Oxford Press.

Bobo, Lawrence D., and Vincent L. Hutchings. 1996. "Perceptions of Racial Group Competition: Extending Blumer's Theory of Group Position to a Multiracial Social Context." *American Sociological Review* 61(6): 951–72.

Bobo, Lawrence D., and James R. Kluegel. 1993. "Opposition to Race-Targeting: Self-Interest, Stratification Ideology or Racial Attitudes?" *American Sociological Review* 58(4): 443–64.

Bobo, Lawrence D., and Mia Tuan. 2006. *Prejudice in Politics: Group Position, Public Opinion and the Wisconsin Treaty Rights Dispute.* Cambridge, Mass.: Harvard University Press.

Bogardus, Emory. 1967. *A Forty Year Racial Distance Study.* Los Angeles, Calif.: University of Southern California.

Bonilla-Silva, Eduardo. 2003. *Racism Without Racists: Color-Blind Racism and the Persistence of Racial Inequality in the United States.* Lanham, Md.: Rowman & Littlefield.

Borjas, George J. 1994. "Long-Run Convergence of Ethnic Skill Differentials: The Children and Grandchildren of the Great Migration." *Industrial and Labor Relations Review* 47(4): 553–73.

Bowles, Samuel, and Herb Gintis. 1977. *Schooling in Capitalist America: Educational Reform and the Contradictions of Economic Life.* London: Routledge & Kegan Paul.

Bradshaw, Brad S., and Frank Bean. 1973. "Trends in Fertility of Mexican Americans: 1950–1970." *Social Science Quarterly* 53(4): 688–96.

Brooks-Gunn, Jeanne, Greg J. Duncan, Pamela Kato Klebanov, and Naomi Sealand. 1993. "Do Neighborhoods Influence Child and Adolescent Development?" *The American Journal of Sociology* 99(2): 353–95.

Brown, Michael K., Martin Carnoy, Elliott Currie, Troy Duster, David B. Oppenheimer, Marjorie M. Schultz, and David Wellman. 2003. *Whitewashing Race: The Myth of a Color Blind Society.* Berkeley, Calif.: University of California Press.

Brown-Coronel, Margie. 2006. "The del Valle Family and Rancho Camulos: Gender, Identity, and Memory in Late 19th-Century Southern California." Ph.D. dissertation, University of California, Irvine.

Brubaker, Rogers. 2004. *Ethnicity Without Groups.* Cambridge, Mass.: Harvard University Press.

Bryk, Anthony S., Valerie E. Lee, and Peter B. Holland. 1993. *Catholic Schools and the Common Good.* Cambridge, Mass.: Harvard University Press.

Bryk, Anthony S., Peter B. Holland, Valerie E. Lee, and Ruben A. Carriedo. 1984. *Effective Catholic Schools: An Exploration.* Washington: National Catholic Educational Association.

Buchanan, Patrick J. 2006. *State of Emergency: The Third World Invasion and Conquest of America.* New York: Thomas Dunne Books.

Buitron, Richard A. 2004. *The Quest for Tejano Identity in San Antonio, Texas, 1913–2000.* New York: Routledge.

Bureau of Economic Analysis. 2005. Regional Economic Accounts, CA1-3 Personal Income Summary. Washington: U.S. Department of Commerce. Accessed at http://www.bea.gov/regional/reis/drill.cfm.

Buriel, Raymond, and Desdemona Cardoza. 1988. "Sociocultural Correlates of Achievement Among Three Generations of Mexican American High School Seniors." *American Educational Research Journal* 25(2): 177–92.

Camarillo, Albert. 1979. *Chicanos in a Changing Society: From Mexican Pueblos to American Barrios in Santa Barbara and Southern California, 1848–1930.* Cambridge, Mass.: Harvard University Press.

———. 1984. *Chicanos in California: A History of Mexican Americans in California.* San Francisco, Calif.: Boyd & Fraser.

Caplan, Barbara. 1987. "Linking Cultural Characteristics to Political Opinion." In *Ignored Voices: Public Opinion Polls and the Latino Community,* edited by Rodolfo O. de la Garza. Austin, Tex.: Center for Mexican American Studies, University of Texas.

Carrigan, William D. 2003. "The Lynching of Persons of Mexican Origin or Descent in the United States, 1848 to 1928." *Journal of Social History* 37(2): 411–38.

Carter, Prudence. 2005. *Keepin' It Real: School Success beyond Black and White.* Oxford: Oxford University Press.

Chapa, Jorge. 1988. "Are Chicanos Assimilating?" In *Anglos and Mexicans,* edited by David Montejano. Berkeley, Calif.: Institute of Government Studies, University of California, Berkeley.

Charles, Camille Z. 2003. "The Dynamics of Racial Residential Segregation." *Annual Review of Sociology* 29:167–207.

Chávez, Linda. 1991. *Out of the Barrio: Toward a New Politics of Hispanic Assimilation.* New York: Basic Books.

Chinchilla, Norma, Nora Hamilton, and James Loucky. 1993. "Central Americans in Los Angeles: An Immigrant Community in Transition." In *In the Barrios: Latinos and the Underclass Debate,* edited by Joan Moore and Raquel Pinderhughes. New York: Russell Sage Foundation.

Chui, Tina W. L., James E. Curtis, and Ronald D. Lambert. 1991. "Immigrant Background and Political Participation: Examining Generational Patterns." *The Canadian Journal of Sociology* 16(4): 375–96.

Citrin, Jack, and Benjamin Highton. 2002. *How Race, Ethnicity, and Immigration Shape the California Electorate.* San Francisco, Calif.: Public Policy Institute of California.

Coleman, James S. 1988. "Social Capital and the Creation of Human Capital." *American Journal of Sociology* 95(Supplement): S95–S120.

Coleman, James S., Thomas Hoffer, and Sally Kilgore. 1982. *High School Achievement: Public, Catholic, and Private Schools Compared.* New York: Basic Books.

Comaroff, John. 1991. "Humanity, Ethnicity and Nationality: Conceptual and Comparative Perspectives on the USSR." *Theory and Society* 20(5): 661–87.

Conchas, Gilberto Q. 2006. *The Color of Success: Race And High-Achieving Urban Youth.* New York: Teachers College Press.

Conley, Dalton. 1999. *Being Black, Living in the Red: Race, Wealth and Social Policy in America.* Berkeley, Calif.: University of California Press.

Cornell, Stephen, and Douglas Hartmann. 1998. *Ethnicity and Race: Making Identities in a Changing World.* Thousand Oaks, Calif.: Pine Forge Press.

Crul, Maurice, and Hans Vermeulen. 2003. "The Second Generation in Europe. Introduction." *International Migration Review* 37(4): 965–86.

Cruse, Harold. 1967. *The Crisis of the Negro Intellectual.* New York: Morrow Paperback Editions.

Dahl, Robert A. 1961. *Who Governs? Democracy and Power in an American City.* New Haven, Conn.: Yale University Press.

Dávila, Arlene. 2001. *Latinos, Inc.: The Marketing and Making of a People.* Berkeley, Calif.: University of California Press.

Davis, Mike. 1990. *City of Quartz: Excavating the Future in Los Angeles.* London: Verso.

De la Garza, Rodolfo O., and Louis De Sipio, editors. 1999. *Awash in the Mainstream: Latino Politics in the 1996 Elections.* Boulder, Colo.: Westview Press.

De la Garza, Rodolfo O., Angelo Falcón, and Chris García. 1996. "Will The Real Americans Please Stand Up: Anglo and Mexican-American Support of Core American Political Values." *American Journal of Political Science* 40(2): 335–51.

De Sipio, Louis. 1996. *Counting on the Latino Vote: Latinos as a New Electorate.* Charlottesville, Va.: University of Virginia Press.

———. 1999. "The Second Generation: Political Behaviors of Adult Children of Immigrants in the United States." Paper presented at the Annual Meeting of the American Political Science Association, September 2–5, 1999, Atlanta, Ga.

———. 2004. "The Pressures of Perpetual Promise: Latinos and Politics, 1960–2003." In *The Columbia History of Latinos Since 1960,* edited by David Gutiérrez. New York: Columbia University Press.

———. 2006. "Latino Civic and Political Participation." In *Hispanics and the Future of America,* edited by Marta Tienda and Faith Mitchell. Washington: The National Academies Press.

Downey, Douglas B., and James W. Ainsworth-Darnell. 2002. "The Search for Oppositional Culture Among Black Students." *American Sociological Review* 67(1): 156–64.

Duncan, Brian, Joseph V. Hotz, and Stephen J. Trejo. 2006. "Hispanics in the U.S. Labor Market." In *Hispanics and the Future of America,* edited by Marta Tienda and Faith Mitchell. Washington: The National Academies Press.

Durand, Jorge, Edward Telles, and Jennifer Flashman. 2006. "The Demographic Foundations of the Latino Population." In *Hispanics and the Future of America,* edited by Marta Tienda and Faith Mitchell. Washington: The National Academies Press.

Economic News & Analysis on Mexico. 2003. "President Vicente Fox Removes Mexico's U.N. Ambassador Adolfo Aguilar Zinser Over Comments on U.S." November 19, 2003. Accessed at http://www.accessmylibrary.com/coms2/summary_0286-32434092_ITM.

Ellis, Mark, and Richard Wright. 1999. "The Industrial Division of Labor Among Immigrants and Internal Migrants to the Los Angeles Economy." *International Migration Review* 33(1): 26–54.

England, Paula. 1992. *Comparable Worth: Theories and Evidence.* New York: Aldine de Gruyter.

Eschbach, Karl, and Christina Gómez. 1998. "Choosing Hispanic Identity: Ethnic Identity Switching Among Respondents to High School and Beyond." *Social Science Quarterly* 79(1): 74–90.

Espinosa, Gaston, Virgilio Elizondo, and Jesse Miranda. 2003. "Hispanic Churches in American Public Life: Summary of Findings." Report. Institute for Latino Studies, University of Notre Dame.

Estrada, Leobardo, Chris García, Reynaldo Flores Macías, and Lionel Maldonado. 1981. "Chicanos in the United States." *Daedalus* 110(2): 103–31.

Evans, William N., and Robert M. Schwab. 1995. "Finishing High School and Starting College: Do Catholic Schools Make a Difference?" *Quarterly Journal of Economics* 110(4): 941–74.

Farley, Reynolds, and Richard Alba. 2002. "The New Second Generation in the United States." *International Migration Review* 36(3): 669–701.

Feagin, Joe. 2006. *Systematic Racism: A Theory of Oppression.* New York: Routledge.

Featherman, David L., and Robert M. Hauser. 1978. *Opportunity and Change.* New York: Academic Press.

Feliciano, Cynthia. 2005. "Educational Selectivity in U.S. Immigration: How Do Immigrants Compare to Those Left Behind?" *Demography* 42(1): 131–52.

Fernández, Roberto, and François Nielson. 1986. "Bilingualism and Hispanic Scholastic Achievement: Some Baseline Results." *Social Science Research* 15(1): 43–70.

Finch, Brian Carl, and William Vega. 2004. "Acculturation Stress, Social Support, and Self-Rated Health Among Latinos in California." *Journal of Immigrant Health* 5(3): 109–17.

Finke, Roger, and Rodney Stark. 2005. *The Churching of America, 1776–2005: Winners and Losers in our Religious Economy.* New Brunswick, N.J.: Rutgers University Press.

Fischer, Claude, Robert Max Jackson, C. Ann Stueve, Kathleen Gerson, Lynne McCallister Jones, and Mark Baldassare. 1977. *Networks and Places: Social Relations in the Urban Setting.* New York: Free Press.

Fishman, Joshua. 1977. "Language and Ethnicity." In *Language, Ethnicity and Intergroup Relations,* edited by Howard Giles. London: Academic Press.

Flores, Richard. 2002. *Remembering the Alamo: Memory, Modernity and the Master Symbol.* Austin, Tex.: University of Texas Press.

Fogel, Walter. 1967. *Mexican Americans in Southwest Labor Markets* (Advance Report 10). Los Angeles, Calif.: Mexican American Study Project, University of California, Los Angeles.

Foley, Neil. 1997. *The White Scourge: Mexicans, Blacks and Poor Whites in Texas Cotton Culture.* Berkeley, Calif.: University of California Press.

Foner, Nancy. 2000. *From Ellis Island to JFK: New York's Two Great Waves of Immigration*. New Haven, Conn.: Yale University Press.

Frank, Reanne, and Patrick Heuveline. 2005. "A Crossover in Mexican and Mexican-American Fertility Rates: Evidence and Explanations for an Emerging Paradox." *Demographic Research* 12(March): 77–104.

Frederickson, George. 1997. *The Comparative Imagination: On the History of Racism, Nationalism and Social Movements*. Berkeley, Calif.: University of California Press.

———. 2002. *Racism: A Short History*. Princeton, N.J.: Princeton University Press.

Freeman, Gary P. 2004. "Immigrant Incorporation in Western Democracies." *The International Migration Review* 38(3): 945–69.

Frey, William, 1999. *Immigration and Demographic Balkanization: Toward One America or Two? America's Demographic Tapestry*. New Brunswick, N.J.: Rutgers University Press.

Fryer, Roland G. 2006. "Acting White." *Education Next* Winter(1): 53–59.

Fryer, Roland G., with Paul Torelli. 2006. "An Empirical Analysis of 'Acting White'." Unpublished Working Paper. Harvard University and National Bureau for Economic Research.

Fuchs, Lawrence H. 1990. *The American Kaleidoscope: Race, Ethnicity, and the Civic Culture*. Middletown, Conn.: Wesleyan University Press.

Gallup Poll. 2001. "Gallup Poll Results." *USA Today*, May 20, 2005. Table 3 for national survey taken June 11–17, 2001. Accessed at http://www.usatoday.com/news/polls/tables/live/0623.htm.

———. 2005. "Poll: Americans Approve of Immigration—In Principle." June 6–25, 2005. Accessed at http://www.gallup.com/poll/1660/Immigration.aspx#1.

Gándara, Patricia. 1995. *Over the Ivy Walls: Educational Mobility Among Low Income Chicanos*. Albany, N.Y.: SUNY Press.

Gans, Herbert J. 1962. *The Urban Villagers; Group and Class in the Life of Italian-Americans*. New York: Free Press of Glencoe.

———. 1979. "Symbolic Ethnicity: The Future of Ethnic Groups and Cultures in America." In *On The Making of Americans: Essays in Honor of David Riesman*, edited by Herbert Gans, Nathan Glazer, Joseph Gusfield, and Christopher Jencks. Philadelphia, Pa.: University of Pennsylvania Press.

———. 1992. "Second-Generation Decline: Scenarios for the Economic and Ethnic Futures of the Post-1965 American Immigrants." *Ethnic and Racial Studies* 15(2): 173–93.

———. 1995. *The War Against the Poor*. New York: Basic Books.

———. 1999. "The Possibility of a New Racial Hierarchy in the Twenty-First Century United States" In *The Cultural Territories of Race: Black and White Boundaries*, edited by Michelle Lamont. Chicago, Ill.: University of Chicago Press.

García, John. 1982. "Ethnicity and Chicanos: Measurement of Ethnic Identification, Identity and Consciousness." *Hispanic Journal of Behavioral Sciences* 4(3): 295–314.

García, Richard A. 1991. *Rise of the Mexican American Middle Class: San Antonio, 1929–1941*. San Antonio, Tex.: Texas A & M University Press.

Gibson, Margaret. 1988. *Accommodation Without Assimilation: Sikh Immigrants in an American High School*. Ithaca, N.Y.: Cornell University Press.

Goldsmith, Pat Antonio. 2003. "All Segregation Is Not Equal: The Impact of Latino and Black School Composition." *Sociological Perspectives* 46(1): 83–105.

Gómez, Laura. 2002. "Race Mattered: Racial Formation and the Politics of Crime in Territorial New Mexico." *UCLA Law Review* 49(5): 1395–416.

———. 2007. *Manifest Destinies: The Making of the Mexican American Race.* New York: New York University Press.

González, Gilbert G. 1990. *Chicano Education in the Era of Segregation.* Philadelphia, Pa.: Balch Institute Press.

González, Gilbert G., and Raul A. Fernández. 2003. *A Century of Chicano History: Empire, Nations, and Migration.* New York: Routledge.

Gordon, Milton Myron. 1964. *Assimilation in American Life: The Role of Race, Religion, and National Origins.* New York: Oxford University Press.

Gratton, Brian. 2002. "Race, the Children of Immigrants and Social Science Theory." *Journal of American Ethnic History* 21(4): 74–84.

Gratton, Brian, and Myron P. Guttmann. 2000. "Hispanics in the United States: 1850–1900. Estimates of Population Size and National Origin." *Historical Methods* 33(3): 137–53.

Grebler, Leo, Joan W. Moore, and Ralph Guzmán. 1970. *The Mexican American People: The Nation's Second Largest Minority.* New York: Free Press.

Greeley, Andrew. 1971. *Why Can't They Be Like Us? America's White Ethnic Groups.* New York: E. P. Dutton.

Green, John C., Corwin E. Smidt, James L. Guth, and Lyman A. Kellstedt. 2005. *The American Religious Landscape and the 2004 Presidential Vote: Increased Polarization.* Pew Forum on Religion and Public Life, Survey Report, February. Accessed at http://pewforum.org/publications/surveys/postelection.pdf.

Griswold del Castillo, Richard. 1993. "Chicano Historical Discourse: An Overview and Evaluation of the 1980s." *Perspectives in Mexican American Studies Volume 4: Emerging Themes in Mexican American Research,* edited by Juan R. García. Tucson, Ariz.: University of Arizona Press.

Guglielmo, Thomas A. 2006. "Fighting for Caucasian Rights: Mexicans, Mexican Americans and the Transnational Struggle for Civil Rights in World War II Texas" *The Journal of American History* 92(4): 1212–37.

Gullickson, Aaron. 2005. "The Significance of Color Declines: A Re-Analysis of Skin Tone Differentials in Post Civil Rights America." *Social Forces* 84(1): 157–80.

Gutiérrez, David. 1995. *Walls and Mirrors: Mexican Americans, Mexican Immigrants, and the Politics of Ethnicity.* Berkeley, Calif.: University of California Press.

Gutiérrez, Ramon. 2005. "Internal Colonialism: An American Theory of Race." *Du Bois Review* 1(2): 281–95.

Guttmann, Myron P., Robert McCaa, Rodolfo Gutiérrez-Montes, and Brian Gratton. 2000. "Los Efectos Demográficos de la Revolución Mexicana en Estados Unidos" ["The Demographic Effects of the Mexican Revolution in the United States"]. *Historia Mexicana* 50(1): 145–65.

Guzmán, Betsy. 2001. *The Hispanic Population.* Washington: U.S. Dept. of Commerce, Economics and Statistics Administration, U.S. Census Bureau.

Hahn, Robert A., Joseph Mulinare, and Steven M. Teutsch. 1992. "Inconsistencies in Coding of Race and Ethnicity Between Birth and Death of U.S. Infants." *Journal of the American Medical Association* 267(2): 259–63.

Hajnal, Zoltan, and Mark Baldassare. 2001. *Finding Common Ground: Racial and Ethnic Attitudes in California.* San Francisco, Calif.: Public Policy Institute of California.

Hale, Henry E. 2004. "Explaining Ethnicity." *Comparative Political Studies* 37(4): 458–85.

Handman, Max S. 1930. "Economic Reasons for the Coming of the Mexican Immigrant." *The American Journal of Sociology* 35(4): 601–11.

Haney López, Ian. 1996. *White By Law: The Legal Construction of Race.* New York: New York University Press.

———. 2003. *Racism on Trial: The Chicano Fight for Justice.* Cambridge, Mass.: Belknap Press of Harvard University Press.

Hannaford, Ivan. 1996. *Race: The History of an Idea in the West.* Washington: Woodrow Wilson Center Press.

Hauser, Robert M., and John Robert Warren. 1997. "Socioeconomic Indexes for Occupations: A Review, Update and Critique." *Sociological Methodology* 27(1997): 177–298.

Hauser, Robert M., Solon J. Simmons, and Devah I. Pager. 2004. "High School Dropout, Race/Ethnicity, and Social Background from the 1970s to the 1990s." In *Dropouts in America: Confronting the Graduation Rate Crisis,* edited by Gary Orfield. Cambridge, Mass.: Harvard Education Publishing Group.

Hechter, Michael. 1975. *Internal Colonialism: The Celtic Fringe in British National Development, 1536–1966.* Berkeley, Calif.: University of California Press.

———. 1985. "Internal Colonialism Revisited." In *New Nationalisms of the Developed West,* edited by Edward Tiryakian and Ronald Rogowski. Boston, Mass.: Allen & Unwin.

Hill, David. 2005. "Hispanics: Faith Trumps Ethnicity." *TheHill.com.* Accessed at http://www.thehill.com/david-hill/hispanics-faith-trumps-ethnicity-2005-03-09.html.

Hirschman, Charles. 2004 "The Origins and Demise of the Concept of Race." *Population and Development Review* 30(3): 385–415.

———. 2005. "Immigration and the American Century." *Demography* 42(November): 595–620.

Hochschild, Jennifer, Traci Burch, and Vesla Weaver. 2006. *Effects of Skin Color Bias in SES on Political Activities and Attitudes.* Unpublished manuscript. Paper presented at the annual meeting of the American Political Science Association, September 2, 2004, Chicago, Ill.

Hodson, Randy, Dusko Sekulic, and Garth Massey. 1994. "National Tolerance in the Former Yugoslavia." *The American Journal of Sociology* 99(6): 1534–58.

Hoffer, Thomas, Andrew M. Greeley, and James S. Coleman. 1985. "Achievement Growth in Public and Catholic Schools." *Sociology of Education* 58(2): 74–97.

Hondagneu-Sotelo, Pierrette. 1994. *Gendered Transitions: Mexican Experiences of Immigration.* Berkeley, Calif.: University of California Press.

Horsman, Reginald. 1981. *Race and Manifest Destiny: The Origins of American Racial Anglo-Saxonism.* Cambridge, Mass.: Harvard University Press.

Huntington, Samuel P. 1996. *The Clash of Civilizations and the Remaking of the World Order.* New York: Simon & Schuster.

———. 2004a. "The Hispanic Challenge." *Foreign Affairs* March/April: 30–45.

———. 2004b. *Who Are We?: The Challenges to America's National Identity.* New York: Simon & Schuster.

Hurtado, Aida, and Charles Arce. 1986. "Mexicans, Chicanos, Mexican Americans, or Pochos . . . Que Somos? The Impact of Language and Nativity on Ethnic Labeling." *Aztlán: A Journal of Chicano Studies* 17(1): 103–29.

Iceland, John, Daniel H. Weinberg, and Erika Steinmetz. 2002. *Racial and Ethnic Residential Segregation in the United States: 1980–2000.* U.S. Census Bureau, Census Special Report, CENSR-3. Washington: U.S. Government Printing Office.

Ignatiev, Noel. 1996. *How the Irish Became White.* New York: Routledge.

Irvine, Jacqueline Jordan, and Michèle Foster. 1996. *Growing Up African American in Catholic Schools.* New York: Teachers College Press.

Jacobsen, Matthew Frye. 1998. *Whiteness of a Different Color. European Immigrants and the Alchemy of Race.* Cambridge, Mass.: Harvard University Press.

Jargowsky, Paul A. 1997. *Poverty and Place: Ghettos, Barrios, and the American City.* New York: Russell Sage Foundation.

———. 2003. "Stunning Progress, Hidden Problems: The Dramatic Decline of Concentrated Poverty in the 1990s." *Living Cities Census Series.* Washington: The Brookings Institute.

Jenkins, Richard. 1997. *Rethinking Ethnicity: Arguments and Explorations.* London: Sage Publications.

Jessen, R. J. 1969. "Some Methods of Probability Non-Replacement Sampling." *Journal of the American Statistical Association* 64(325): 175–93.

———. 1970. "Probability Sampling with Marginal Constraints." *Journal of the American Statistical Association* 65(330): 776–96.

Jiménez, Tomás. 2004. "Negotiating Ethnic Boundaries: Multiethnic Mexican Americans and Ethnic Identity in the United States." *Ethnicities* 4(1): 75–97.

———. 2005. "Immigrant Replenishment and the Continuing Significance of Ethnicity and Race: The Case of the Mexican Origin Population." *Center for Comparative Immigration Studies* Working Paper 130. San Diego, Calif.: University of California.

Johnson, David R., John A. Booth, and Richard J. Harris, editors. 1983. *The Politics of San Antonio: Community, Progress, and Power.* Lincoln, Neb.: University of Nebraska Press.

Kao, Grace, and Marta Tienda. 1995. "Optimism and Achievement: The Educational Performance of Immigrant Youth." *Social Science Quarterly* 76(1): 1–19.

Kasinitz, Philip. 1992. *Caribbean New York: Black Immigrants and the Politics of Race.* Ithaca, N.Y.: Cornell University Press.

Keefe, Susan E., and Amado M. Padilla. 1987. *Chicano Ethnicity.* Albuquerque, N.M.: University of New Mexico Press.

Keith, Timothy Z., and Ellis B. Page. 1985. "Do Catholic High Schools Improve Minority Student Achievement?" *American Educational Research Journal* 22(3): 337–49.

Kellstedt, Lyman A. 1974. "Ethnicity and Political Behavior: Inter-Group and Inter-Generational Differences." *Ethnicity* 1(4): 393–415.

Kluckhohn, Florence Rockwood, and Fred L. Strodtbeck. 1961. *Variations in Value Orientations.* Evanston, Ill.: Row, Peterson.

Knight, Alan. 1990. "Racism, Revolution and Indigenismo: Mexico, 1910–1940." In *The Idea of Race in Latin America, 1870–1940,* edited by Richard Graham. Austin, Tex.: University of Texas Press.

Kozol, Jonathan. 2005. *The Shame of The Nation: The Restoration of Apartheid Schooling in America.* New York: Crown.

Ladányi, Janos, and Ivan Szelényi. 2006. *Patterns of Exclusion: Constructing Gypsy Ethnicity and the Making of an Underclass in Transitional Societies of Europe.* New York: Columbia University Press.

Lakoff, George, and Mark Johnson. 1980. *Metaphors We Live By.* Chicago, Ill.: University of Chicago Press.

Lamare, James. 1982. "The Political Integration of Mexican American Children: A Generational Analysis." *The International Migration Review* 16(1): 169–88.

Lamont, Michelle, and Virág Molnár. 2002. "The Study of Boundaries in the Social Sciences." *Annual Review of Sociology.* 28(1): 167–95.

Lansdale, Nancy S., and R. S. Oropeza. 2002. "White, Black or Puerto Rican? Racial Self-Identification among Mainland and Island Puerto Ricans." *Social Forces* 81(1): 231–54.

Laurie, Heather, Rachel Smith, and Lynne Scott. 1999. "Strategies for Reducing Nonresponse in a Longitudinal Panel Survey." *Journal of Official Statistics* 15(2): 269–82.

Lieberson, Stanley. 1980. *A Piece of the Pie: Blacks and White Immigrants Since 1880.* Berkeley, Calif.: University of California Press.

———. 2000. *A Matter of Taste: How Names, Fashions and Culture Change.* New Haven, Conn.: Yale University Press.

Lieberson, Stanley, and Mary Waters. 1988. *From Many Strands: Ethnic and Racial Groups in Contemporary America.* New York: Russell Sage Foundation.

Limerick, Patricia. 1987. *Legacy of Conquest: The Unbroken Past of the American West.* New York: Norton.

Lin, I-Fen, Nora Schaeffer, and Judith Seltzer. 1999. "Causes and Effects of Nonparticipation in a Child Support Survey." *Journal of Official Statistics* 15(2): 143–66.

Linton, April. 1994. "A Critical Mass Model of Bilingualism Among U.S.-Born Hispanics." *Social Forces* 83(1): 279–314.

Long, Mary. 1996. "San Antonio v. Rodríguez and the Next Twenty Years of State Court Cases." Ph.D. dissertation. Loyola University.

López, David E. 1982. *The Maintenance of Spanish over Three Generations in the United States.* Los Alamitos, Calif.: National Center for Bilingual Research.

———. Forthcoming. "Whither the Flock? The Catholic Church and the Success of Mexicans in America." In *Religion and Immigration,* edited by Richard Alba, Albert Raboteau, and Josh DeWind. New York: New York University Press.

López, David E., and Ricardo D. Stanton-Salazar. 2001. "Mexican Americans: A Second Generation at Risk." In *Ethnicities: Children of Immigrants in America,* edited by Rubén Rumbaut and Alejandro Portes. Berkeley, Calif.: University of California Press.

López, David, Eric Popkin, and Edward Telles. 1996. "Central Americans: At the Bottom, Struggling to Get Ahead." In *Ethnic Los Angeles,* edited by Roger Waldinger and Mehdi Bozorgmehr. New York: Russell Sage Foundation.

Macías, Reynaldo. 1985. "Language and Ideology in the United States." *Social Education* 49(2): 97–100."

Madsen, William. 1964. *The Mexican-Americans of South Texas.* New York: Holt, Rinehart and Winston.

Martínez, George A. 1997. "The Legal Construction of Race: Mexican-Americans and Whiteness." *Harvard Latino Law Review* 2(Fall): 321–47.

Martínez, Oscar J. 1975. "On the Size of the Chicano Population: New Estimates 1850–1900." *Aztlán: International Journal of Chicano Studies Research* 6(1): 43–67.

Massey, Douglas S. 1985. "Ethnic Residential Segregation: A Theoretical Synthesis and Empirical Review." *Sociology and Social Research* 69(3): 315–50.

———. 2004. "Review of Who Are We? by Samuel P. Huntington." *Population and Development Review* 30(3): 543–8.

Massey, Douglas S., and Nancy A. Denton. 1987. "Trends in the Residential Segregation of Blacks, Hispanics and Asians: 1970–1980." *American Sociological Review* 52(6): 802–25.

———. 1993. *American Apartheid: Segregation and the Making of the Underclass.* Cambridge, Mass.: Harvard University Press.

Massey, Douglas S., Jorge Durand, and Nolan J. Malone. 2003. *Beyond Smoke and Mirrors: Mexican Immigration in an Era of Economic Integration.* New York: Russell Sage Foundation.

Massey, Douglas S., Camille Zubrinsky Charles, Garvey Lundy, and Mary J. Fischer. 2003. *The Source of the River: The Social Origins of Freshmen at America's Selective Colleges and Universities.* Princeton, N.J.: Princeton University Press.

Matute-Bianchi, Maria Eugenia. 1986. "Ethnic Identities and Patterns of School Success and Failure Among Mexican Descent and Japanese-American Students in a California High School: An Ethnographic Analysis." *American Journal of Education* 95(1): 233–55.

McCaa, Robert. 1997. "Families and Gender in Mexico: A Methodological Critique and Research Challenge for the End of the Millennium." Presented at IV Conferencia Iberoamericana Sobre Familia: Historia de Familia. September 21–22, 1997, Universidad Externado de Colombia Centro de Investigaciones Sobre Dinámica Social, Bogotá, Colombia.

McLemore, Dale, and Ricardo Romo. 1985. "The Origins and Development of the Mexican American People." In *The Mexican American Experience: An Interdisciplinary Anthology,* edited by Rodolfo de la Garza. Austin, Tex.: The University of Texas Press.

Menchaca, Marta. 1993. "Chicano Indianism: A Historical Account of Racial Repression in the United States." *American Ethnologist* 20(3): 583–603.

Miles, Robert. 1989. *Racism after Race Relations.* London: Routledge.

Milkman, Ruth. 2006. *L.A. Story: Immigrant Workers and the Future of the U.S. Labor Movement.* New York: Russell Sage Foundation

Mirandé, Alfredo. 1977. "The Chicano Family: A Reanalysis of Conflicting Views." *Journal of Marriage and the Family* 39(4): 747–56.

Montejano, David 1987. *Anglos and Mexicans in the Making of Texas: 1836–1986.* Austin, Tex.: University of Texas Press.

———. 2004. "Who is Samuel P. Huntington? Patriotic Reading for Anglo Protestants Who Live in Fear of the Reconquista." *The Texas Observer,* August 13, 2004. Accessed at http://www.texasobserver.org/article.php?aid=1727.

Moore, Joan W. 1967. "Political and Ethical Problems in a Large-Scale Study of a Minority Population." In *Ethics, Politics and Social Research,* edited by Gideon Sjoberg. Cambridge, Mass.: Schenkman Publishing.

———. 1970. "Colonialism: The Case of the Mexican Americans." *Social Problems* 17(4): 463–72.

Moore, Joan W., and Raquel Pinderhughes, editors. 1993. *In the Barrios: Latinos and the Underclass Debate.* New York: Russell Sage Foundation.

Muñoz, Carlos. 1989. *Youth, Identity, Power: The Chicano Movement.* London: Verso.

Murguía, Edward. 1982. *Chicano Intermarriage: A Theoretical and Empirical Study.* San Antonio, Tex.: Trinity University Press.

Murguía, Edward, and Edward E. Telles. 1996. "Phenotype and Schooling Among Mexican Americans." *Sociology of Education* 69(October): 276–89.

Myers, Dowell. 2007. *Immigrants and Boomers: Forging a New Social Contract for the Future of America.* New York: Russell Sage Foundation.

Myrdal, Gunnar. 1944. *An American Dilemma.* New York: Harper and Row.

Naboa, Julio. 2005. "On the Westside: A Portrait of Lanier High School During World War II." In *Mexican Americans and World War II,* edited by Maggie Rivas-Rodríguez. Austin, Tex.: University of Texas Press.

Nagel, Joane. 1994. "Constructing Ethnicity: Creating and Recreating Ethnic Identity and Culture." *Social Problems* 41(1): 152–76.

———. 1996. *American Indian Ethnic Renewal: Red Power and the Resurgence of Identity and Culture.* New York: Oxford University Press.

Nakano-Glenn, Evelyn. 2002. *Unequal Freedom: How Race and Gender Shaped American Citizenship and Labor.* Cambridge, Mass.: Harvard University Press.

National Center for Education Statistics. 2007. *Status and Trends in the Education of Racial and Ethnic Minorities.* Washington: U.S. Department of Education. Accessed at http://nces.ed.gov/pubsearch/pubsinfo.asp?pubid=2007039.

Navarro, Armando. 1995. *Mexican American Youth Organization: Avant-Garde of the Chicano Movement.* Austin, Tex.: University of Texas Press.

Neal, Derek. 1997. "The Effects of Catholic Secondary Schooling on Educational Achievement." *Journal of Labor Economics* 15(1): 98–123.

Neidert, Lisa J., and Reynolds Farley. 1985. "Assimilation in the United States: An Analysis of Ethnic and Generation Differences in Status Attainment." *American Sociological Review* 50(6): 840–50.

Ngai, Mae E. 2004. *Impossible Subjects: Illegal Aliens and the Making of Modern America.* Princeton, N.J.: Princeton University Press.

Noyelle, Thierry, and Thomas M. Stanback, Jr. 1984. *The Economic Transformation of American Cities.* Totowa, N.J.: Roman & Allanheld.

Oakes, Jeannie 2005. *Keeping Track: How Schools Structure Inequality.* New Haven, Conn.: Yale University Press.

Office of Immigration Statistics. 2003. *Yearbook of Immigration Statistics.* Washington: U.S. Department of Homeland Security.

Ogbu, John, editor. 1978. *Minority Education and Caste: The American System in Cross-Cultural Perspective.* New York: Academic Press.

Olivas, Michael A. 2006. *Colored Men and Hombres Aquí: Hernández vs. Texas and the Emergence of Mexican American Lawyering.* Houston, Tex.: Arte Publico Press.

Oliver, Melvin L., and Thomas M. Shapiro. 1995. *Black Wealth/White Wealth: A New Perspective on Racial Inequality.* New York: Routledge.

Omi, Michael, and Howard Winant. 1986. *Racial Formation in the United States: From the 1960s to the 1980s.* New York: Routledge & Kegan Paul.

Ono, Hiromi. 2002. "Assimilation, Ethnic Competition and Ethnic Identities of U.S.-Born Persons of Mexican Origin." *The International Migration Review* 36(3): 726–45.

Orfield, Gary. 1993. *The Growth of Segregation in American Schools: Changing Patterns of Separation and Poverty since 1968.* Alexandria, Va.: National School Boards Association.

————, editor. 2004. *Dropouts In America: Confronting The Graduation Rate Crisis.* Cambridge, Mass.: Harvard Educational Press.

Orfield, Gary, and John Yun. 1999. *Resegregation in American Schools.* Cambridge, Mass.: The Civil Rights Project, Harvard University.

Ortiz, Vilma. 1994. "Women of Color: A Demographic Overview." In *Women of Color in American Society,* edited by Maxine Baca Zinn and Bonnie Thornton. Philadelphia, Pa.: Temple University Press.

————. 1996. "The Mexican Origin Population: Permanent Working Class or Emerging Middle Class?" In *Ethnic Los Angeles,* edited by Roger Waldinger and Mehdi Bozorgmehr. New York: Russell Sage Foundation.

Ortiz, Vilma, and Estela Ballon. 2007. "Longitudinal Research at the Turn of the Century: Searching for The Mexican American People." *Sociological Methods and Research* 36(1):112–37.

Oyserman, Daphna, Markus Kemmelmeier, Stephanie Frybers, Hezi Brosh, and Tamera Hart-Johnson. 2003. "Racial-Ethnic Self Schemas." *Social Psychology Quarterly* 66(4): 333–47.

Pager, Devah. Forthcoming. "The Sociology of Discrimination." *Annual Review of Sociology.*

Palloni, Alberto, and Elizabeth Arias. 2004. "Paradox Lost: Explaining the Hispanic Adult Mortality Advantage." *Demography* 41(3): 385–415.

Panunzio, Constantine. 1942. "Intermarriage in Los Angeles, 1924–33." *American Journal of Sociology* 43(5): 690–701.

Park, Robert E. 1926. "The Urban Community as a Spatial Pattern and a Moral Order." In *The Urban Community: Selected Papers from the Proceedings of the American Sociological Society, 1925,* edited by Ernest W. Burgess. Chicago, Ill.: The University of Chicago Press.

————. 1930. "Assimilation, Social." In *Encyclopedia of the Social Sciences,* edited by Edwin Seligman and Alvin Johnson. New York: Macmillan.

Passel, Jeffrey. 2005. "Estimates of the Size and Characteristics of the Undocumented Population." Washington: Pew Hispanic Center Report.

Perl, Paul, Jennifer Z. Greely, and Mark M. Gray. 2004. "How Many Hispanics are Catholic? A Review of Survey Data and Methodology." Working Paper. Washington: Center for Applied Research in the Apostolate.

Perlmann, Joel. 2005. *Italians Then, Mexicans Now: Immigrant Origins and Second-Generation Progress, 1890 to 2000.* New York: Russell Sage Foundation.

Perlmann, Joel, and Roger Waldinger. 1997. "Second Generation Decline? Children of Immigrants, Past and Present—A Reconsideration." *International Migration Review* 31(4): 893–922.

Perry, David, and Alfred Watkins. 1977. *The Rise of the Sunbelt Cities.* Beverly Hills, Calif.: Sage Publications.

Pettigrew, Thomas. 1979. "Racial Change and Social Policy." *Annals of the American Academy of Political and Social Science* 441(1): 114–31.

Phinney, Jean, and Juana Flores. 2002. "Unpackaging Acculturation: Aspects of Acculturation as Predictors of Traditional Sex Role Attitudes." *Journal of Cross-Cultural Psychology* 33(3): 319–30.

Pollock, Mica. Forthcoming. *Because of Race: How Americans Debate Harm and Opportunity in Our Schools.* Princteon, N.J.: Princeton University Press.

Population Reference Bureau. 2006. *World Data Sheet.* Accessed at http://www.prb. org/pdf06/06WorldDataSheet.pdf.

Portes, Alejandro. 1998. "Social Capital: Its Origins and Applications in Modern Sociology." *Annual Review of Sociology* 24: 1–24.

Portes, Alejandro, and Robert L. Bach. 1985. *Latin Journey: Cuban and Mexican Immigrants in the United States.* Berkeley, Calif.: University of California Press.

Portes, Alejandro, and Rubén Rumbaut. 2001. *Legacies: The Story of the Immigrant Second Generation.* Berkeley, Calif.: University of California Press.

Portes, Alejandro, and Alex Stepick. 1994. *City on the Edge: The Transformation of Miami.* Berkeley, Calif.: University of California Press.

Portes, Alejandro, and Min Zhou. 1993. "The New Second Generation: Segmented Assimilation and its Variants." *Annals of the American Academy of Political and Social Science* 530(1): 74–96.

Purnell, Thomas, William Idsard, and John Baugh. 1999. "Perceptual and Phonetic Experiments on American English Dialect Identification." *Journal of Language and Social Psychology* 18(1): 10–30.

Pycior, Julie L. 1997. *LBJ and Mexican Americans: The Paradox of Power.* Austin, Tex.: University of Texas Press.

Redfield, Robert. 1960. *The Little Community and Peasant Society and Culture.* Chicago, Ill.: University of Chicago Press.

Reimers, Cordelia. 1985. "A Comparative Analysis of the Wages of Hispanics, Blacks and Non-Hispanic Whites." In *Hispanics in the U.S. Economy,* edited by George J. Borjas and Marta Tienda. New York: Academic Press.

Reimers, David. 1985. *Still the Golden Door: The Third World Comes to America.* New York: Columbia University Press.

Reskin, Barbara F. 1993. "Sex Segregation in the Workplace." *Annual Review of Sociology* 19: 241–70.

Rieff, David. 2006. "Nuevo Catholics." *New York Times Magazine.* December 24, 2006.

Rindfuss, Ronald R., and James A. Sweet. 1977. *Postwar Fertility Trends and Differentials in the United States.* New York: Academic Press.

Rivas-Rodríguez, Maggie, editor. 2005. *Mexican Americans and World War II.* Austin, Tex.: University of Texas Press.

Rodríguez, Clara. 2000. *Changing Race: Latinos, The Census, and The History of Ethnicity in the United States.* New York: New York University Press.

Rodríguez, Gregory. 1996. *The Emerging Latino Middle Class.* Malibu, Calif.: Institute for Public Policy, Pepperdine University.

Roediger, David R. 1999. *The Wages of Whiteness: Race and the Making of the American Working Class.* London: Verso.

———. 2005. *Working Toward Whiteness: How America's Immigrants Became White.* New York: Basic Books.

Romano, Octavio I. 1968. "The Anthropology and Sociology of the Mexican-Americans: The Distortion of Mexican-American History." *El Grito: A Journal of Contemporary Mexican American Thought* 2(1): 13–26.

Romo, Harriet D., and Toni Falbo. 1996. *Latino High School Graduation: Defying the Odds.* Austin, Tex.: University of Texas Press.

Rosales, Rodolfo. 2000. *The Illusion of Inclusion: The Untold Political Story of San Antonio.* Austin, Tex.: University of Texas Press.

Rosenfeld, Michael J. 1998. "Impacts of Migration: Mexican Immigrants and Mexican American Political Assimilation." In *Migration Between Mexico and the United States: Binational Study.* Mexico City and Washington: Mexican Ministry of Foreign Affairs and the U.S. Commission on Immigration Reform.

Roybal, Edward R. 1966. "Remarks to the U.S. House of Representatives." 89th Congress, 2nd sess.

Rubel, Arthur J. 1966. *Across the Tracks: Mexican-Americans in a Texas City.* Austin, Tex.: University of Texas Press.

Ruíz, Vicki L. 1998. *From Out of the Shadows: Mexican Women in Twentieth-Century America.* New York: Oxford University Press.

———. 2004. "Tapestries of Resistance: Episodes of School Segregation and Desegregation in the U.S. West." In *From Grassroots to the Supreme Court: Exploration of Brown. V. Board of Education and American Democracy,* edited by Peter Lau. Durham, N.C.: Duke University Press.

Rumbaut, Rubén G. 2006. "The Making of a People." In *Hispanics and the Future of America,* edited by Marta Tienda and Faith Mitchell. Washington: National Academies Press.

Rumbaut, Rubén G., and Alejandro Portes. 2003. "Introduction—Ethnogenesis: Coming of Age in Immigrant America." In *Ethnicities: Children of Immigrant in America,* edited by Rubén G. Rumbaut and Alejandro Portes. Berkeley, Calif.: University of California Press.

Rumbaut, Rubén G., Douglas S. Massey, and Frank D. Bean. 2006. "Linguistic Life Expectancies: Immigrant Language Retention in Southern California." *Population and Development Review* 32(3): 447–60.

Ryang, Sonia, editor. 2000. *Koreans in Japan: Critical Voices from the Margin.* London and New York: Routledge.

San Miguel, Guadalupe. 1987. *"Let All of Them Take Heed": Mexican Americans and the Campaign for Educational Equality in Texas, 1910–1981.* Austin, Tex.: University of Texas Press.

Sánchez, George J. 1993. *Becoming Mexican American: Ethnicity, Culture, and Identity in Chicano Los Angeles, 1900–1945.* New York: Oxford University Press.

Sandberg, Neil C. 1974. *Ethnic Identity and Assimilation: The Polish-American Community; Case Study of Metropolitan Los Angeles.* New York: Praeger.

Sanders, Jimy. 2002. "Ethnic Boundaries and Identity in Plural Societies." *Annual Review of Sociology* 28:327–57.

Santa Ana, Otto. 2002. *Brown Tide Rising: Metaphors of Latinos in Contemporary American Public Discourse.* Austin, Tex.: University of Texas Press.

Santa Barbara News Press. 2004. Obituary for Tamotsu (Tom) Shibutani, August 13, 2004.

Saragoza, Alex. 1987. "The Significance of Recent Chicano-Related Historical Writings: An Appraisal." *Ethnic Affairs* 1(1): 24–62.

Schlesinger, Arthur. 1992. *The Disuniting of America.* New York: W. W. Norton.

Schneider, Barbara, Sylvia Martínez, and Ann Owens. 2006. "Barriers to Educational Opportunities for Hispanics in the United States." In *Hispanics and the Future of America,* edited by Marta Tienda and Faith Mitchell. Washington: National Academies Press.

Schultz, April. 1992. *Ethnicity on Parade: Inventing the Norwegian American Through Celebration.* Amherst, Mass.: University of Massachusetts Press.

Segura, Denise. 1994. "Inside the Work Worlds of Chicana and Mexican Immigrant Women." In *Women of Color in American Society*, edited by Maxine Baca Zinn and Bonnie Thornton. Philadelphia, Pa.: Temple University Press.

Sewell, William H., and Robert M. Hauser. 1975. *Education, Occupation, and Earnings: Achievement in the Early Career.* New York: Academic Press.

Shibutani, Tamotsu, and Kian M. Kwan. 1965. *Ethnic Stratification: A Comparative Approach.* New York: Macmillan.

Skerry, Peter. 1990. "Hispanic Job Discrimination Exaggerated." *Wall Street Journal,* April 27, 1990, 12.

———. 1993a. "The New Politics of Assimilation." *City Journal* 3(Fall): 6–7.

———. 1993b. *Mexican Americans: The Ambivalent Minority.* New York: Free Press.

Skrentny, John D. 2002. *The Minority Rights Revolution.* Cambridge, Mass.: The Belknap Press of Harvard University Press

Slayden, James. 1921. "Some Observations on Mexican Immigration." *Annals of the American Academy of Political and Social Science* 93(1): 121–26.

Small, Steve. 1994. *Racialized Barriers: The Black Experience in the United States and England in the 1980s.* London: Routledge.

Smith, Anthony. 1990. *The Ethnic Revival in the Modern World.* Cambridge: Cambridge University Press.

Smith, James P. 2003. "Assimilation Across the Latino Generations." *The American Economic Review* 93(2): 315–19.

Smith, James P., and Barry Edmonston. 1998. *The Immigration Debate: Studies on the Economic, Demographic and Fiscal Effects of Immigration.* Washington: National Academy Press.

Smith, Tom. 1990. *Ethnic Images.* General Social Survey, Technical Report 19. Chicago, Ill.: National Opinion Research Center, University of Chicago.

Soja, Edward W. 1989. *Postmodern Geographies: The Reassertion of Space in Critical Social Theory.* London: Verso.

Sollors, Werner. 2000. *Interracialism: Black-White Intermarriage in American History, Literature and Law.* Oxford: Oxford University Press.

Solórzano, Daniel. 1995. "The Baccalaureate Origins of Chicana and Chicano Doctorates in the Social Sciences." *Hispanic Journal of Behavioral Sciences.* 17(1): 3–32.

South, Scott J., Kyle Crowder, and Erick Chávez. 2005. "Migration and Spatial Assimilation Among U.S. Latinos: Classical Versus Segmented Trajectories." *Demography* 42(3): 497–21.

Stanton-Salazar, Ricardo, and Sanford Dornbusch. 1995. "Social Capital and the Reproduction of Inequality: Information Networks among Mexican-origin High School Students." *Sociology of Education* 68(1): 116–36.

Steele, Claude M., S. K. Spencer, and Joshua Aronson. 2002. "Contending with Group Image: The Psychology of Stereotype and Social Identity Threat." *Advances in Experimental Social Psychology* 34: 379–440.

Stevens, Gillian. 1985. "Nativity, Intermarriage, and Mother-Tongue Shift." *American Sociological Review* 50(1): 74–83.

———. 1992. "The Social and Demographic Context of Language Use in the United States." *American Sociological Review* 57(2): 171–85.

Stone, John. 1979. "Introduction: Internal Colonialism in Comparative Perspective." *Ethnic and Racial Studies* 2(3): 255–9.

Suárez-Orozco, Marcelo M. 1987. "Toward a Psycho Social Understanding of Hispanic Adaptation to American Schooling." In *Success or Failure? Learning and the Language Minority Student,* edited by Henry T. Trueba. New York: Newbury House.

Sue, Christina, and Edward Telles. 2007. "Assimilation and Gender in Naming." *American Journal of Sociology* 112(5): 1383–415.

Suro, Roberto, and Jeffrey Passell. 2003. "The Rise of the Second Generation: Changing Patterns in Hispanic Populations Growth." Washington: Pew Hispanic Center.

Suro, Roberto, Richard Fry, and Jeffrey Passell. 2005. "Hispanics and the 2004 Elections: Population, Electorate, and Voters." Washington: Pew Hispanic Center.

Tafoya, Sonya. 2002. "Mixed Race and Ethnicity in California." In *The New Race Question: How the Census Counts Multiracial Individuals,* edited by Joel Perlmann and Mary Waters. New York: Russell Sage Foundation.

Takaki, Ronald. 1989. *Strangers from a Different Shore: A History of Asian Americans.* Boston, Mass.: Little, Brown.

Telles, Edward. 2004. *Race in Another America: The Significance of Skin Color in Brazil.* Princeton, N.J.: Princeton University Press.

———. 2006. "Mexican Americans and the American Nation: A Response to Professor Huntington." *Aztlán: A Journal of Chicano Studies* 18(2): 167–84.

Telles, Edward, and Edward Murguía. 1990. "Phenotypic Discrimination and Income Differences Among Mexican Americans." *Social Science Quarterly* 71(4): 682–96.

Thernstrom, Stephan, and Abigail Thernstrom. 1997. *America in Black and White: One Nation Indivisible.* New York: Touchstone.

Tienda, Marta. 1995. "Latinos and the American Pie: Can Latinos Achieve Economic Prosperity?" *Hispanic Journal of Behavioral Science* 17(4): 403–29.

Tienda, Marta, and Faith Mitchell, editors. 2006. *Hispanics and the Future of America.* Washington: National Academies Press.

Tolnay, Stewart, and E. M. Beck. 1995. *A Festival of Violence: An Analysis of Southern Lynchings, 1882–1930.* Urbana, Ill.: University of Illinois Press.

Trejo, Stephen J. 1997. *Why Do Mexican-Americans Earn Low Wages?* Santa Barbara, Calif.: Chicano/Latino Working Poor Project, Center for Chicano Studies.

Tremblay, Marc, and Hélène Vézina. 2000. "New Estimates of Intergenerational Time Intervals for the Calculation of Age and Origins of Mutations." *American Journal of Human Genetics* 66(2): 651–8.

U.S. Bureau of the Census. 1966. "Characteristics of the South and East Los Angeles Areas: November 1965." Current Population Reports, Series P-23, No. 18. Washington: U.S. Government Printing Office.

———. 2002. Current Population Survey. *Voting and Registration in the Election of November 2000: Population Characteristics.* Current Population Reports, Series P-20, Number 542. Washington: U.S. Government Printing Office.

U.S. Immigration and Naturalization Service. 2005. Statistical Yearbook of the Immigration and Naturalization Service, 2003. Washington: U.S. Government Printing Office.

Valdes, Guadalupe. 2000. "Bilingualism and Language Use Among Mexican Americans." In *New Immigrants in the United States: Readings for Second Language*

Educators, edited by Sandra Lee McCay and Sau-ling Cynthia Wong. New York: Cambridge University Press.

Valdez, Avelardo. 1983. "Recent Increases in Intermarriage by Mexican American Males in Bexar County, Texas, from 1971–1980." *Social Science Quarterly* 64(1): 136–44.

Valencia, Richard R. 2002. "The Plight of Chicano Students: An Overview of Schooling Conditions and Outcomes." In *Chicano School Failure and Success: Past, Present, and Future,* edited by Richard R. Valencia. London: Routledge/Falmer.

Valencia, Richard R., Martha Menchaca, and Rubén Donato. 2002. "Segregation, Desegregation and Integration of Chicano Students: Old and New Realities." In *Chicano School Failure and Success: Past, Present, and Future,* edited by Richard R. Valencia. London: Routledge/Falmer.

Valenzuela, Angela. 1999. *Subtractive Schooling: U.S. Mexican Youth and the Politics of Caring.* Albany, N.Y.: State University of New York Press.

Vargas, Zaragosa. 2005. *Labor Rights are Civil Rights: Mexican American Workers in Twentieth-Century America.* Princeton, N.J.: Princeton University Press.

Veltman, Calvin. 1983. *Language Shift in the United States.* Berlin: Mouton.

Vigil, James Diego. 1988. *Barrio Gangs: Street Life and Identity in Southern California.* Austin, Tex.: University of Texas Press.

———. 1997. *Personas Mexicanas: Chicano High Schoolers in a Changing Los Angeles.* Fort Worth, Tex.: Harcourt Brace College Publishers.

Waldinger, Roger. 2003. "Transforming Foreigners into Americans." *Diaspora* 12(2): 247–72.

———. 2007. "Foreigners Transformed: International Migration and the Remaking of a Divided People." In *The New Americans: A Guide to Immigration Since 1965,* edited by Mary Waters and Reed Ueda. Cambridge, Mass.: Harvard University Press

Warner, Lloyd, and Leo Srole. 1945. *The Social Systems of American Ethnic Groups.* New Haven, Conn.: Yale University Press.

Waters, Mary C. 1990. *Ethnic Options: Choosing Identities in America.* Berkeley, Calif.: University of California Press.

———. 1999. *Black Identities: West Indian Immigrant Dreams and American Realities.* New York: Russell Sage Foundation.

Waters, Tony. 1999. *Crime and Immigrant Youth.* Thousand Oaks, Calif.: Sage Publications.

Watkins, Susan Cotts, and Andrew S. London. 1994. "Personal Names and Cultural Change." *Social Science History* 18(2): 169–209.

Williams, Norma. 1990. *The Mexican American Family: Tradition and Change.* Dix Hills, N.Y.: General Hall.

Willis, Paul. 1981. *Learning to Labor: How Working Class Kids Get Working Class Jobs.* New York: Columbia University Press.

Wilson, Frank. 2005. *Race, Class and the Postindustrial City.* Albany, N.Y.: State University of New York Press.

Wilson, William Julius. 1978. *The Declining Significance of Race: Blacks and Changing American Institutions.* Chicago, Ill.: University of Chicago Press.

———. 1987. *The Truly Disadvantaged: The Inner City, The Underclass, and Public Policy.* Chicago, Ill.: University of Chicago Press.

Wimmer, Andreas. 2002. *Nationalist Exclusion and Ethnic Conflict: Shadows of Modernity.* Cambridge: Cambridge University Press.

———. 2007. "Elementary Forms of Ethnic Boundary Making: A Processual and Interactionist Approach." Unpublished manuscript. Department of Sociology, University of California Los Angeles.

Winant, Howard. 1994. *Racial Conditions: Politics, Theory, Comparisons.* Minneapolis, Minn.: University of Minnesota Press.

Wirth, Louis. 1938. "Urbanism as a Way of Life." *American Journal of Sociology* 44(1): 1–24.

Wojtkiewicz, Roger A., and Katherine M. Donato. 1995. "Hispanic Educational Attainment: The Effects of Family Background and Nativity." *Social Forces* 74(2): 559–74.

Womack, John, Jr. 1991. "The Mexican Revolution, 1910–1920." In *Mexico Since Independence,* edited by Leslie Bethell. Cambridge: Cambridge University Press.

Yancey, William L., Eugene P. Ericksen, and Richard N. Juliani. 1976. "Emergent Ethnicity: A Review and Reformulation." *American Sociological Review* 41(3): 391–403.

Ybarra, Lea. 1982. "When Wives Work: The Impact on the Chicano Family." *Journal of Marriage and the Family* 44(1): 169–78.

Ybarra-Frausto, Tomás. 1999. "The Chicano Cultural Project Since the 1960s" (Interview). In *La Vida Latina en L.A.: Urban Latino Cultures,* edited by Gustavo Leclerc, Raul Villa, and Michael J. Dear. Thousand Oaks, Calif.: Sage Publications.

Yinger, Milton. 1985. "Ethnicity." *Annual Review of Sociology* 11(August): 151–80.

———. 1994. *Ethnicity: Source of Strength? Source of Conflict?* Albany, N.Y.: State University of New York Press.

Zavella, Patricia. 1987. "Women's Work and Chicano Families: Cannery Workers of the Santa Clara Valley." Ithaca, N.Y.: Cornell University Press.

Zhou, Min, and Carl L. Bankston III. 1998. *Growing up American: How Vietnamese Children Adapt to Life in the United States.* New York: Russell Sage Foundation.

Zúñiga, Victor, and Rubén Hernández-León, editors. 2006. *New Destinations: Mexican Immigration to the United States.* New York: Russell Sage Foundation.

=== Index ===

Boldface numbers refer to figures and tables.

and socioeconomic prospects, 4;
underclass, xxiii, xxv, 42, 154–5,
271. *See also* middle class; working class
code-switching, 192–4
college completion rates: by
generation-since-immigration,
108, **109, 114**; and parental expectations, **121,** 121–2; and racial
comparison, 106, **107,** 115–6, 269,
270, 271
Comaroff, John, 23
Cornell, Stephen, 21, 25, 223
cross-sectional study, 46–47, 216
Cubans, 12, 39
cultural deficiency theory, 74
culture: acculturation, 33, 185–6, 200,
209–10, 242; and assimilation,
87–89, 198, 202, 209–10, 272,
281–2; and assumptions of isolation, 74; birth names, 196–9, 210,
308, 340n36; and educational
attainment, 120–2; and ethnic
boundaries, 160; family values,
204–6; fertility and pro-natalist
values, 202–4; holiday celebration, 207–9, 228; internal colonialism's barriers to, 29–30;
introduction, 185–6; music,
favorite, 206–7; and racialization,
14, 101-2, 242; rural vs. urban,
186; and salience of ethnic identity, 226; vs. social boundaries, 25.
See also language; religion and
religiosity

Dahl, Robert, 240, 241, 254
deindustrialization, xxiii, 98, 145, 147
De la Garza, Rodolfo, 239, 241–42
Democratic Party, 247–53
Denton, Nancy A., 163
De Sipio, Louis, 241–2
Díaz, Porfirio, 80
discrimination: and acculturation, 242;
based on Spanish accent, 193; as
boundary reinforcer, 78, 84; culture and racialization, 14; in education, 79, 89–90, 131–3, 232,

235–6, 331n112, 332–3n136,
336n51; gender variations in perception of, 281; historical perspective, 76–77, 78–79, 331n113, 117,
332–3n136; and identity, 227–8,
237; in labor market, 135–6; and
language, 186, 188; perception of,
231–6, 313; in political participation, 238; and racialization, 4, 15,
22; residential, 149, 160, 161, 193;
and skin color, 233–4, 282; and
social stigmatization, 287; and
urban areas, 100; voter, 238–9;
WWII-era moves to reduce, 85
dissimilarity index in residential segregation, **162,** 162–3
downward assimilation, 5, 32, 33, 131,
154, 188.
dropout rates, high school. *See* high
school graduation rates

earnings, personal, 139–43, **144, 153**
economy: and education, 126–7;
employment patterns, 137–9, 143,
145–8; and ethnic boundary
strength, 25; ethnic enclaves,
32–33, 42; focus on, 21–22; impact
on integration, 278–9; industrial
restructuring, xxiii, 96–101, 137–9,
156–7; and involuntary nature of
assimilation, 31; research assumptions from 1960s, xxii–xxiii;
undocumented workers' effect
on, 255, **256,** 257–8, 318n21; and
urban area, 137–9. *See also* labor
market; socioeconomic status
education: and age, 128; assimilation
over historical time, 269, **270,** 271;
attainment determinants, 301;
bilingual, 188; cultural deficits,
120–2; discrimination in, 79,
89–90, 131–3, 232, 235–6, 331n112,
332–3n136, 336n51; and educational segregation, 123–6; effect
on assimilation, 32, 265–6, 267,
268, 274–7, 279, 280; and gender,
128, 129, 281; generational
changes in attainment, 33, 104–5,
108–10; and generation-since-